Fiscal Policies
in
Economies
in
Transition

Edited by
Vito Tanzi

WITHDRAWN

International Monetary Fund
Washington, D.C.

© International Monetary Fund, 1992

Library of Congress Cataloging-in-Publication Data

Fiscal policies in economies in transition / edited by Vito Tanzi.
  p. cm.
  Includes bibliographical references and index.
  Contents: v. 1. Policies.
  ISBN 1-55775-191-9
  1. Fiscal policy—Europe, Eastern. 2. Post-communism—Europe, Eastern.
3. Fiscal policy—Africa. 4. Post-communism—Africa. 5. Fiscal policy—
Asia. 6. Post-communism—Asia. I. Tanzi. Vito.
  HJ1000.F56   1991
  336.3'0947 — dc20   91-40994
                                                              CIP

This book's cover and its interior
were designed by the IMF Graphics Section.
David Driscoll of the IMF's External Relations Department
edited the book for publication.

Price: US$24.50

Please send orders to:
International Monetary Fund, Publication Services
700 19th Street, N.W., Washington, D.C. 20431, U.S.A.
Tel.: (202) 623-7430   Telefax: (202) 623-7201

FOREWORD

One of the most dramatic political and economic developments of recent years has been the realization on the part of the citizens of many centrally planned economies that central planning cannot lead to economic well-being and to democratic and open societies. The successful economic and social transformation of these countries will not be easy. It will require great effort and perseverance on the part of policymakers; it will also require the solution to many technical problems never before discussed by economists, and the creation of new institutions.

From the beginning the IMF has assisted these countries with technical advice and, where appropriate, with financial assistance. One aspect that has required particular attention is the establishment of fiscal institutions as a prerequisite to good fiscal policy. Some institutions that are essential to the proper functioning of a market economy were not needed, or were needed in very different forms, by the centrally planned economies. Until efficient fiscal institutions are fully in place, the conduct of macro-economic policy will be difficult. Many mistakes can be made in the process of creating these fiscal institutions, which could reduce the chance for a successful economic policy. Such mistakes should be avoided.

This book brings together some of the knowledge in the fiscal area accumulated by individuals who have been closely involved with this historical process of transformation. As long as this knowledge remains in confidential reports to specific countries, or in the memory of a few individuals, it will not be as useful to the community at large as it could be. Lessons learned in one country may be useful to other countries. And many individuals outside the Fund can benefit from this knowledge. I am hopeful that this book, dealing with such a topical and important subject, will help make the road to a market economy less bumpy.

Michel Camdessus
Managing Director
International Monetary Fund

iii

Contents

Introduction
Vito Tanzi

One of the important but least-known functions of the International Monetary Fund is the provision of what is broadly and not precisely described as "technical assistance." Technical assistance comprises many heterogeneous activities, ranging from those associated with the setting up of statistical systems and central banks to those associated with the setting up of fiscal institutions and the reform of public finances. Much of this activity is largely invisible to outsiders since it is often carried out quietly and discreetly. It rarely makes the news, even though there is growing evidence that the policymakers of the Fund's member countries attach importance to it and that the receiving countries derive significant benefits from it. When this activity results in the writing of reports, these are written for the specific use of the most senior economic policymakers of the member countries. Because of their confidentiality, these reports are never available to the general public and are generally available to only a few key individuals.

It is natural that the individuals who are engaged in these activities often come to acquire a detailed and profound knowledge of the relevant area since they have access to information that is rarely available to others. The authors of the papers contained in this book have been deeply involved with technical assistance and, in more recent years, with technical assistance to the countries that are now generally called "economies in transition." These authors have spent much time in these countries studying their fiscal systems and assessing possible reforms. With one exception, all the authors have been associated with the Fiscal Affairs Department of the Fund, which is the department through which the Fund provides technical assistance in the fiscal area. Since technical assistance is closely connected with the creation of institutions and with policy reform in general, it is natural that the authors of these papers have a bias for the practical over the theoretical. The papers have been written to provide guidance to the policymakers in their reform effort rather than to provide classroom material for academic discussion. Thus, there is little abstract theorizing in them. Still, they should be useful to all those who have a genuine interest in understanding what is really going on in the economies in transition and to those who want to influence that process. It is, thus, the hope of the editor that the interest in this book will extend beyond those directly involved with fiscal reform in these countries and that this book will increase the general awareness about the obstacles and the possibilities faced by these countries. Incidently, the group of economies in transition extends beyond the countries of Central and Eastern Europe and includes some from other continents. Much of the focus in this volume is, however, on the Central and Eastern European countries.

As in the past couple of years, the Fiscal Affairs Department intensified its work in the transforming of planned economies; it became evident that the amount of knowledge of the fiscal systems of these countries and of the way in which those systems might develop was very limited. This lack of knowledge was likely to lead to mistakes on the part of economists advising these countries. The institutional limitations to policy changes were likely to be ignored, and unrealistic expectations about how soon new policies could be implemented would be created. In fact, the early talk about "big bang" solutions was largely the result of ignorance of the real situation. In fiscal policy, there cannot be any big bang solution since, before new policies can be introduced, new institutions must be created. And the creation of these new institutions will require a lot of effort and time. This realization provided a strong reason to make available to a wider audience some of the knowledge accumulated by those engaged in technical assistance in the fiscal area. The Fund could provide an important service to the general public, as well as to the policymakers of the relevant countries, by making some of this material generally available. An additional reason was that those who received the technical assistance reports would often not remain in their job for long so that the benefit of this assistance might be reduced by this lack of continuity.

In a period when "planning" has lost much of its allure, it must be admitted that this is a fully planned book. The content of edited books is rarely fully planned, since the editors of these books must rely on papers already available (often those presented at conferences) and can thus only marginally influence the content and the coverage of the papers. These papers often do not provide a cohesive whole. The genesis of the present book, however, is somewhat different. All the papers were written for this volume in response to specific instructions by the editor. As a consequence, they form a homogeneous body, covering all the major facets of fiscal policy. The book is likely to provide the most comprehensive treatment of fiscal issues in economies in transition now available in print.

The book is made up of three parts. The first part, consisting of four chapters, deals with general effects of fiscal policy, including the financing of the deficit, the management of public debt, and the fiscal implications of privatization of public enterprises. The second part, consisting of seven chapters, deals with revenue aspects in general, and especially with the setting up and the reform of tax systems. In fact, to be successful, the process of transformation of these economies must include the replacement of a revenue system that consists largely in the transfer of funds from relatively few surplus enterprises to the government to one that is based on the contribution of a very large number of taxpayers. One quick lesson learned from early work in these countries is that modern and market-economy types of tax systems have to be developed almost from scratch. The third part consists of five chapters dealing broadly with public expenditure. Once again, the lack of modern institutions in the budgetary area is highlighted.

Chapter 1, by Chand and Lorie, is a broad survey of fiscal issues in economies in transition. It is a kind of introductory overview. It covers the main feature of financial and fiscal policies under classical central planning, the consequences of partial reforms, the obstacles to market-oriented reform, and the requirements for a successful transition to a market economy.

The second chapter, by Adrienne Cheasty, covers an area that has received little, if any, attention so far, namely, the financing of growing fiscal deficits in countries that were not supposed to have deficits, that had experienced little, if any, deficits in the past, and that, as a consequence, did not have the institutions to absorb in a noninflationary way large fiscal deficits. Cheasty provides interesting data on five East European countries. She shows that it will be difficult for those countries to finance substantial deficits in noninflationary ways since central bank financing will almost inevitably have to play a large role in financing the deficits. In a way, the situation of these countries is similar to that of poorer developing countries with undeveloped capital markets and limited possibilities of placing bonds with the public. Foreign financing is also likely to be limited. Cheasty shows that the method by which budget deficits are financed will be an important determinant of the success of the stabilization efforts. Through a simulation exercise she shows the effects of financing alternatives on the fiscal deficit itself, on the inflation rate, and on the trade balance. The importance of foreign financing in reducing the cost of the transition is highlighted.

Chapter 3, by Mark Allen, also deals with a topic that has attracted almost no attention, namely, the management of the existing and growing domestic debt. He shows that, as time passes, the value of government-owned assets is becoming progressively lower while the government is nationalizing large and growing liabilities. Thus, the net worth of the public sector appears progressively lower. Examples of these liabilities are bad bank loans to the enterprise sector and bank losses arising out of housing credit extended at very low fixed interest rates. Thus, old debt is being added to newly created debt arising out of current fiscal deficits. This process is not complete so that the full extent of public debt is yet not known. The need to develop financial markets to encourage financial saving is stressed.

Chapter 4, by Richard Hemming, deals with a topic that, unlike those in Chapters 2 and 3, has received and continues to receive a lot of attention, namely, privatization. The privatization of state enterprises has been considered by many as a sine qua non for the transformation of these economies. It would generate resources for the government, it would create incentives for the enterprises to become more efficient, and it would remove from the management of those enterprises bureaucrats still ideologically committed to central planning. Without privatization it is unlikely that the public enterprises of these countries could meet the challenge of world competition. Unfortunately, so far, progress in this area has been slow. The reasons for privatization and the difficulties faced are discussed by Hemming's chapter, which also assesses the fiscal implications of privatization.

Chapter 5, by Krister Andersson, is a kind of introductory chapter to the chapters dealing with taxation. Andersson highlights efficiency considerations in the setting up of tax systems, considerations that may be ignored owing to the preoccupation with revenue or to the temptation on the part of policymakers to pursue some sort of industrial policy or some social objectives through the tax system. The debate between broad-based systems and special incentives is addressed, and some important tax incentives issues are discussed. A key question in this chapter is the kind of tax system that would contribute to a favorable investment climate.

Chapter 6, by Milka Casanegra, Carlos Silvani, and Charles Vehorn, addresses the issue of taxation from the angle of administrative feasibility. These authors argue that fundamental changes must take place in the institutions that deal with tax administration, and they outline some of these changes. New institutions must be created; staff must be trained; new procedures must be developed; and modern techniques must be introduced. All this will take a lot of effort and much time. The possibility of making mistakes will be particularly high in this area. Without a total restructuring of the tax administration, the reform of the tax system along the lines of market economies will remain a dream. This is a chapter that should be read by all tax experts from advanced market economies who are pushing their own ideas of a proper tax system on the economies in transition. And, of course, it should prove useful to the policymakers of those countries charged with reforming the tax systems.

Chapter 7, by Ved Gandhi and Dubravko Mihaljek, is a broad introductory chapter on the need for and the scope of tax reform in economies in transition. Noting that taxation has attracted little attention on the part of those who have written on the centrally planned countries, it argues that socialist economies in transition need tax reform and need it immediately. It goes on to discuss the role of various taxes and the reforms in other sectors required to make tax reform possible. For example, there is a loose link between tax reform, price reform, financial reform, external sector reform, and factor market reforms. This chapter discusses objectives and constraints of tax reform in the short run and over the longer run.

The following three chapters—Chapters 8, 9, and 10—by Leif Muten, Alan Tait, and Van-Can Thai, discuss respectively the three groups of taxes that will play a major role especially over the next few years, namely, income taxes, value-added taxes, and foreign-trade taxes.

Chapter 8, by Leif Muten, starts by outlining the role of income taxes in centrally planned economies. These taxes were not used to redistribute income, as their objective was achieved through more direct means, but to discourage private activities. The promotion of incentives was not an objective of policy, and the concept of income and profit was vague and not in accordance with accounting or economic concepts. In market economies, these taxes should be based on objective concepts, should be efficient, and possibly, should be consistent with the achievement of new objectives, such as an improvement in income distribution. Muten discusses various questions that must be addressed in the process of reforming these taxes.

Value-added taxes are likely to play a large role in the future of the tax systems of the economies in transition because of revenue needs and, especially for the Eastern European countries, because of their desire to get closer to European tax structures. Alan Tait's Chapter 9 is a careful evaluation of the prospects for the introduction of these taxes. He indicates that all the Eastern European countries have declared their intention to introduce value-added taxes soon and some have already done so. Tait discusses the obstacles faced in this process and outlines the structure of the tax that, in his view, is the best feasible one. Issues related to the size of the base and the structure of the rates receive careful attention. He cautions that the attempt to pursue objectives other than revenue generation through value-added taxes is bound to lead to value-added taxes that are far from efficient. Mistakes made at the time of introduction of the tax will be difficult to correct at a later time.

Foreign trade taxes play an important role in developing countries but not in industrial countries. In centrally planned economies, they did exist but their role was largely limited to insulating domestically controlled prices from variations in international prices and to obtaining trade concessions from other countries. In economies in transition, import duties may come to play roles closer to those played by these taxes in developing countries, namely, revenue generation and the protection of particular industries. The chapter by Van-Can Thai analyzes the role of foreign trade taxes in economies in transition. He reviews the recent role of tariffs in the reform of several of these countries and discusses the future role of tariffs as well as of export taxes and subsidies. Since this chapter deals with issues that have received almost no attention, it fills an important gap in the general knowledge.

The transformation of the economies of the previously centrally planned countries will be accelerated if foreign direct investment is attracted to these countries and if it brings needed capital, technology, and managerial skills. What are the factors that attract foreign direct investment? And what role can taxation play? These questions have often been raised in connection with developing countries. In Chapter 11, Erik Offerdal addresses the same questions within the context of economies in transition. He discusses the role of tax incentives, describes the current situation, and makes recommendations for further tax reform. He cautions that foreign direct investment will generate serious complications for a tax administration already strained by the changes taking place.

Chapter 12, by Ke-Young Chu and Robert Holzmann, surveys some general issues concerning public expenditure. It discusses the level of total expenditure in economies in transition as well as their structure. It shows that the level of public expenditure has been somewhat higher in these countries than in market economies owing largely to the role of transfers to families and enterprises. The transition to a market economy will require a redefinition of the role of government. The new role will almost surely be smaller. The macroeconomic situation and the probable decline in tax revenue will require a reduction in public spending, especially in transfer payments. Over the medium run such a reduction will not be easy.

The chapter by A. Premchand and L. Garamfalvi assesses the strength of budget and accounting systems in centrally planned economies and the extent to which these fiscal institutions can be adequate during the transition to a market economy. Their conclusion is that major reform will be necessary since the institutions that prevailed under central planning will prove to be wholly inadequate in the new situation. Once again these reforms will take time. As they put it: "...the recent experience with institutional developments suggests that it is a medium-term task, more suited to long-distance running than to sprinters." Premchand and Garamfalvi provide a careful outline of the changes that will be needed.

The question of social security in economies in transition is addressed by George Kopits in Chapter 14. He points out that "ironically, countries that have lived for decades under socialism are experiencing a social security crisis of major proportions." It is unlikely that the fiscal resources that will be available to these countries in future years will be sufficient to finance existing social security programs. Inevitably, major reforms aimed at reducing and restricting benefits will become essential if fiscal crises are to be avoided. This chapter provides a careful analysis of the problems for various programs such as old-age pensions and health related schemes and outlines future options for reform. Kopits emphasizes that stop-gap adjustments will not provide a solution and that fundamental reforms are necessary.

The transformation of the centrally planned economies will bring about major changes in income distribution and in living standards. Some groups are likely to experience unacceptable cuts in living standards. It is thus necessary that, especially during the period of transition, social safety nets are put into place so as to protect the most vulnerable groups. Chapter 15, by Ehtisham Ahmad, addresses this important topic. It discusses various options, such as cash compensation and means testing, categorical transfers and allowances, limited rationing, and other means for protecting the vulnerable groups. The likely prospect that tax revenue will fall during the transition makes it essential that whatever option is chosen, it cannot be a fiscally expensive one.

The last chapter, by Hewitt and Mikaljek, addresses an issue of growing importance in these countries, namely, the fiscal arrangements between the central government and the local government. How will the transition to a market economy affect the existing assignments of fiscal functions and power-sharing arrangements between different levels of government? Chapter 16 addresses this question. For sure, the transition is likely to lead to an increased role for the local governments. But then, how will they get their revenues? And what precisely will be their expenditure responsibilities? Hewitt and Mikaljek provide some answers.

PART I

General Aspects

CHAPTER 1 ═══════════════════════════

Fiscal Policy

Sheetal K. Chand and Henri R. Lorie

It is understandable that the authorities in the former centrally planned economies (CPEs) of Eastern Europe should still hold varying views on the role to be played by the state once they have completed their transition to a market economy. Reassuringly, the experience of countries in Western Europe provides a menu of institutions and social contrivances that have enabled their market economies to operate relatively smoothly, while promoting innovation, economic growth, and equity, despite some differences in social beliefs. Today, they offer a broad picture of where the former CPEs of Eastern Europe are headed in their endeavor to emulate and rejoin the rest of Europe.

What is far less charted, however, is the transition path to a market economy that minimizes economic and social cost. This problem is especially acute given the wide gap between the initial starting point of these economies and the desired market economy. Not only the institutional framework, but human attitudes and intellectual capital, will all have to be largely revamped. In essence, the situation faced by countries exiting from central planning can be compared to that of a building that has been constructed on an inadequate set of foundations, which can support only a much smaller structure than an alternative set of foundations (the market-oriented set). The main problem is how to change the foundations so that a larger building is attainable. While a rush to replace the foundations runs the risk of collapse—the building will then have to be constructed from the ground up—excessive gradualism will stunt desired growth. The trick to avoid losing too much of the old building while replacing the foundations quickly is to support those parts of the building that can be retained (such as the production of basic consumption [wage] goods), with temporary scaffolding. According to this analogy, promoting the desired transition will require a number of temporary interventions. The issue is which ones.

11

This paper considers the fiscal policy requirements—and their sequencing—for economies in transition. Since so much depends on initial conditions, the paper starts with an assessment of the role, characteristics, and consequences of financial and fiscal institutions and policies under classical and reformed central planning up to early 1990. It then examines the initial situation at the outset of the transition to a market-oriented economy, the macroeconomic reforms introduced, and some key fiscal implications. A strategy of fiscal reform for managing the transition, viewed as part of the overall reform effort, is subsequently developed.

Financial and Fiscal Policies Under Classical Central Planning

Main Features

In the early years after the Second World War, the Eastern-bloc countries were subject to *classical* central planning.[1] Based on an almost exclusive state ownership of means of production, the state determined what to produce and how to produce, leaving no role to markets and the price mechanism. Such decisions were made by the plan which also set out the investment strategy for the country. The plan emphasized almost exclusively quantitative targets, and although these were valued through the use of prices, the latter were set administratively and kept rigid for long periods of time. Consequently, they generally did not reflect relative scarcities and opportunity costs. The performance of state enterprises was measured by how well they met the quantitative targets. The *incentive structure*—including bonuses to workers and management—was geared to output maximization and over-fulfillment of the plan rather than to efficiency and innovation. Insofar as prices were based on costs plus mark-up, there was little incentive for cost minimization. In cost calculations, capital was largely viewed as a free good from the individual enterprises' point of view, a perspective reinforced by extremely low interest rates and the arbitrary transfers of depreciation funds to the budget.

The monetary counterpart of classical central planning was reflected in the annual financial plans. These consisted of the state budget, credit plan, cash plan, and the foreign exchange plan. Subordinated to the physical plan, they mostly served as accounting instruments to facilitate the implementation of physical transactions, control the enterprises' activities, and

---

[1]For a fuller description, see Gregory and Stuart (1986) and Wanless (1985).

enforce accountability. Inter-enterprise transactions were effected through immediate debiting and crediting of largely earmarked accounts in the monobank, which also provided limited financing for working capital and sometimes investments as specified ex ante in the plan. In general, enterprises had little freedom in the use of their bank deposits, while strictly regulated wage funds limited the injection of cash in the economy through wage increases. Furthermore, most of the enterprises' savings and investments were intermediated through the state budget—in particular, through the full transfer of the enterprises' residual income. However, households constituted an exception since they exerted independent control on their cash holdings and savings account deposits. Thus, the balance between households' income and expenditure was directly affected by monetary aggregates, together with their decisions regarding how much to save or to spend.[2]

State Budgets

Public policy objectives of the Eastern bloc focused on (i) the implementation of a development strategy aimed at rapid industrialization and "extensive" economic growth;[3] (ii) the generous provision of public goods in areas such as education, health, culture, and transportation virtually free of charge; (iii) the state commitment to take care of the young, old, and sick through a comprehensive system of social security and welfare benefits; and (iv) the implementation of an egalitarian approach to income and consumption that would also release resources for the growth process. Money wages tended to be low and fairly uniform, but accompanied with a significant non-cash component in the form of subsidized access to basic necessities such as food, shelter, heating, electricity, and transportation. The emphasis of the budget was thus on allocative and redistributive functions of fiscal policy. The need for a stabilization function was limited, except when supply side and terms of trade shocks occurred, or when there was a demand imbalance emanating from the household sector.[4] However, major financial imbalances were to result from the partial attempt to reform classical central planning.

The pursuit of the above objectives was generally done without recourse to inflationary financing. This required that large budgetary outlays be matched by equally large receipts, particularly in connection with

---

[2]See Ofer (1989).

[3]This relies heavily on the absorption of available labor and natural resources rather than on the "intensive" use of these resources.

[4]See, for example, Fetherston (1983).

the redistributive and financial intermediation roles assumed by the state budget. Total revenue and expenditure in the Eastern-bloc countries consistently amounted to 50–60 percent of GDP (except in the case of the U.S.S.R. and Yugoslavia for whom those ratios are lower) which was about 10 percentage points higher than observed for the typical European Community (EC) country. However, on excluding from revenue that part of receipts that can reasonably be estimated as the return from state capital, and from expenditure most subsidies and noninfrastructural capital outlays, these aggregates fall below those of EC countries. Both revenue and expenditure would also be further reduced by eliminating certain "grossing-ups" at the enterprises' level that do not exist in Western fiscal systems.[5] A better approximation is then obtained of the true extent of the state's delivery of public goods and services and ability to raise resources to finance such activities, as generally understood in market economies. This is distinct from the issue of the state's influence over the economy, which of course was pervasive in the former Eastern-bloc countries.

Public policy directions and their requirements largely determined the structure of budgetary revenue and expenditure as well as the institutional framework to implement the budget. Only a few of their salient features can be highlighted here. On the revenue side, receipts from profits, the turnover tax, and social security or payroll taxes accounted for the bulk of revenue. The low wage policy, low interest rates, and the "socialist" accounting practices pursued tended to inflate the enterprises' residual income (despite sometimes high payroll taxes) that was transferred to the budget. Turnover taxes and subsidies were defined as the difference between administratively set wholesale and retail prices. In addition to being a key revenue mobilizing instrument, they could be used to regulate incipient demand and supply imbalances resulting from the mismatch between planner's and households' preferences.[6] The compression of wages and salaries left little room for income taxation, which was used instead to impose punitive marginal tax rates on self-employed professionals, artists, and businesses so as to reduce such incomes to public sector levels. Emphasis on administered trade specialization within the Council for Mutual Economic Assistance (CMEA) left no role for tariff protection, while imports of consumer goods from the west faced strict quantitative restrictions which, in conjunction with administratively set prices, also

---

[5]These concern, in particular, subsidized inputs and the nonpecuniary component of wages.

[6]Luxuries tended to carry high turnover taxes while necessities were subsidized. Vertical equity was therefore maintained while horizontal equity was protected through income transfers according to family needs.

allowed the state to collect scarcity rents. Generally, the dissociation of domestic prices of tradables from their international prices led the state to collect revenues (pay subsidies) on foreign trade through the so-called equalization fund. The high concentration of economic activity in a small number of state enterprises and the expected close adherence to the "plan" facilitated the control and payment of tax liabilities to the budget.

On the expenditure side, subsidies and social security outlays represented large shares of total expenditure, each reaching in most cases 20–30 percent, or equivalent to some 10–15 percent of gross domestic product (GDP) each.[7] Subsidies applied mainly to certain consumption goods and to certain industrial inputs, while pensions, disability benefits, and child allowances accounted for the whole of social security outlays. Unemployment benefits were little used since the state guaranteed some form of employment to all, while the welfare programs as a whole could be limited given the extent of price subsidies and universality of social benefits. In part the horizontal equity and anti-poverty objectives were addressed through universal family benefits (including child allowances). Generally, the goal of reducing the poverty "gap," defined as the percentage of the population living below the deemed subsistence level, was to a large extent achieved. Investment outlays were also substantial, the largest part being implemented through the budget, including both infrastructure and fixed capital formation in enterprises. Criteria for determining the allocation of investment emphasized objectives and gave little consideration to rates of return as an intertemporal allocative device.[8]

Partial Reforms and Their Consequences

Changes in Incentive Structure

The several partial attempts at reforming central planning during the last quarter century were motivated by (i) the increasing exhaustion of "extensive" growth potentials as evidenced by declining growth rates, despite sustained high investment rates; and (ii) the growing awareness of the inefficiencies and lack of innovation associated with the centralized decision and incentive system, which continued to broaden the competitive gap with the West.[9]

---

[7]The latter, in countries where social security benefits were mainly provided through the budget; in others, such as the U.S.S.R., the enterprises carried a large share of social security outlays.

[8]See Tanzi (1991) for the argument that CPEs have mobilized too much savings by the state and misallocated it.

[9]For the case of the U.S.S.R., see Ofer (1990).

A key element of the partial reforms was the shift in the incentive structure that was to accompany the decentralization of decisions toward enterprises. The *plan* would no longer provide detailed specifications on what and how much to produce, and the importance of state orders was reduced. Instead, the enterprises were given greater flexibility in input, employment and wages, and investment policy decisions, and were told to "maximize profits." Both the payment of bonuses and creation of development funds to finance the enterprises' own investment projects were directly linked to the generation of cash-flow surpluses.

The new incentive structure was supported by changing the system of profits transfers to the budget to one increasingly determined by parametric rules (i.e., tax rates), although these still tended to be differentiated among sectors and even enterprises.[10] In consequence, the enterprises rather than the state became the recipient of the residual income from economic activity, even though the state remained the owner of the capital. However, another consequence of the devolution of certain investment decisions to enterprises was that capital expenditures of the state budget could also be curtailed.

The partial reform programs aimed at establishing a closer correspondence between domestic wholesale prices (still fixed administratively) and international prices, using a more uniform set of exchange rates. The objective was to improve efficiency by eliminating price distortions. This policy exposed the nonprofitability of certain sectors under the prevailing exchange rates. However, the failure to apply a tight budget constraint on the enterprises led not to a more desirable reallocation of capital, but to the emergence of deficits financed by the budget through operating subsidies, or by the banking system. Furthermore, while some production subsidies were removed by increasing wholesale prices above international prices in order to cover costs, the result often conflicted with the egalitarian objectives of the authorities who consequently did not pass through the adjustment to retail prices on consumer necessities. The decline in production subsidies would therefore be offset by higher consumer subsidies. Exchange rate overvaluation also necessitated larger export subsidies for trade with both the CMEA and the convertible area. Hence, the partial reforms had only little impact in reducing total subsidy outlays, which remained consistently around 10–15 percent of GDP throughout most of the CMEA until 1990 (Table 1).

---

[10]The differentiation acted perversely as profitable enterprises were subjected to high rates and less profitable enterprises to lower rates.

Ultimately, the partial reforms failed because most of the features of central planning were still retained. At best, they may have permitted some cost minimization. However, the reforms failed to introduce genuine market and price liberalization, so that there was no price-based mechanism to avoid shortages. Both the official exchange rates and interest rates continued to be largely dissociated from the real value of the domestic currency and capital, necessitating the administrative allocation of foreign exchange and credit. The reforms also left untouched state ownership of the means of production, but weakened rather than strengthened the rights and effective control of the state as owner of the capital in enterprises. As a result, the decentralization of decisions conferred greater responsibility to managers, but with less accountability. Nor did the risk of enterprise bankruptcy impose discipline as the banking system willingly accommodated the financing needs of enterprises. In this climate, and with the prevalent incentive structure, managers tended to devote resources to bargaining with the state so as to make their enterprises more "profitable," including negotiating tax preferences and subsidies, and colluding with the workers to generate and share short-run cash-flow surpluses. Insofar as higher profits generated in this manner financed greater investments, resource allocation was not necessarily improved. Cheap, accessible credit encouraged extensive capital investment and inventory accumulation, and even supported the granting of money wage increases, with negative spillovers on the balance of payments, which led to rising foreign indebtedness. Although the partial reforms modified incentives, they did so in a manner that increasingly violated the macroeconomic balance between demand and supply. The improvement in incentives was incomplete and not complemented by the development of new instruments for control and influence.

Stabilization Policies

Under classical central planning, the sources of macroeconomic imbalances took largely the form of supply shocks and external terms of trade shocks. In particular, overly ambitious plan targets were frequently underfulfilled, creating shortages, which for inputs could lead to further shortages in the production of goods that depended upon them.[11] These shortages were managed by administratively reallocating outputs and inputs

---

[11]For an informative account of stabilization problems in planned economies, see Wolf (1985a).

Table 1. Fiscal Data for Eastern European Countries, General Government, 1980–90

(Period averages; in percent of GDP)

	Bulgaria		Czechoslovakia		Hungary		Poland		Romania		U.S.S.R.		Yugoslavia
	1985–89	1990	1980–89	1990	1982–89	1990	1984–89	1990	1981–89	1990	1985–89	1990	1980–89
Total revenue	57.7	55.7	56.4	56.6	60.6	58.1	46.8	43.9	45.7	38.6	43.8	42.7	33.5
Individual income taxes	4.0	4.2	6.9	6.6	1.9	6.3	0.8	0.6	0.1	0.0	4.0	4.5	1.7
Enterprise taxes	20.2	19.2	17.0	12.4	10.7	7.6	10.1	12.4	15.6	7.4	14.5	13.0	1.4
Social security contributions and payroll tax	9.6	10.5	7.0	13.1	13.2	15.9	10.3	3.0	11.9	14.4	3.4	4.7	17.9
Domestic taxes on goods & services	13.0	10.4	17.1	17.4	18.8	16.4	12.7	6.3	10.5	12.0	11.7	12.7	8.2
Taxes on international trade	3.8	3.7	1.5	1.4	3.4	3.4	2.3	0.6	0.0	0.0	7.0	5.1	3.0
Other revenue	7.1	7.7	7.0	5.5	12.5	8.4	10.6	20.9	7.6	4.8	3.1	2.7	1.2
Total expenditure and net lending	61.0	66.9	57.9	61.2	61.9	58.3	48.7	40.1	40.7	39.6	50.7	50.6	33.0
Consumption	26.1	30.3	24.0	26.9	22.7	23.7	…	…	14.8	16.6	25.7	24.7	…
Interest payments	1.7	10.5	0.0	0.2	1.6	3.0	…	…	0.4	0.0	0.3	0.9	…
Subsidies	15.6	15.9	14.2	13.8	16.4	10.0	15.8	7.3	7.6	8.0	7.2	7.9	…
Social security	10.2	13.2	12.4	13.7	13.2	17.6	9.2	9.0	1.3	7.2	9.3	12.8	…
Capital expenditure	9.7	5.6	7.3	6.7	8.0	4.1	6.5	2.9	16.6	7.8	8.2	4.4	…
Extrabudgetary	46.5	−180.0	…	…	…	…	…	…	…	…	…	…	…
SURPLUS/DEFICIT (−)	−2.4	−8.6	−1.5	−4.7	−1.4	−0.2	−2.0	3.8	4.9	−1.0	−6.9	−7.9	0.4
Memo Item:													
Enterprise tax less subsidies	4.5	3.3	2.8	−1.3	−5.7	−2.3	−5.7	5.2	14.3	0.2	5.1	0.2	…

Sources: Staff estimates.

[1]1989 estimated, 1990 planned.

and by imports, often to the benefit of enterprises and at the expense of households. Without price flexibility, shortages often resulted in further rationing and forced accumulation of money balances, and stimulated the emergence of black market activities, although frequent attempts were made to control such activities. Generally, the credit and cash plans exerted tight control which limited the extent of such disequilibria. The same was true for imbalances attributable to terms of trade shocks, although here the impact might have been more severe because with fixed domestic prices, the deterioration in the terms of trade did not affect the position of households and enterprises, but was entirely reflected in the budgetary outcome since *net* revenue from import price differences, in particular, declined. However, households would eventually be hit since deliveries to the domestic market would be reduced by the requirement of generating higher exports to pay for unchanged volumes of planned imports of inputs.[12]

The looser financial policies generally accompanying partial reforms, particularly with regard to credit, and the more expansive wage policies, added an "excessive demand" dimension to the stabilization problems of reformed CPEs. As a result of the perverse interaction between partial reform measures and the maintenance of key economic and institutional features of central planning, shortages intensified. One consequence was to induce destabilizing responses as enterprises and households tried to protect themselves by building large inventories of inputs and goods.

On the budget side, the partial reforms led in most cases to a significant decline in receipts from enterprise profits, reflecting both tax policy changes and a fall in the profits base itself. The latter tended to reflect on one hand the growth of wages outpacing productivity gains and, on the other hand, the impact of external shocks, in particular terms of trade deterioration. These developments also led in many cases to a decline in enterprise net of tax savings despite a general reduction of the state's take in the income generation of enterprises.

The current balance of the state budget was, however, less affected as government consumption expenditures, including maintenance of the physical, education, and health infrastructure were curtailed. Reflecting the impact of higher real wages, the buildup of a monetary overhang,[13]

---

[12]See Wolf (1985b).

[13]There may have been two components to this overhang: one reflecting the spillover effect on money demand of shortages in the goods' market; and the other, the voluntary build-up of money balances under repressed financial markets for the purpose of purchasing durables, particularly under conditions of limited availability. See Blanchard and others (1990).

and possibly a perceived decline in state provision of life-cycle needs, observable households' savings, on the other hand, tended to rise markedly. This facilitated the financing of the capital outlays, although state budget Capital expenditures were often curtailed at the same time as investment decisions were devolved to enterprises, whose total domestic investment remained high. Hence, decentralization under the partial reforms contributed to the emergence of a large imbalance between saving and investment at the level of enterprises. The state budget's role in the emergence of that disequilibrium was in most countries secondary, at least until the very end of the experiment with the partial reforms.[14]

Onset of Market-Oriented Reform

The essence of a comprehensive market reform, in addition to relying on widespread private ownership, is the recourse to flexible prices and markets for reconciling demands and supplies for goods and services and for allocating scarce resources. This represents a fundamental systemic change from the use of bureaucratic methods to achieve the reconciliation in a context of rigid prices. However, while there is a gain in efficiency and, through reliance on the profit motive, a more effective exploitation of technological advances, the potential for instability becomes more generalized. The state gives up direct control over the demands and supplies of major sectors of the economy, who may now behave in ways that do not ensure that the productive capacity of the economy is always adequately utilized. The price that transactors must be willing to pay in a market economy in return for greater economic freedom involves both the heightened risks of business failure and less job security. At the same time, the emergence of a private sector and private forms of ownership, together with the likely initial large price adjustments, can lead to massive redistributions of income and wealth that may not accord with widely held equity goals. Such problems are likely to be made more difficult by the interaction between inherited institutions and practices and the new reality of market reform, which need to be examined first.

Legacy

The past weighs heavily on the former centrally planned economies as they transit to market-oriented economies with regard to (i) the productive and incentive environment; and (ii) the institutional environment.

---

[14]A major exception is the U.S.S.R., for whom a large increase in subsidies accompanied partial price reforms.

Production and Incentive Structure

The characteristics of production, including the amount and allocation of capital, are essentially given at the outset of the transition, and are likely to be adjusted only gradually over the medium term. However, given the new set of relative prices for factors and inputs, unrestrained profit maximization, especially on the part of monopolies, could lead to massive disruptions in output, employment, and the relative shares of wages and profits. With the very large terms of trade shifts (see below), there is a high probability of "corner solutions" and negative value added at the level of individual enterprises.[15] This suggests that welfare could decline markedly in the short run. Furthermore, the initial phase of the transition to a market economy will take place in an environment where the state still looms extremely large as owner of most enterprises and controller of regulatory and licensing arrangements. Lacking ownership rights, the profit-oriented incentives could operate perversely to encourage managers of potential candidates for privatization to exploit a monopoly position and siphon away funds and contracts for their own use. As long as the relationships between the state enterprises, government, and banking system have not been clarified, and new market-oriented tax arrangements put in place, the incentive structure is likely to remain ambiguous, with possible perverse results.

Inherited Fiscal Institutions

The revenue and expenditure systems that are inherited are not geared to the requirements of a market economy. Expenditure, which has a pervasive effect on resource allocation, needs to be contained and directed to new goals, while the tax design will have to be adapted to the new realities, taking account of market-based reactions.

Virtually all the elements of the traditional tax system will have to be overhauled. For instance, the profit tax is mostly concerned with the transfer to the budget of the state enterprises' surpluses, according to their individual means. Consequently, exemptions, multiple rates, and special privileges abound that would be harmful for efficiency and revenue mobilization, in a context where the taxpayer is free to organize his activities. The discriminatory income tax rates that apply to the private sector are not supportive of their activities and will have to be reformed. The turnover tax in its old form (i.e., levied as a wedge between fixed retail and producer prices) cannot deal with free—and consequently variable—

---

[15]See, in particular, the argument of McKinnon (1989).

prices. Revenue from price and so-called coefficient differences on international trade and transactions cannot survive the liberalization of trade practices and prices, nor the unification of applicable exchange rates, and new trade-related taxes will need to be established. However, with trade channeled through monolithic trading enterprises, essential customs functions have been neglected.

A major casualty of the interaction between the inherited institutions and the liberalizing reform is likely to be the tax on profits, a mainstay of the pre-reform revenue system, which could exhibit severe erosion. Furthermore, enterprises on being further decentralized would tend to exercise greater autonomy in the management of their cash flow and resist the transfer of profits to the state. In the meantime, the reform process will encourage the establishment of privately run enterprises. However, the tax administration is only geared to taxing state enterprises, with virtually no capacity to tax a rapidly growing number of private, profit-motivated firms. The latter will find it in their interests to practice tax avoidance and evasion, especially if they continue to be subjected to highly confiscatory tax rates. State enterprises themselves could exploit weaknesses in the taxation of private enterprises by manipulating transfer prices and shifting profits to them. Potentially severe revenue losses could also result from a failure to rebase the turnover tax to the new flexible price environment, which would include the introduction of appropriate excise duties and customs levies.

In addition to a declining revenue performance, the weaknesses in the tax system would hamper attainment of the equity goals that are so prominent in the centrally planned economies. The abandonment of direct means of ensuring consistency with the equity goals through wage and price controls places the onus for achieving consistency on less direct fiscal instruments such as taxes. However, neither tax policy nor its administration are geared to effectively taxing undesired distributions of incomes and windfalls, such as various forms of capital gains, that will become possible in a free market environment. Furthermore, since transactors will be free to choose how to respond to market signals, the inherited tax system could induce highly inefficient responses that will exact a heavy cost from the economy.

The expenditure side generates several limitations to be overcome. Typically, outlays have been incurred in pursuit of goals laid down in the plan, but the abandonment of planning will require new approaches to the determination of goals and means. In particular, unless there is substantial downsizing of government, decentralization will not be a success. Furthermore, the systems of budgeting and expenditure management are geared to control and accountability of the outlays specified in the plan rather than encouraging spending agencies to formulate their budgets flex- *account'y* ibly within the given totals so as to get value for money and avoid waste. *vs* Traditional procedures for monitoring state enterprises focus more on *efficiency* whether quantities actually produced and sold warrant the level of subsidies or turnover tax payments that have been planned, and on whether profit transfers to the budget are in line with targets, rather than on genuine indicators of efficiency and profitability.

Government is also massively involved in the transactions of the economy through widespread commitments and interventions in the form of implicit subsidies (and taxes), implicit contracts, and contingent liabilities. For example, interest and exchange rates were not only administratively determined under central planning, they were also set at highly repressed levels in accordance with the plan's objective of rapid (and import dependent) industrialization, as well as cheap housing, implying large implicit subsidies for the beneficiaries and large implicit taxes on exporters and savers. Similarly, low wages reflected a quid pro quo between the government or state enterprises and the households regarding the provision of pension and family benefits on an unfunded basis, low prices for necessities, and free education and health care. The undoing of these implicit contracts, even if accompanied by higher wages for the working population, would hurt particularly hard the old and households with young children. Examples of contingent liabilities of the state budget relate to the unfunded provision of disability insurance and unemployment compensation insurance, and the extension of borrowed foreign exchange to enterprises without requiring them to assume the exchange rate risk.

Macroeconomic Consequences

At the time the reform is initiated the initial conditions are likely to be grim. A history of partial and inconsistent reforms in an environment of increasingly lax financial policies, difficulties in mobilizing foreign financing, and a deteriorating external economic environment bring to the forefront both the stabilization and restructuring needs. The latter are compounded by the severe terms of trade losses faced by several of the economies as a consequence of moving to world market pricing for their oil and other imports (as well as for often previously overpriced uncompetitive exports). For some of the economies this has led to an acute shortage of foreign exchange that has necessitated very large devaluations. Imports have been priced out of reach of much of the economy, which has led to import curtailment and the loss of domestic production.

On initiating the reform, three major price groupings are likely to undergo major adjustment—the exchange rate, interest rates, and goods prices—so as to more closely accord with demand and supply conditions and international prices. The adjustment of prices would initially be toward "parallel" market prices and hence involve overshooting. Such adjustment will have both balance sheet or stock effects and repercussions for flows that may create serious imbalances in the macroeconomy and especially for the budget. If not promptly attended to, the result could be a further destabilization and distortion of the economy. Thus, a policy of depreciating the exchange rate, while required to create the conditions for an improvement in the balance of payments, could cause a contraction, insofar as the price level is moved up and the price of imported inputs rises, leading to an unwanted redistribution of assets and income. A similar outcome could result from an abrupt increase in interest rates. This could be especially problematic in cases where the balance sheet structure of the entity reflected past ad hoc relations with the State, for example, highly leveraged debt instead of equity.

A contraction would reduce revenue, while increasing pressure on the social safety net; positive interest rates would also directly increase the debt service burden. Financial instruments are required to alleviate such consequences, while promoting the objectives of reform. The dilemma is that for some time to come the reforming economies will have to rely on fiscal policies, as the principal means for both containing the economic contraction and promoting structural change and equity goals. Monetary and credit policies and financial institutions would be too weak in the initial stages. However, for the budget to be deployed as an effective instrument, any adverse repercussions on the budget itself of the market-oriented reforms will first have to be contained, on which some suggestions are developed in the next section.

Fiscal Policies to Manage the Transition

The fiscal policy challenge of the transition is to contribute to the stabilization effort without delaying the fiscal restructuring necessary, which in part involves strengthening the fiscal instrument itself. The budget should provide incentives for economic recovery, in particular the growth of the private sector, and contribute to improving the economic and administrative infrastructure. Since little can be done in the short run to change fiscal institutions, especially the tax administration and budgeting practices, fiscal policies have to be formulated taking this constraint into account. Furthermore, the structural adjustment will have to be phased in such a way that revenues will continue to be collected and essential functions maintained. Some temporary fiscal instruments will have to be developed for the short run to help stabilize the economy and to ease the transition on the supply side, so as to buy time for the more desirable longer-term restructuring of the fiscal instruments. Fiscal measures are also needed for the early consideration of equity issues arising out of the adjustment process so as to promote a consensus in favor of reforms, in societies that continue to be very sensitive to social justice and harmony.

Improving Fiscal Institutions

Abandoning centralized control in favor of indirect instruments in a market economy will necessitate a different fiscal approach insofar as the concern becomes one of influencing behavior. With regard to tax policy, a number of steps can be taken immediately. First, the tax reform should eliminate the discriminatory taxation of private sector activities at penalty rates, in order to encourage its rapid development. In addition, price liberalization must be accompanied by a rebasing of the turnover tax system, preferably into an ad valorem sales tax, broadly based and with one or two rates only. Immediate elimination of the multitude of exemptions and special privileges for the different categories of taxation is also essential to present from the start an even playing field. Furthermore, measures to protect the revenue base, particularly during the initial period of large price inflation, must be instituted at the outset. More fundamental reforms, such as the formulation of a value-added tax (VAT) system, would be undertaken in due course.[16]

A critical requirement is to develop government administration, and the tax administration in particular, so as to handle tasks in a market environment, which will include new enforcement procedures. Such institutional adjustment will take years, since it requires comprehensive reorganization and retraining and recruitment of appropriate staff. However, some crucial initial steps can be taken to strengthen the tax administration as it applies to existing—mostly state-owned—enterprises. A more effective monitoring system to fill the gap left by the abandonment of central planning is required. This is especially important with regard to the state enterprises, which will now enjoy greater autonomy and, given their monopoly powers, be in a position to exploit the liberalization process. Appropriate incentives to motivate civil servants should also be provided. However,

---

[16]For an overview, see Tanzi (1991).

the initial adjustment in prices is likely to cause considerable erosion in real salary levels. Hence, to motivate tax officers in particular and to reduce any incentive to engage in corrupt practices, special facilities will need to be given to them such as revenue-related bonuses.

The budget formulating agencies will have to develop a separate capability for undertaking cost-benefit evaluations of expenditure programs, rather than rely on central planning determinations. As this is likely to take time, while new opportunities will arise for a misallocation of resources, expenditure control and accountability will have to be stressed in the initial stages. Since the bureaucracy will be geared to a different perception of its functions, considerable confusion is likely to result. This could adversely affect outlays in critical areas such as operations and maintenance, and the provision of social benefits. Putting in place an adequate social safety net to cope with the new hardships requires reshaping the existing social security and welfare system and creating new facilities and skills. Both to comply with the budget constraint and to promote market determined wage bargaining, benefits will increasingly have to be targeted to those whose needs are greatest and means smallest. This will require considerable reorganization of existing administrative mechanisms that are geared to providing generalized benefits.[17]

Institutional practices for financing a budget deficit and managing cash will also need to be reformed to accommodate a market economy. The budget can no longer be financed through monetary accommodation, since the proceeds would not now be automatically sterilized through forced savings. Spending agencies will have to change their operating procedures to cope with this hard budget constraint. The practice of holding large amounts of cash on deposit by different departments, while at the same time owing large debts to the banking system, will no longer be practical, given that the spread between lending and deposit interest rates will now be much higher and government will be paying more for its loans. To save costs, more effective cash management will be needed. More generally, the practice of different departments and state enterprises running up arrears with each other should be curtailed.

Stabilization Role

Most observers agree that in the initial stages the budget, as the principal instrument for stabilizing the economy, should be used (i) to withdraw liquidity from the economy, or at least not contribute additional liquidity;

---

[17]Kopits (1991).

and (ii) to provide resources for the rehabilitation of the rest of the economy.

While the above policies would tackle the "flow" stabilization problem, some attention must also be devoted to the 'stock' stabilization problem. The cumulated fiscal imbalances of the past, at rigidly fixed and increasingly unrealistic prices, were partially sterilized through rationing and the buildup of a substantial monetary "overhang." For example, in the U.S.S.R., this is estimated to amount to some 25 percent GDP in 1990.[18] The means for tackling the stock aspect of the stabilization problem involve essentially fiscal policy options, with budget ramifications that extend well into the future.[19] At least in theory, price liberalization combined with tight flow constraints should take care of the "one-step" price adjustment. However, this could be problematic since it might involve an overshooting of prices and bear adverse distributional and inflationary expectations consequences.

Alternative means to eliminate the monetary overhang would be (i) monetary reform, and (ii) an aggressive interest rate policy. The first approach, which has not generally been adopted (with the partial exception of the Soviet Union), is the equivalent of a 100 percent tax on (part of) money holdings (earmarked for repayment of the state budget indebtedness vis-à-vis the banking system). If the "frozen" deposits of state enterprises are the ones confiscated, this would leave resources for privatization. The second approach of raising interest rates should make it more attractive to hold money balances, thereby lessening the potential inflationary effect of price liberalization. However, the public debt service burden would rise, and unless offset by additional revenue measures or higher interest recoveries on government's own lending, could necessitate monetary financing.[20] The end result could be a validation (and more) of the inflation process that the high interest rate policy was supposed to prevent in the first place. In practice, a combination of elements of all three alternatives may be considered.

The earlier analysis of this paper points to the emergence of severe macroeconomic disequilibria following decentralization at the level of state enterprises. Given the medium-to-long-run nature of privatization and incentive reforms, state intervention and control in this sector will remain critical in the short term and should focus on subjecting them to a

---

[18]See International Monetary Fund (1991).

[19]These issues are also discussed in Calvo and Frenkel (1991).

[20]The possibility that rising prices may accentuate the "flow" disequilibrium by worsening the fiscal balance is also discussed by Fisher and Gelb (1990).

hard budget constraint. In addition, it will be necessary to impose: (i) quantitative limits on net bank credit; (ii) a moratorium on new investments of state enterprises—including stock building—and their financing pending a clarification of the price incentive environment (i.e., relative price stability), with a few exceptions such as for telephone and other utility companies; and (iii) the temporary continuation of a wage and incomes policy dictated from above.

Aside from its role discussed above in combating inflation, the budget also could play a critical role in maintaining an acceptable level of output. At a minimum, the production of wage goods needed to sustain basic consumption should be protected during the initial period, while markets are emerging, and there is considerable confusion and uncertainty as to the binding relative prices. This also argues for caution in allowing the emergence of large wage differentials across and within state enterprises. Of course, to the extent that price liberalization removes consumer subsidies—and related budgetary outlays—the price of basic wage goods will rise, which could be offset by granting an income supplement of the same amount. The once-and-for-all replacement of a large array of separate subsidies by a wage supplement of the same amount is a good measure as it expands the choice set of individuals and thereby enhances efficiency and welfare and should be undertaken at the outset. From a budgetary standpoint this is costless. However, separately, some reduction in the newly defined level of real wages may be necessary to take account of a terms of trade deterioration. Broadly, the basic thrust of the fiscal and other measures should be to ensure that there is adequate demand for domestic wage goods, on which the livelihoods of so many depend.

Policies to Ease Transition on the Supply Side

Extensive liberalization could exert serious adverse effects in the short run on production and the financial situation of enterprises, households, and ultimately the banking system. The budget, through its outlays, could play an important role in cushioning temporarily some of the more extreme effects so as to create a breathing space for the desired supply side responses to occur.

One example concerns the likely uncompetitiveness of a number of manufacturing and industrial sectors, including consumer goods and agro-industrial products, which under the old regime were protected by strict quantitative restrictions, but will bear the immediate shock of trade liberalization. For many of these enterprises, devaluation and wage restraint might not be enough to make them viable in the new environment, given their high import content and lack of substitutability with foreign counter-parts. Yet, it might be that limited amounts of resources spent to restructure and improve product specification, quality, and marketing could improve their marketability. Clearly, this process would require some time and resources. Merely eliminating price distortions is likely to have only limited impact on resource reallocation in the short run, and could even cause disruptions, particularly since credit and capital markets will be very imperfect for some time. One way out, of course, would be to provide temporary operating and restructuring subsidies. An alternative would be to re-internalize the operating subsidy by introducing *temporary* duties on competing imports. The resulting budgetary receipts could in turn be used for other costs of restructuring.[21]

Another (related) example concerns the domestic pricing of petroleum products during the transition to a market economy. Full pass-through of external developments in this area involves two major shocks (i) the increase of border prices for petroleum imports from the Soviet Union to their international levels; and (ii) the massive devaluation of the domestic currency, with its often recognized element of initial "overshooting." Generally, domestic prices of petroleum products for industrial users (for which the taxes are often rebated) would increase in percentage terms by the full amount of the increase in import costs, but the percentage increase could be substantially less for households if existing excises are on a specific rather than ad valorem basis. Since the double shock in domestic petroleum prices for industrial users could be the main factor underlying the unprofitability of a significant part of the manufacturing sector, tempo-rary subsidization of industrial users would ease the transition to an even-tual full pass-through. The temporary operation of a dual exchange rate could also be an implicit and non-budgetary way to operate this scheme, which would be financed by the implicit taxation of exports for which the more appreciated exchange rate would apply. An alternative and more transparent approach would be to have a temporary but explicit bud-getary subsidy, which will, however, need to be financed.

A third example concerns the implications of the move toward more realistic or market-determined interest rates. Obviously, this is a key mechanism to ensure a more efficient allocation of capital and to encour-age private savings. How fast should holders of "old loans," whether households' housing finance or enterprises' investment credit, be required

---

[21]Given the likely short-run price inelasticities, what matters most is that the policy decision to eventually eliminate the price distortions is clearly announced and perceived as irrevocable.

to meet the new interest rate conditions? There seems to be no reason to postpone the adjustment for households that would receive offsets in the form of interest income on deposits and a compensatory (partial) increase in salaries.[22] However, enterprises could face both profitability and cash-flow problems. To the extent that these constraints could be remedied through restructuring, there may be a case for temporary interest subsidies. In general, explicit subsidies would be preferable to the relief that could be provided by the capitalization of interest obligations due. This is because the nontransparency of the latter would not easily allow a distinction between enterprises in temporary versus permanent difficulties (which should obviously be liquidated) and ultimately lead to a further weakening of the banks' balance sheet. In addition, since capitalization of interest would need to be accommodated within previously established credit ceilings, they would crowd out legitimate credit demand from new starting firms of the private sector.[23]

Other budget outlays could also be applied to removing bottlenecks that impede the adjustment process, for example, the economic and administrative infrastructure, so as to increase exports and encourage foreign investors. It would be desirable to invest in critical aspects of human capital neglected under central planning, such as commercial and business studies. Another key requirement is to make banks and credit institutions responsive to the needs of the productive sector—especially the new private ventures. This would require (i) training and retraining of their staff; and (ii) a cleanup of the banks' balance sheets, without which bank activities would remain stifled and foreign participation and privatization of financial institutions would be very difficult. The budget would have to meet a significant part of the cost, for instance, in the form of a swap of government securities against nonperforming assets of the banking system, leading to higher budgetary interest expenditures. However, since the financial conditions of the enterprises determine the health of the banks, financial sector restructuring and the emergence of a viable com-

---

[22] Of course, there is the possibility—especially for the short run—that the increase in interest rates is such that mortgage payments exceed temporarily many times the share of total income they used to represent. In this case, explicit or implicit subsidy may need to be granted, together with arrangements to capitalize part of the interest due.

[23] To the extent that a large portion of accounting profits of banks represents income associated with capitalization of interest payments, it is unclear whether these so-called profits could or should be fully taxed, adding to the lack of transparency.

petitive banking system should follow rather than precede enterprise restructuring and price reform.[24]

In principle, privatization of the large state enterprise sector need not involve net outlays for the budget. However, this will depend on the state of their balance sheets and whether, after proper accounting, the state enterprises show a positive net worth that the private sector is willing to pay for. Of course, from a structural point of view, privatization is a critical requirement and it may be necessary to incur some initial outlays to get the process moving.

Safety net outlays are also likely to increase during the transition period, in particular, unemployment benefits and welfare payments for a much larger group of people. Over the medium term, the social security and welfare system must be adapted to the characteristics and needs of a market economy where (i) income differentials will rise, implying that certain segments of the population will be in a better position to provide for themselves; and (ii) economic insecurity will increase, necessitating greater attention to social insurance and poverty alleviation. The first implies that some savings in social expenditures could be obtained by reducing the universal nature of many benefits that existed under central planning—such as child and maternity allowances—and increasing the targeting of such outlays. Obviously, market-oriented safety net and redistributional policies (including through the tax system) should avoid providing disincentives to working and risk taking of a socially productive nature.

Revenue Mobilization

The fiscal requirements for stabilization and promoting the needed supply response can only be met through efficient revenue mobilization. However, the shift of enterprise-related outlays, such as subsidies for inputs and previous nonpecuniary components of wages, from the budget to enterprises will reduce their income and hence the profit transfers to the budget. Such transactions represent a netting out of what was being shown on a gross basis in the budget.[25] Revenue will further decline in step with the decline in enterprise income as a consequence of terms of trade deterioration and the initial decline in economic activity accom-

---

[24]See Fisher and (1990). Since, on the other hand, the needs of the emerging private sector would be immediate, new private banks with foreign participation would have to fill the gap.

[25]For this reason, it would be a mistake to believe that elimination of subsidies would, pari passu, allow a reduction in statutory taxation.

panied by reduced productivity and labor hoarding. In addition, price liberalization will not correspondingly increase enterprises' receipts since part of that liberalization will involve substitution of sales receipts for subsidy receipts, while input costs would rise. Accordingly, the share of profits could decline even if nominal wages increase by less than the consumer price index (CPI) (the latter includes the removal of subsidies). Of course, a sufficient decline in real wages could increase the share of profits even though aggregate income declined.

What is critical for the fiscal outcome is that on a net basis there be an adequate revenue flow from the enterprises to the budget. This will require that firm discipline be exercised on the state enterprises. With the abandonment of central planning, there would be a natural tendency for them to retain as much of their disposable income as possible. The scope for this becomes greater with the mandatory market-oriented changeover in the system of accounting and taxation. Typically, the change to a more accurate accounting system would lead to a reduction of the profit tax base because (i) previously non-deductible expenses such as interest will become deductible; and (ii) a market-oriented accounting system is prudential, that is, concerned with recognizing contingent costs which would also be deductible. To preempt such sources of deterioration of the tax base, stricter tax accounting regulations will be needed. The adoption of a new system of taxation with lower statutory rates is also necessary to provide appropriate signals to the private sector. While the new rates should be applied uniformly to both the private and public sectors, special measures will be required to ensure an adequate transfer of resources from the state enterprises. Since in the immediate future the state will remain owner of their capital, it should be entitled to receive, in addition to the profits tax, a share of the *after-tax* profits of the state enterprises as a dividend.

Generally, financing additional adjustment-related expenditures through the taxation of windfall gains that also result from this adjustment appears to be a fruitful way of containing the distortive effects of taxation and raising additional revenue needed. Potentially significant sources of such windfalls could include the hard currency gains from certain exports and the liquidation of the excess inventories traditionally held by firms in a command economy that are no longer needed in a market system. A revenue source not to be neglected would be the taxation of higher interest incomes accruing to holders of large bank deposits, and of higher bank profits, which would result from the pursuit of a high-interest-rate policy in the short run. Taxation of the households' consumption of petroleum products could also be increased, including by moving to an ad valorem basis. Furthermore, since many new opportunities will arise in a liberalized market context for making money and enjoying windfalls, the tax system will have to play a larger role in achieving an equitable distribution of income and wealth. In addition to individual income tax progressivity, some forms of capital gains tax may be envisaged.[26] However, recourse to such devices should be limited, at least in the initial stages, so as to fully encourage nascent private initiatives and to comply with administrative expectations.

Concluding Remarks

The former CPEs have embarked on a bold journey toward a market economy in order to improve their future growth prospects. This requires a fundamental transformation of the economy and the development of new productive relationships. Inevitably, resources will have to be released from former activities, many of which will cease to be viable, and there will be some loss of production in the transition, while the economy is being regenerated. However, it is imperative that the transition not be too painful nor too prolonged, or the consensus for reform will unravel. This places a heavy premium on successfully managing the transition.

The basic requirements for initiating a market economy are that prices and markets be comprehensively liberalized and that transactors be free to trade to their mutual advantage. This will be highly beneficial, but the earlier sections have demonstrated that the initial effects could be devastating. This is essentially because the abandonment of central planning demolishes the incentive structure that ensured performance under the old system, whereas the market based incentive system will take time to establish itself as new forms of behavior will have to be learnt and new institutions created. In the interregnum there could be unfortunate consequences from the interaction between the institutions that are inherited and the liberalizing reforms.

Thus, output could decline by more than is warranted by the need to respond to the relative price adjustments of the reform, since it takes time to undertake the massive reallocation of capital and labor made necessary by the relative price adjustments. Further contraction in output would result if such price adjustments also cause aggregate demand to decline precipitately, as could occur if there are major redistributions in purchasing power and assets between different sectors and classes. In particular, a price liberalization accompanied by extensive decentralization could lead

---

[26]For a different view, see Kornai (1990) who sees little merit to a progressive income tax for countries in transition.

to excessive price adjustments that reflect monopoly power, because of inevitable delays in breaking up traditional monopoly structures. Monopoly profits will then rise at the expense of labor's income and consumption, which would adversely affect their demand for wage goods and promote stagnation.

It is likely that tax revenue will be adversely affected by the negative macroeconomic effect of the terms of trade deterioration and changes systemic to the transition to a market environment at a time when pressures on social expenditure will increase. Tax bases will further erode in the interim context of weakening enforcement and compliance, while new tax systems are being established. Hence, the net contribution of enterprises in particular to the budget could well decline from their pre-reform levels, even if the large budget subsidies of the past to them are being eliminated. Such pressures on the budget limit the contribution that fiscal policy can make to the restructuring of the economy.

Thus, in the short term the outcome from a "big bang" approach could involve escalating prices, a massive contraction in output, and a deteriorating fiscal situation. Unless checked, the last could pave the way to hyperinflation. However, attempts at checking the fiscal deterioration, for example, by further reducing maintenance and other state outlays, rigidly maintaining the nominal anchor of mandated wages, or postponing outlays necessary for the restructuring of the economy (and in particular of the enterprise and banking sectors), could worsen the depression and delay the restructuring. A vicious circle would result, with escalating stagflation and increasing political tensions. Needless to add, this would not be a climate conducive to badly needed foreign investment, however generous the foreign investment laws.

An alternative strategy, which is implied by the discussion in earlier sections, would be to initiate the various elements of the big bang, but to accompany it with a number of temporary interventions to contain unwarranted adverse effects, in other words to mediate the transition. The previous sections have given several examples of such interventions that would limit disruptions to the economy, while containing demands on the budget. It is important that such interventions, which should be carefully thought through, not subvert the reforms. To the extent possible, the interventions should be market based. For example, in the area of price adjustments, pending the breakup of monopoly firms, some watchdog form of surveillance could be exercised in place of direct controls. This could be related to a tax on excess profits, analogous to the frequently employed tax on excess wages. The decentralization should not merely be an opportunity for firms to generate monopoly profits by raising prices and reducing output. On the contrary, firms should be encouraged to respond adequately to the new incentives to produce for the market. For a variety of reasons they may resist doing so, which should be countered by appropriate state supervision in the interim. However, the temptation to reinstitute direct controls, such as state orders for production, should be resisted as a retrograde step. Instead, the measures should be market related and could include even firing managers.

There must also be effective surveillance of the redistribution of resources in the initial stages of reform so as to ensure that there is adequate purchasing power in the economy and, in particular, that real wages are not excessively eroded so that there is demand for the basic consumption goods that the economy produces. There must also be surveillance to prevent speculative forces from derailing the adjustment. An appropriate wage policy, combined with checks on the monopoly power of enterprises, will reduce the need for social support outlays, an essential requirement if resources for the restructuring of the economy are to be made available.

References

Blanchard, O., and others "Reform in Eastern Europe," Report of the WIDER World Economy Group (November 1990).

Calvo, G., and J. Frenkel, "From Centrally Planned to Market Economies: The Road from CPE to PCPE," IMF Working Paper 91/17 (Washington: International Monetary Fund, 1991).

Fetherston, Martin J., "Fiscal Developments and Issues in Selected Centrally Planned Economies," IMF Working Paper 83/72 (Washington: International Monetary Fund, 1983).

Fisher, S., and A. Gelb, "Issues in Socialist Economy Reform," World Bank Working Paper WPS 565 (Washington: World Bank, 1990).

Gregory, P., and R. Stuart, *Soviet Economic Structure and Performance* (New York: Harper and Row, 1986).

International Monetary Fund, World Bank, and European Bank for Reconstruction and Development, *A Study of the Soviet Economy*, Vol. 1 (Paris: OECD, February 1991).

Kopits, G., "Fiscal Reform in European Economies in Transition," IMF Working Paper 91/43 (Washington: International Monetary Fund, April 1991).

Kornai, J., *The Road to a Free Economy: Shifting from a Socialist System: The Case of Hungary* (New York: Norton, 1990).

Lipton, D., and J. Sachs, "Creating a Market Economy in Eastern Europe: The Case of Poland," Brookings Papers on Economic Activity I: 1990 (Washington: Brookings Institution, 1990), pp. 75–133.

McKinnon, R., "The Order of Liberalization for Opening the Soviet Economy," Report prepared for the International Task Force on Foreign Economic Relations (New York, April, 1989).

Ofer, G., "Budget Deficit, Market Disequilibrium, and Soviet Economic Reforms," *Soviet Economy* (June 1989), pp. 107–61.

——, "Macroeconomic Issues of Soviet Reforms," Working Paper No. 222, The Hebrew University of Jerusalem (1990).

Tanzi, V., "Tax Reform and the Move to a Market Economy: Overview of the Issues," in *The Role of Tax Reform in Central and Eastern European Economies* (Paris: OECD, 1991).

——, "Mobilization of Savings in East European Countries: The Role of the State," in *Economics for the New Europe*, ed. by Anthony B. Atkinson and Renato Brunetta (London: Macmillan, 1991).

Wanless, P.T., *Taxation in Centrally Planned Economies* (London and Sydney: Croom Helm, 1985).

Wolf, T. (1985 a), "Economic Stabilization in Planned Economies," *Staff Papers,* International Monetary Fund, Vol. 32 (March 1985), pp. 78–131.

————, (1985 b), "Exchange Rate Systems and Adjustment in Planned Economies," *Staff Papers,* International Monetary Fund, Vol. 32 (June 1985), pp. 211–47.

CHAPTER 2

Financing Fiscal Deficits

Adrienne Cheasty

Before perestroika in the Soviet Union and the Velvet Revolution in Eastern Europe, fiscal deficits in planned economies either did not exist or were very small. The strains of the shift to indirect instruments of demand management and of structural reform have typically widened budget gaps in economies in transition. Consequently, policymakers in these economies must now deal with the issue of financing their budget deficits.

This paper discusses budgetary financing issues relevant to economies in transition. It begins with a description of government financing in planned economies prior to the reforms at the end of the 1980s. The small financial gaps of the pre-reform period are explained by reference to the philosophy and mechanics of the planning system. It then discusses the effect of the transition on financing needs—through emerging budget pressures—and on governments' ability to finance their deficits as the transition evolves. It describes simulations, which illustrate the consequences for a transition economy of the financing alternatives open to it, and then discusses the implications of these consequences for countries actually in transition. Economic conditions prior to the reforms and the credibility of the reforms turn out to be important inputs to a government's decision about the type of budget financing it should adopt. Hence, depending on their macroeconomic circumstances, economies presently in transition may find themselves with optimal financing packages very different from those of their neighbors.

The countries discussed in this paper are Bulgaria, Czechoslovakia, Poland, Romania, and the U.S.S.R.[1] However, the paper draws more fully on U.S.S.R. experience, for two reasons. First, the Soviet budget remained relatively close to the classical planning system until perestroika. And

---

[1] Yugoslavia has been omitted from the study because its federal system and high inflation made comparative analysis of the data difficult.

second, perhaps ironically, the U.S.S.R. was the first of this group to begin the transition. Important restructuring laws that heavily shocked the Soviet budget were introduced in 1985–86, soon after Gorbachev's accession; apart from in Poland, practically no transition-related restructuring took place in the other countries before 1989.[2]

Before the Reforms

Size of Financing

Unlike in Western industrial economies, governments in planned economies typically had a positive net position in their domestic banking system, tiny bond issues, and a foreign debt that was practically completely linked to productive sector liabilities. Historically, overall public debt has been small, despite the centralization of activity in the public sector. Table 1 shows the financing behavior of the transition economies between 1985 and 1990.[3] Deficits (measured in the table by total financing) tended to be small in terms of GDP, and cyclical. The beginning of the transition is signaled by the emergence of much higher deficits in 1989 and 1990. The outliers are Romania, which ran large surpluses in order to eliminate its national debt, and the Soviet Union from 1986 on. In the first half of the 1980s—before perestroika—the Soviet state budget deficit had always remained below 2 percent of GDP.

What financing there was, was practically all domestic, with the exception of Bulgaria in 1985–86. Bulgaria's net foreign inflows reflected its relatively weak and dependent position in CMEA trade. The U.S.S.R., on the other hand, registered negative net foreign financing, because of its lending program abroad. By far the largest share of domestic financing came from the banking system. This trend has continued into the transition. In 1989, bank financing covered the whole budget deficit in all countries except Czechoslovakia. And in 1990, all of Czechoslovakia's deficit was financed by bank credit. As discussed below, banking system finance did not have the same economic impact as in Western economies; rather, in effect it was akin to nonbank financing. But bank financing since 1989, on the other hand, can be directly compared with money growth in Western economies, with the same undesirable inflationary consequences.

---

[2]Unless otherwise noted, all information regarding the U.S.S.R. is taken from International Monetary Fund (1991).

[3]The rationale for the classification of financing in the table can be found in Tanzi (1985).

Table 1. Economies in Transition: Financing of Government Operations[1]

(In percent of GDP)	1985	1986	1987	1988	1989	1990[2]
Bulgaria						
Financing	0.8	2.6	−1.2	0.9	0.6	9.3
Foreign	1.1	1.7	−1.1	−1.2	−1.3	4.3
Domestic	−0.3	0.9	0.0	2.0	1.9	5.0
Bank	−0.3	0.9	0.0	2.0	1.9	3.3
Nonbank	—	—	—	—	—	1.6
GDP (billion leva)	326	344	365	383	404	434
Czechoslovakia						
Financing	0.5	0.8	0.5	2.4	8.9	4.4
Foreign	—	—	—	—	—	—
Domestic	0.5	0.8	0.5	2.4	8.9	4.4
Bank	0.4	1.6	0.7	2.6	6.9	4.4
Nonbank	0.1	−0.7	−0.2	−0.1	2.0	0.0
GDP (billion koruny)	677	695	711	740	760	835
Poland						
Financing	...	0.3	0.8	0.0	5.4	−3.5
Foreign	...	0.7	0.1	−0.2	−0.3	−0.7
Domestic	...	−0.4	0.7	0.3	5.7	−2.8
Bank	...	−0.4	0.7	0.3	5.1	2.8
Nonbank	...	0.0	—	—	0.5	−5.6
GDP (billion zlotys)	8,576	12,953	16,940	29,629	96,549	581,225
Romania						
Financing	...	−4.5	−7.0	−5.9	5.6	...
Foreign	...	—	—	—	—	...
Domestic	...	−4.5	−7.0	−5.9	5.6	...
Bank	...	−4.5	−7.0	−5.9	5.6	...
Nonbank	...	—	—	—	—	...
GDP (billion lei)	...	844	850	854	794	...
U.S.S.R.						
Financing	2.4	6.2	8.4	9.2	8.7	7.6
Foreign	−1.0	−1.1	−0.9	−0.6	−0.5	−0.4
Domestic	3.3	7.3	9.2	9.8	9.2	7.9
Bank	3.8	7.9	9.7	10.0	9.7	6.0
Non-bank	0.8	0.4	0.7	0.9	0.9	1.9
Overfinancing	−1.3	−1.0	−1.1	−1.1	−1.3	0.0
GDP (billion rubles)	777	799	825	875	924	1,000

[handwritten annotations: "= surplus" above 1987 Bulgaria figures; "= deficit" pointing to 9.3 in 1990 Bulgaria Financing]

Source: IMF staff estimates.

[1] These figures are not precisely comparable across countries. In particular, the coverage of government may differ between countries.

[2] Figures for 1990 are provisional outturns or budgeted amounts.

Nonbank financing was minimal because of the absence of financial assets and a domestic capital market. In the planning system, enterprise funds were not fungible, and, apart from sporadic bond issues, savings deposits were the only financial store of value available to individuals. Thus, in Bulgaria, Poland, and Romania, there was no nonbank financing; in Czechoslovakia, nonbank financing was negative because the government decided to honor obligations and retire bonds issued prior to 1956. Even in the Soviet Union, with its much discussed money and wealth overhangs, inflationary bank financing has been accelerating. Bond purchases outside the banking system did not rise above 1 percent of GDP until 1990.

Significance of Financing

In order to understand the apparent stability of the fiscal equilibrium in these otherwise vulnerable economies, it has to be stressed that the insignificance of the budget deficit was a direct consequence of the successful functioning of the planning system. In the planning system, fiscal policy may be seen as having two goals: redistribution and stabilization. Planning theory focuses only on the redistributional objective.[4]

However, since planned economies were subject to exogenous shocks, both in internal supply and from the rest of the world, the budget also had to stabilize the economy against these shocks.[5]

An awareness of the budget's stabilization function is important for interpreting overt budget financing in planned economies. Deficits, and the need to finance them, appeared only when shocks were so large or unexpected that the budget could not cushion them. In this sense, an explicit budget deficit in a planned economy was a measure of the *net* extent to which administered prices were irreconcilable with true economic costs.

---

[4]The function of the tax/subsidy structure of the budget was to shift resources among sectors as dictated by the economy's social welfare function. Since the budget was conceived purely as the instrument of redistribution (rather than a donor or recipient), efficient and successful redistribution would imply that the budget always remained in balance.

[5]Consumers and producers could be insulated completely from any movement in economic variables such as world prices or scarcity costs—as long as the budget absorbed the shock by passively allowing revenue collection from price-wedge taxes and open-ended subsidy payments on account of price differentials to vary. Inasmuch as the shock had to be internalized into the economy, its impact could be redistributed, through changes in the prices that determined budgetary revenues and expenditures, to whatever sector the government felt could bear it with least cost. If prices were changed without an adjustment in the credit plan, stabilization through the budget implied redistribution as well. But since credit to enterprises, for example, tended to be automatic and inexpensive, enterprises were often relatively indifferent to price changes. With, or in the absence of, redistribution, stabilization/insulation could theoretically be complete without the emergence of a measured budget deficit. (This contrasts with Western budgets, where the extent of stabilization is measured by the fiscal stance—some normalized measure of the deviation from balance—i.e., by the extent to which the budget must be financed.)

Because of the sometimes ad hoc methods of equilibrating the budget, two conceptual types of planned economy budget deficit should be distinguished: the ex ante deficit and the ex post deficit.

The *ex ante deficit* emerged when a shock—for instance a bad harvest requiring grain imports at higher world prices—caused the budget plan to become inconsistent with budget equilibrium. Frequently, re-equilibration was achieved by price changes that required higher credit to the enterprises affected by them, by one-time demands on the reserve funds of governments, by measures that would have to be reversed, or by creative accounting. In such cases, the instruments used to reattain balance seemed a lot closer to the Western convention of budget financing than they did to ordinary revenue and expenditure (and are discussed below as "camouflaged" or "indirect" financing), though overt financing remained very small.

The *ex post budget deficit* gave rise to actual recorded financing. The ex post deficit may be said to measure the extent to which the planning mechanism was unable to use identified sectors to cushion the shock, and was forced to let it diffuse through the macroeconomy. Within the ex post deficit, a further precision must be made. Typically, though not always, when planned economies' statistics are adjusted to western rules of accounting, the observed ex post deficit widens.[6] This is because planned economy convention counted as revenues many items that would be called financing by Western governments. On the other hand, uses of financing, such as debt amortization, were included as expenditures, so that the net effect of a reclassification to Western standards could in a few cases be to reduce the observed deficit. The data in Table 1, to the extent possible, have been adjusted to follow western accounting norms.

Thus, a conceptually complete discussion of budget financing in planned economies would have to cover three categories of financing: identified financing to cover the reported budget deficit; financing camouflaged as above-the-line budget items; and indirect financing in terms of ad hoc measures to reconcile the original plan with the post-shock expected budgetary outturn. In the transition, however, an important first step in adopting Western standards of budget management must be to make all financing explicit. The various components of planned economy financing are delineated in the paragraphs immediately below, but when discussing financing methods during the transition, it is assumed that financing needs will have been made transparent in the budget.

---

[6]For a discussion of deficit measurement in Western economies, see Blejer and Cheasty (1991).

Budget Financing

Foreign Financing

In the budgets of this group of economies prior to the transition, gross foreign inflows to government were counted as revenues, regardless of whether they were loans extended by foreigners, repayments of loans granted by the domestic government in the past, interest on outstanding loans, or grants. Likewise, all foreign outflows were classified as expenditures. Hence, no foreign financing appeared in published budget reports.[7]

The foreign financing included as revenue came from Western banks, CMEA-area banks, and in the form of aid from other CMEA-governments (practically uniquely from the U.S.S.R.). Given the centralized structure of foreign trade in the classical planned economy, and the small budget gaps, a very large share of recorded foreign inflows was trade related, and its equivalent in Western economies would not have been treated as public sector financing.[8] Because of the links to trade, the maturity structure of foreign inflows differed from in the West: for instance, in 1989, about 33 percent of Soviet debt had a term of less than one year (mainly suppliers' credits), compared with 12 percent or less for all countries included in the *World Bank Debt Tables*.[9]

Apart from differences in its structure, hard-currency financing was comparable to equivalent financing elsewhere. Financing in nonconvertible currencies from CMEA-area banks, on the other hand, had the distinguishing characteristic of being somewhat under the control of CMEA governments. Given that CMEA-area prices and quantities traded were negotiated between countries, by protocol and consistent with their five-year plans, outstanding balances in favor of one country could be eliminated in the next round of protocols by price and quantity adjustments. In this sense, the CMEA countries may broadly be seen as parts of a common redistributive budgetary mechanism, which differed only from the domestic budget instrument in that price renegotiation through redrafting CMEA protocols was a far more cumbersome way of returning to budgetary equilibrium. Hence, not just total public debt, but also its foreign component (the accumulation of deficits in the "external budget balance") ten-

---

[7]A reclassification of foreign financing according to Western norms eliminates a large share of hitherto unidentified revenues and expenditures in the Soviet budget.

[8]Of course, it would not have borne public sector guarantees.

[9]World Bank (1989), Vol. 1, p. 78. The classifications of debt are not fully comparable.

ded to be smaller than gross trade flows would suggest, since surplus and deficit countries could, purely by accounting measures, reverse their financial imbalances from year to year.

The effect of administered prices on concessional foreign flows recorded (positively or negatively) in planned economy budgets is particularly noteworthy. Specifically, budgeted foreign aid has been very small, despite a Western conviction that Soviet economic aid to its satellites has been hugely significant. The Soviet budget recorded rub 1.7 billion in total foreign aid in 1987, including both economic and military aid. This amounted to 0.4 percent of total budgeted expenditure and was equivalent to US $2.8 billion at the official exchange rate. The C.I.A. estimated that Soviet economic aid to Cuba alone in 1987 amounted to US $4 billion (C.I.A. (1989), Table 157). The C.I.A. calculation compares the value in world prices of Soviet-Cuban trade transactions and describes the net benefit as financing for Cuba. This is indisputable from the economic point of view, but the fact remains that the explicit drain on the Soviet budget (and its counterpart, the recorded financing of the Cuban budget) has been insignificant.

Domestic Bank Financing

Bank financing for the budget was provided both directly and indirectly. Direct bank financing was a simple matter, since planned economies administered the financial arm of the plan through a monobank (Gosbank in the U.S.S.R.). Conceptually, direct credit to government was seen as having two economic components: the use of the savings deposits of the private sector and "free" credit.

Owing to shortages of both goods and opportunities for investment in most planned economies, the savings rate of individuals tended to be high and stable. The private sector almost always ran a significant surplus.[10] In the Soviet system, this characteristic was recognized. Planners took into account, at the conceptual level, that this surplus could finance deficits elsewhere in the economy without generating inflation. Thus, credit to government was divided into the conceptual offset of the banking system's part of the private sector surplus—which bore interest (albeit low), and expansionary (free) credit, which bore no interest. The economic impact of the bank credit to government that was "backed" by the build-

---

[10]For instance, households' saving as a share of disposable money income in 1988 was 16.5 percent in Poland and 11.1 percent in Bulgaria. Czechoslovakia, with a ratio of 4.2 percent, was an exception because its government espoused a policy of minimizing consumer goods shortages.

up of saving deposits was as if the savers had bought bonds. Prior to 1987, recourse to expansionary credit was unknown; bank financing of the government's deficit did not exceed the private sector surplus. Its appearance in Soviet statistics in 1987 signaled either the miscalculation in the plan of the resource balance in the economy, or the government's loss of control over resources as the private sector's savings became more liquid and savings deposits became more volatile.

Indirect bank credit financed the ex ante deficit in several ways.

Ad hoc taxes. First, if a potential deficit was recognized, the discretionary nature of the tax system allowed planners to demand higher contributions from firms than specified in the plan. Since the monobank traditionally automatically accommodated firms' needs for credit, bank borrowing was the easiest way for firms to meet their plan targets despite the less favorable tax environment. Inasmuch as that happened, the higher taxes collected to bring the budget back into balance were really disguised bank lending. Western budget convention (for example, IMF (1984)) distinguishes revenue from financing in that revenue does not increase government liabilities, and therefore adds to government net worth.[11] But in planned economies, the distinction between the assets and liabilities of enterprises and government was far less clear-cut. For instance, in 1986 and again in 1990, the Soviet government was forced to cancel or take over rub 70 billion in debt of enterprises and agricultural organizations, which had been paying taxes while becoming insolvent. This rub 140 billion in debt write-off may be considered a preliminary indicator of the extent to which tax receipts were not really revenue, but merely financing, in the sense that government was eventually held liable for the funds it had taken from the productive sector.

Use of government reserve funds. A second disguised source of financing in the planning system was the use of the reserve funds of local governments as contributions to budget revenue. In other words, local governments could be asked to use their accumulated savings from their operations of previous years to finance expenditures. Since these funds had no liabilities attached (unlike running up an overdraft in the same savings account would have had) they were considered revenues and not financing. Nevertheless, their use weakened government's net credit position in the banking system.

In this particular case, planned economy budget accounts clearly misstated the economic impact of the deficit. The use of reserve funds showed up as increased revenue only when it was going to finance expen-

---

[11]For a discussion of this definition, see Blejer and Cheasty (1991).

diture (otherwise remaining outside the budget, dormant in bank accounts). Hence, the above-the-line budget record of recourse to these funds suggested a strengthening of revenues and fiscal strictness, rather than the loosening of fiscal policy that Western-style accounting would have indicated.

Permeable nongovernment accounts. A third instrument, even more indirect than the above sources of bank financing (and an issue that is likely to remain unresolved), is the unidentified financing from the use of other, "nongovernment" accounts in the banking system. In an organic state, the concept of integrity of accounts did not exist in the same way as in Western financial systems; in particular, the bank accounts of state sector entities (including enterprises) that happened to be in surplus were sometimes used for ad hoc financing of particular programs or projects. In the extreme, thus, all the financial resources of the economy were potential government funding.

In analyzing the role of the banking system in funding planned economy governments, it is also useful to understand the administrative mechanism by which the budget was financed. At the beginning of the budget year, the government's expenditure account was allocated enough credit to cover all of its planned expenditures for the whole year. Hence, expenditures could be carried out regardless of the pace of revenue collection.[12] This administrative system for credit allocation often led to over-financing of the realized budget deficit.[13] In any year, there was a possibility that expenditures would fall short of planned targets—particularly because, in government as in other sectors, expenditure targets tended to be political statements and therefore biased upward, compared with the more usual downward bias resorted to by Western governments to get their budgets approved. When expenditures fell short, the financing that had been placed in the expenditure account would not be exhausted at the end of the year. In deficit years in particular, there was strong pressure from the center to save on expenditures. Hence, paradoxically, the bigger the

---

[12]In planning terms, this system was efficient, because it meant that financial or timing inconsistencies in the plan could not hold up production that depended on budgetary participation. However, such a system sacrificed all possibilities of financial control—both monitoring and adjustment. Thus, while the automatic pre-financing mechanism may have been costless when deficits were low and early warnings would not have changed government policy much, it became inadequate for budget management as soon as the transition created uncertainties in revenue collection and new expenditure needs.

[13]Table 1 shows that the Soviet budget was over-financed by more than 1 percent of GDP every year since 1985.

recorded deficit, the more likely that deficit was to have been over-financed.

Nonbank Domestic Financing

Domestic financing from outside the banking system also had direct and indirect components.

Direct nonbank financing in the form of bond sales to households was the most common way of financing the small deficits in the classical planning system.[14] These sales were small, but sufficient. They carried a very low interest rate, but were salable to a quasi-captive market, since few alternative assets existed. In some cases, the addition of a lottery feature (premium bonds) raised the expected interest rate, while keeping the coupon in line with planning norms. And, in recent years, commodity bonds have been issued, providing as part of their return warrants to purchase difficult-to-get consumer goods, such as washing machines and cars. (Commodity bonds are particularly profitable for government, because warrants to buy are valuable to the private sector but not to government, which has to implement some distribution mechanism for the goods that are in short supply. The sale of commodity bonds is like a sale of quota rights.)

Indirect nonbank financing occurred when the ex ante deficit was financed by the extraordinary taxation of firms or individuals, in cases where these did not have access to credit to cover their increased financial burden. Again, the organic nature of the system meant that the weakening of the financial position of any entity in the system was potentially equivalent to an increase in government liabilities; the distinction between taxation and financing was more blurred than in the West.

Financing Needs and Costs

Increase in Financing Needs

Table 1 makes it clear that planned economies have been unable to cope with the impact of the transition on the budget. The fiscal deficit rose by more than 5 percent of GDP in all countries (except the U.S.S.R. where it was already high) in 1989 or 1990; and practically all of these deficits

---

[14]Depending on the accounting system, bond financing might also be classified as revenue.

were financed by credit. The causes of the increase in financing needs are multi-faceted.[15]

(a) Profit taxes fell because enterprises' profits dropped, and many enterprises expect to go bankrupt.

(b) To alleviate the deteriorating financial situation of enterprises, governments have in many cases felt it necessary to sacrifice profit taxes further, by cutting rates and offering incentives and exemptions.

(c) Production began to shift to the private sector, before a tax base encompassing this new source of income could be developed.

(d) To avoid the costs of price liberalization being absorbed by the budget—as were price shocks in the past—the tax/subsidy price differential system has to be dismantled. The countries in this group have been slow to make rates explicit, with consequent revenue leakages as governments began to lose control of prices.[16] And, as soon as rates are made transparent, the high rates have to be lowered—for political reasons and to avoid a wholesale shift to a black market.

(e) There are also pressures to ease the burden of higher liberalized prices by reducing individual taxes. For example, in order to compensate for price increases in April 1991, the U.S.S.R. cut the tax rate on individuals from 13 to 12 percent, raised the threshold, and increased exemptions.

(f) On the expenditure side, budget pressures have also mounted. Unemployment has emerged—adding social safety nets to entitlements.[17]

(g) Indexation of pensions in the wake of price adjustments is also costly for the budget.[18]

---

[15]The effect of the transition on the financing needs of planned economies moving to the market has been widely discussed (for instance, in Tanzi (1991), Blejer and Szapary (1990), McKinnon (1991)) and is covered in other papers in this volume. Hence, the topic will be dealt with relatively briefly here.

[16]The most costly example of leakage is the Soviet budget's footing the bill for the lag between increases in wholesale prices (at the end of 1990) and retail price adjustments (that did not take place until April 1991). This "stabilization" is estimated to have cost the budget rub 20–25 billion.

[17]Cuts in subsidies usually do not offset unemployment costs, since cuts have typically been accompanied by direct compensation to the population, in the form of direct income supplements or food stamps.

[18]Empirically, pension support is creating a serious problem for the group of economies covered in this paper. In the late 1980s, across the CMEA, there was a wave of reforms of social insurance schemes and pension funds, with big upward adjustments in pensions. (See, for instance, Prust and others (1990) on Czechoslovakia, and JSSE, Vol. 1, Appendix III.1–3 on the Soviet Union. Bulgaria and Romania also introduced pension reforms in 1990.) Even without indexation, the pension reforms created a large new stock of obligations that budgets going into the transition were ill-equipped to handle. (For instance, in the U.S.S.R., social

(h) Finally, the objective of the transition, to renew growth in transitional countries, is to be achieved mainly through structural adjustment. But structural reform places a heavy charge on the budget for new infrastructural investment in areas such as telecommunications and the distribution system, and because of the need for conversion of defense industries, the repair of oil pipelines, the retooling of strategic foreign-exchange-earning fuel industries, and pollution control.

The conclusion from this list of developments can only be that the transition is already putting heavy pressures on budget balances, and that these are unlikely to be alleviated in the near term. Despite strong arguments for not running a fiscal deficit in an economy trying to shift from state control to private activity, and despite severe fiscal retrenchment in some of the countries in this group, financing needs are likely to remain high. The question is to which source of financing should transition countries turn? The rest of this section discusses the effects that the transition may have on the various financing options.

Foreign Financing Needs

CMEA countries are seeking more convertible-currency foreign financing. Because of the change in the trade regime and the payments system, a higher share of their debt will henceforth have to be borrowed in Western capital markets and serviced in dollars at world interest rates. The shift to hard-currency financing has also eliminated the possibility of negotiated adjustments to prices of tradables in order to keep external obligations small. Hence, for a given level of trade, the size of external debt may be expected to rise.

Parallel with and to some extent linked to the change in the payments system has been the deterioration in the credit ratings of CMEA countries, particularly the U.S.S.R.'s. Foreign exchange shortages led to the emergence of arrears, which in turn made further borrowing problematic. Thus, not only must planned economies change the structure and increase the size of their foreign borrowing, but each dollar of foreign borrowing will be forthcoming with an interest premium.

From the point of view of the budget, however, the reasons for foreign borrowing should become fewer. Before, the budget/government was responsible for foreign financing of practically all trade. Now there is a strong argument, both in terms of financial prudence on the part of the

---

welfare expenditures were 8 percent of GDP in 1989, and were projected to amount to 12 percent of GDP in 1991, with benefit indexation (International Monetary Fund (1991), Appendix III.1–3).

government, and in terms of teaching firms to budget properly as market entities, to let firms do as much of their own financing as possible—preferably, without a government guarantee. The argument is reinforced by the fact that domestic resource costs to the budget of financing external public debt have shot up, as planned economies have undertaken large devaluations in their move towards convertibility and external competitiveness. To say that the motives for foreign borrowing have been reduced in number is not, however, the same as saying that foreign financing in the budget should necessarily shrink. Indeed, as discussed in the next section, under some circumstances, foreign budget support may be a relatively attractive option for governments of economies in transition.

Domestic Financing

Transition economies have not yet developed domestic markets for government bonds. This is evident from their dependence on bank credit to finance their escalating 1989 and 1990 deficits. It is a central dilemma of the transition that, at a time when resources should be shifted to the private sector, not only are government financial needs increasing but, at the same time, the demand for saving instruments is sure to be affected by the change in the characteristics of the economy. Three key elements should be kept in mind in the cultivation of domestic financing sources during the transition: the appropriate level of a market-clearing domestic interest rate, the size of existing public debt, and the behavior of the public.

Domestic Interest Rate

For economies in transition, the domestic interest rate may differ significantly from world rates for several reasons. Historically, interest rates have been kept very low in undeveloped domestic capital markets with few alternative assets, and capital has been kept from moving abroad by strict controls. Since these controls typically are not lifted until late in the transition, and since savers have to learn to seek the highest return internationally, there could be a period at the start of the transition when the government could capture the private sector surplus at lower than the international cost of capital.

Table 2 shows representative nominal interest rates on credits for the five countries under discussion. At the end of 1990, it seemed that the use of the domestic interest rate as a tool to attract and ration funds had practically not begun. It is remarkable how little rates have changed, particularly when compared with the acceleration in inflation.

Table 2. Indicators for Assessing Financing Options

	1985	1986	1987	1988	1989	1990[1]
Bulgaria						
Trade balance (In billions of U.S. dollars)	−0.4	−0.8	−1.0	−1.0	−1.2	−0.8
Reserves/convert. imports (Months)	6.9	5.2	3.4	4.8	3.8	1.5
External debt (In billions of U.S. dollars)	3.2	4.7	6.1	8.2	9.2	10.0
Convert. debt stock/exports (Percent)	80	141	152	187	227	310
Domestic interest rate (Credits in percent)	...	4.6	4.4	4.5	4.7	5.2
CPI change (Percent)	1.7	3.5	2.7	2.5	6.4	26.3
Czechoslovakia						
Trade balance (In billions of U.S. dollars)	0.7	0.2	—	−0.1	0.3	−0.4
Reserves/convert. imports (Months)	3.0	3.3	3.6	4.2	4.9	0.7
External debt (In billions of U.S. dollars)	4.6	5.6	6.7	7.3	7.9	7.6
Convert. debt stock/exports (Percent)	91	99	114	114	115	109
Domestic interest rate (Credits in percent)	5.0	5.1	5.1	5.1	5.7	5.6
CPI change (Percent)	...	0.5	0.1	0.2	1.4	14.2
Poland						
Trade balance (In billions of U.S. dollars)	...	−0.4	−0.2	0.2	0.3	1.5
Reserves/convert. imports (Months)	...	2.5	3.9	4.3	4.1	6.8
External debt (In billions of U.S. dollars)	...	33.5	39.7	39.1	41.4	48.5
Convert. debt stock/exports (Percent)	...	570	580	490	500	400
Domestic interest rate (Credits in percent)	...	6.3	6.5	10.5	36.3	62.0
CPI change (Percent)	...	17.1	31.1	73.9	639.6	249.3
Romania						
Trade balance (In billions of U.S. dollars)	1.4	1.9	2.3	3.5	2.7	−0.7
Reserves/convert. imports (Months)	0.9	2.1	6.3	4.0	8.0	2.6
External debt (In billions of U.S. dollars)	6.9	6.9	6.1	2.0	0.1	0.1
Convert. debt stock/exports (Percent)	110	116	118	33	2	6
Domestic interest rate (Credits in percent)	...	5	5	5	5	5
CPI change (Percent)	...	0.7	1.2	2.6	0.9	...
U.S.S.R.						
Trade balance (In billions of U.S. dollars)	1.3	3.6	8.2	4.8	−0.1	...
Reserves/convert. imports (Months)	5.9	7.6	7.3	6.4	5.0	...
External debt (In billions of U.S. dollars)	28.9	31.4	39.2	43.0	54.0	52.2
Convert. debt stock/exports (Percent)	102	111	117	121	139	128
Domestic interest rate (Credits in percent)	2.2	2.4	2.3	2.2	2.8	2.8
CPI change (Percent)	...	2.0	1.3	6.0	2.0	4.8

Source: IMF staff estimates.

[1] Figures for 1990 are provisional or budgeted amounts.

As the transition continues, however, and interest rates are liberalized, there are reasons why the domestic interest rate might exceed the international rate. First, the uncertainties of the transition create political risk and currency risk (inasmuch as other currencies are available to domestic savers), so that a risk premium over the base (pre-transition) rate is likely to emerge. Second, the scrapping of the financial plan implies that all sectors of the economy will, for the first time, be competing for loanable funds. Responsibility for investment is typically shifted from government to state enterprises, joint ventures usually require sizable domestic counterpart funds to all foreign investment, and privatization has to be financed by somebody. Hence, deficit bond-financing may be expected to push up the interest rate by a crowding-out factor intrinsic to the transition.[19] Third, it cannot be taken for granted that the pre-transition rate in a shortage economy was market clearing. Thus, even in the absence of a risk-premium and crowding-out pressures from the emerging private sector, the domestic interest rate could well rise as the financial system develops. Finally, large relative price changes are likely to affect the domestic price level with a feed-back to wages that exacerbates inflation pressures and increases nominal domestic debt service.

Existing Domestic Debt

If domestic interest rates have to rise substantially to reflect the shortage of domestic capital, the cost of domestic debt service could seriously hurt the stabilization effort.

In the Soviet system, for instance, it is possible that the domestic debt situation is already explosive. Planned public debt by the end of 1990 was rub 586 billion, or 59 percent of GDP. Projected inflation for 1991 is at least 60 percent, given the price increases that took place in April 1991. If the government were to pay even a 2 percent real rate of interest on all of the debt, its interest bill alone in 1991 would come to more than 6 times the measured 1990 deficit—a deficit which the authorities were already unable to finance by bonds, and which has begun to generate inflation.[20]

---

[19]If the transfer of investment responsibilities to firms is matched by a cutback in government expenditure, pressure on interest rates will be less. In transition countries, however, the offset has been small. For instance, Soviet government investment expenditure dropped by only 5 percent between 1987, the year the Law on State Enterprises (introducing autonomy in enterprise investment) was introduced, and 1989.

[20]The simulations in the next section are unrealistically conservative in that they do not assume any debt service on debt incurred prior to 1991.

On the other hand, if positive real rates are not offered, domestic bond financing of the 1991 budget is unlikely to be feasible.

It should be stressed that the level of the interest rate is relevant not only for determining the cost of nonbank domestic debt but also of credit to government. There is a strong temptation for government not to pay market rates on the credit it uses, particularly when this credit comes directly from the central bank. The Soviet Union pays no interest on unbacked credit from Gosbank, and only 2.8 percent on credit conceptually backed by private savings. In Poland, the state budget does not pay interest on central bank credit; and in Bulgaria, interest rates on government borrowing are 0.5–2.5 percent, compared with rates to 4–5 percent for other sectors. But the costs of this credit cannot be avoided, in present value terms. If the central bank has to bear them, its financial position will be weakened and ultimately threatened to the point that the government has to reinject capital. Its true financing need will become apparent in the form of a stock injection—which could well be even more costly to pay for.[21]

Public Debt in Transition Economies

Several behavioral factors could conceivably temper upward pressures on the domestic interest rate. In the group of countries under discussion, governments' ability to avoid inflationary financing in the near future while meeting debt service obligations may depend on two temporary institutional anomalies. First, savers appear to continue to have money illusion, as is suggested by the reported maintenance of savings rates despite the growing divergence between inflation and interest rates seen in Table 2. Second, transition governments seem able to create a de facto subordination of old debt to new debt, in the sense that new debt is already being offered on more attractive terms without the old debt immediately being rolled over. This segmentation of debt will be possible only as long as domestic capital markets remain undeveloped, and capital controls are enforced. The two characteristics are specific to early-transition economies, and both will disappear as the transition evolves.

It has also been argued that interest rate pressures during the transition will be alleviated by a growing willingness of the public and of firms to hold assets. As the "enterprise funds" system of accounting and financial

---

[21]The correct measure of the fiscal deficit in a case where the central bank is subsidizing government credit is a consolidated balance that includes all quasi-fiscal activities of the central bank. On this point, see Robinson and Stella (1991).

their newly fungible funds. Individuals could also be induced to save, both because a wider array of assets will begin to be offered on more attractive terms—as privatization and borrowing enterprises create mutual funds and nongovernment bonds, and because people must be uncertain about the future. Also, inasmuch as the demand for money rises, the danger from inflation will diminish.

The composition of the public's portfolio will, of course, be influenced by its inflationary expectations. It is possible that transition economies have the advantage over Latin American economies that their people have not developed inertial inflationary expectations in the wake of a long history of failed stabilization programs.[22] This would also explain some amount of apparent money illusion. If inflationary expectations remained easy to influence downwards, it could be argued (as in Dornbusch and Wolf (1990), and Edwards (1991)) that a one-time bout of inflation, which would ease the realignment of relative prices, eliminate a monetary over-hang, and remove any domestic debt overhang from impeding privatization, would be an attractive financing option—compared with bond finance. Its advisability would depend on the forcefulness with which the government was able to stabilize, once the objectives of the inflation had been achieved.

The size of existing government domestic debt could itself have a rigidi-fying impact on inflationary expectations. A heavy real domestic government debt burden (replacing external debt after the debt crisis) created a credibility problem in domestic stabilization for Argentina, Brazil, and Mexico that transition economies have not yet had to face. If the government's liabilities are mainly domestic, it always has the attractive option of inflating away their real value. When the public recognizes this, its inflationary expectations become harder to keep low, and the equilibrium domestic interest rate rises (Calvo (1988)). This effect would worsen the real domestic debt service bill (and therefore the fiscal deficit) as long as the government committed itself to avoiding inflation. In general, thus, transition countries with high existing public debts are likely to face relatively higher costs of future public deficits because of adverse expectational effects, regardless of whether they finance the deficits by bank credits or bonds.

---

[22]Though see Edwards (1991) for an opposing view.

Privatization

Several countries envisage revenues from privatization as a major source of financing budget gaps during the transition. The question of the size and timing of privatization revenues is too large a topic to be properly addressed in this paper. However, some points may be made here—with the general thrust that receipts from privatization are not an appropriate source of budget financing.

It is likely that stabilization is a prerequisite—rather than an accompaniment—for structural reform. The slow pace of privatization and foreign investment in transition economies so far suggest that base economic conditions and a credible assurance of future stability are necessary before real estate in transition economies becomes an attractive asset. If this is so, the budget will have to be satisfactorily financed before significant privatization revenues can be expected. This point leads to the more general problems of timing and predictability in privatization. A budget that relies on such lumpy and uncertain revenues is not in line with the discipline of western budget management.

Furthermore, the revenues, by definition, will be temporary. At a time when governments have to design completely new menus of permanent budget priorities, it would be dangerous to introduce longrun programs such as unemployment insurance with transitory financing. The use of privatization revenues to cover permanent programs would not merely simply postpone the day of reckoning, but could tempt policymakers to be more generous with, for instance, social programs, than their economy can afford in the long run.

Finally, privatization could be construed as the disposal of public wealth. If the proceeds from the sale of public assets are used to finance current outlays, then government net worth will decline. A weakening in the government balance sheet could be injudicious for governments who wish to increase their debt in the short term. An alternative suggestion has been that the revenues be used to retire government debt, that is, to strengthen the fiscal balance sheet, in order to facilitate new financing.

Financing Alternatives

The method by which budget deficits are financed will be an important determinant of the success of the stabilization efforts that must play a large role in economic reform. Though true for all economies, this is worth elaborating for the case of economies in transition, in order to highlight the choices confronting them. This section discusses the implications of simulations which show the effects of financing alternatives on the fiscal

deficit itself, the inflation rate and the trade balance. The simulations—
from a realistic base situation—illustrate how the future of the economy is
not neutral to the financing package. The formal framework underlying
the simulations is outlined in the appendix.

To isolate the effect of the option chosen to finance the budget deficit
on the success of the transition, the simulations assume that the government runs a deficit in the first year of the transition, and from then on
maintains a restrictive fiscal policy in the sense that the primary balance is
kept in equilibrium. Only the debt service ensuing from the first year's
deficit perpetuates the deficit; that is, the deficit in years $t+1$ on measures
the impact of debt service on the fiscal balance. Likewise, the inflation rate
shown measures only the impact on inflation from the deficit, through its
financing; and analogously for the trade balance. In this sense, the framework is quite partial, and cannot be taken as a representation of the general evolution of an economy in transition.[23]

As an illustration that does not diminish the generality of the results, the
initial values of the simulation model are set to equal approximately the
corresponding Soviet measures for 1991.[24]

Table 3 shows the effects of 11 different financing scenarios on the
budget deficit, the inflation rate, and the trade balance. The scenarios
distinguish between the impacts of choosing foreign, domestic nonbank,
domestic bank financing, or a combination. They also examine the influence of the domestic interest rate regime and the underlying real growth
rate of the transition economy on the consequences of financing a deficit
domestically or externally. The main conclusions from the simulation
results are listed here.

Foreign financing is the option that creates the smallest burden on
future budget balances, and in that restricted sense, minimizes the cost of
the transition.[25] In reality, however, this will be the case only when the
domestic interest rate exceeds the world interest rate, and the exchange
rate can be supported. Because foreign financing (in these simulations)
corresponds to a relaxation of the resource constraint, it relieves inflationary pressures. However, the cost to the economy is the buildup of external

---

[23]Perhaps the most important omission is a treatment of the exchange rate,
which is assumed fixed. However, it is clear that domestic inflation, and the
build-up of external debt if there is a trade deficit, will have a strong impact on the
sustainability of the exchange regime, and therefore on the relative domestic
resource costs of domestic and foreign debt service.

[24]The values are for T, G_{prim}, GDP_{t-1}, and M^s_{t-1}. Specifically, the rub 250 billion
deficit projected for the state budget in 1991 (for instance, in Aslund (1991)) was
taken as given, and T and G_{prim} extrapolated from it.

[25]The deficit in years $t+1$ on is lower in scenario (1) than in (2)–(4).

Table 3. The Impact of Financing Options on the Economy

$t =$	(1991) Base year	(1992) 2nd year	(1995) 5th year	(2000) 10th year
(1) All foreign financing				
Deficit (As percent of GDP)	−16	−2	−2	−4
Inflation rate	−2	−2	−2	−2
Trade balance (As percent of GDP)	−16	−2	−2	−4
(2) All domestic bank financing				
Deficit (As percent of GDP)	−13	−4	−6	−7
Inflation rate	23	32	78	249
Trade balance (As percent of GDP)	0	0	0	0
(3) All domestic non-bank financing				
Deficit (As percent of GDP)	−16	−3	−6	−16
Inflation rate	−2	−2	−2	−2
Trade balance (As percent of GDP)	0	0	0	0
(4) Equal shares of each type of financing				
Deficit (As percent of GDP)	−15	−3	−4	−6
Inflation rate	6	8	16	37
Trade balance (As percent of GDP)	−5	−1	−1	−2
(5) Equal shares/high domestic interest				
Rate deficit (As percent of GDP)	−15	−5	−8	−13
Inflation rate	6	9	23	77
Trade balance (As percent of GDP)	−5	−2	−3	−4
(6) All foreign financing/high domestic interest rate (Same as low rate case)				
+				
(7) Deficit (As percent of GDP)	−16	−2	−2	−4
Inflation rate	−2	−2	−2	−2
Trade balance (As percent of GDP)	−16	−2	−2	−4
(8) All domestic financing/high domestic interest rate				
Deficit (As percent of GDP)	−14	−6	−13	−20
Inflation rate	11	17	55	279
Trade balance (As percent of GDP)	0	0	0	0
(9) All domestic financing/low domestic interest rate				
Deficit (As percent of GDP)	−14	−3	−4	−7
Inflation rate	11	13	25	63
Trade balance (As percent of GDP)	0	0	0	0
(10) All foreign financing/high growth				
Deficit (As percent of GDP)	−17	−2	−2	−5
Inflation rate	−7	−8	−9	−13
Trade balance (As percent of GDP)	−17	−2	−2	−5
(11) All domestic financing/high growth				
Deficit (As percent of GDP)	−15	−3	−6	−9
Inflation rate	6	9	26	97
Trade balance (As percent of GDP)	0	0	0	0

debt from the consequent trade deficit. Since the trade balance actually deteriorates over time, the economy would have to become increasingly export-oriented to prevent a debt crisis from emerging.

Hence, foreign financing will be an attractive option to transition economies: to the extent that they can get concessional financing; if capital at home is particularly scarce and its domestic return high; if the trade balance is relatively healthy and prospects for expanding markets are rosy; if they have a low initial external debt; if inflation is considered likely and if avoiding it is a high priority.

In simulation (2), *domestic bank financing* generates accelerating inflation, and eventually hyperinflation, because of the inflation component of interest payments. On the plus side, a buildup of external debt is avoided—at least for a while,[26] and the real value of government debt incurred at the beginning of the transition is steadily eroded. (This can be seen indirectly by the fact that the level of the deficit as a share of GDP—that is, the real interest burden—remains lower than in the case (simulation (3)) where debt is financed by domestic bond issue.) Note that an important reason for the accelerating inflation in this simulation is that the government paid market interest rates on its bank debt, as it would have to bondholders, thus putting further pressure on the budget balance.

Since the government is assumed to return to primary balance after the first year, inflation is fueled only by debt service. It is clear that, to stop the inflation, the government would have to begin to finance interest payments as well from sources other than the banking system. In that sense, bank financing is, at best, a temporary option.

Domestic bank financing is usually the option adopted when external debt is high; domestic interest rates are high and foreign concessional financing is ruled out (usually because of the presence of external debt); domestic public debt is already high—often a prime cause of the high domestic interest rates—and difficult to roll over; reserves are low, so that protecting the trade balance retains a high priority; and it is believed that the economy can tolerate inflation.

Domestic nonbank financing would appear to be the most prudent option for deficit finance. Like foreign financing, it avoids inflationary pressure; like domestic bank financing, it substitutes for pressures on the trade balance and a buildup of external debt. Its main problem, of course, is its deflationary impact on the rest of the economy—only part of which can be seen in this framework. According to simulation (3), if the Soviet

---

[26]It must be remembered that in this extreme scenario, inflation is the cost of running a fiscal deficit while forgoing all imports. This policy choice could be pursued by keeping the economy completely closed or by maintaining a fully flexible exchange rate regime. If transition economies try to bankroll their fiscal deficits while pursuing liberalization on the external side, bank financing will lead to some (lower) inflation and some deficit on the trade balance.

Union succeeded in financing its projected 1991 budget deficit purely by issuing domestic bonds, then, by the year 2000, the real burden on the economy of its interest payments would have grown from 3 percent to 16 percent of GDP.[27] Some of the burden is due to an increase in the real domestic interest rate to reflect crowding out,[28] and some is due to deflation. This evolution implies an evident failure of the transition objective of reducing the presence of the state in the economy. If the government has such a heavy demand for private sector funds, privatization will be difficult to finance. Thus, undue reliance on nonbank financing in the transition is the scenario likely to maximize enterprise bankruptcy.

These consequences suggest that domestic nonbank financing may be relatively least costly when: credit to the private sector is difficult to control; domestic supply is relatively elastic; foreign financing is relatively expensive; existing domestic debt is low; other assets are scarce; transitional inflation is high or inevitable; and money illusion has not been eliminated by past inflation.

The choice between financing methods cannot be independent of the *domestic-world interest differential.* A comparison of scenarios (4) and (5)—the deficit financed in equal shares domestically and from abroad, but with first low and then high domestic interest rates—shows that a high domestic cost of capital makes deficit-financing far more burdensome. In the high-interest case, the budget deficit remains higher, the inflation rate grows faster (because some of the interest bill ends up being financed by bank credit), and the trade balance is worse (since some of the interest bill ends up being covered by foreign resources).

When foreign financing is not available, as in simulations (8) and (9), the behavior of the domestic interest rate becomes a crucial indicator of whether a fiscal deficit can be sustained during the transition. A high domestic interest rate makes inflation and the deterioration of the budget balance even more extreme than in simulation (5). (Simulations (6) and (7) show that when foreign financing is unconstrained, the level of the domestic interest rate is irrelevant.)

It is clear from simulations (4)–(9) that, for countries in transition, any policies that bring the domestic (market) interest rate down will enhance the government's ability to finance its deficit. This is one reason why the financial reform many transition economies are engaging in is of vital

---

[27]This occurs despite continued real growth of 2 percent a year. In reality, crowding-out would be likely to depress GDP growth, so that the weight of interest in GDP would be even higher.

[28]The crowding-out parameter, arbitrarily chosen to be 0.2, could well be much higher in transitional economies with very inelastic supply.

importance. Likewise, any policy that encourages voluntary savings, and reduces perceived risk, will help in the overall stabilization effort.

The economy's *real growth rate* also makes a difference to the consequences of financing a fiscal deficit. Simulations (10) and (11) show the outcome of foreign and domestic financing, respectively, for an economy growing at 7 percent a year in real terms, compared with the 2 percent real growth rate assumed so far. Predictably, inflation pressures are lower. In (10), the rapid deflation would be likely in reality to lead to an exchange rate revaluation.[29] In (11), the effects of bank financing on the price level are less extreme because of the relaxation of supply constraints.

Financing the Budget

Table 2 presents economic indicators useful for assessing the capacity of the group of countries under study to finance fiscal deficits from the various options open to them. The trade balance and foreign reserves measure countries' capacity to service foreign debt. The debt stock figures give an idea of the long-run sustainability of foreign financing. The domestic interest rate (preferably the domestic-foreign differential) should signal relative scarcities of foreign and domestic capital. Alternatively, the inflation rate-interest rate differential indicates the financial liberalization necessary before a government can expect to attract its private sector surplus. A high inflation rate also suggests that an expansionary push from the budget would be inappropriate. Moreover, the higher present and past inflation rates are, the lower the likely breathing space from continued money illusion.[30]

Of the group, *Czechoslovakia* and *Romania* would appear relatively suited to soliciting foreign financing, with some reservations.[31] The two countries have little external debt, both absolutely and compared with

---

[29]Because the simulations hold the exchange rate fixed, simulation (10) compared with (1) suggests somewhat misleadingly that financing a deficit from abroad leads to a fiscal deficit higher in terms of GDP in (10) than in (1). A revaluation would generate a corresponding decline in the domestic cost of external debt service.

[30]Data on domestic debt stocks and monetary overhangs would have been useful but were not available.

[31]Among transition economies, Eastern Germany, (not included in the tables because comparable data are not available) seems well placed to take advantage of foreign financing. Eastern Germany scores high on access to concessional financing and to new markets, and pressure to avoid inflation.

their export earnings.[32] This would suggest that both are "good risks" for foreign lenders. Both have a history of healthy hard-currency trade balances, though they were affected by the systemic deterioration of external positions in 1990. Although not shown in the data, the transferable ruble balances of both have been relatively healthy (particularly Czechoslovakia's), suggesting that they may be less burdened than partner countries in the shift to convertible currency payments. On the other hand, reserves in both countries dropped precipitously in 1990, a warning that high foreign debt service might not be easy to sustain. Czechoslovakia differs from Romania in that it had a sophisticated and broadly based industrial base with strong linkages to other parts of the ex-Austrian Empire prior to the introduction of planning. These links were backed by a regional capital market which shows signs of being resuscitated.

Comparing foreign financing with domestic options, it appears that, in Czechoslovakia, private activity is emerging relatively strongly, with consequent pressure on domestic credit markets. Privatization, at least of small-scale shops and enterprises, became significant in 1990. Hence, the potential for crowding-out could be an important argument against domestic nonbank financing. However, despite the fact that a new interest rate structure was put in place in 1990 as part of financial reform, there has been little movement in the domestic interest rate to substantiate the problem.[33] As in other countries, the Czechoslovak inflation rate began to accelerate, implying that expansionary domestic finance could have costs beyond those of a fiscal deficit financed with foreign resources. On the other hand, analysts have found no evidence of a monetary overhang in Czechoslovakia, because, unlike other CMEA economies, the Czechoslovak government pursued conscious policies to equilibrate the market for consumer goods. Hence, inflation in Czechoslovakia should be more short-lived than, for instance, in Poland.

In Romania, the domestic interest rate is still institutionally set. The contraction of the domestic economy to prepay foreign debt would suggest that the supply of domestic capital in Romania must be particularly limited. On the other hand, unlike in Czechoslovakia, no alternative sav-

---

[32]The indicators fall short of a complete picture of financing capacity particularly because they do not deal with CMEA trade or obligations. It is likely, however, that former CMEA obligations will be renegotiated, and that from now on trade and borrowing will require convertible currency.

[33]The lack of response to interest liberalization is most likely due to the de facto debt subordination referred to in the section on "Financing Alternatives," above. The Czechoslovak Government is attempting to protect existing rates on mortgages and other targeted loans.

ing instruments—such as privatized assets—have yet emerged, so what demand for bonds there is would naturally finance government. While no current data on inflation are available, diverging black market and state prices for consumer goods, together with increasing saving rates at a time when real deposit interest rates were falling, suggest there is a monetary overhang. Moreover, enterprises received an expansionary boost in 1989–90 in the form of an effective write-off of accumulated losses. There-fore triggering inflation by money issue to finance the budget could, on the one hand, help to equilibrate the narrowly based goods markets but on the other, release a price spiral with stronger effects than the money injection would suggest.

Relative to Poland and Bulgaria, the *U.S.S.R.* also has a manageable foreign debt, on the criterion of the debt/export ratio. This is in line with the international rule-of-thumb that oil exporters are good credit risks. However, Soviet debt is large in absolute terms; moreover, a trade deficit emerged in 1989. Uncertainty about the size and future of the Soviet Union, and questions about the status of existing debt, imply that the large absolute foreign debt may deter foreign lenders. Further, the unsustain-able differential between the exchange rate at which debt is serviced (rub 1.8/US $1) and the "free" rate (rub 28/US $1) suggest that the per-ceived domestic resource costs of foreign debt service may weigh more heavily on the budget in the future. Plans to make the ruble convertible will, even in the absence of higher foreign debt service bills, put pressure on foreign reserves, which have anyway been falling since 1986. Conces-sional financing large enough to cover a significant portion of projected budget gaps also seems further away from the U.S.S.R than from Eastern European countries who are smaller and perceived as being more inevita-bly committed to market reforms.

The prospects for domestic financing are also limited. The Soviet Union's domestic debt is also large—equivalent to nearly 60 percent of 1990 GDP.[34] Hence, domestic budget financing at competitive rates would be expensive for the budget balance. Besides, there are indications that competitive rates could be high by historical Soviet standards. In 1990 the government planned to finance a rub 60 billion deficit by bond issue, but, even after a doubling of the interest rates offered midway through the year, the bonds were taken up only by the captive banking system.

---

[34]This ratio is not comparable to debt/GDP ratios in other countries because government liabilities held by the monetary authorities are not netted out. (See Guidotti and Kumar (1991), pp. 2 ff.)

Since the existence of such a large debt may keep inflation expectations—and interest rates—high whether or not budget financing is expansionary, there may be no escape from inflation in the U.S.S.R. Besides the possible unsustainability of Soviet debt, the inflationary tendencies from disequilibria in Soviet goods markets are also considered substantial.[35] The difficulties in financing the Soviet deficit by non-monetary means are not an argument in favor of a large Soviet budget deficit financed by money creation. Given the pressures on the value of the ruble, any budget deficit, regardless of how it is financed, may be more costly in the U.S.S.R. than in the other countries in the group.

Table 2 suggests that Bulgaria and Poland may find it necessary to rely mainly on domestic financing. Their foreign debt is high (310 percent and 400 percent of 1990 exports, respectively), making it relatively difficult for them to seek further financing abroad. Astonishingly, Poland's debt, in absolute terms, is practically as big as the Soviet Union's. Bulgaria, in particular, has low reserves—though not as low as Czechoslovakia's in 1990—and they have been dropping in terms of exports since 1988. Moreover, its balance on convertible trade is the worst in the country grouping.

Of the group, Poland and Bulgaria experienced the highest inflation in 1990. Poland's was even higher in 1989, making it probably more vulnerable to new monetary shocks, if long-term inflationary expectations have been raised. However, Poland's inflation had the not unimportant side-effects of significantly reducing its real domestic debt, and eliminating the monetary overhang. Poland is also likely to differ from Bulgaria in the size of its informal markets, which depend significantly on western contacts. These markets, which were an important brake on inflation when they were legalized at the beginning of the transition, have eased Poland's supply constraint. Black markets in Bulgaria, Romania, and the U.S.S.R. are said to be far smaller as a share of economic activity, meaning that aggregate supply is likely to be correspondingly less elastic. Financial restructuring in Poland is also further evolved than in these other countries: since mid-1990 preferential credits have been reduced and the interest rate has become an important instrument in determining the allocation of funds. Hence, an attempt by Poland to finance future budget deficits by bond issue would be facilitated by supply cushions to reduce crowding-out, and the existence of a more responsive capital market. On the other hand, Poland can no longer rely on money illusion and capital controls to

---

[35]It is estimated that Soviet households have an overhang of rub 160 billion— one third of their financial wealth (International Monetary Fund (1991), Vol. 1, p. 389).

keep debt service bills low. In Bulgaria, where alternative assets remain few, government bonds, even at low or negative rates, may be an acceptable saving instrument in the near term.

Conclusions

The conclusions on financing possibilities for economies in transition are orthodox. Transition economies are like Western economies: no budget deficit is costless, regardless of how it is financed. Governments will have to assess economic preconditions and rank the costs of the different types of financing—a buildup of external debt and foreign exchange pressures versus inflation versus the continued large presence of government in the economy because of crowding-out. The argument above shows that for most countries there is no clear-cut ranking. Countries, such as Czechoslovakia, with few disequilibria going into the transition and a credible commitment to market transformation, could finance a budget deficit from any source at lower cost than, say, the U.S.S.R. or Bulgaria, for whom both foreign and domestic resources are scarce.

Conclusions for management of the macroeconomy are also predictable. If a budget deficit has to be financed, supporting measures in other parts of the economy that minimize its costs will be valuable. Financial reform—including the development of the interest rate instrument and of domestic capital markets—can help, as can a prudent credit policy. Rationalization of currency markets and the shift to a sustainable exchange rate will ease pressures on the trade balance and increase international creditworthiness. For countries with high external debt or arrears, an orderly regularization of external obligations is likely to be a prerequisite for any access to further foreign financing.

On the administration of budgetary financing, one or two messages are important. First, all financing should be made transparent, below the line in the budget, so that the size and costs of the budget deficit cannot be ignored. Second, the government should withdraw from "off-balance-sheet activities" such as trade financing guarantees, that are no longer appropriate in a market-style economy where government's role in production is reduced. More generally, the scope and limitations of the public sector should be clearly delineated. Third, at the administrative level, improvements in budget control translate into a reform of the automatic financing mechanism. The system whereby credit to cover total budgeted spending was placed at the disposal of the government from the outset of the year has to be changed, and procedures for monitoring the joint evolution of receipts and expenditures put into place.

Finally, and most important, there are strong economic arguments for not running a budget deficit during the transition. In a reform program aimed at shifting production and command over resources from the state to a new and fragile private sector, a continuing public sector deficit can be interpreted as a failure to achieve the objectives of the reform. The discussion of financing sources in this paper assumed that, because of the pressures outlined above, budget deficits will be an inevitable feature of the transition for most planned economies. If deficits could be avoided, the transition could be easier.

References

Aslund, Anders, "Moscow's New Power Center," *New York Times*, April 19, 1991.

Blejer, Mario I., and George Szapary, "The Evolving Role of Tax Policy in China," *Journal of Comparative Economics*, September 1990.

———, and Adrienne Cheasty, "The Measurement of Fiscal Deficits: Analytical and Methodological Issues," *Journal of Economic Literature*, December 1991.

Calvo, Guillermo, "Servicing the Public Debt: The Role of Expectations," *American Economic Review*, September 1988, pp. 647–51.

Central Intelligence Agency, *Handbook of Economic Statistics*, 1989.

Dornbusch, Rudiger, and H. Wolf, "Monetary Overhang and Reforms in the 1940s," NBER Working Paper 3456 (Cambridge, Massachusetts: National Bureau of Economic Research, 1990).

Edwards, Sebastian, "Stabilization and Liberalization Policies in Eastern Europe: Lessons from Latin America." Paper presented at the IRIS-IPR Conference on Eastern European Reform, Prague, March 1991.

Guidotti, Pablo E., and Manmohan S. Kumar, *Domestic Public Debt of Externally Indebted Countries*, IMF Occasional Paper 80 (Washington: International Monetary Fund, 1991).

International Monetary Fund, *A Manual on Government Finance Statistics* (Washington: International Monetary Fund, 1984).

———, IBRD, OECD, and EBRD, *A Study of the Soviet Economy* (Paris: OECD, February 1991).

McKinnon, Ronald, "Financial Control in the Transition to a Market Economy." Paper presented at the IRIS-IPR Conference on Eastern European Reform, Prague, March 1991.

Prust, Jim, and others, *The Czech and Slovak Federal Republic: An Economy in Transition*, IMF Occasional Paper 72 (Washington: International Monetary Fund, 1990).

Robinson, David J., and Peter Stella, "Amalgamating Central Bank and Fiscal Deficits," in *How to Measure the Fiscal Deficit: Analytical and Methodological Issues*, ed. by Mario I. Blejer and Adrienne Cheasty (Washington: International Monetary Fund, 1991).

Tanzi, Vito, "Fiscal Management and External Debt Problems," *External Debt Management*, ed. by Hassanali Mehran (Washington: International Monetary Fund, 1985).

———, "Tax Reform and the Move to a Market Economy: Overview of the Issues," in *The Role of Tax Reform in Central and Eastern European Economies* (Paris: OECD, 1991).

World Bank, *World Debt Tables*, 1989–90 (Washington: World Bank, 1989).

Appendix

Financing Alternatives for the Budget Deficit

The budget deficit (D) is the excess of government non-interest spending (G_{prim}) and interest payments on public debt (i) over revenue (T).

$$D = G_{prim} + i - T. \tag{1}$$

It can be financed by foreign inflows (FF), domestic nonbank financing (NBF), or, as a residual, by domestic bank financing (BF),

$$BF = D - FF - NBF. \tag{2}$$

If the deficit is financed from abroad, the budget must pay i_w as interest on the debt incurred. If it is financed by domestic bond issue, debt service costs are i_{dom}. In order to attract domestic financing in the newly liberalizing system, i_{dom} must be adjusted to equilibrate the demand and supply of loanable funds:

$$i = i_w + i_{dom}. \tag{3}$$

In light of the discussion in "Financing Alternatives," above, a risk premium (ρ), a crowding-out parameter (γ) and domestic inflation (π) help to determine the domestic interest rate. The base domestic real rate $(\bar{r})$ is shown to be independent of the world real interest rate, as a proxy for the other effects discussed there:

$$i_{dom} = \bar{r} + \rho + \gamma(NBF/GDP) + \pi. \tag{4}$$

If the budget deficit is financed by printing money (BF), the money supply will grow. It is assumed that monetary policy is accommodating, in the sense that, in the absence of a fiscal deficit, it would grow in line with real growth (g) and inflation:

$$M^s = M^s_{t-1}(1 + \pi_{t-1})(1 + g) + BF. \tag{5}$$

Note that bank financing is the only influence of the deficit on the money supply. Implicit here is another important assumption—that all foreign financing is matched by imports, and therefore affects the trade balance (*TB*) directly and uniquely.

$$FF = -TB. \tag{6}$$

Inflation is the change in the money supply less real growth. This formulation assumes that demand for real balances grows with real income[36] and that velocity is constant.

$$\pi = M^s - g. \tag{7}$$

Finally, nominal *GDP* rises in line with an exogenous real growth rate, and inflation.

$$GDP = GDP_{t-1}(1 + g)(1 + \pi). \tag{8}$$

---

[36]Not a very realistic assumption. However, as discussed in Section III, the direction of changes is hard to predict.

CHAPTER 3

Government Debt Management
Mark Allen

Recognized government domestic debt played a very small role in the traditional centrally planned economy.[1] State budgets were expected to be in balance or surplus in normal times, and recorded deficits were usually financed out of the surpluses of previous years held on deposit with the monobank. At times, particularly during the Stalinist period, bonds and other forms of state loans were floated to which the general population was expected to subscribe, but this form of finance did not generally outlast the 1950s. Some countries, for example both the Soviet Union and China during the 1980s, issued government paper to be held compulsorily by state enterprises. While the recorded budgets indicated relatively little use of domestic financing, the state as a whole did acquire liabilities off the budget, largely in the form of currency issue and deposits. These in turn were backed by the assets of the banking system, the soundness of which did not normally need to be tested.

The economic transformation now occurring in the countries of Central and Eastern Europe involves, among other things, redrawing the lines of demarcation between the government and the nongovernment sectors of the economy. The establishment of a market economy also requires clarity as to the assets and liabilities of the various economic agents. Thus, as part of the process of demarcation, the issue of the extent of government debt is acquiring great importance. Determining the liabilities of the government inherited from the past is a process of political and economic trial and error, and the full size of the bill in each individual country will only be known after some time. By then, it will be mixed with the new liabilities incurred by the governments during the transformation process itself.

---

[1] In this paper, issues relating to the management of foreign debt are ignored.

In the first part of the paper, the question of the extent and nature of the inherited government debt are treated. Issues related to incurring and managing new domestic debt by governments are treated next. The following section treats the forms in which government debt in the economies in question has been issued, and the final section discusses some general issues connected with the management of government domestic debt and the transformation process.

Old Debt

Public-Sector Debt

The economic transformation process that the countries of Central and Eastern Europe are going through involves redrawing the boundary between the public sector and the rest of the economy. In essence, the bulk of the banking system and the state enterprise sector are to be transferred to private hands or put beyond the reach of direct government control and responsibility. The governments of the region start the process with a certain inheritance of public-sector assets and liabilities, the latter reflecting the claims of the public and private sector on the government, on government agencies, and on the state-owned banking system.[2]

The net public debt inherited by the governments of the region is the difference between the size of their liabilities and the value of their assets. At the start of the transformation process it was generally thought that the value of the assets (primarily in the form of the state-owned enterprise sector's physical assets) would clearly exceed the value of the liabilities. As time goes on, it is becoming less and less obvious that the value of these assets that the state can realize exceeds the sum of the liabilities now outstanding. Among the most difficult challenges of this transition period is for governments to maximize the transfer value of the assets they are handing over to the private sector, so that the net debt they definitively assume is minimized.

Bad Bank Loans to Enterprise Sector

The counterpart of a large part of the hitherto unrecognized debt of the governments in these countries is bad bank loans. To the extent that these loans are clearly bad, the commercial banks will have to be recapitalized. They could do this gradually by making profits through wide spreads, but

---

[2]See Pablo E. Guidotti, and Manmohan S. Kumar, *Domestic Public Debt of Externally Indebted Countries*, IMF Occasional Paper 80 (Washington: International Monetary Fund, 1991), p. 10.

this may not be possible if the banks are to compete with new banks that do not have such poor loan portfolios. It may also be undesirable to deal with the consequences of past lending decisions by taxing current borrowers and depositors. The only practical way for this recapitalization to be done is through an injection of funds by the government, in essence replacing a bank claim on the enterprise with a bank claim on the government. In some cases, the government privatization agency takes over the claim as part of the financial restructuring of the enterprise needed for privatization.

In most countries, the link between the assumption by the government of liabilities of privatized enterprises and the government's receipts from privatization sales has been clearly made. Czechoslovakia is to manage privatization through State Property Funds, which are expected to run surpluses, offsetting the government's debt. The receipts from privatization in east Germany are to accrue to the Treuhand and to be used to offset the costs of the Treuhand's operations and assumed liabilities. In Hungary, the proceeds from privatization are to be largely devoted to paying off government debt.

With time, the net value of the enterprises being privatized looks smaller and smaller. On the asset side, the increasingly depressed activity levels and management problems in such enterprises are reducing the market value of the future stream of earnings. Also with time, it is increasingly difficult to keep the assets of the enterprises together as going concerns. On the other side, the extent of the liabilities is becoming clearer. The most extreme example is perhaps the case of the east German Trust Fund (Treuhandanstalt).[3] In order to privatize, it is taking over part of the financial liabilities of the former German Democratic Republic on a case-by-case basis; it has had to guarantee bank credit for working capital purposes to keep many enterprises from closing down; it has had to give title insurance, protecting new owners against any claims from former owners; it has had to take on all liabilities for past environmental damage; and it has had to take over part of the costs of shedding labor under west German law. While some of these conditions are peculiar to east Germany, others apply to all the countries of the region.

In some cases, the government has taken certain loans to state enterprises off the balance sheets of the commercial banks. Thus, in Czechoslovakia, it was decided as of March 1991 to take over inventory

---

[3]See Leslie Lipschitz, and Donough McDonald, eds., *German Unification: Economic Issues*, IMF Occasional Paper 75 (Washington: International Monetary Fund, 1990), p. 7–9.

credits and put them into a special Consolidation Bank for gradual amortization, with any associated costs to be covered out of the revenue of State Property Funds.

The most extensive cleaning of the balance sheet of the banking system has occurred in Romania. Because of the unorthodox financial practices of the Ceauşescu regime, the new government inherited substantial government deposits and an enterprise sector highly indebted both to the banks and to each other. In the first half of 1990, banks were instructed to write off two thirds of unserviceable enterprise debt, using government deposits for the purpose. The most of the remainder was refinanced by the National Bank of Romania. Later, it was decided that the government would take over this debt and supply the National Bank in return with nonnegotiable government instruments. These are to be retired through the Enterprise Restructuring Fund, financed by the revenues from the sale of state assets, and a tax on the revaluation of enterprise stocks as of November 1, 1990.

Specific Debts

Apart from the general issue of the assumption by the government of the bad debt of the enterprise sector, the governments have also recognized explicitly certain specific debts to the banking system. One of these is *housing credit* and the losses arising from such lending. In some countries, housing loans were extended at low, fixed interest rates. This was possible as most deposits were at low rates, which remained virtually unchanged for many years. With the sharp rise in interest rates, which formed part of the adjustment programs in the countries in question, the housing banks and funds found themselves having to pay much more for their deposits than they were earning on their assets.

In the case of Hungary, at the end of 1989, the government purchased such mortgages from the National Savings Bank by issuing market-rate nonnegotiable Housing Fund bonds. In Poland, rapid inflation eroded much of the value of housing debt. New housing loans, however, bear a high nominal interest rate, a large part of which is capitalized with part being purchased by the government.

Another form of loss to banks that has been explicitly recognized as government debt in several countries is *valuation losses* on banks' unbalanced foreign exchange positions. This problem was particularly serious in Poland, where the domestic banks have considerable foreign exchange liabilities to residents. The foreign exchange was deposited in Bank Handlowy, which in turn sold it to the government over the years to meet the country's balance of payments obligations. As the zloty has been devalued, the banks have retained a foreign exchange claim on Bank Handlowy, but the latter simply booked a loss to its valuation account. In the 1991 budget, provision was made for the Polish Government to issue some US$5 billion worth of foreign currency denominated bonds to Bank Handlowy to give it an asset that will allow it to reduce the degree of currency mismatch on its books.

In Czechoslovakia, the government took over the losses of the main foreign trade bank, the Obchodni Bank, after the devaluation at the start of the adjustment program. With the adoption of the deutsche mark by the German Democratic Republic on July 1, 1990, a similar valuation loss arose, caused by the different exchange rates applied to different items on the balance sheets of east German banks.[4] The net effect was a claim of east German banks on the Equalization Fund of DM 26.5 billion. Valuation losses are also an issue in Bulgaria.

Some claims taken over by the government resulted from *foreign debt servicing*. In the case of Poland, most foreign debt servicing was done by Bank Handlowy, and such debt was, until 1990, a liability of the bank, although the government reimbursed the bank for the cost of debt service. Some arrears in this reimbursement occurred in 1989 and 1990, and these are being settled by issuing explicit government debt to the bank. The 1989 arrears have been covered by the issue of two-year paper, not bearing interest, but with the principal indexed to the consumer price index. The 1990 debt is to be covered with part of the foreign currency bond issue mentioned above.

Some *past export activity* has resulted in financial institutions holding assets of dubious worth. In Czechoslovakia, the government took over export credits from the books of the State Bank. In Poland, consideration is being given to the issue of government paper in exchange for the transferable ruble assets of the National Bank.

Broader Liabilities

The above transactions involve the government's issuing debt to banks to allow them to meet their liabilities. Similar issues arise in connection with other institutions with financial liabilities, insurance companies, and pension funds. Both insurance companies and pension funds in Eastern Europe have tended to operate on an unfunded basis, covering their current outlays with their premium or contribution income together with

---

[4]See Lipschitz and McDonald (1990), p. 146.

bank credit or budget transfer. As part of the process of establishing a market economy, consideration is being given to putting such institutions on a self-financing basis.

The case of insurance companies is very similar to that of banks, which require a certain capitalization to ensure their soundness to protect policy holders from the danger of failure. At present, the value of insurance companies' assets is considerably less than their liabilities. This raises the question of the need for capital injection by the government. A further issue is the absence of appropriate domestic assets for insurance companies in the region to invest in. While the emerging property and equity markets should make some assets available to insurance companies, long-term government bonds are also needed. In 1991, Romania plans to borrow from the insurance companies to cover part of the budget deficit, issuing new financial instruments in the process.

The issues in the case of pension funds are rather more complicated. Up to now, the pension system has enjoyed a state guarantee. Pension entitlements earned to date represent a long-term liability of the government. Suggestions have been made that this liability be explicitly recognized by the government, which would issue long-term paper to the pension funds, as was done in Chile. Pension funds would then be able to finance pensions out of earnings on this asset, as well as current contributions, and instead of a regular transfer from the budget.

While this proposal would help in the development of a well-funded pension industry after the U.S. model, it would reduce the government's flexibility considerably and could entail certain dangers. Most Western European countries operate unfunded state pension schemes, which do not create serious problems. It may be difficult and unadvisable for the government to quantify explicitly existing pension liabilities in the current uncertainties about the countries' income levels. Providing an asset that will ensure a certain real value of pensions will be difficult and expensive. Furthermore, putting such a large sum at the disposal of pension funds with no experience in asset management would require a major supervisory effort by the governments, one for which they are ill equipped.

New Debt

The governments of Central and Eastern Europe are also incurring new debt, in addition to recognizing the old debt discussed in the previous section. Some debt is incurred as the result of budget deficits. Other debt is being issued in order to create the financial instruments needed for better monetary management. Finally, the inability to make a clean break with the past may mean that the process of assumption of obligations cannot be limited to those established before the new governments took power.

The fiscal situation in Central and Eastern Europe is precarious. The need for government social and investment expenditure is self-evident, while the revenue base is suffering from the disruptions caused by the changes in tax collection systems and the erosion of the old revenue base in the state sector. While the governments are running tight fiscal and monetary policies, the assumption of new domestic debt seems inevitable. Governments are trying to find new debt instruments to replace part of their reliance on bank borrowing to cover their deficits.

As the banking system develops and as central banks try to run more market-based monetary policies, a need has appeared for money market instruments. A policy of issuing short-term paper to fill this need and to permit the central bank to perform open market operations has been followed in all the countries of the region. Hungary was the first country to do this, with 90-day treasury bills sold since 1988. In Poland, the role of potential money market instruments was first filled by the National Bank of Poland bills, issued from mid-1990 in one-month and then two-month maturities through regular auctions. More recently, the government has displaced the central bank on this market by auctioning its own one-and two-month treasury bills. Bulgaria and Czechoslovakia plan to issue short-term Treasury bills during the course of 1991.

It is not easy for the governments of the region to make a clean break with the past. Policies have in general tried to make state enterprises and banks fully responsible for their current decisions and to bear any financial consequences. Not only that; to the extent possible such economic agents have been expected to take responsibility for the decisions of the past, with the government taking over obligations only when its liability could be clearly shown or when the case was in extremis.

However, with the vast bulk of employment accounted for by the state sector, with some towns totally dependent on one state-sector employer, with the tax base dependent on flows from state enterprises, with a need to prevent the disruption of the banking system by a flood of bankruptcies, and with a need to keep enterprises in as going concerns for privatization purposes, governments are finding themselves obliged to moderate the pace at which state enterprises are allowed to fail. The clearest example of this has been east Germany, where the Treuhand has guaranteed considerable liquidity credits to enterprises to keep them functioning. So far, such explicit public support has not been available in the other countries. However, as enterprises lose creditworthiness, there is similar pressure on governments elsewhere to extend guarantees to such borrowing. Beyond that it would seem that the governments of the region are not prepared to allow major domestic banks to fail as a result of the burden of past debt or of providing sufficient resources to keep the state sector going.[5]

The inability to make a clean break with the past, or the unacceptability of its consequences, means that the governments are running considerable moral hazard. They are accumulating considerable implicit contingent liabilities that will probably be called sooner rather than later. This problem is likely to be with the countries of the region throughout the transition period. Two conclusions seem to follow. The first is the need for the countries to run as small a deficit as possible to provide room for the hidden deficit that is building up and which will become visible at some point, and to limit the accumulation of explicit guarantees to the extent possible. The second is that the cost of recognizing too much old debt may be offset by the gains from rapid privatization that such recognition would facilitate.

Management of Government Debt

Most recognized domestic government debt in Eastern and Central Europe is held by financial institutions, principally by banks, in the form of bank credit to the government or its agencies. The issue of government paper is as yet in its infancy. However, as already mentioned, some forms of government paper do exist, and others are being developed.

Various considerations govern the appropriate structure of government debt and the form of the instruments that should be issued. The government will clearly want to keep the cost of debt service as low as possible, consistent with the holders of such debt doing so voluntarily. The form in which government debt is issued can help stimulate the development of financial markets, a point that is discussed further below. The government will normally seek to issue instruments that give it flexibility in financing. Finally, the instruments should be such as to allow government debt operations to be transparent. On this last point, the explicit recognition of the obligations of the government forms a major element of the transformation process in the economies of Eastern and Central Europe. Making the debt and the government's servicing obligations transparent serves also to make the dilemmas and problems of macroeconomic policy that much clearer.

---

[5]Apart from any implicit guarantee of bank solvency, the countries of the region are all in the process of establishing explicit deposit insurance schemes.

Following the OECD Committee on Financial Markets, government paper may be divided into the marketable and the nonmarketable.[6] As far as marketable paper is concerned, the governments of Central and Eastern Europe have issued a certain amount of short-term instruments, largely for the purpose of creating instruments for money market purposes. Some countries have issued treasury bills of up to one-year maturity. In the uncertain economic conditions now prevailing in the region, governments have generally considered it too difficult to persuade investors to hold long-term domestic paper. In Poland some indexed marketable state bonds of indefinite maturity are still outstanding, which can be used to purchase the stock of privatized enterprises at a discounted price.

Nonmarketable instruments constitute the main form of government debt, most of which is in the form of bank loans. As mentioned above, nonmarketable paper or promissory notes have been issued by several governments to financial institutions to cover losses arising from certain past operations for which the government is now assuming the responsibility. There is little or no nonmarketable debt held by personal investors, since state savings banks mobilized savings deposits rather than selling savings bonds issued by the government.

As far as primary sales techniques are concerned, governments have mainly resorted to auctions for treasury bills and to private placements when they replace certain bank claims with some form of government paper. So far little use has been made of tap issues of government paper or of consortium techniques in the primary market, and this probably reflects the absence of secondary markets in government paper.

The adjustment and transformation programs of the region are designed, among other things, to end financial repression and establish confidence in domestic currencies. In this context, interest rates have been high in both nominal and real terms. This has meant that the interest rates on new instruments have also had to be high. The issue of short-term treasury bills to provide instruments for the development of a money market have been designed to help establish benchmark interest rates for the economies. With bank balance sheets needing strengthening, the governments have had to pay market interest rates on their liabilities to banks. The relatively high short-term interest rates and the uncertainty surrounding medium-term economic conditions has made it hard to issue fixed interest market-rate government debt obligations with maturities longer

---

[6]Committee on Financial Markets, Group of Experts on Government Debt Management, *Government Debt Management: Debt Instruments and Selling Techniques* (Paris: OECD, 1983), p. 11.

than a year. Longer-term obligations have either been at floating rates or the principal has been indexed to the cost of living, as in the case of certain bonds issued in Poland.

Developing longer maturity government paper will be helpful for a number of reasons. It will in particular allow the financing of budget deficits with an instrument that is a more distant substitute for money, and reduce the amount of paper that the government will have to roll over. It will also help provide a benchmark for investors for the longer-run cost of capital. However, before this can happen on any scale, government anti-inflationary policies will need to achieve credibility.[7]

As the financial structure of the countries of the region changes, there will be a need for longer-term, low-risk, financial instruments that will maintain their value. Already local insurance companies face the lack of suitable instruments to invest in, with alternative assets, such as stocks, being scarce and very risky, and the property markets not being fully developed. While assets issued by foreign debtors and institutions would be suitable assets, the authorities have been cautious about removing restrictions on capital transactions for fear of destabilizing the balance of payments. Since it may be difficult to issue fixed rate paper to be held by such institutions, governments may have to meet this need by issuing index- or exchange rate-linked paper.

Should Government Debt Be Welcomed?

Development of Financial Markets

While the inheritance of a large stock of government debt means that the budget has to mobilize resources to service the debt, the positive aspects of the large debt stock have not yet been fully appreciated in the region. Government debt, being free of credit risk and being available in large quantities, can be used to stimulate the development of financial markets. In the developed OECD countries, it is those with the largest government debt markets that have experienced the fastest rates of financial market innovation.

The potential for financial market development has been recognized as far as the money markets are concerned. As already discussed, most of the countries have started to introduce short-term government or central bank paper to provide an instrument to banks to manage their liquidity,

---

[7]For a discussion of the maturity of government debt in indebted developing countries, see Guidotti and Kumar (1991), p. 20–3.

and the intention is progressively to move to open-market operations for monetary control to replace the moral suasion and administrative limits now applied. In this process, there may be a temptation to increase the demand for government paper artificially by requiring banks to hold government paper, as part of their reserve requirements or for other purposes.[8] To the extent that this is done, the market for government paper loses some of its ability to provide a benchmark for interest rates in the economy, and the government may finance its deficit through implicit and nontransparent taxes on financial institutions.

In building the infrastructure for privatization of state enterprises, the governments of the region have opened or reopened stock exchanges, to create a secondary market for enterprise shares. So far they have taken little or no advantage of these markets to establish a secondary market for government paper. Were they to do so, they could greatly contribute to establishing deeper, more liquid financial markets, that would be of use, not only in financing the government, but also in mobilizing capital for privatization and the development of the private sector.

As a first step, governments could secure part of their debt to the banking system and encourage banks to sell this debt through the stock exchange to private sector investors and institutions. This would probably require government assistance in ensuring that properly capitalized brokers operated on the market, and that it remained liquid. As already discussed, there is a considerable potential demand for government paper outside the banking system, and such a mechanism could help the government tap these sources of funds. Encouraging banks to sell their claims on the government to other investors would help free resources for credit operations directed to the private sector. The increasing depth of such a market would both increase the information content of the interest rate and facilitate the financing of any budget deficit. With the commercial banks rather inexperienced and cartelized, interest rates determined on a market with private capital are likely to be a more reliable guide to the true cost of money.

A further important consequence of the active encouragement of a secondary market for government debt is that it would attract capital to the stock market and the primary market, which could help in mobilizing the financial and human resources needed for an extensive stock issue program as part of privatization. It would help in generating experience

---

[8]See Guidotti and Kumar (1991), p. 11, for a discussion of compulsory bank reserves as part of public sector debt, whether or not such reserves are remunerated.

for the securities industry in trading in an instrument free of credit risk, and would help provide the basis for the development of hedging instruments that will be of use to the private sector.

Can the Debt Be Serviced?

As yet we do not know the true size of the government's debt in the countries of Eastern and Central Europe. Until the governments are able to draw the line between the obligations of the state and those of the rest of the economy in a credible and definitive fashion, the full extent of the debt burden on the governments of the region will not be known, nor the ability of the governments to service this debt.

The governments of Eastern and Central Europe are generally being very cautious about the amount of old debt that they are explicitly recognizing. This is both sensible and understandable. The formal recognition of debt by the government is probably expansionary, as it reduces the degree of uncertainty of an economic agent about his net worth. Banks and enterprises unsure about whether the government will recognize a claim are likely to be more cautious in their activities than those that have such certainty. In principle, the assumption of liabilities by the government should be limited to those incurred under the old system, to avoid the problem of moral hazard. However, it is becoming increasingly difficult to draw the line between losses incurred as a result of recent decisions and those being incurred now because of decisions taken in the past.

The rapid recapitalization of the banking system is required to strengthen it and make it more able to pursue its roles as the mobilizer and allocator of savings. Too large a capitalization could put too many resources at the disposal of the banks, making it more difficult to continue a policy of credit restraint. Writing off too many of the banking system loans to the state enterprise sector involves a transfer of assets to the enterprises, and these assets may not be held in trust for the state. If such a debt reduction is done as part of the process of privatization, it may be reflected in an increase in revenues from privatization of a similar amount, but this is likely to be the case only if the privatization process is sufficiently transparent and competitive.

Governments in the region are engaged in a process of cautiously determining the extent of their obligations. That they should be cautious is essential for macroeconomic reasons. By removing uncertainty as to who will bear the cost of past operations, it makes those relieved of the burden think that they have more money (*pace* Ricardian equivalence). Such operations also create moral hazard, in that those who think the govern-

relieved them of a claim once may incur new claims in the expectation that the government will also relieve them of these claims. Nevertheless, once the government does recognize a liability, it should make this recognition as transparent as possible and restructure the debt in such a way as to promote the development of financial markets. This will also serve the government's turn as it will help develop more flexible ways to manage the fiscal situation.

CHAPTER 4

Privatization of State Enterprises
Richard Hemming

Privatization is a central feature of the structural reform programs being adopted throughout Eastern Europe. The idea that transferring state activities to the private sector can help solve some of the problems associated with government intervention in the economy gained considerable popularity during the 1980s. Unfortunately, the expectations created by the rhetoric have yet to be fulfilled, largely because the preconditions for successful privatization—relating mainly to institutional development—are demanding. The worldwide economic impact of privatization therefore remains modest. Even the landmark program in the United Kingdom—albeit of considerable importance as an example of what can be achieved by way of privatizing large public monopolies—resulted in only around 20 enterprises, together accounting for about 5 percent of value added, being divested to the private sector over more than ten years. In contrast, the recently announced privatization program in Poland aims to reduce state ownership of more than 7,000 enterprises—which swamp the rest of the nonagricultural economy—by about half over three years. How can such an ambitious objective be achieved?

If the countries of Eastern Europe were similar to Western countries in terms of their economic, legal, and financial structure, and privatization followed already established practices, the outlook would indeed be discouraging. There has, however, emerged a consensus that the transition from a planned economy to a market economy is unlikely to occur without extensive and rapid privatization, and that improving enterprise efficiency will be difficult in the absence of effective markets. Finding solutions to the institutional problems that could stand in the way of progress

Note: The author is grateful to Dieter Bös for his comments on an earlier draft of this paper.

is therefore of crucial importance. So too, in emerging democracies, is establishing broad-based social and political support for privatization. Much of the widespread interest in privatization in Eastern Europe concerns these aspects of the process.

Unlike the other papers in this volume, the following discussion is not dominated by fiscal issues, which are only part of a much wider set of considerations that bear upon the privatization debate. But the fiscal implications of privatization are immense. These arise not so much from the direct budgetary impact of asset transfers, but more from the broader consequences if the burden on the economy of a large and inefficient state enterprise sector is not relieved.

The paper is organized as follows: It begins with a discussion of the issues that have arisen in devising the broad privatization strategy being adopted throughout Eastern Europe. Privatization is then linked to other policies supporting the transformation process. More specific issues are raised in the context of an assessment of available privatization options, which are then illustrated by reference to country experience. Particular attention is paid to the Polish program; at the time of writing, this was the most fully articulated privatization strategy in Eastern Europe.

General Issues

Why Privatization?

Structural reform in Eastern Europe is geared ultimately toward improving efficiency in resource allocation through increased reliance on markets. This requires bold measures across a broad front to liberalize economic activity. In Western-type mixed economies, private ownership of a firm or industry is not in principle a prerequisite for increasing its exposure to market forces; public enterprises can be subjected to private competition. However, the general presumption is that liberalization can proceed faster and the resulting efficiency gains will be greater if liberalization is accompanied by privatization (Vickers and Yarrow (1988)). In the case of Eastern Europe, there is broad agreement that privatization is a necessity. Previous attempts to combine decentralized coordination with state ownership—so-called reform communism—suggest that without the incentive of private ownership, liberalization does not lead to effective competition. Consequently, the guidance of the command economy is removed, but efficient markets do not emerge to provide guiding signals in its place. Developing a market economy must therefore begin with the privatization of state enterprises.

State enterprises lie at the heart of planned economies: investment and production plans for the economy are implemented at the enterprise level; nonagricultural incomes derive primarily from enterprises; and enterprises pay most of the taxes that finance other state activities. In performing these functions, state enterprises in planned economies have developed the most extreme incentive failures that have led for calls to privatize their Western counterparts. Moreover, things became worse as a result of the increased operational autonomy extended to enterprises. The shift to reform communism led to an enormous amount of discretionary power being vested in managers—who often owe their position to political patronage—and workers. While the enterprise sector was invigorated, autonomy was directed not so much toward maximizing profit but more to the pursuit of activities that serve the self-interest of politicians, managers, and workers. Statutory protection from domestic and international competition, and a soft budget constraint to shield enterprises from the consequences of their inefficiency, created a sheltered environment in which a wide range of rent-seeking activities could flourish.

The stabilization policies now being adopted in most countries of Eastern Europe are having an immediate impact on state enterprises. Lowering inflation that had become endemic since the partial implementation of market reforms, and in some cases had reached the hyperinflation stage with the elimination of most price controls, necessitated tight monetary and fiscal policies. Enterprises straight away found their ability to borrow constrained by higher interest rates and reduced access to preferential credit, while the government was forced to harden its budget constraint—by withdrawing discretionary tax privileges and limiting subsidies—because lower output and increased unemployment strained budgetary finances. The resulting discipline on enterprise finances was in most cases reinforced by some form of wage policy.

State enterprise reform in general, and privatization in particular, is part of a more comprehensive reform package geared toward interdependent stabilization and structural objectives. Given that state ownership has accommodated inefficient enterprises, privatization is regarded as necessary to consolidate the financial discipline imposed on enterprises during the stabilization phase. The principal fear is that labor unrest forces a relaxation of wage policy, which sets off a wage-price explosion. As regards structural issues, privatization is probably the only way of quickly establishing private property rights and offers the prospect of effective corporate control of enterprise behavior, which are closely related features of a properly functioning market economy.

Property Rights

Under classical planning, state enterprises are unambiguously regarded as state-owned property, however vaguely this may be defined. As indicated above, the onset of reform communism created new problems. The separation of ownership and control typically gives rise to principal-agent problems, which emerge when owners (in this case the state) are distanced from their agents (in this case managers and workers) and are not therefore properly informed about their behavior. Rent-seeking activities are the usual consequence. Reform communism increased the scope for rent seeking. Moreover, in many cases the reforms also confused property rights, as decision-making powers typically associated with ownership were transferred to managers and workers of smaller enterprises, but the legal claim to enterprise ownership was not conveyed in the process. Principal-agent problems were thus compounded by uncertainty regarding property rights. Under threat of losing such rights—imaginary or not— managers and workers often reacted with extreme forms of rent seeking, effectively stripping the assets of the enterprises that employed them.

Privatization in the first instance requires the state to affirm its ownership of enterprises. At the same time, the state needs to restrain the response of managers and workers to this clarification of property rights. But the importance of establishing property rights extends beyond the need to effect a change in enterprise ownership. It is these rights—which cover the control of the assets, the claim on the income they earn, and freedom of disposal—that legitimize the notion of a market. Privatization therefore needs to be supported by appropriate property and contract laws that are enforced through the courts, to reassure the private sector that the property rights it obtains are protected.

Corporate Control

Managers who owe their position to political connections or an affinity to economic planning will have their weaknesses exposed by the market. Competition to sell goods and services will sometimes signal such weaknesses to owners of firms in the form of poor profitability, who can then take corrective actions. It is, however, only with very small firms that owners have the day-to-day involvement which provides for such direct monitoring. In the case of large corporations, the threat of bankruptcy is the only disciplining mechanism provided by the product market. But with a diversified ownership an enterprise can stay in business for a long time before actually going bankrupt. It is the role of the capital market to signal not only shortcomings of management but also ineffective oversight on the part of owners long before bankruptcy looms large. The basic function of the capital market is to trade property rights, a need which has not yet arisen in Eastern European economies. Privatization can be the catalyst for the establishment of capital market institutions, like stock exchanges. It is important that such institutions be appropriate to requirements; there is no need to import many of the more esoteric features of Western models. Capital market development should be geared primarily toward achieving effective corporate control.

An important issue arises concerning the form of privatization best suited to this objective. Disposing of enterprises in small lots allows for the spreading of risk and will encourage share trading from the outset, but the more diversified the ownership structure, the greater the likelihood of principal-agent problems. A more concentrated ownership—especially if enterprises are placed with carefully selected owners—enhances the prospects for control, as the new owners take an active interest in the performance of the enterprise. But this could hinder development of the capital market because the volume of trading will be light, which in turn limits the future role of the capital market in signaling profitable opportunities for ownership change. This dilemma is addressed in more detail below.

Is Speed of the Essence?

There is a continuing debate about the pace at which privatization should occur. Many of the proponents of rapid privatization argue that the potential efficiency gains associated with private ownership and well-functioning product and capital markets are so large that the benefits will be felt from the very beginning. The view of opponents is that immediate efficiency gains from privatization are likely to be small and associated more with product market discipline—and especially increased exposure to foreign competition—than with the role of the capital market. In particular, they doubt the institutional capacity of emerging capital markets to correct an initially inappropriate structure of ownership. They also question where good new managers are going to come from (Kornai (1990)). It is therefore concluded that new owners and managers should be put in place on a case-by-case basis, with a view to ensuring that the longer-term benefits of privatization are realized. To a degree, these misgivings are shared even by the most vigorous supporters of rapid privatization. The issue, however, turns on more than economic and bureaucratic considerations. Most important, it is feared that with a more measured pace political opposition will capitalize on the costs of privatization and the whole process will grind to a halt (Lipton and Sachs (1990)). Rapid privatization will diffuse such opposition, both by reducing some of its costs—for example, because the potential for asset stripping is lower—and by immediately establishing some of its benefits—for example, the right of property ownership.

At What Cost?

While rapid privatization is tailored to compelling objectives, these objectives are not to be achieved without regard to the resulting costs. The unacceptable costs of rapid privatization may be either social or economic, although the two are related. Moreover, both usually imply political costs. A sharp increase in unemployment, especially in the heavy industrial sector, is an inevitable result of privatization. This should of course be reversed in the longer term, as reform measures begin to create new employment opportunities in services, trade, and light industry. However, the short-term transition has to be handled carefully. In particular, creating pockets of high employment—in certain regions, for example—may require special measures, such as relocation incentives for industry and accelerated housing construction to encourage labor mobility, as well as an expansion of social programs to cushion the impact of adjustment.

More generally, if privatization is expected to exacerbate an already unequal distribution of wealth because enterprises end up mainly in the hands of those who have personally profited from a position of power under the previous system, this could undermine the social support for the process from the outset. Similarly, while access to foreign capital and expertise is recognized to be crucial, there are judged to be limits to the level of foreign involvement that is socially acceptable. Reflecting these concerns, it is advocated that privatization should involve a sharing of wealth among the population. However, the mechanism by which such sharing is achieved must be economically sound.

Since privatization is motivated in part by a desire to improve the efficiency of state enterprises, there is a natural presumption that it is desirable from an economic standpoint. If an enterprise is sold at its fair market value, this is indeed the case, since everybody can benefit from efficiency improvements not achievable under state ownership. The problem, of course, is that an equitable sharing of national wealth is inconsistent with selling enterprises at close to their market value. This requires free disposal, or at least heavily discounted sales. But if the state has to give away all or part of an enterprise it is forgoing revenue, which would be fiscally irresponsible if either essential expenditure programs have to be curtailed as a consequence, or bad taxes have to be levied to pay for them. Moreover, it would compromise stabilization objectives if the government has to resort to unsustainable deficit financing or if the implied redistribution of wealth leads to a consumption boom.

Fiscal Considerations

The fiscal aspects of privatization—especially when it involves the free disposal of enterprises—is a subject of some concern. When the state disposes of an enterprise it will no longer receive dividends and profits from that enterprise. On the other hand, it will not have to provide subsidies. Assuming that the same taxes are paid after privatization—and setting aside any problems arising from the changed time profile of receipts—the state will be no better or worse off in the long run if it receives for the enterprise a sum equivalent to the present value of the forgone net income (Hemming and Mansoor (1988)). This sum is likely to be less than the market value of the enterprise, which should reflect the increased profitability expected under private ownership. If improved profitability is in prospect, privatization can help the budget in the long run. Nevertheless, selling an enterprise is under most circumstances likely to yield an immediate cash flow benefit. But since this largely compensates for future income that will no longer be received, the disposition of sale proceeds is important.

If privatization receipts are used to purchase other income-earning assets or to repay debt, tax increases (or expenditure cuts) will not be needed in the future. The implications for the budget are precisely as outlined above. Using them instead to finance a tax cut or higher consumption—assuming only limited scope for expenditure cuts later— will require higher taxation in the future, to compensate for forgone net income. Free disposal of enterprises will also lead to increased taxation in the future, for the same reason. It would therefore appear that there is little to choose between sales (at any price) and free disposal in the long term, since their principal difference lies in the time profile of taxation each implies. This, however, ignores the benefits of tax smoothing, which reduces the efficiency costs of taxation and argues in favor of selling enterprises and using the proceeds to restore the government's net worth (von Furstenberg (1990)). Moreover, free disposal also has the disadvantage that it can create a budgetary problem in the short term, which has to be addressed through tax and expenditure adjustments. Fortunately, there would appear to be enough scope for the reform of tax and expenditure policy in Eastern Europe to suggest that the design of a privatization strategy is unlikely to hinge on its budgetary consequences, either in the short term or the long term.

Policy Environment

Economic Policies

Privatization cannot be planned and executed in a vacuum. Although it may be necessary for the creation of a successful market economy, the preceding discussion confirms that it is far from sufficient. A commitment to stabilization is clearly essential, both as a precondition for structural reform and to provide a more favorable basis for economic decision making. In particular, high and variable inflation rates, together with impending balance of payments difficulties, tend to discourage both domestic and foreign investment. In this connection, successful agreement on the reduction of an excessive debt burden—as in the case of Poland—should provide an impetus to investment.

The key objectives of structural policy reform should be to create an environment where the private sector is free to make business decisions; where market signals guide such decisions; where available savings, including those from abroad, are channeled to their most productive use; and where essential state activities are not an impediment to the private sector. Price and trade liberalization, financial deregulation, and tax reform are therefore of critical importance. Indeed, trade policy takes on special significance as most of the economies of Eastern Europe attempt to adjust to the loss of the traditional export markets implied by the change in CMEA trading arrangements and economic collapse in the U.S.S.R. However, while a liberal trade regime—both at home and abroad—will expose domestic enterprises to import competition and provide access to new foreign markets, domestic markets cannot fully develop without the removal of internal barriers to competition.

Competition Policy

To promote domestic competition requires a package of measures to facilitate easy entry to and exit from an industry. Legal restrictions on the disposition of labor and capital should be relaxed; it is especially important that bankruptcy be recognized as a legitimate means of exit. Company law, commercial and investment codes, and employment contracts will therefore have to be rewritten. But given that the economies of Eastern Europe are dominated by large state monopolies, even all the above measures may not be sufficient to create competition. Existing enterprises could take advantage of market domination, an existing network of business contacts, preferential arrangements with suppliers, and a cushion of financial resources to preclude the development of effective competition. Under such circumstances, an appropriate competition policy should have three aspects: the forced breakup of monopolies, the promotion of small private business, and regulation.

A number of countries have broken up the largest monopolies at an early stage of the reform process. In particular, state trading enterprises have proved relatively easy to dismantle and subsequently to privatize. For example, some 60,000 shops have already been leased or sold in Poland following the dismantling of retail cooperatives (Sachs (1991)). While there is considerable scope for increasing competition in the trade sector through this means, progress in the industrial sector could be rather slow. It may therefore be important to directly encourage and support the start-up of new production activity, especially through the creation of specialized advisory and financial institutions. Given that it may prove impossible to break up some monopolies, or there could be potential for monopolies to re-establish, regulation is necessary to protect consumers' interests and to prevent new businesses from being driven out of the market through unfair competition. The creation of an office to monitor trading practices is the natural response.

Enterprise Policies

State enterprise sectors in Eastern Europe will inevitably remain large for a number of years to come. Even if the institutional capacity existed to accelerate the pace of privatization, many enterprises are not in a fit condition for sale, while others for a variety of reasons (strategic importance, natural monopoly characteristics) will not be privatized. There is therefore a need for measures to make enterprises ready for privatization and for policies to ensure that enterprises which must remain in the state sector are forced to effect improvements in efficiency. Without such policies, privatization plans will be frustrated either because some enterprises will not find buyers or continued inefficiency in the state sector places an unacceptable burden on the private sector.

In many countries, it is intended that the state assert its ownership rights by transforming enterprises into wholly state-owned joint stock companies. The fact that this is sometimes referred to as commercialization—as opposed to the more natural corporatization—is intended to convey the behavioral justification for this change in ownership structure. In the interim period prior to privatization, enterprises should be subjected to the oversight of independent directors charged with provisional responsibility for corporate control. While it is desirable that management and workers are closely monitored in the transition period—to protect the enterprise's assets and to preserve its market value—issues arise as to who should appoint the directors and their ability and incentive to fulfill this function.

Also, many enterprises will need restructuring prior to sale. This extends beyond breaking up large enterprises. Because of heavy indebtedness, outdated equipment and poor management, some enterprises may appear to have bleak prospects; however, with appropriate financial, technical, or organizational restructuring they can be made viable. But even with restructuring, there are some enterprises that could not survive competition and would have no value to the private sector as going concerns; such enterprises are therefore clear candidates for liquidation. The question that arises concerns whether the state or a new private owner should be responsible for restructuring and liquidation. While common sense suggests that the state should restructure or liquidate enterprises only where it stands to gain, the issue then turns on the expertise of the state in general, and temporary directors in particular, to make well-informed decisions about structural change.

In the case of enterprises that for economic or other reasons remain permanently in the state sector, Eastern Europe faces problems shared the world over. While there is some scope for competition to discipline state enterprises—by contracting out and franchising contestable activities—administrative policies are generally unavoidable. These typically involve measures to limit political interference, to specify clear performance targets, to increase management autonomy and accountability, to eliminate unproductive labor practices, to improve performance incentives, and to impose a tight budget constraint. However, it has in most countries proved difficult to implement such measures, which only serves to emphasize the importance of successful privatization.

Social Policies

With the prospect of a sharp increase in unemployment during the possibly prolonged transition, social policies take on special significance. Adequate unemployment compensation must be provided, but without creating work disincentives that could inhibit an efficient matching of labor supply and demand. Retraining and job placement programs will also be required. At the same time, other social programs must be enhanced, to avoid an unfair distribution of the burden of adjustment. The retired, disabled, and other disadvantaged groups already live close to the poverty line, and are the worst affected by the policy of subsidy reduction, especially where it affects the prices of basic food, housing, and other essential items of consumption.

Privatization Options

Criteria for Success

The preceding discussion has referred to various aspects of privatization that have to be considered in judging whether the process is a success. While not intended as a checklist against which the available options in Eastern Europe should be assessed, the following emerge as the main questions that should be asked:

(i) Is effective control of enterprises established?

(ii) Does privatization attract social support?

(iii) Are adverse economic consequences avoided?

While not answered in a systematic manner, these questions underlie the analysis that follows.

Market Sales

Privatization in Western economies has typically taken the form of market sales, either through public offering or private placement. Offering shares for public sale to the population requires all the elements of a modern financial system to be in place if it is to proceed reasonably quickly. As indicated above, Eastern Europe lacks even rudimentary capital markets. Moreover, valuation is meaningless with highly distorted markets; existing regulatory standards require that little information of help to potential investors is routinely provided by enterprises; and there are few nationals with the ability to interpret such information if it were available. These problems also preclude the auctioning of shares as an alternative to a pre-priced share offer. And even if a share offer or auction were feasible, enterprise ownership would be restricted to a handful of already wealthy individuals with the resources to buy shares. This would also be the likely outcome of efforts to sell state enterprises through direct placement. As indicated earlier, ownership concentration may be desirable from the point of view of establishing effective control over the management of enterprises, especially if the new owners have a record of responsible entrepreneurship. It is, however, more reasonable to expect that many potential buyers will have accumulated their wealth through the abuse of power and privilege, and such sales will simply reinforce existing inequalities. The resulting social and political resistance to privatization will be compounded by any suspicion that valuable state assets are being sold for less than they are really worth. In this context, spontaneous privatization at little or no cost by enterprise management has been widely disparaged. Selling to foreigners meets similar opposition, with mutually beneficial deals negotiated between managers and foreign partners again being singled out for particular scorn. However, heavy foreign participation in the domestic economy is probably less of a threat than commonly feared. Indeed, the cautious stance currently being adopted by foreign investors—who as yet do not see a sufficiently reassuring economic, social, and political environment to encourage large-scale investment— should cause more serious concern, since it could deprive Eastern Europe of much-needed access to capital, modern technology, and management expertise.

A suggested response to the problems of market sales, and in particular those arising from a shortage of investable funds, is to lower the sale price deliberately to bring it into line with available resources. It has been suggested, for example, that subsidized credit be made available to purchase shares. Of course, this cannot compensate for valuation difficulties and for problems associated with the availability and interpretation of information. Moreover, extending the range of activities qualifying for preferential credit is inconsistent with the thrust of financial sector reform. Indeed, if the objective is to achieve a broad-based share ownership despite a low level and unequal distribution of financial resources, free disposal is probably a better way to proceed, but only if the other shortcomings of market sales are overcome in the process or addressed through accompanying measures. But the prospect of free disposal raises the issue of who should get what.

Worker Self-Management

Most notably in Hungary and Poland, reform communism has been associated with the creation of workers' councils which exercise a considerable measure of control over enterprises, including some scope to dispose of assets. Equating this with ownership rights, workers in both countries have been pressuring for enterprises to be formally transferred to them. However, because the rest of the population also has a notional claim to enterprise ownership, it is generally believed that transferring enterprises to workers, who are already regarded by many as fortunate to work for a state enterprise, is unfair. Moreover, despite the clear interest workers should have in the financial future of the enterprises they own, the available evidence—for example, from Yugoslavia—suggests that such concern is secondary to their own terms and conditions of employment. While worker self-management is likely to be limited—mainly to some highly labor-intensive activities—workers' demands for preferential consideration under other privatization options are proving irresistible.

Free Disposal

Distributive justice is clearly well served by the free disposal of shares to the population, although—to the extent direct sales are possible—distributing the cash proceeds of privatization to the population may be preferable. Free disposal also has the advantage that it can be relatively quickly implemented, insofar as it does not presume a functioning capital market. Although the government forgoes revenue in the form of sales proceeds, if the poorest are able to liquidate their share allocations, this can substitute for social transfers from the budget. This in turn implies that the size of fiscal adjustment which must normally accompany free disposal can be smaller. It is also to be expected that consumption will respond to the increase in private sector wealth and the relaxation of liquidity constraints associated with free disposal. While the boost to consumption is potentially large (Borensztein and Kumar (1991)), the macroeconomic risks are generally judged to be modest; in any event, the need to tighten financial policies if increased consumption threatens to be destabilizing is recognized.

While attractive in principle, free disposal raises a number of practical issues. Distributing shares directly to the population is difficult without valuation, since there are otherwise no clear criteria for deciding how shares should be allocated. One solution is to distribute privatization vouchers rather than shares, which can then be exchanged for shares obtained in a competitive auction. This establishes a relative value of enterprises—expressed in vouchers—but does not place an absolute value on either enterprises or vouchers, which must await the creation of capital market institutions and the commencement of share trading. For this reason, vouchers need not be denominated in money, although this may be felt necessary to secure initial support for the program. But the absolute value established by an auction using money-denominated vouchers is illusory; trading might establish a lower value, which could then be a source of unnecessary resentment toward privatization.

Whichever approach is adopted, the resulting ownership structure of enterprises and the relative values established in the auction is unlikely to reflect well-informed judgments about the current position of each enterprise and its prospects. Moreover, the widely dispersed pattern of ownership that results will not permit effective control. It is therefore necessary, at least initially, to entrust these responsibilities to those who can fulfill them better—in the early discussion of the Polish program it was suggested that either holding companies or financial intermediaries could play this role.

Holding Companies

One suggestion is that state enterprises to be privatized should be grouped under umbrella organizations, most obviously taking the form of state-owned holding companies (Blanchard and Layard (1990)). The population would receive shares in the holding companies or vouchers which could be exchanged for shares; the holding companies would then be responsible for preparing enterprises for privatization, including their restructuring. As enterprises are increasingly exposed to market discipline and their value is revealed, privatization would proceed and the holding companies could be progressively dissolved. Shares in the holding companies would in the process be translated into a diversified portfolio of enterprise shares. A private ownership structure more conducive to effective control will emerge as enterprise shares are traded on the capital market. The problem with this approach is that without an effective mechanism for control of the holding companies, there is nothing to ensure that they will function in the best interests of investors. The final impact may be no more than the insertion of an additional layer of bureaucracy into the existing system, which only increases the potential for incentive failures at a time when their cost to the population is becoming more transparent.

Financial Intermediaries

Another suggestion—which does not necessarily preclude an initial role for holding companies—derives from the successful part played by banks in Germany and Japan as core investors in major companies. However, rather than relying on banks, the proposal is that recipients of vouchers would lodge them with, and thus become owners of, new private sector financial intermediaries—subject to appropriate financial regulation—who would have the exclusive right to bid for enterprise shares through auction (Frydman and Rapaczynski (1990)). Vouchers could after a period be converted into a portfolio of the shares—essentially a unit trust—held by each intermediary. The trading of shares, first by the intermediaries and then by individuals, would stimulate evolving capital markets.

In a variant of this proposal, vouchers would in addition be distributed to existing financial institutions—who could also use them to bid for shares in the auction—to broaden the range of core investors (Lipton and Sachs (1990)). An additional advantage of distributing vouchers to state-owned financial institutions—which are often undercapitalized—is that the government can reduce expenditure related to the recapitalization necessary for their subsequent privatization. While this type of proposal combines widespread ownership and social justice with the prospect of effective control and efficiency improvements, the following discussion of the current status of the Polish privatization program—for which the Lipton/Sachs approach was devised—illustrates the still numerous difficulties of implementation.

Country Programs

Poland

The legal framework for privatization in Poland was established in June 1990, with the passing of the Privatization Law. By the end of the year, a provisional program was outlined (Government of the Republic of Poland (1990)). Reflecting the strengths and weaknesses of the available options, the proposed program has a somewhat eclectic character. It has four aspects: enterprise commercialization; mass privatization; direct sale of some large enterprises; and the privatization of small- and medium-sized enterprises.

Upon their commercialization—that is, conversion into wholly state-owned joint stock companies—each enterprise will be subject to the oversight of a Board of Directors appointed jointly by the State Treasury and enterprise employees. It is expected that the majority of state enterprises will eventually be commercialized. Larger enterprises will in the main be subject to mass privatization, with new investment groups being created to manage enterprise shares on behalf of the population. Where appropriate and feasible, some large enterprises will be subject to more traditional methods of privatization, whereby they will be valued and then sold through public offer, by arrangement to a willing buyer, or as a joint venture. Traditional methods will also be used for some medium-sized enterprises, while a wider range of techniques—including leasing, which has been the norm in the already extensively privatized retail sector—will be applied to privatize smaller enterprises.

Each of the four aspects of the proposed program has raised issues, many of which have yet to be resolved. As regards commercialization, the intention is that this should be voluntary. But given that workers' councils will be broken up, it has been necessary to offer workers some incentive to volunteer, in this case a tranche of shares on concessional terms and the possibility of a less restrictive wage policy. As a last resort, government reserves the right to force commercialization on an enterprise. A problem also arises concerning the structure of the new Boards. Many enterprises will be commercialized long before they are privatized, and in the interim they should undergo necessary restructuring and become increasingly exposed to market discipline. There are, however, doubts as to whether much headway can be made by inexperienced directors who may be preoccupied with primarily looking after the often-competing interests of the state and enterprise employees.

Mass privatization is the most problematical part of the program. The initial intention was to distribute nominally denominated vouchers equivalent to 30 percent of enterprise shares to the population and to selected financial institutions, principally the social insurance fund and some commercial banks. Part of the remaining 40 percent of shares was to be allocated to enterprise employees upon commercialization—either 20 percent of shares would be sold to them at a 50 percent discount or they would receive 10 percent of shares free of charge. The residual shares would then be managed by the investment groups on behalf of the Treasury. After further consideration, it has now been decided that investment groups will receive 60 percent of enterprise shares, each holding 33 percent of the shares of some enterprises—for which they will act as lead shareholder—and a smaller quantity of shares in many other enterprises. A maximum of 10 percent of shares will be distributed to employees free of charge. The Treasury will retain the remaining 30 percent of shares (Government of the Republic of Poland (1991)). Every Polish citizen will receive a participation certificate in each investment group. Trading in certificates and new shares issued by the investment groups will commence in mid-1993. For the most part, the above changes offer a clearer affirmation of the importance attached to the core investor principle, reflect the problems involved in attaching nominal values to vouchers, and respond to the lack of enthusiasm shown by financial institutions toward the original proposals. However, the principal uncertainty—concerning the prospects for attracting international expertise to set up and manage the investment groups—remains roughly the same.

In the case of direct sales, the major issue concerns the role of foreign investors. It is widely recognized that foreign investment is essential to the transformation process, and the recent relaxation of the foreign investment law reflects this. Moreover, with a shortage of domestic savings—household deposits with the banking system amount to less than 15 percent of the book value of the enterprise sector—a large foreign stake in directly privatized enterprises must be actively sought. However, the Privatization Law initially required approval for foreign equity holdings in excess of 10 percent; notwithstanding this requirement, the relaxation of the extent to which foreign investors will be free to acquire a significant share of Polish capital remains unclear. With small and medium-sized enterprises, the principal concern has been the scope for spontaneous privatization because of inadequate monitoring by the government. To control better the privatization process, without having to slow down the pace of implementation, its administration is being decentralized.

Czechoslovakia

A voucher scheme remains the cornerstone of the Czechoslovak privatization program. Between 40 percent and 80 percent of the equity in 1,000–2,000 of the largest enterprises will be distributed through vouchers. The exact amount will depend upon the success achieved in finding foreign partners and otherwise arranging direct privatization deals. Vouchers will not be issued to all citizens, but will instead be sold for a nominal sum. Through this means, it is hoped that voucher holders will take a keener interest in the privatization process and the performance of the enterprises they will ultimately own. In the first instance, a limited number of shares will be made available through a series of auctions, with a rough initial valuation of enterprises to convey information about the enterprises to potential investors. As the auctions proceed, and investors gain more experience of the way a capital market operates, it is expected that share trading will commence and additional shares can be sold on the market for cash rather than vouchers. The state intends, however, to retain a minority shareholding in many large enterprises. Other forms of privatization will supplement the voucher scheme, and there has already been substantial progress with small-scale privatization through auctions of shops, restaurants, and other business in the service sector.

Hungary

Privatization in Hungary began in late 1988, with the passing of legislation allowing enterprises to be transformed into joint stock companies as a prelude to privatization. However, there followed a flood of spontaneous privatizations, as the management of many enterprises exploited opportunities to take them over or to enter into lucrative deals with foreign partners. While patently inequitable, spontaneous privatization was nonetheless defended by those who felt that it was not a high price to pay for reducing the role of the state in the economy. In the end, however, the critics prevailed, and to prevent the privatization process from falling into further disrepute, the direction of policy was shifted. By mid-1989, spontaneous privatization was under control, and a government-led strategy was being put into place (Schwartz (1991)).

A new State Property Agency (SPA) was set up in 1990 to oversee the privatization process. The government's program emphasizes the sale of enterprises, with a view to using the proceeds to reduce debt. Vouchers are to be avoided. Nevertheless, the goal is to achieve a reduction in state ownership to below one half of total assets in the competitive sphere of the economy by 1993. Privatization is to proceed through three main avenues. Small shops and restaurants will be auctioned in early 1991. The SPA will sell large enterprises through active privatization programs. Two such programs, each involving about 20 enterprises, were launched during 1990. For smaller enterprises, privatization initiated by the enterprises or other interested buyers will be encouraged, with the SPA role limited to ensuring that the enterprise concerned is appropriately valued and that the process is transparent. The Hungarians are adopting a liberal attitude to foreign participation in the privatization process, because foreign investment is attached enormous importance if modernization needs are to be met. For this reason, there are special incentives for foreign investors and administrative procedures will be streamlined. State assets will be disposed of free of charge only to public agencies, such as social insurance funds, but with a corresponding reduction in subsidies.

Concluding Comments

Bold privatization programs in Eastern Europe are a necessary risk. But having attached the economic transformation flag to the privatization mast, the objective is to minimize the chance of failure. Political commitment—the fragility of which has undermined privatization in many developing countries—is unquestionable. This also makes it easier to take the measures necessary to manage any adverse social and economic consequences. Many of the remaining difficulties are practical. Poor organization and a shortage of experienced administrators are a major obstacle. There are limits to the extent foreign expertise can be used; it lacks local knowledge, is expensive, and may even crowd out local talent.

Yet to a degree it is unavoidable, especially in connection with institution building. Stock markets, investment funds, auctions, etc., require foreign involvement. However, it is one thing to create institutions; it is quite another thing for them to function properly. But if the public has confidence in its rights to own, control, and undertake transactions in private property, this will go a long way toward establishing faith in the institutions which allow these rights to be exercised and making them work.

References

Blanchard, Olivier J., and Richard Layard, "Economic Change in Poland," Centre for Economic Policy Research Discussion Paper No. 432 (June 1990).

Borensztein, Eduardo, and Manmohan S. Kumar, "Proposals for Privatization in Eastern Europe," *Staff Papers*, International Monetary Fund (Washington), Vol. 38 (1991).

Frydman, Roman, and Andrej Rapaczynski, "Markets and Institutions in Large Scale Privatizations," paper presented at a conference on Adjustment and Growth: Lessons for Eastern Europe, held in Pultusk, Poland (October 4–5, 1990).

Government of The Republic of Poland, *Program for the Privatization of the Polish Economy* (Warsaw, December 1990).

———, *Mass Privatization—Proposed Program* (Warsaw, June 1991).

Hemming, Richard, and Ali M. Mansoor, *Privatization and Public Enterprises*, IMF Occasional Paper 56 (Washington: International Monetary Fund, January 1988).

Kornai, Janós, *The Road to a Free Economy* (New York: W.W. Norton and Company, 1990).

Lipton, David, and Jeffrey Sachs, "Privatization in Eastern Europe: The Case of Poland," *Brookings Papers on Economic Activity*, Vol. 2 (Washington: Brookings Institution, 1990).

Sachs, Jeffrey D., "Accelerating Privatization in Eastern Europe," paper presented at the World Bank Annual Conference on Development Economics, held in Washington, D.C. (April 25–26, 1991).

Schwartz, Gerd, "Privatization: Possible Lessons from the Hungarian Case," *World Development*, 19 (1991).

Vickers, J.S., and G.K. Yarrow, *Privatization: An Economic Analysis* (Cambridge, Massachusetts: MIT Press, 1988).

von Furstenberg, George M., "Pareto-Optimal Privatization for Gaining Political Support," Indiana University Working Papers in Economics No. 90–050 (November 1990).

PART II

Revenue

CHAPTER 5

Efficiency Considerations in Tax Policy
Krister Andersson

The recent opening up of markets in many countries places new and greater demands on the tax structure. More integrated financial markets make the allocation of resources more sensitive to differences in national tax rates. Differences in tax regimes between countries can result in capital flows across countries affecting both the location of investments and ownership of capital. Taxation of income from business activities as well as taxation of financial flows across countries has therefore received much more attention now than it did only a few years ago. As the previously centrally planned economies embark on economic reforms, their tax structures need to promote a more efficient allocation of capital between sectors within their countries and across borders. In the tax reform process, it is important to consider which tax parameters have a large impact on the net rate of return paid to the investor. However, it is also important to take into account the overall complexity of the tax system and whether it is possible to administer the tax rules. During the 1980s, the pace of tax reform was rapid in OECD countries. Countries which had centrally planned economies now have a unique opportunity to opt for the simplified broad-based tax systems which the Western countries have introduced.

Economic Efficiency

Tax reform efforts in most West European countries have focused on capital income taxation and taxes on consumption. The top marginal income tax rates have been reduced, and in some cases drastically, to mitigate adverse effects on labor supply. With high taxes on wage income in the past, untaxed economic activities, leisure activities, and black market activities tended to increase and erode the tax base.

To create an efficient system of capital taxation, policy makers must consider the effects of taxation on savings and investment. A reduction in the after-tax return to capital, for instance by taxing interest and dividend income, is equivalent to making future consumption relatively more expensive and therefore tends to decrease savings. Income taxes also affect savings by lowering private disposable income causing a reduction in both present consumption and savings. For a net borrower, taxes lower the after-tax cost of borrowing which tends to increase borrowing and increase consumption. The overall effect on private savings of taxation of capital income is ambiguous and the effect on national savings depends on how the government uses its tax revenues.

If the tax system results in a decrease in the level of household savings and if the economy is closed, the equilibrium interest rate will rise which will decrease the demand for investment capital. In an open economy, however, capital can flow in from abroad so the investment level depends on the prevailing world market interest rate and not only on domestic savings. Taxes on the return to savings will therefore have only a limited impact on the investment level. However, the ownership of capital may be affected.

The tax system also affects investment. Different tax treatment for different types of assets is likely to have a large impact on investment opportunities and the composition of the investor's portfolio. Estimates of the size of misallocation of resources owing to different tax treatment in different sectors are in the range of less than one percent of GNP up to several percent of GNP. Since the growth rate of the economy may be affected, the distortions are believed to be substantial and very costly, both in terms of allocation of resources and in revenue terms.[1]

Empirical evidence of taxes' impact on savings and investment and the resulting capital flows across countries indicate the part of the flow of portfolio capital from Japan to the United States during the 1980s that can be attributed to tax factors. Japan taxed the use of capital more heavily than the United States, while the United States taxed its residents more heavily on their savings than Japan did. The tax systems therefore encouraged capital to flow from Japan to the United States.[2]

To assess whether a tax system encourages savings and investment relative to the tax system of other countries, a framework has been developed which permits evaluation of the overall impact of taxes and of various tax incentives on the rate of return of capital. By incorporating and

---

[1]For a survey of different models for tax policy, see Pereira and Shoven (1988).
[2]Bovenberg and others (1990).

combining different taxes and by including tax provisions and the economic environment in which the tax system operates, the impact of each tax system on incentives to locate investments in various countries can be illustrated. Such a methodology is described below.

The User Cost of Capital

To assess the impact of taxation on incentives to invest, three different layers of taxes must be considered. First, the taxes at the corporate level, second, shareholder taxes, and, third, for investment flows across borders, taxes imposed on foreign investors.

At the corporate level, besides the statutory corporate tax rate, the rules of how to calculate taxable profits are very important for the after-tax return the investor can receive. Interest payments are generally deductible when calculating taxable profits, while dividend payments are not. This leads to the so-called double taxation of dividends. Dividends are paid out of after-tax profits, and dividends are then taxable at the shareholder level. Most OECD countries allow for some double taxation relief for equity-financed investments. Tax depreciation for fixed assets also plays a major role in determining the after-tax return for the investor. Other important factors at the corporate level are investment grants and different methods of deferring tax payments through allocation funds (such as investment funds). The use of grants and funds have, however, been drastically reduced in the OECD countries during the 1980s.

At the shareholder level, taxes on interest, dividend income, and capital gains matter. Changes in these tax rates may cause the investor to prefer to receive his return in a different form. It has, for instance, been argued that the increase in the capital gains tax rate in the United States in connection with the Tax Reform Act of 1986 encouraged distribution of profits rather than retention of profits.[3]

The third level of taxation that affects investment decisions is taxes imposed on foreign investors. Many countries levy withholding taxes on dividend and interest remittances from the source (host) country to the

---

[3]The impact of dividend taxation on the cost of capital depends on which view on dividend taxation is believed to be most relevant. According to the "new" view of dividend taxation, assuming that corporations generally adopt profit retentions rather than new share issues as the marginal source of equity finance, dividend taxes do not distort investment decisions and amount to a lump-sum tax on existing rather than new capital. According to the "old" view of dividend taxation, dividend taxes do matter since new share issues are assumed to be the marginal source of equity finance. It is an empirical question which view more closely resembles corporate behavior. See Sinn (1987 and 1990).

resident (home) country of the investor. These withholding taxes may in some cases be credited against tax liabilities in the home country when foreign-source income is subject to further taxation at home. Several EC countries and the United States adhere to the residence principle, taxing income wherever it is derived from, but the foreign tax credit is typically limited to the residence country's own tax rate on the same kind of income. For portfolio investment there is typically no credit for the underlying foreign corporate income tax. The final tax liability may also depend on the form in which the investment income is received. Interest income and dividend income are often taxed at an equal rate while capital gains, in particular capital gains from exchange gains and losses, may escape further taxation.

By combining several different taxes and by incorporating tax provisions in a consistent way, it is possible to develop a framework that permits evaluation of the overall impact of taxes and of possible tax changes on the required rate of return on the last unit of fixed capital.[4] Such calculations attempt to capture the effect of the tax system and do not incorporate the effect of other potential factors in the investment decision, such as the availability of a suitable labor force or the quality of infrastructure, and more important, the effect of differential risk. However, it is possible to see the impact of broad interaction of the tax system and the macroeconomic environment.

For a given after-tax rate of return, the before-tax rate of return can be expressed as an explicit function of tax parameters and the resultant difference between the two rates of return can be used to calculate the effective marginal tax rate. The difference between the before-tax rate of return and the after-tax rate of return is often referred to as a tax wedge. The tax wedge can be explained by defining three rates of return: the required before-tax rate of return on investment, p, the market return (after corporate taxes), r, and the after-tax rate of return to the saver, s. All these returns are measured in real terms. In the case of debt finance, the market return corresponds to the real interest rate, and for equity financing, it amounts to the real return on equity (taking into account dividends and expected capital gains) before shareholder taxes. The total tax wedge, wt, can therefore be thought of as consisting of two parts:

$$wt = wc + wi = (p - r) + (r - s) = p - s$$

where wc denotes the corporate tax wedge and wi the investor's wedge.

---

[4]See, for example, King and Fullerton (1984).

When cross-border investments are considered, it is more useful to separate the total tax wedge into a host country tax wedge and a home country tax wedge. The host country levies corporate taxes but often also withholding taxes on dividend and interest payments. The home country, in turn, either exempts or taxes these returns, typically subject to some form of double taxation relief.

The corporate tax wedge is derived from the neoclassical theory of investment behavior, where firms carry out investments until the before-tax rate of return, p, is at least sufficient to cover the cost of finance and the tax payments.[5] In general, the corporate tax system tends to favor debt financing while capital gains taxation at the investor's level often leads to a favorable tax treatment of the part of investment financed with retained earnings. The framework used here allows us to incorporate these effects and compare tax wedges for different sources of financing.

A Cross-Country Comparison

Figure 1 (and Table 1 in the appendix) shows that Hungary and Poland have the largest total tax wedge for an equity-financed investment in machinery among the countries included in the study.[6] A similar picture is found for many of the economies in transition. Both Hungary and Poland provide relatively conservative depreciation rules for tax purposes and the depreciation allowances are calculated by using the straight-line method based on historical costs.[7] The same method is used in Austria, Greece, Portugal, and Spain, while the others permit declining-balance depreciation. However, Austria allows an additional 20 percent in depreciation allowances in the initial year and Spain has an investment tax credit of 5 percent. These provisions are very important in present value terms for the user cost of capital. Ireland has very generous depreciation allowances, but since the corporate tax rate is only 10 percent, the decrease in tax liability is limited. Finland and Turkey allow for acceler-

---

[5]The expression for p is derived from the equality between the after-tax marginal benefit and the marginal cost of an investment project: $(1 - tc)(p + \delta) = (1 - k - tc \times z)(\tau - \pi + \delta)$. Therefore $p = (1 - k - tc \times z)(\tau + \delta - \pi)/(1 - tc) - \delta$ where tc = statutory corporate tax rate, k = investment grant, z = present value of depreciation allowances, τ = nominal discount rate, δ = economic rate of depreciation, π = expected rate of inflation, and p = required before-tax real rate of return.

[6]A summary of the countries' tax system can be found in Table 1 in the appendix.

[7]The rate of depreciation used for Hungary is 12 percent. The average rate of depreciation for investment in machinery may be as low as 6.5 percent. This would make the total tax wedge for Hungary considerably larger.

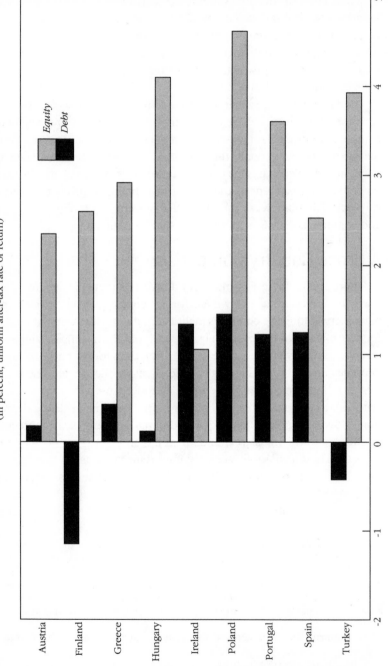

Figure 1. Total Tax Wedge on Investments in Machinery, 1990

(In percent; uniform after-tax rate of return)

ated depreciation and in Turkey the value of the depreciation allowances is enhanced by indexation of the depreciable base.

The results for Ireland deserve closer scrutiny. In contrast to other countries, a debt-financed investment in Ireland carries a *larger* tax burden than equity-financed investment owing to the combination of a small subsidy at the corporate level and the relatively heavy home taxation of interest income as compared with taxation of equity capital at the investor's level. The Irish case therefore clearly demonstrates the importance of the statutory corporate tax rate; the higher the tax rate, the larger is the value of interest deductions and the larger the subsidy for debt-financed investment at the corporate level.

Broad-Based System Versus Special Incentives

In order to promote investment, many countries have introduced special tax preferences for some investors or types of investments. As it turns out, investment tax credits, capital expensing, and accelerated depreciation are very effective in lowering the cost of capital but they may induce windfall gains to investors and they tend to erode the tax base. The proliferation of tax preferences undermines the tax system's revenue collecting capacity and may lead to allocative distortions, and a very careful examination is therefore necessary before any such preferences are introduced. As they embark on tax reform, formerly centrally planned economies have a golden opportunity to avoid the experience of West European countries that made extensive use of investment tax preferences from the 1950s through the 1970s. Instead, these countries may opt for broader tax bases with low tax rates in order to limit national as well as international distortions in the allocation of resources and to protect their revenue base. The cost of capital framework allows us to assess which types of tax incentives are most effective in lowering the user cost of capital. As an example of how the user cost of capital framework can be used to evaluate tax policy options for economies in transition, let us look at Hungary as a case study. The results are, however, generally applicable to economies in transition.

Hungary has undertaken major tax reform efforts during the last three years. The personal income tax and value-added tax were introduced on January 1, 1988, followed by the enterprise profit tax, effective January 1, 1989. Hungary has a statutory corporate income tax rate of 40 percent, a straight-line depreciation method for investments in machinery and buildings and provides a two-year loss carryover. The overall system of corporate taxation imposes a relatively heavy burden on investments since the tax depreciation rules for fixed assets are conservative with a relatively long assets life for tax purposes.[8]

To offset the restrictive treatment of tax losses and depreciation, Hungary has granted tax preferences to foreign-owned enterprises. Foreign investors receive tax concessions ranging from a 20 percent reduction in the corporate tax rate to a complete five-year tax holiday. In addition, accelerated depreciation has been increased to 30 percent (from 20 percent earlier) and the eligible asset categories have been broadened to include most advanced industrial equipment. Hungary also gives foreign-owned companies a rebate equal to the underlying tax on the reinvested profits of the foreign shareholder.

The relatively heavy tax burden on domestic investments led in 1990 to the introduction of special rules for private entrepreneurs. Under this legislation, Hungarian businessmen can opt for special tax treatments which enable them to depreciate assets over as short a period as two years and to reduce their tax rate by 50 percent. The resulting tax system is complex with similar assets having different tax treatment depending on form of business and ownership. The tax system gives rise to large distortions of the allocation of investments and capital. Eventually, more and more of the businesses will be transformed into tax-favored enterprises with adverse revenue implications.

Some Possible Tax Policy Measures

The possible designs of tax incentives are virtually unlimited. A common form of tax incentives is the *investment tax credit*. It is earned as a percentage of eligible expenditures. If Hungary were to introduce a general tax credit of 1 percentage point, the total tax wedge of 4.1 percentage points would be reduced to 3.8 percentage points, a reduction by some 6.6 percent (see Figure 2). The effect is relatively large since the tax credit is received up front. The tax credit is usually applicable only to new investments and the cost of capital for old, existing capital is therefore not affected. There is no windfall gain to existing capital owners.

If the *useful life of an asset for tax purposes* is shortened by one year, the total tax wedge is reduced by almost 8 percent. Incentive deductions differ from tax credits in that they reduce the income subject to tax rather than the actual tax payment. It is, however, administratively difficult to separate new investments from old existing capital. If this is attempted, there is a need to keep track of the rules in force at the time an asset was

---

[8]This is a feature shared by almost all formerly centrally planned economies. See the paper on Income Tax Reform by Leif Mutén in this volume.

Figure 2. Decrease in Total Tax Wedge, Equity Financed Investment
(Changes in percent)

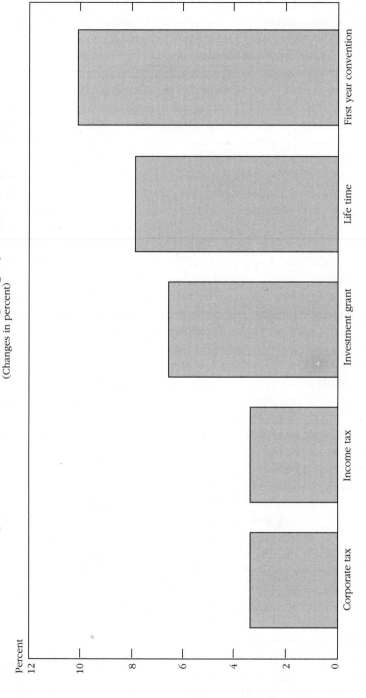

Note: For the corporate tax and the income tax, a 1 percentage point decrease, for the investment grant a 1 percentage point increase, and for asset life a reduction by one year. For first year convention, an increase from on average 40 percent deductability to 100 percent.

purchased or installed. The United States is one country that applies different depreciation rules depending on the prevailing rules at the time of purchase. Complicated rules have had to be enacted to prevent abuse in form of sell-lease-back arrangements and swaps of assets between firms. Given the limited resources for tax administration and the large demands for information and control, especially for the numerous newly formed enterprises in economies in transition, it does not seem advisable to have different tax treatment of different vintage capital. Allowing short asset life for tax purposes for certain investors or certain activities creates similar administrative difficulties and should therefore also be resisted.

Another aspect of depreciation of fixed assets for tax purposes is to what extent *depreciation during the purchase year* is allowed. Many countries prorate depreciation and limit depreciation to the period the asset has been owned or installed. By allowing full depreciation irrespective of date of purchase, the tax depreciation period can be shifted forward and therefore increase in present value terms. If Hungary applied this method, as Finland and Ireland among others do, the total tax wedge would be reduced by over 10 percent. Only new investments would be affected, thereby avoiding any windfall gain to existing owners of capital. If introduced, the rule should be applied to all sectors of the economy, minimizing sectoral distortions.

An important component in the tax system, especially for the international allocation of capital, is the *statutory corporate tax rate*. It has a direct impact on financial marginal source decisions and the allocation of taxable income from multinational firms. Since interest charges are deductible when ascertaining corporate profits, interest charges tend to be deducted in jurisdictions with a high statutory corporate tax rate while profits subject to transfer pricing tend to be allocated in jurisdictions with a low statutory corporate tax rate. A 1 percentage point lower statutory corporate tax rate in Hungary would reduce the total tax wedge on an equity-financed investment by some 3.5 percentage points and the difference between debt and equity-financed investments would decrease. The reason for this is that the value of interest deductions would decrease as the corporate tax rate is reduced. If the *income tax rate at the shareholder level* is lowered by 1 percentage point on interest income, dividend income, and capital gains, the total tax wedge would decrease by a similar 3.5 percentage points.

Another form of incentives which would lower the user cost of capital includes preferential tax rates for particular sources of income. A related measure is tax holidays for certain types of ventures. Administrative problems occur in identifying what is a new business since existing businesses can restructure to appear as new businesses. These incentives make the tax system more complex and cause uncertainty about the stability of the tax structure. New measures may be introduced for competing industries and long-term planning may therefore become more difficult.

Effectiveness Versus Efficiency

From the calculations above, it is clear that there is a need to decrease the total tax wedge on investments in Hungary and in Poland. Introducing an investment tax credit, accelerated depreciation, or preferential tax rates would indeed reduce the tax wedges significantly and increase investment incentives. However, even if these measures are effective in lowering the cost of capital it doesn't mean that they are efficient means. The arguments against preferential tax treatment for some investors or investment projects are well known from the economic literature. It is difficult for the government to pick "the winners," and it can be questioned whether the winners really need any tax concessions. Tax preferences lead to a less efficient allocation of resources and result in a need for other taxes to be higher to compensate for forgone revenues. The heavier tax burden on other sectors of the economy tends to make the tax system more distortionary. The different tax treatment across sectors and types of businesses also leads to extensive tax planning and rearrangements to qualify for tax preferences. For instance, if foreign investors are given preferential tax treatment, there is an incentive for domestic investors to undertake their investments with the help of a foreign partner. The decrease in tax liability can then be divided up between the domestic and foreign partners. In general, more educated and well informed citizens will be more able to make use of tax preferences.[9]

The international experience is that tax incentives may generate less investment than the government loses in revenues.[10] An important reason for the cost inefficiency of tax incentives is the fact that they are available to all qualifying investments. A large part of investments would have

---

[9]This aspect of the tax system should not be underestimated. During the 1970s and 1980s, high income earners in Sweden made such extensive use of deductions for interest payments that the government would have raised more revenue by not taxing capital income at all. Low-income earners reported taxable capital income while high-income earners invested in low-taxed or tax-exempt assets while fully deducting interest payments on loans taken to finance these investments. See Andersson (1987).

[10]A Canadian study evaluating an investment tax credit for the Cape Breton Island found that a generous three-year tax credit of 60 percent generated only $75 of investment for every $100 of government revenue cost. See Canadian Department of Finance (1990).

occurred in any event. Measures that target marginal investments have been hard to implement. If the cost of misallocation of resources is included, tax incentives become even less attractive. Similar results have been found for tax holidays.

Furthermore, preferential tax treatment inevitably makes the tax system more complex. This aspect is particularly important for economies in transition. Their capability to administer a new tax system with numerous new taxpayers is naturally limited in the short run. It takes time to train tax inspectors and to form an appropriate organization to provide tax information to the public, assess tax payments, audit returns, and collect taxes. It is a difficult task to form an appropriate organization, and an excessively complex tax system could make the tax system inoperable for several years. The need to report information to the authorities results in reporting costs for taxpayers, and the registration of such information with the tax authorities can become an overwhelming task, leaving fewer resources for actual tax control and tax audits.

Another justification for simple broad-based taxes is the uncertainty created by a tax system full of special rules. Political pressure groups will form over time and, as a consequence, tax concessions may be eroded or extended to competitors. The perceived fairness of the tax system will almost certainly be questioned and activity in the underground economy could increase. As a result, governments may be forced to implement second best solutions, such as minimum taxes, which add to the complexity of the tax system and themselves may be arbitrary and distortionary.

Tax preferences tend to proliferate, and as the revenue base decreases, higher taxes have to be imposed on other sectors of the economy. There is often a good reason behind each single new tax concession. Usually, the concessions show that the entire tax system needs to be overhauled, yet the proliferation of concessions is harmful to economic efficiency. The rules of the game are changing and tax changes will affect both asset values and income flows. Eventually, when all sectors have received preferential tax treatment, what has been achieved is a tax system with lower rates, but the tax base may not be the appropriate one. A more efficient tax system with low rates and a broad base could generally be achieved with lower economic and administrative costs, if not introduced in a piecemeal fashion.

If special tax incentives are dismissed, other tax measures may have to be used. While the average total tax wedge for the seven European economies included in Figure 1 (excluding Hungary and Poland) was some 2.7 percentage points, Hungary had a total tax wedge around 4.1 percentage points and Poland around 4.6 percentage points. The large tax wedges in

Poland and Hungary can to some extent explain why these countries have found it necessary to introduce a number of tax concessions, in particular for foreign investors. Given a certain revenue requirement, other investors, primarily domestic investors, have had to pay even higher taxes.

The Hungarian tax system could be reformed in a number of ways to achieve a total tax wedge similar to that in other European countries, without resorting to tax concessions for certain investors. The main reason for the large tax wedge in Hungary and in Poland is the assumed long asset life time for tax purposes. If Hungary introduced a first year convention allowing full depreciation the first year irrespective of purchase date, and if a faster depreciation method was introduced, twice the straight line method in combination with a statutory corporate tax rate of 35 percent (40 percent at present), the total tax wedge would be reduced from 4.1 percentage points to 2.7 percentage points, the average for the other seven European countries in Figure 1.

Such a proposal may be costly in revenue terms and therefore calls for careful consideration before it could be put forward. However, it serves as an illustration that broad-based, non-distortionary measures are a good alternative to specific incentives to attract certain types of investors or investments. Tax concessions are also costly in revenue terms and they hamper economic efficiency. The introduction of tax preferences also makes it more difficult to reform the tax system since some of the concessions are of a contractual nature and can therefore not be taken away in a tax reform. A country entering a transitional period is therefore well advised to opt for a broad-based low rate tax system rather than introducing preferences and facing a difficult reform process later on.

Other Aspects of the Tax System

Although the cost of capital calculations capture key aspects of the tax system, a number of important features have been left out. One such feature is the treatment of losses. Most countries allow for carry-forward of losses to future years and some allow for carry-back to previous tax years. Restrictions usually apply to the time period during which losses may be carried over and sometimes also to the amounts which may be claimed. The provision of carry-forward of losses is especially important for countries in transition, where new areas of economic activity are opening up and private enterprises may incur initial losses in an uncertain investment climate.

Another important aspect of the tax system is the tax treatment of inventory. Some countries allow LIFO valuation, for instance Austria (if not contradicted by the facts), Belgium, Germany, Greece, Portugal, and the United States. In a period of rising prices, the cost of supplies is higher, and therefore net income lower, under LIFO than under FIFO, and hence LIFO results in lower taxes. It is, however, beyond the scope of this study to assess the impact of inventory evaluation on the user cost of capital.

Perhaps the most important factors for the investment environment in economies in transition are, however, overall macroeconomic conditions and the stability and transparency of rules and regulations. The tax system can contribute to this by allowing general rather than specific provisions, thereby ensuring that the revenue base is not eroded, which inevitably leads to destabilizing tax changes in the future. Also, the tax system, as well as other regulatory provisions, should be transparent in the eyes of the investor, with no scope for a negotiated settlement of tax liabilities, as was the practice formerly in centrally planned economies. Once the institutions are established and markets are integrated the tax system may play an increasing role in the ability of these countries to attract capital and to promote adequate domestic levels of saving and investment. If domestic savers bear a relatively heavy tax burden, more investment is financed abroad and a larger share of the capital stock is owned by foreigners. Furthermore, if saving and investment decisions are influenced to a large extent by tax considerations, the resulting low level of savings reflects an inefficient allocation of resources.

Conclusions

The opening up of markets in formerly centrally planned economies could result in increased worldwide competition for capital. A central question is to what extent the tax system should contribute to a favorable investment climate. Some countries have chosen to offer a variety of tax concessions, especially to foreign investors, while maintaining a relatively large tax burden for domestic investors. From the points of view of revenue and efficiency, it would be better to introduce a uniform, stable, and transparent tax treatment of all investors. However, the cost of capital calculations undertaken in this study serve to illustrate the need for further tax reform in countries such as Poland and Hungary, to achieve a more efficient allocation of resources and a more competitive tax system. Since many others of the economies in transition are in a similar situation, these tax policy suggestions may be applicable to other countries as well.

Economies in transition should adopt realistic and simple capital cost recovery allowances (in line with economic depreciation), and some kind of loss carryover provision should be allowed. Further, consideration could be given to lower statutory tax rates as permitted by revenue constraints, and to indexation of both assets and liabilities for tax purposes, so as to reduce the distortionary bias of high rates of inflation in favor of debt-financed investment in short-lived assets (including inventories) and against equity-financed longer-lived fixed assets. The alternative approach, followed in certain countries of lowering investment costs by providing up-front investment grants or the reliance on tax holidays, is to be avoided. It creates distortion between different types of investments and forms of businesses and ownership. Valuable resources would be spent on tax planning rather than making appropriate market decisions and the allocation of resources would be distorted.

The administrative and institutional constraints in economies in transition are such that a complex tax system with special treatment for different investors, sources of finance, or investment projects should be resisted. The use of tax preferences results in vast resources being used to inform the public and control details on tax forms, and expensive staff time is spent on assessing whether a taxpayer qualifies for special treatment. It is important to use available tax inspectors for audits and on site inspections to assess whether revenue and cost figures are reasonable. The credibility of the tax system will to a large extent depend on how it is enforced. The expansion of the private sector with many new private entrepreneurs and small businesses presents a particular problem which would be greatly exacerbated by detailed and complex tax rules. Furthermore, as international experience shows, incentives can easily proliferate, are very difficult to target, and result in revenue erosion. The formerly centrally planned economies should therefore carefully consider whether a simplified broad-based tax system with relatively low rates is not better suited for their economic development than preferential tax treatment for various investors.

References

Alworth, J., "Capital Mobility, the Cost of Capital under Certainty and Effective Tax Rates in Europe," *Finnish Economic Papers*, Vol. 1 (1988).

Andersson, K., "Sweden," in *Comparative Tax Systems: Europe, Canada, and Japan*, ed. by Joseph Pechman (Arlington, VA: Tax Analysts, 1987).

———(1991a), "Integrating Corporate and Shareholder Taxes," *Tax Notes*, Vol. 50, No. 13, April 1 (1991).

———(1991b), "Taxation and the Cost of Capital in Hungary and Poland," *Staff Papers*, International Monetary Fund, Vol. 38 (June 1991).

Auerbach, A., "The Cost of Capital and Investment in Developing Countries" (Washington: Public Economics Division, World Bank, 1990).

Boadway, R., N. Bruce, and J. Mintz, *Taxes on Capital Income in Canada: Analysis and Policy*, Canadian Tax Paper No. 80 (Toronto: Canadian Tax Foundation, 1987).

Bovenberg, L., and others, "Tax Incentives and International Capital Flows: The Case of the United States and Japan," in *Taxation in the Global Economy,* ed. by A. Razin and J. Slemrod for NBER (Chicago: University of Chicago Press, 1990).

Canadian Department of Finance, *Economic Efforts of the Cape Breton Investment Tax Credit* (Ottawa: Department of Finance, 1990).

Coopers and Lybrand, *International Tax Summaries, A Guide for Planning and Decisions* (New York: John Wiley and Sons, various issues).

Devereux, M., and M. Pearson, *Corporate Tax Harmonization and Economic Efficiency,* Institute for Fiscal Studies, Report Series No. 35 (Cambridge: Woodhead-Faulkner, 1989).

Hall, R., and D. Jorgenson, "Application of the Theory of Optimum Capital Accumulation," in *Tax Incentives and Capital Spending,* ed. by G. From (Washington: Brookings Institution, 1971).

International Bureau of Fiscal Documentation, *Guides to European Taxation* (Amsterdam: International Bureau of Fiscal Documentation, various issues).

King, M., *Public Policy and The Corporation* (London: Chapman and Hall, 1977).

————, and D. Fullerton, eds., *The Taxation of Income from Capital: A Comparative Study of the United States, the United Kingdom, Sweden and West Germany* (Chicago: University of Chicago Press, 1984).

Pereira, A., and J. Shoven, "Survey of Dynamic Computational General Equilibrium Models for Tax Policy Evaluation," *Journal of Policy Modeling* (1988), 10(3), pp. 401–36.

Poterba, J., "Tax Policy and Corporate Saving," in *Brookings Papers on Economic Activity,* 2:1987 (Washington: Brookings Institution, 1987).

Price Waterhouse, *Corporate Taxes—A Worldwide Summary* (New York: Price Waterhouse, various years).

Sinn, H.W., *Capital Income Taxation and Resource Allocation* (Amsterdam: North-Holland, 1987).

————, "Taxation and the Cost of Capital: The "Old" View, the "New" View, and Another View," NBER Working Paper No. 3501 (Cambridge, Massachusetts: National Bureau of Economic Research, 1990).

Tanzi, V., and L. Bovenberg, "Is There a Need for Harmonizing Capital Income Taxes Within EC Countries," in *Reforming Capital Income Taxation,* ed. by Horst Siebert (Tübingen: J.C.B. Mohr, 1990).

Appendix

Assumptions in the Calculations of the User Cost of Capital

The calculations[11] presented below focus on portfolio investment by a "typical European investor" (undertaken by individuals or institutions). Such investment is likely to be more sensitive to the after-tax rate of return than direct investment.[12] The study examines the minimum gross rate of return necessary for an investment to yield a given uniform after-tax rate of return. The corresponding tax wedges for both an equity-financed and a debt-financed investment are presented for investment in machinery.

As an illustration, it is assumed that the expected rate of inflation is equal across countries while the nominal interest rate is endogenous, so as

---

[11]For a more detailed description of assumptions, see Andersson (1991b).

[12]It can be argued that decisions to undertake direct investment are also influenced by market strategies and long term planning.

to accommodate effective tax rate differentials. Thus, the nominal interest rate is calculated so that investments yield the same after-tax real rate of return to the investor irrespective of the country in which he invests. This assumption enables us to highlight differences in the required gross rate of return to yield a given real net rate of return.[13] It is assumed that the investor receives the same after-tax real rate of return on a debt-financed investment and on an equity-financed investment, thus ignoring the presumed higher risk associated with equity financing. The fraction of new shares in an equity-financed investment is assumed to be 10 percent in all countries. This assumption means that taxes levied on dividends are relatively unimportant since 90 percent of an equity-financed investment is assumed to be in the form of retained earnings. Increasing the share financed by issuing new equity (which is equivalent to assuming a higher dividend payout ratio), the overall level of taxes on equity capital would be higher.[14]

The investor is assumed to face the same home country tax liability irrespective of the country in which he invests. The tax rate on dividend income is assumed to be 20 percent, equal to the tax rate on interest income. The accrued capital gains tax rate is assumed to be 8 percent, the same as the capital gains tax rate on exchange gains and losses.[15] These tax rates chosen are broadly in line with marginal tax rates faced by a typical European investor. In practice, an infinite number of investment channels exist, resulting in a wide range of marginal tax rates. Although each investor would have different tax rates and his particular profit or loss situation (including income from other sources) may also influence his effective tax rate, the intent is only to present a broad view of the effects of the tax systems on investment, and not to evaluate the precise tax implications for any particular investor.[16]

---

[13]Real after-tax rates of return are not necessarily equalized across countries. Nevertheless, the assumption serves to illustrate the size of the tax wedges when a common requirement is made on the net rate of return.

[14]For a discussion of factors influencing the dividend payout ratio, see Andersson (1991a).

[15]Capital gains are normally taxed upon realization and not as they accrue. The accrued capital gains tax rate has been calculated from the statutory capital gains tax rate, and by assuming a rate of realization of 10 percent of the gains per year. The accrued capital gains tax rate is, in present value terms, assumed equal to the capital gains tax upon realization.

[16]Given the assumption that the investor faces the same home tax country liability irrespective of the country in which he invests, the chosen tax parameters are of little practical significance when evaluating relative investment incentives across countries.

Table 1. Effective Taxation of Income from Investment in Machinery, 1990
(With uniform inflation rate and after-tax rate of return)[1]

	Austria		Finland		Greece		Hungary		Ireland		Poland		Portugal		Spain		Turkey	
	Debt	Equity	Debt	Equity	Debt	Equity	Debt	Equity	Debt	Equity	Debt	Equity	Debt	Equity	Debt	Equity	Debt	Equity
Required rate of return	17.18	19.34	15.87	19.59	17.44	19.93	17.12	21.10	18.33	18.05	18.42	21.60	18.23	20.61	18.23	19.51	16.59	20.95
After-tax rate of return	2.00	2.00	2.00	2.00	2.00	2.00	2.00	2.00	2.00	2.00	2.00	2.00	2.00	2.00	2.00	2.00	2.00	2.00
Total tax wedge	0.18	2.34	-1.13	2.59	0.43	2.92	0.12	4.10	1.33	1.05	1.43	4.61	1.22	3.61	1.23	2.51	-0.42	3.94
Host tax wedge	-1.82	1.62	-3.13	1.86	-1.57	2.20	-1.88	3.37	-0.67	0.32	-0.57	3.88	-0.78	2.88	-0.77	1.78	-2.42	3.21
Corporate tax wedge	-1.82	1.56	-3.13	1.82	-2.68	2.13	-1.88	3.37	-0.67	0.32	-1.68	3.84	-2.54	2.85	-1.88	1.75	-3.58	3.21
Withholding tax wedge	—	0.06	—	0.04	1.11	0.07	—	—	—	—	1.11	0.04	1.76	0.03	1.11	0.03	1.16	—
Home tax wedge	2.00	0.72	2.00	0.73	2.00	0.72	2.00	0.73	2.00	0.73	2.00	0.73	2.00	0.73	2.00	0.73	2.00	0.73
Corporate tax rate	30.00	30.00	42.00	42.00	40.00	36.00[2]	40.00	40.00	10.00	10.00	40.00	40.00	40.00	40.00	35.00	35.00	47.80	47.80
Host withholding tax rate																		
Dividends	20.00	20.00	15.00	15.00	25.00	25.00	—	—	—	—	15.00	15.00	12.00	12.00	10.00	10.00	10.00	10.00
Interest	—	—	—	—	10.00	10.00	—	—	—	—	10.00	10.00	15.00	15.00	10.00	10.00	10.00	10.00
Tax depreciation rate	10.00	10.00	30.00	30.00	16.80	16.80	12.00	12.00	10.00	10.00	10.00	10.00	12.50	12.50	10.00	10.00	20.00	20.00
Method[3]	SL	SL	DB	DB	SL	SL	SL	SL	DB	DB	SL	SL	SL	SL	SL	SL	DB	DB
First year convention[4]	0.75	0.75	1.00	1.00	0.50	0.50	0.40	0.40	1.00	1.00	0.50	0.50	1.00	1.00	0.50	0.50	1.00	1.00
Initial deduction[5]	20.00	20.00	—	—	—	—	—	—	30.00	30.00	—	—	—	—	—	—	—	—
Investment tax credit	—	—	—	—	—	—	—	—	—	—	—	—	—	—	5.00	5.00	—	—
Nominal interest rate (endogenous)	10.00	10.00	10.00	10.00	11.11	11.11	10.00	10.00	10.00	10.00	11.11	11.11	11.77	11.77	11.11	11.11	11.11	11.11
Expected rate of inflation																		
Host country	6.00	6.00	6.00	6.00	6.00	6.00	6.00	6.00	6.00	6.00	6.00	6.00	6.00	6.00	6.00	6.00	6.00	6.00
Home country	6.00	6.00	6.00	6.00	6.00	6.00	6.00	6.00	6.00	6.00	6.00	6.00	6.00	6.00	6.00	6.00	6.00	6.00

Sources: International Bureau of Fiscal Documentation; Coopers and Lybrand; Price Waterhouse; and various national sources.

[1] Rates of return, tax wedges, tax depreciation rate, initial deduction, and investment credit are expressed in percent of asset value; corporate tax rate as a percent of taxable income; and withholding tax rate is in percent of taxable remittance. Interest and inflation rates are shown in annual percentage changes.

[2] Only undistributed profits are liable to the corporate tax.

[3] SL = straight-line method; DB = declining-balance method.

[4] Determines to what extent an acquired asset is depreciable when acquired. A value of 1 indicates that a whole year's depreciation is allowed whenever purchased. A value of 0.5 indicates that the purchases are prorated, with on average half a year's deduction.

[5] In addition to regular first-year depreciation.

It is assumed that the investor has a sufficient home country tax liability to credit foreign withholding taxes. Furthermore, integration of corporate and personal taxes have only been taken into account in those cases where such integration extends to a foreign investor. Economic depreciation is assumed to occur at a constant geometrically declining annual rate of 15 percent. Depreciation for tax purposes has been incorporated explicitly, including the extent to which depreciation is allowed during the year of purchase.[17] The generosity of investment grants has decreased in all of the countries and only Spain among the countries considered still allows for a general investment grant. Almost all the countries in the sample allow for accelerated rates of tax depreciation or investment grants for specific types of investments or investments in certain regions. These industry-specific and regional provisions have not been included in the study.

In Table 1, five tax wedges are presented: the corporate tax wedge; the withholding tax wedge; the resulting host tax wedge; the home tax wedge; and the total tax wedge. The required pre-tax real rate of return, which consists of the cost of finance, p, gross of the economic rate of depreciation, δ, and the real rate of return after all taxes, s, are also presented. The tax wedges are calculated as the difference between the before- and after-tax rate of return. A negative number indicates a net subsidy through the tax system. Table 1 also provides a summary of the different countries' tax systems.

------

[17]The so-called first year convention may have a relatively large impact on the cost of capital since a larger depreciation in the first year is worth more in present-value terms than a deferred depreciation allowance.

CHAPTER 6

Modernizing Tax Administration

Milka Casanegra de Jantscher, Carlos Silvani, and Charles L. Vehorn

Several countries in Eastern Europe and elsewhere throughout the world are moving toward economies that rely less on central planning and more on a market orientation. As these countries in transition (CITs) transform their economies, the share of tax revenues collected from government enterprises should decline and tax collections from the private sector should increase, provided that compliance can be enforced in that sector. If taxes cannot be effectively enforced in the private sector, these countries may find themselves facing major future revenue shortfalls.

To face this challenge, the tax administrations of these countries will be compelled to make fundamental changes in the way they collect government revenue.[1] Because of state ownership, a major role of the tax administration in socialist countries was to verify that the correct amount of revenue was transferred from one government account to another. With reforms toward a more market-oriented economy, the tax administration will have to shift resources into ensuring the compliance of an increasing number of private enterprises that will be responding to market incentives rather than incentives created by the economic plan. This shift from simple verification of transfers to more challenging compliance activities will demand entirely new skills and abilities from tax officials and a totally different operational strategy from the tax administration. The purpose of this chapter is to analyze the effects of tax reform on tax administration as the economy becomes more market oriented. The analysis proceeds in

---

Note: The authors appreciate the useful discussion and concrete description of tax administrations provided by Isaias Coelho, Francois Corfmat, John Crotty, Adrien Goorman, and Graham Holland.

[1] Tax administration here includes domestic tax collection, but does not include international trade taxes collected by the customs administration.

three steps. First, we describe in general terms the current status of tax administration in countries that functioned with centrally planned economies.[2] Next we analyze the changes necessary to modernize tax administration so that it can function more effectively in light of all the other reforms occurring throughout the economy.[3] Finally, we discuss institutional obstacles to the changes needed, both from within the tax administration and from other institutions outside the tax administration's domain.

Current Conditions

The implications of state ownership permeate through the basic practices and procedures of tax administrations in these countries. The state is entitled to all of the profit from state-owned enterprises. Whether the state receives this profit as tax revenue or as dividend payment, the total resources available to the state will be the same. Thus, the relationship between the tax assessor (or auditor) and the state-owned enterprise's tax accountant is less adversarial than in market-oriented economies, primarily because the two are both employed by the state. This type of ownership also allows the state to make discretionary ex post changes to the tax code (Gray (1990)). In China, for example, tax authorities can impose an adjustment tax on top of the enterprise income tax. This tax is intended to be an equalizer that compensates for differential profitability, so rates vary depending on the particular circumstances of each enterprise (Blejer and others (1991)).

Another feature of state ownership is that the number of taxpayers is relatively small compared with countries with market-oriented economies. Most tax revenue is obtained from the few large state-owned enterprises or collectively owned enterprises through turnover taxes and a profits tax. State-owned banks play a major role in monitoring the tax payments of these state-owned enterprises; in some countries in transition banks will not release funds to the state-owned enterprises to pay wages until these have paid taxes due. However, it will be difficult for this prac-

---

[2]This description is based primarily on discussions with government tax officials at the various levels of tax administration in several countries in transition during IMF technical assistance missions.

[3]There does not seem to be complete agreement in the literature on where restructuring of the tax system fits in the sequencing of economic reform. Some argue that the early development of an effective tax system is necessary (Calvo and Frenkel (1991)), while others, acknowledging the interdependence of factors, argue that macroeconomic stabilization, price reform, and privatization are of primary importance (Genberg (1991)).

tice to continue, given the growth envisaged in the private sector, including the creation of privately owned banks. The prospects of privatization have led to subdivision of state-owned enterprises and the creation of numerous small and medium-sized enterprises, which will be subject to the profits tax and the value-added tax (VAT). For example, in Bulgaria the number of such enterprises has increased from 1,200 to 1,800 over the past year, while the number of registered small firms has increased by more than tenfold from 14,000 to 140,000 over the past 18 months. In addition, more heavy reliance is expected to be placed on individual income taxes, primarily collected from withholding of wages and salaries. Individual income taxpayers will clearly see their tax burden, in some cases for the first time. As Kornai (1990) has noted, however, citizens in these countries are not used to paying taxes, so tax administrators and policymakers should anticipate attempts to dodge taxes and design tax systems that do not test citizens' loyalty.

The remainder of this section describes in general terms the organizational structure of tax administrations in countries in transition, discusses the major tax administration functions, and presents a table summarizing the current conditions of tax administration for selected countries in transition.

Organization

In most of the countries in transition, tax administrations have three important organizational features. First, they generally are organized according to the type of taxpayer or the type of tax, rather than by the functions of tax administration (e.g., collection, audit, appeals). Second, they are organized hierarchically usually on three geographical levels: headquarters, regional, and local. Third, they perform additional activities normally outside the purview of modern tax administrations. With respect to the first feature, a country may have one division that collects all of the taxes from state-owned enterprises and another division may collect all of the taxes from individuals. In some countries one tax official is in charge of performing all the main tax administration functions (assessment, collection, and audit) with respect to a group of state-owned enterprises, but the productivity of that employee tends to be lower than productivity under an organizational structure that would allow employees to specialize. This way of organizing, coupled with the fact that local tax officials have discretion in granting tax relief in some cases, also creates the potential for serious abuses in a market-oriented economy. Modern tax administrations are more likely to be organized along functional lines. For example, the collection division, in principle, should record and control payment of all taxes irrespective of the type of tax or type of taxpayer.

With respect to the geographical levels, the headquarters level consists of a relatively small number of staff who perform both tax policy work and the overall supervision of tax administration. In some cases the headquarter's supervision of the other levels is loosely structured, lacking clear lines of authority. For example, the Director of Turnover Taxes is not required to coordinate with the Director of the Profits Tax when issuing directives to the regional levels. Staff at the regional level generally supervise the local tax offices, although in some countries, Bulgaria and Poland for example, regional tax offices may also be responsible for administering the taxes paid by the major taxpayers, the state-owned enterprises. Staff at the local level actually deal with most taxpayers and perform the functions associated with tax administration.

The control that the headquarters level has over the regional and local levels varies by country. In some cases local tax administrators who collect both central government and local government taxes are employees of the local government; in other cases the central government tax department controls all the tax staff, who collect all taxes some of which are earmarked for the central government and some to the local government. In contrast to many countries with market-oriented economies, the different levels of government in countries in transition ordinarily do not have (i) general revenue sharing formulas designed to treat jurisdictions equitably or (ii) separate tax administrations to collect specific taxes allocated to a given government level. This lack of a controllable revenue base may constrain local governments in obtaining sufficient resources to provide local public goods that satisfy the specific demands of residents.

A third feature of the organizational structure is that tax administrators are asked to perform activities that are usually considered outside the realm of modern tax administrations. One responsibility is to audit the performance that each state-owned enterprise makes with respect to the economic plan. While this type of audit satisfies the need to centralize economic information and to ensure the economic plan is being followed, it has very little in common with the type of audits conducted by tax auditors in market-oriented economies. Another responsibility that should not be part of tax administration is the allocation of tax revenue to various government (provincial and local) budgets. Poland, for example, has developed complicated agreements between levels of government that allocate so much of tax "a" from enterprise "b" to local government "c" for purpose "d." As a consequence, the incentive to create these enterprises is not solely based on estimates of the founders that the enterprise will become profitable. Instead, a market-driven profit incentive is replaced by an incentive to increase local government tax revenue. If the enterprise is not profitable, the founders are not held accountable because the enterprise can obtain benefits from state-provided subsidies, known as the "soft budget constraint" for struggling firms. A third responsibility, which is a consequence of the soft budget constraint, is that tax administrations must audit the subsidy. In Hungary, for example, auditors devote a great deal of time attempting to ensure that the subsidy was properly used, that is, put in the correct fund and then spent on appropriate activities prescribed by the fund.

Systems and Procedures

One of the major challenges for tax administrators of countries in transition is moving the staff from a tradition of manual systems and outdated tax administration procedures to a more modern administration that includes reliance on computerized systems. This shift will affect almost every employee, from the one who records the name of new taxpayers in the registration book, to the one who checks the taxpayer's account to make sure that the tax due column equals the tax paid column. To perform their jobs efficiently by taking full advantage of the technology being introduced, all the tax staff will have to undergo extensive retraining to acquire new skills and abilities. While each subsystem of the tax administration process will undergo fundamental change, we have selected the major functions to describe the current conditions and illustrate the extent to which systemic change will be needed: registration, returns processing, collection, audits, penalties, and appeals.

(i) *Registration.* In most countries in transition, when a taxpayer registers at the local tax office it assigns a local number to the taxpayer—as opposed to a national taxpayer identification number (TIN)—and establishes a folder file.[4] All of the year's tax returns, payment slips, and any other relevant forms are kept in this folder file. In modernizing tax administration systems and procedures, it is important to establish a national taxpayer identification number, which is the essential key to identify all documents related to a taxpayer. The taxpayer identification number facilitates computerization of the taxpayer register and the taxpayer master file, where basic data items are stored, so that the tax administration no longer has to rely on the documents and forms in a taxpayer's folder as the only source of data. Reliance on documents in a folder file, as discussed

---

[4] Only a few countries in transition like Bulgaria have national taxpayer identification numbers.

below, can make the collection and auditing processes more cumbersome.

(ii) *Returns processing.* Whenever a tax is due, the taxpayer will either bring the tax return or a notice of assessment[5] to the local tax office, a post office, or a bank, if the current law allows payment at places other than the tax office. If the taxpayer is a state-owned enterprise, tax officials may visit the enterprise and in some cases help fill out the tax return. If, on the other hand, the taxpayer is an individual and has questions about how to fill out the tax return properly, the tax office provides only limited assistance. In one tax office the only assistance individual taxpayers received consisted of a properly filled out return being placed on the bulletin board as an example for taxpayers who were confused. Most local tax offices simply do not have adequate facilities to provide taxpayer services for taxpayers other than the state-owned enterprise. In general, the process of filing returns is cumbersome for both the tax administration and the taxpayer. Moreover, the notion that tax administrations should attempt to reduce taxpayer compliance costs by providing information and assistance, simplifying procedures, or requiring only a minimum amount of information on a return is not clearly understood or appreciated.

When the local tax office receives a return, it is placed in a folder file rather than sent through a process that captures essential data from the return. Processing the return by computer would establish the necessary data files to support other administrative subsystems. These subsystems include creation of a taxpayer master file, identification of stopfilers, identification of delinquent accounts, and selection of taxpayers for audit.

(iii) *Collection.* The tax collection process, while difficult to generalize, usually requires that the taxpayer physically make a trip to either a tax office, a post office, or a bank (paying taxes by mailing a check and the tax return to the tax administration is not advisable in countries with unreliable postal services). When payment is made at a bank, for example, the taxpayer brings the payment slip to the bank clerk who will stamp or sign the payment slip, accept the tax payment, and give the taxpayer 1 copy of the payment slip as a receipt. Other copies of the payment slip go to the bank and the tax office. In China, however, the process is more cumbersome. The taxpayer first goes to the tax office where 6 copies of the payment slip must be prepared. The taxpayer, after leaving 1 copy at the

---

[5]In some countries, such as Bulgaria and Czechoslovakia, the taxpayer fills out a tax declaration, which provides the tax authorities with relevant economic information. The tax authorities then compute the tax due and send a notice of assessment to the taxpayer. This process differs sharply from a self-assessment system where one document serves as both a tax return and a payment slip.

tax office, takes the remaining 5 copies to the bank where he or she makes the payment. Of the remaining 5 copies, 1 goes to the taxpayer, 2 to the bank, and 2 to the tax office to verify that the correct amount was paid.

When payment is made at banks, the usual procedure followed by bank clerks is to batch together groups of payment slips using rubber bands along with an adding machine tape for each batch showing the total amount paid. These batches are then sent to the tax office where a tax clerk verifies the total and verifies that those funds were placed in the government account. Also, lists of stopfilers are created by comparing those who paid with those who should have paid. Tax officials then visit the taxpayer in person or send a reminder notice before the lapse of several payment periods. These predominantly manual processes have worked reasonably well, mainly because of the relatively small number of state-owned enterprises.

As the number of taxpayers grows, however, it will become almost impossible to design reliable and timely procedures for detection of stop-filers and delinquent taxpayers unless the collection system is computerized. For example, if a tax return is misfiled or the whole folder file of a taxpayer misplaced, then the tax staff will have to spend time trying to find the lost item or visit the taxpayer to ask if the taxpayer can verify that payment has been made. With more taxpayers, more folder files are likely to be lost, and more time must be spent in the nonproductive activity of finding lost items or visiting taxpayers to obtain payment verification. With computerization the tax administration can store returns in batches that are cross-referenced to taxpayer identification numbers. This eliminates the problems associated with filing each return in the taxpayer's folder, including the problem of detecting stopfilers in a timely fashion, since the information is on the computer in the taxpayer master file.

(iv) *Audit.* In most centrally planned economies audit coverage is extremely broad, especially for state-owned enterprises where coverage is often 100 percent.[6] Because the number of large taxpayers is relatively small, it is possible for tax officials to visit almost every one of these firms annually to check tax compliance and evaluate the firm's progress in meeting the targets under the annual plan.[7] As these economies become more

---

[6]These audits, as discussed in more detail below, are not the same as tax audits in Western countries.

[7]State-owned enterprises tend to be large because they employ an autarkic production strategy where almost every component part is produced in-house. This inefficient strategy contrasts sharply with economies like Korea's, where small and medium-sized enterprises abound, and Japan's, just-in-time (*kanban*) produc-

market oriented, tax officials will have to select firms for audit because they will not have sufficient resources to provide 100 percent coverage of all the rapidly expanding new enterprises. These new enterprises will include many small and medium-sized firms and service-oriented activities, which by their very nature are harder to tax. From a macroeconomic perspective, the share of GDP that is most difficult to tax will come from sectors that are experiencing the highest growth rates (Tanzi (1991b)). In Poland, for example, the share of GDP in 1987 for all sectors except construction and industry was 47.8 percent, whereas in Spain, Portugal, and Greece this same share was from 62.7 to 70.2 percent of GDP (Lipton and Sachs (1990)). Therefore, it will be very important to properly select taxpayers for audit and develop a wide range of audit methods.

One of the most significant reforms of the tax system is the move toward greater reliance on self-assessment. Adopting a value-added tax, for example, will mean that traders must assess their own tax liability and be able to document their tax calculation if audited. Under the previous system of turnover taxes, the tax rates were so numerous and changed sometimes unexpectedly that many taxpayers did not bother to keep up with the changes. Because of this complexity, the taxpayer relied on a tax official to visit the state-owned enterprise and assess the tax based on the various commodities produced by the enterprise. If the taxpayer quibbled about certain aspects of the assessment, the tax official and taxpayer would sometimes negotiate a reasonable amount. Tax administrators and taxpayers did not view these discussions from an arm's length perspective, partly because both were employed by the state (International Monetary Fund, and others (1990)).

Another important change in auditing will be in the criteria that tax auditors use to render their judgments. In countries in transition, audits were based on targets in the enterprise's annual plan. Actual performance was compared to expected performance and deviations had to be justified. In effect auditors were auditing the plan rather than the tax liability of state-owned enterprises. Many countries in transition have already abandoned the requirement of an annual plan, so auditors no longer have a common set of criteria on which to base their assessments. However, auditors have not yet developed separate audit strategies for tax obligations nor learned how to use modern audit techniques, for example, how to find and identify evidence of underreporting.

---

tion process, where small highly specialized firms provide the necessary components in a timely fashion (Lipton and Sachs (1990)).

(v) *Penalties.* Most of the countries in transition have penalties for a taxpayer's failure to meet his or her obligations under the tax laws. However, the penalties rarely go beyond a general interest payment to specific automatic fines for specific tax offenses. In Bulgaria, until recently, the general interest penalty was 0.03 percent a day (slightly less than 10.7 percent a year), which was exceedingly low given its inflation rate of over 60 percent a year.[8] In contrast, most Western countries have adopted detailed penalty structures with relatively high interest on taxes in arrears, administrative penalties for various tax infringements (failure to file, failure to pay, failure to withhold, or failure to produce books), and court-imposed fines or imprisonment for fraudulent behavior. In addition, some countries grant the tax administration the authority to temporarily close firms for certain tax violations.

(vi) *Appeals.* While the penalties in centrally planned economies may be low, taxpayers have little room to maneuver once they are penalized. Independent tax courts to hear a taxpayer's complaint only exist in a few countries in transition like the U.S.S.R. and Mozambique. A taxpayer with a dispute typically has three levels of appeal. At the first level, the head of the local tax office hears the appeal. If an auditor made an overzealous tax assessment, that assessment could be amended through a negotiation between the head of the local tax office and the taxpayer. If a solution is not reached at the local level, the taxpayer can take the case to the second level of appeal—the head of the provincial tax office. If the taxpayer still is unhappy with the decision, he or she can go to the Minister of Finance, who is the final arbiter.

Summary of Current Conditions

Table 1 summarizes the current tax administration conditions for selected countries in transition. In contrast to modern tax administrations, these tax administrations have placed heavy reliance on manual systems and procedures and have conducted audits of the economic plan that do not employ tax auditing methods. As the economies of countries in transition become more market oriented and as the private sector grows, the outdated tax administrations will experience increasing difficulty in coping with new taxpayers and new taxes. To fulfill their mission, these tax administrations will be forced to modernize in several different functional areas simultaneously.

---

[8]Now the penalty has been changed to the prime interest rate plus the daily rate described above.

Table 1. Basic Features of Tax Administration in Selected Countries in Transition

	Algeria	Angola	Bulgaria	China	Mozambique	Poland	U.S.S.R.
Organization							
Hierarchical Structure	2 levels	3 levels	3 levels	3 levels	2 levels	3 levels	2 levels
Divisional Structure	by function	by type of taxpayer	by type of taxpayer	by type of tax	by type of tax	by type of tax	by type of tax
Responsibilities other than tax administration		Yes	Yes		Yes	Yes	
Registration		Computerized registration	Manually prepared registry	Manually prepared registry	Manually prepared registry	Manually prepared registry	Manually prepared registry
Taxpayer Identification Number (TIN)	Separate identification systems for each tax	No TIN	National TIN	Local TIN	Local TIN	Local TIN	Local TIN
Procedures for processing tax returns and accounting for revenue collected	Primarily manual	Primarily manual	Primarily manual	Primarily manual	Primarily manual	Primarily manual	Primarily manual
Payment	At tax office	At tax office	State-owned enterprises pay at banks. Other taxpayers pay at banks, tax offices, or post offices.	Through banking system	At tax office	State-owned enterprises pay at banks. Other tax-payers pay at tax offices or post offices.	Through banking system
Audit	Less than 2% coverage for state-owned enterprises	No more than 25% coverage	100% coverage for state-owned enterprises	100% coverage for state-owned enterprises	100% coverage for desk audits; less than 100% coverage for field audits	100% coverage for state-owned enterprises	100% coverage for state-owned enterprises; 100% for desk audits of all taxpayers
Appeals	1 level—no tax court	Up to the Ministry of Finance level—no tax court (in practice)	3 levels—no tax court	5 levels—top level is a tax court that has just been created	2 levels—top level is a tax court	3 levels—no tax court	3 levels—including a tax court
Extent of Computerization	Limited computerization only for statistical purposes	Limited computerization at Ministry of Finance	Extremely limited computerization	Limited computerization	Limited computerization	Implementing computerization on all levels of the tax administration	Extremely limited computerization

Sources: Discussions with various tax officials in these countries.

Steps Needed to Modernize Tax Administration

Changes in Organizational Structure

With increasing demands on the tax administration, the present organizational structure will hamper managerial initiatives to allocate resources more productively. This will thwart the tax administration's efforts in promoting voluntary compliance through well-organized taxpayer assistance and enforcement programs. A fundamental departure from the old methods of tax administration is needed. The old methods included too many labor intensive procedures that can now be computerized and too many activities that were superfluous to the basic mission of a tax administration. A new organizational structure that concentrates solely on collecting the taxes due according to the law is an effective way to signal to all tax administrators that fundamental changes are being made. Along with a modern organizational structure, it would also be desirable to elevate the status of the tax administration to a semi-autonomous organization within the Ministry of Finance. This would help to enhance the image of the tax administration and remove the conception that tax administration work is of a somewhat menial nature. It would also allow the tax administration to pay competitive salaries, thus enabling it to attract and retain highly qualified tax officials.

Most modern tax administrations are organized on a functional basis. As a long-term goal, a functional organization of a tax department should cut across all taxes. However, in the short term, a tax department could be organized by type of tax. Over both the short term and the long term, the tax department should include a separate unit to deal with the largest taxpayers, thus ensuring adequate control over a major share of tax revenue.

Organizing by function has at least three advantages. First, it increases productivity by allowing employees to develop special skills with respect to the function they perform. Second, it provides a system of checks-and-balances where one tax official does not handle all the functions of a given taxpayer. China is currently experimenting with an organizational structure where the audit function is separate from the assessment function. If the tax assessor makes an incorrect assessment under this new organizational structure, it is likely to be discovered by another tax official when an audit is conducted. Third, a functional organization enables the tax department to operate more effectively. For example, if a taxpayer has failed to pay the VAT, corporate tax, and withholding tax, the collection problem is handled by one individual in the collection section, not by three different people in three different sections.

Figure 1 illustrates one way to view the interrelationship among the various tax administration responsibilities as blocks in a pyramid. The size of each block represents the potential number of citizens affected by each major responsibility of tax administration. At the base of the pyramid is taxpayer services, that is, taxpayer information assistance, and education. With the help of the media, the tax administration can raise the tax consciousness of all the citizens in the country. If citizens understand their obligation under the tax law, then the probability that returns are filed accurately is increased. The functions of returns processing and collection deal with fewer citizens, those currently required to pay taxes or submit returns. The audit function affects a small subset of taxpayers—those selected for audit. Those taxpayers who fail to comply with the law and are penalized have the right of appeal. A long-term goal of a tax administration should be to make the number of taxpayers involved in the penalties and appeals process as small as possible. However, when new taxes are being implemented, it is important to have a massive enforcement effort to reach this long-term goal. Thus, a pyramid with a broad base and a narrow apex represents a tax administration that has been relatively successful in fostering voluntary compliance.

Introduction of Electronic Data Processing

As mentioned before, the current tax administration systems of manual processing will have great difficulties in coping with the rapid expansion in the number of taxpayers and the administrative changes imposed by the new tax laws. How is the tax administration going to be able to process all of these new tax returns in a timely fashion without computers? The first crucial step is to design a broad administrative framework before making decisions related to computerization. Computerization is a necessary but not a sufficient condition for the improvement of a tax administration's effectiveness, that is, reducing noncompliance. There are several cases where computer capacity was increased, but did not improve the tax administration's effectiveness because the system was not properly designed or properly used. Critical mistakes can be made if hardware or software specifications are established before the broad administrative framework is designed. In the absence of such a framework, computerization may impose constraints that result in a situation where the tax administration is serving the computer, thus in effect putting the cart before the horse.

Figure 1. Building an Effective Tax Administration

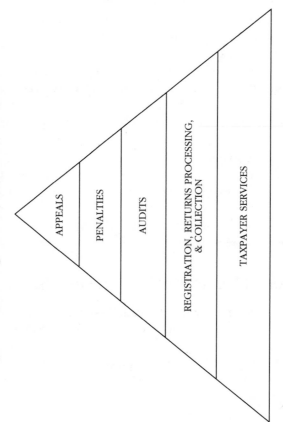

Note: Each block in the pyramid represents the potential number of taxpayers affected by the particular tax administrations responsibility.

In designing a broad administrative framework, current constraints and available resources should of course be considered. Issues such as the following should be addressed:

- How are taxpayers to be identified? Should the taxpayer identification number be the same for all taxes, or should there be a different number for each tax? Should branches or subsidiaries of enterprises have the same taxpayer identification number?

- How will taxpayers determine and pay their taxes? Should taxpayers assess their own taxes on a tax return, thus eliminating the need for a notice of assessment? Should taxpayers be allowed to submit tax returns and payments to either the tax office, or the bank, or the post office, or only to one of these?

- How should tax data be collected and verified? Should tax data be entered into the computer at the local tax office level, or at the place of payment if different from a tax office (bank or post office), or at the headquarters level of the tax administration? Should tax data be verified at the local tax office level, or at the place of payment, or at the headquarters level of the tax administration?

- How should the processing systems for different taxes be designed? Should the systems for processing personal income tax returns, profits tax returns, and VAT returns be the same?

The above questions are a few examples of a much longer list. They are presented here simply to illustrate that many significant administrative decisions must be made before a complete computer system is designed. The answers to these questions depend, to a certain extent, on the current conditions of the tax administration. What is desirable as a long-term goal may not be feasible in the short term. For example, as a long-term goal only one taxpayer identification number should be issued to a taxpayer. In order to achieve this goal, a short-term solution may be advisable such as introducing new taxpayer identification numbers in phases—first to those taxpayers subject to the VAT and later to those taxpayers subject to other taxes. Self-assessment is an important long-term goal, but a modified self-assessment system may be used to cut down on errors made by taxpayers in calculating their individual income taxes. In this system, taxpayers would continue to file yearly returns specifying income from all sources and other pertinent data, and the tax administration would use computers to calculate the taxes due or refund payable. With respect to the processing systems for different taxes, the goal should be to make the systems as similar as possible. This eases the burden on the tax administration and reduces taxpayer compliance problems.

Without an overall administrative framework a computer system cannot be designed to serve adequately the needs of the tax administration. A complete computer system should have a number of subsystems that process tax returns and payment through the various steps to ensure that accurate records of taxpayer accounts are maintained in a timely fashion. These systems include the following:

taxpayer registration,

accounting systems,

current ledger accounts,

control of arithmetical errors,

control of stopfilers,

control of refunds,

selection of taxpayers for audit,

control of penalties, and

a system to track appeals.

Since the task of completely computerizing the tax administration is formidable, it is advisable to approach the conversion to computers in stages. The administrative systems that demand the highest priority are (i) establishing a taxpayer register, taxpayer identification numbers, and a master file and (ii) processing returns and payments smoothly. These systems should be implemented in the first stage, but designed to be consistent with the overall systems framework previously discussed. Also, these systems will provide the foundation on which the tax administration will build all the other computer systems, including those that establish controls for stopfilers, delinquent accounts, and unregistered taxpayers.

Developing the Audit Function

As the structure of economic activity shifts away from large state-owned enterprises to new and smaller enterprises, modern audit procedures must be adopted with specific guidelines to address different conditions, for example, auditing large enterprises versus auditing small enterprises or VAT audits versus income tax audits. These new procedures, while important, are not as time critical as other functions, such as returns processing and collection. Audits should not be performed until sufficient data has been gathered from the tax return and other sources of information, so the auditor can visit the taxpayer with sufficient background information.[9] Also, because most tax codes contain a three- to five-year statute of limitations, taxes can be assessed and collected for prior years if audits reveal underpayment.

The first step in developing the audit function, however, is to realize that the tax administration cannot cope with auditing 100 percent of the taxpayers. If it attempted to, audits would be so superficial that only the most flagrant abuses would be detected. So an audit strategy must be developed. In developing this strategy various questions should be addressed. How many firms and individuals should be audited each year? What is the mix between audit methods (single-item audits versus in-depth audits)? Who should be audited? How often should firms and individuals be audited?

Audit coverage (the percentage of taxpayers audited per year) may vary by class of taxpayer and type of tax, but to the extent that resources are available the coverage should include cases related to each type of tax and each category of taxpayer. For example, frequent audits may be advisable for the largest, say, 100 enterprises because these enterprises will probably account for an extremely large share of total tax revenue. However, small and medium-sized enterprises should not be neglected. Experience has shown that a broad audit coverage has a positive effect on compliance of all taxpayers (Casanegra de Jantscher and Silvani (1990)). Since audits of the profits tax are generally more complicated and time consuming than VAT audits, profits tax coverage should be less than VAT coverage.[10]

Audit coverage can be increased by choosing an appropriate mix among different audit methods. More single-item audits relative to the number of in-depth audits will increase coverage (Silvani (1991)). This approach can be particularly effective if many auditors have not sufficiently mastered the more complicated audit techniques that are needed to conduct in-depth audits.

Selection of taxpayers for audit should follow some guidelines, using pertinent information to identify taxpayers with the highest probability of having additional tax liability. For example, taxpayers could be selected for a VAT audit depending on the type of business and where they are ranked by their markup ratio.[11] Audits should be conducted on those taxpayers with the low ratios, especially those with ratios less than one,

---

[9]However, for the VAT, it is also important to make visits to the taxpayers' premises to ensure that they properly keep basic records and issue invoices for all sales.

[10]Another reason for broader audit coverage of the VAT is that VAT revenue will most likely be larger than profits tax revenue.

[11]The markup ratio is annual sales divided by annual purchases.

which means that purchases exceed sales, a situation that is not sustainable over the long term.

It is also important to realize that the audit function will evolve as tax officials develop more information on taxpayer behavior and learn how to use a wide variety of audit tools. In the United States the Internal Revenue Service (IRS), for example, conducts special audits under the Taxpayer Compliance Measurement Program (TCMP) to generate information that could improve their selection of taxpayers for audit. Using data from this program, the IRS identifies certain line items on the various tax forms where taxpayers tend to understate income or overstate deductions. These items are given statistical weights and a mathematical formula, called a discriminant function, generates a score for each tax return. Those returns with the highest discriminant function scores are audited first. While IRS audit coverage for the individual income tax dropped from 2 percent in 1978 to 1 percent in 1988 as audit resources declined, audits became more efficient owing to refinements in the discriminant function. Thus, returns selected for audits that produced no change after the audit dropped from 25 percent to 14 percent (Dubin, Graetz, and Wilde (1990)). Hungary is currently in the process of developing its own DIF to select income taxpayers for audit based on tax return information.

Adoption of Sound Penalty Structure

A tax system where self-assessment plays a major role must be complemented by a strict enforcement of penalties and a fair appeals process. A sound penalty structure should include financial and nonfinancial penalties for both civil and criminal offenses (Tait (1988)). Examples of offenses include failure to register, failure to file, failure to pay the full amount, and negligent or fraudulent behavior. The amount of the penalty should be automatic in most cases and sufficiently high to deter evasion. However, a well-designed penalty structure may fail to deter evasion unless taxpayers see that penalties are being rigorously and fairly applied. It is also important, especially in an inflationary environment, to settle cases as soon as possible rather than wasting time as the taxpayer attempts to delay payment. In Colombia, for example, the penalties are very high but the taxpayer is given the opportunity to close the case quickly by amending the return in exchange for a significant penalty reduction. The taxpayer has the right to dispute the penalty, but if he loses the dispute the size of the penalty rises substantially.

One important concern of tax officials in countries in transition is how to enforce both the current and proposed tax laws. With economic upheavals in so many sectors and the expectation that tax laws will change dramatically in the direction of lower rates, taxpayers in countries like Bulgaria have been less inclined to pay taxes at the old rates. If tax authorities are unsure or tenuous with respect to their enforcement authority, then tax revenues could be severely eroded during the transition processes as taxpayers attempt to take advantage of the situation.[12]

To avoid erosion of the tax base from increased evasion, the tax authorities need to strengthen enforcement efforts, applying sanctions fairly and with sufficient publicity. If other taxpayers see the results of those who fail to meet their obligation under the law, tax base erosion can be limited. The IRS, for example, publishes data on the results of enforcement. In 1987 the IRS imposed 22.9 million penalties on an estimated 6 percent of individual and corporate taxpayers totaling $5.3 billion (Internal Revenue Service (1988)).

Adoption of Fair Appeals Process

At the same time that enforcement is strengthened, taxpayer rights must not be diminished. The appeals process should allow the taxpayer a chance to voice his or her case before the tax administration, and, if not fully satisfied with the results, before some institution outside the tax administration. An objective and independent institution, such as a tax court, needs to be established to balance taxpayers' rights with the rights of the tax administration. Countries like Argentina, Bolivia, Chile, and the United States have three levels of appeal—the first level with the tax authorities and the other two with various courts (Tax Court and Supreme Court). Canada, Germany, and Mexico have four levels—the first level with the tax authorities and the other three with various courts (Tax Court, Federal Court, and Supreme Court). (See International Bureau of Fiscal Documentation (1987–89).)

Institutional Obstacles

Within Tax Administration

A major institutional obstacle within the tax administration will be the total amount of time that must be spent in reorganizing, retraining, and reallocating personnel. The success of the change from manual processing of returns to computerized systems is dependent on all staff being retrained so that they fully understand how the new system works. Also, a

---

[12]If reduction in revenue is observed, it will be difficult to sort out how much is due to fiscal policy and how much to increased evasion.

fundamental reorientation is needed among current auditors to change their mode of thinking from economic audits of the central plan to true tax audits, where the goal is to detect underreporting of taxes. In addition, those personnel performing other administrative functions, but demonstrating the potential to learn audit techniques, should be shifted to the audit function because many labor-intensive administrative functions will be computerized. Creating more auditors from the current tax staff will help to foster the ultimate goal of tax administration—maximizing voluntary compliance. However, the chances of achieving this goal will be hampered if the tax staff are mistrustful, do not fully understand the changes, or feel that their job security is being threatened.

Another potential institutional obstacle is lack of coordination among international agencies and industrialized countries in providing technical assistance to countries in transition. If the tax administration of a country in transition receives technical assistance from various sources, it could adopt an inconsistent set of systems and procedures because one technical advisor was unaware of the advice provided by another. Suppose one technical advisor designs a subsystem implicitly assuming that all processing will be centralized while another advisor designs a different subsystem assuming processing will be decentralized. It may only become apparent that the two subsystems are inconsistent when the tax administration attempts to run the whole system. Also different tax policy advice can have significant implications for tax administration—a system of final withholding and few returns for the personal income tax versus a system with exemptions and deductions that result in almost all taxpayers filing a return. Technical advice is usually more effective if one international organization develops with the authorities a framework for tax administration reform and acts as the liaison for all technical assistance in this area. This arrangement reduces the possibility of making inadvertent mistakes.

Outside Tax Administration

One major institutional obstacle, to a certain extent outside of the tax administration, is the process for drafting the new tax laws, mainly income taxes and the VAT. While the tax administrations of countries in transition may voice their concern, they cannot control how the pressures from various vested interest groups are worked out. Many tax reforms do not result in tax simplification, but instead complicate the work of tax administrators (Bird (1989)). If, for example, too many tax exemptions are placed in the law, the tax administration may not be capable of proper enforcement. Also, if for equity reasons the marginal rates are set relatively high, this will provide a greater incentive to evade and make the law more difficult to enforce. Policymakers in Hungary complicated their new tax laws by allowing special preferences to certain vested interest groups (Tanzi (1991a)). Now they are considering a second round of reform to reduce the number of distorting tax preferences created in the first round of reform. It would be better for countries in transition to adopt simple taxes—with a broad base and low rates—to give the tax administration the chance to adjust to the new system.

The current accounting standards pose a second obstacle. State-owned enterprises use an accounting system that does not accurately reflect profit (total revenue minus total expenses) because the system was designed to meet targets of the central plan rather than reveal to stockholders the enterprise's financial position. Certain items that should be included in costs, such as salaries of managers, advertising, and inputs outside the plan, are disallowed because they are considered a discretionary use of profit (Prust, and others (1990)). This practice inflates profits and raises tax liability above what it would otherwise be. The whole system of accounting needs to be reformed, but the shape and timing of these reforms could profoundly affect tax revenues. Also both tax auditors and business accountants will need sufficient training in the new accounting system.

A third obstacle is the current state of uncertainty surrounding intergovernmental relations.[13] Provincial and local governments in most countries in transition do not have an adequate tax base. As these governments become more independent, they must obtain a tax base or develop realistic revenue-sharing formulas to provide constituents with local public goods and services. The central government's tax administration will be affected by how intergovernmental relations are resolved. Many questions remain to be answered. Will tax officials from the central government collect local government taxes? Will tax officials from the local governments collect central government taxes? Will there be separate tax authorities? Will separate audits be performed on taxes due to the local governments and taxes due to the central governments?

Conclusions

Tax administrations in countries in transition should view the transition period as an opportunity to build a completely new institution. Central planning and state ownership reduced tax administration to simply val-

---

[13]The push for local government autonomy is most pronounced in Yugoslavia and more moderate in Bulgaria, Czechoslovakia, Hungary, and Poland (Kopits (1991)).

idating the transfer of funds from one governmental unit to another. Economic reforms currently underway will force the tax administration to drastically alter its relationship with taxpayers, especially with regard to the audit and collection functions. A major challenge for countries in transition will be to develop tax systems that facilitate rather than complicate compliance. This means that those who make tax policy should understand the trade-offs between the conflicting goals of economic efficiency, equity, and administrative ease. Ease of compliance and administration is best supported by adopting relatively simple taxes with low rates, broad bases, and few exemptions. Supporting compliance also means that those who administer the new taxes should strive to keep procedures, such as tax filing and payments, as simple as possible.

Since it is difficult to change from the old familiar ways to new approaches, many of the personnel in the tax administration will want to apply the old systems and procedures to the new taxes. But this would be a mistake. So the tax administration must send a clear signal to its employees that tax administration must change if it is to be effective, that is, minimize noncompliance. One way to convey this message is to completely change the organizational structure, moving more toward organization based on functional lines and to elevate the hierarchical status of the institution. At the same time, new systems and procedures that take full advantage of computerization should be established. This will lead to prompt identification of stopfilers and delinquent taxpayers and will free tax staff for more productive uses, particularly in the area of audits. In adopting new computer systems, however, it is important to determine first how this new technology can be used to enhance the smooth functioning of tax administration. Without developing a comprehensive strategy of how the basic administrative functions will be accomplished (for example, should banks receive payment, should tax documents be organized in folder files or batch files?) and then setting priorities, the tax administration could end up serving the computers rather than the converse.

All staff, especially those reallocated to more productive areas, must be trained. Training is particularly important in the area of audits where no computer can replace the investigative mind of a competent auditor. To facilitate the auditors' job, the laws and regulations should be clearly written with a set of well-defined tax offenses and penalties that should be automatically applied in most cases. Complementing the penalty structure should be a fair appeals process that allows the taxpayer opportunity to have his or her case reviewed by an independent body, usually a tax court.

All of these reforms will take time to develop. New institutional structures cannot be created in a few months or even in a few years. But a well-designed strategy that (i) develops the guidelines for the tax administration, (ii) provides a foundation for various administrative functions, and (iii) sets priorities will help to ensure that progress is made in an organized manner while setbacks and miscalculations are kept to a minimum.

References

Bird, Richard M., "The Administrative Dimension of Tax Reform in Developing Countries," in *Tax Reform in Developing Countries*, ed. by Malcolm Gillis (Durham: Duke University Press, 1989).

Blejer, Mario, and others, *China: Economic Reform and Macroeconomic Management*, IMF Occasional Paper 76 (Washington: International Monetary Fund, 1991).

Calvo, Guillermo A., and Jacob A. Frenkel, "From Centrally Planned to Market Economies: The Road from CPE to PCPE," *Staff Papers*, International Monetary Fund (Washington), Vol. 38 (June 1991), pp. 268–99.

Casanegra de Jantscher, Milka and Carlos Silvani, "Guidelines for Administering a VAT," *International VAT Monitor* (December 1990).

Dubin, Jeffrey A., Michael A. Graetz, and Louis L. Wilde, "The Changing Face of Tax Enforcement, 1978–1988," *Tax Lawyer*, Vol. 43 (Summer 1990), pp. 893–914.

Genberg, Hans, "On the Sequencing of Reforms in Eastern Europe," IMF Working Paper 91/13 (Washington: International Monetary Fund, 1991).

Gray, Cheryl W., "Tax Systems in the Reforming Socialist Economies of Europe," Working Paper WPS 501 (Washington: World Bank, September, 1990).

Internal Revenue Service, *Annual Report 1987* (Washington: May 1988).

International Monetary Fund, and others, "The Economy of the USSR: Summary and Recommendations," joint report prepared by the IMF, IBRD, OECD, and EBRD at the request of the Houston Summit (Washington: International Monetary Fund, 1990).

International Bureau of Fiscal Documentation, Amsterdam, various years 1987–1989.

Kopits, George, "Fiscal Reform in European Economies in Transition," IMF Working Paper 91/43 (Washington: International Monetary Fund, 1991).

Kornai, János, *The Road to a Free Economy Shifting from a Socialist System: The Example of Hungary* (New York: W. W. Norton & Company, 1990).

———,"The Affinity Between Ownership Forms and Coordination Mechanisms: The Common Experience of Reform in Socialist Countries," *Journal of Economic Perspectives*, Vol. 4, No. 3 (Summer 1990), pp. 131–47.

Lipton, David, and Jeffrey Sachs, "Creating a Market Economy in Eastern Europe: The Case for Poland," *Brookings Papers on Economic Activity* (Washington: The Brookings Institution, 1990).

Prust, Jim, and others, *The Czech and Slovak Federal Republic: An Economy in Transition*, IMF Occasional Paper 72 (Washington: International Monetary Fund, 1990).

Silvani, Carlos, "Improving Taxpayer Compliance," paper presented at a Conference on Tax Administration in CIAT Countries (Segovia, Spain, June 1991).

Tait, Alan A., *Value Added Tax: International Practice and Problems* (Washington: International Monetary Fund, 1988).

Tanzi, Vito (1991a), "Mobilization of Savings in Eastern European Countries: The Role of the State," in *Economics for the New Europe*, ed. by Anthony B. Atkinson and Renato Brunetta (London: Macmillan, 1991).

——— (1991b), "Tax Reform and the Move to a Market Economy: Overview of the Issues," in *The Role of Tax Reform in Central and Eastern European Economies* (Paris: OECD, 1991).

Wanless, P. T., *Taxation in Centrally Planned Economies* (London: Croom Helm, 1985).

CHAPTER 7

Scope for Reform of Socialist Tax Systems

Ved P. Gandhi and Dubravko Mihaljek

Unlike some other market-oriented reforms, such as privatization, price, and foreign-trade reforms, tax reform in socialist economies in transition has not attracted much attention from economists.

There seem to be, at least, three reasons for the neglect of tax reform. First, unlike private property, convertibility, and capital markets, all of which have to be created from scratch, socialist economies already have tax systems which, it is argued, they only need to reorganize. The assumption is that they should be capable of doing this generally on their own by closely following the tax laws of developed market economies. Second, tax reform is a relatively technical and complex subject, where details are extremely important but hard to design without a thorough understanding of the agents' behavioral patterns and the institutional setup of the economy in question. Many professional economists have, therefore, found tax reform too difficult a subject to write about and advise on.[1] Third, reforms of exchange rate, monetary/credit, and wage policies are considered of far greater and immediate importance for the macroeconomic stability of socialist economies in transition than the reform of taxation systems.

This paper attempts to argue that socialist economies in transition need tax reform and need it immediately. This is because: (1) the existing systems of taxation in socialist economies are not tax systems in the usual sense and are, in fact, quite incompatible with a market-oriented econ-

---

Note: The authors have greatly benefited from discussions with Howell Zee at various stages of the preparation of this paper.

[1]Even in the otherwise vast traditional literature on central planning, there are only a few references to fiscal issues, let alone tax reform. See, for example, Davies (1979), Holzman (1962), Kaser (1970), and Ofer (1989).

omy; (2) tax reform can actually facilitate and support many other economic reforms which are necessary for economic restructuring; and (3) tax reform is essential for macroeconomic stability in the transition period.

These arguments are elaborated in the first part of this paper. Major objectives and constraints of tax reform in the short run as well as the long run are identified in the following section. A few alternatives for tax reform and the elements of a tax system appropriate for socialist economies in transition are outlined in the final section.

Need for Tax Reform

Systematic analysis of the prerequisites of transition from a socialist to a market economy suggests that tax reform is not only a necessary condition for transition but is a part of a minimum package of reforms that need to be simultaneously implemented in order to launch the transition process.[2] The need for tax reform in socialist economies in transition arises for, at least, three reasons.

Incompatibility

The first reason why tax reform is a necessary condition for transition lies in the incompatibility of socialist tax systems with a market-oriented economy. A few illustrations will suffice. As one example, in socialist economies, laws of taxation are subservient to laws on wages, input and output prices, production targets, and so forth. Frequently, when wages and input prices are raised, rates of taxes are reduced to accommodate them instead of raising product or consumer prices. As another example, in socialist economies, the authorities can simply announce the tax (many times they do not even need to do that) and it becomes law; there is little or no need for taxpayer education or to seek their acceptance. As a last example, the state is often all knowing of who the taxpayers are or what their economic characteristics are, and this makes tax administration all so very easy. None of these characteristics of the tax system is applicable to taxation in a market-oriented economy.

Furthermore, the structures of dominant tax instruments of a socialist economy are irrelevant to a market-oriented economy. Table 1 contains data on sources of tax revenues in socialist countries of Central and Eastern Europe for 1989 and reveals the dominance of the enterprise profits

---

[2]See Genberg (1991), Kornai (1990), Levine (1989), McKinnon (1989, 1990), Mihaljek (1990a), Nuti (1990), Ofer (1989), and Svejnar (1989).

Table 1. Composition of Tax Revenue in Central and Eastern Europe, 1989

	Enterprise Profit Tax	Personal Income Tax	Turnover Tax	Trade Taxes	Social Security Contributions	Total Tax Revenue
			(As percent of total tax revenue)			(As percent of GDP)
Bulgaria	47.3	8.3	22.7	1.6	19.5	49.3
Czechoslovakia[1]	34.3	9.6	30.1	4.4	13.2	50.7
Hungary	14.3	10.2	35.9	8.2	29.2	49.0
Poland	27.7	9.2	24.2	3.0	23.6	36.8
Romania	26.2	16.0	34.7	2.4	20.5	42.4
U.S.S.R.	32.0	11.5	30.7	16.1	9.2	41.0
Yugoslavia[1]	14.8	21.4	20.8	9.3	22.0	33.2
Average	28.1	12.3	28.4	6.4	19.6	43.2
OECD	7.9	31.8	30.2	1.3	24.4	38.1
LDCs[2]	18.2	11.5	25.9	29.3	13.7	19.2

Sources: National data; and IMF, *Government Finance Statistics Yearbook* (various years).
[1] 1988.
[2] Unweighted average of 124 developing countries for the period 1980–88.

tax and the turnover tax in these countries. This, by itself, tells little about the irrelevance to market economies of the socialist system of taxation. For this, detailed provisions pertaining to taxes in European and non-European socialist countries, and the manner in which they were administered, prior to the initiation of the economy's market orientation, have to be analyzed. Major provisions of these two taxes as well as social security taxes, personal income taxes, and foreign trade taxes are highlighted below.

Enterprise Profits Tax

Several features distinguished the enterprise profits taxes of socialist economies from normal corporate income taxes existing in market economies. (1) In the definition of the tax base, one or more categories were usually directly determined by planners. For example, in the U.S.S.R., deductions from profits were calculated as the difference between the amount of profits provided for in the enterprise's financial plan and the amount of such profits that were actually used for capital outlays and repayment of loans. In Bulgaria, the Council of Ministers usually established the minimum amount of the general profits which should be realized by each state enterprise. Indirectly, the level of profits was affected by wages, interest rates, exchange rates, and pricing policies. (2) Extreme arbitrariness (from the economic point of view) was present in the definition of allowable expenses, exemptions, and deductions and this, in turn, served as an open invitation to bargaining. As an example, in Poland, the list of exemptions and deductions was particularly elaborate, and the tax base of certain enterprises was adjusted by the addition of expenses and losses which were considered "unjustified" and "unwarranted," while the tax was reduced for other enterprises by the application of various allowances and reliefs (viz., to exporters, producers of children's clothing and shoes, and even to providers of hairdressing and dry cleaning services). (3) The practice of differentiating the applicable tax rates, by branches of industry and even by enterprises, was widespread. In Romania, for example, tax rates were differentiated across ministries, centrale, and enterprises with a view to evening out the profitability of the respective subordinate economic units. (4) In many socialist countries, as the enterprises were not in competition with those abroad, the highest tax rates were well above the levels commonly observed internationally (e.g., 70 percent in Angola and Viet Nam; 75–80 percent in Czechoslovakia and Poland). (5) The liability of the enterprise profits tax could be, and often was, waived if an enterprise could show a financial need. Clearly, none of these characteristics is consistent with a market economy.

In addition to an explicit enterprise profits tax, enterprises in socialist economies in transition were also often taxed "implicitly." The government, depending on its revenue needs, often set producer prices for goods and services with a markup over money wages and other costs. This markup determined the enterprises' economic surplus, which was automatically deposited with the state bank (because the means of production were owned or controlled by the state), and which implicitly became revenue and financed the general government budget or an economy-wide investment fund (see McKinnon (1990)). As the state was both the tax collector and the taxpayer, the payment of profits tax as well as other budgetary contributions of enterprises were often negotiated and determined ex post at levels consistent with the planned allocation of resources between enterprises and industries within the public sector.

For an enterprise profits tax to function as it normally does in a market economy, there has to be a restructuring of property rights and state-owned enterprises have to be legally distinguishable from the state management apparatus. Otherwise, the earnings of socialized enterprises will be indistinguishable from those of the Treasury, and enterprises will not be able to legally challenge the explicit and implicit profits taxes imposed on them.

Thus, before a market economy can be ushered in, the links between the enterprises and authorities would need to be severed. The arbitrary, and more or less automatic, transfers of profits to the treasury and/or subsidies to enterprises would need to be replaced by a transparent and legally binding (on both the tax collector and the taxpayer) enterprise profits tax. In addition, the enterprise profits tax will have to be structured in such a way as to create a "level playing field" for all investors. Clear definition of property rights will also help the establishment of enterprise autonomy and financial discipline. Thus, from the point of view of sequencing, the issues relating to the restructuring of property rights will have to be given the highest priority.

Turnover Taxes

In socialist countries, where most prices are fixed by the government, turnover taxes are not really taxes. Instead, they represent predetermined margins between the producer and consumer prices.[3] From an analysis of

---

[3]See, for example, Raiklin (1988), and Alexashenko (1990).

the turnover tax structure in selected socialist countries in transition, the tax appears to have been expressed in three ways:[4] (1) as the retail-wholesale price differential (this has been the most widely used method); (2) in a specific form (i.e., as a fixed amount on specified products); or (3) as an ad valorem rate applied to some measure of turnover.

As a result, the number of turnover tax rates tended to be almost as great as the number of different commodities. Moreover, the effective rates kept on changing over time with changes in price differentials. The example of Bulgaria illustrates this point. Until 1988, the turnover tax was levied according to the differential between the wholesale and retail price, the latter having been set by the state authorities for about 23,000 goods and services. The instability that was introduced by frequent changes in turnover tax rates was serious and would be unacceptable in a competitive market economy. Competitiveness between enterprises would also suffer if their inputs and outputs were subject to hundreds, perhaps thousands, of different tax rates.

The number of transactions to which the reduced rates of turnover tax or exemptions from turnover tax were applied also was great. Thus, the tax base tended to be narrow and turnover tax revenues were generally raised from a few selected commodities. The tax on alcohol in the U.S.S.R., for example, generated about 40 percent of turnover tax revenue and 13 percent of total tax revenue in the early 1980s. As a result, the authorities' anti-alcohol campaign had serious budgetary consequences during 1985–88.

Despite this complexity, the collection of turnover taxes remained remarkably efficient (see Tanzi, (1991)). Since the only legal form of payment between the enterprises and retailers was transfers on accounts in the state bank, and since prices were administratively fixed and the volume of their turnover closely monitored, there was practically no possibility for tax evasion nor of tax arrears. The banks would simply reduce the outstanding balances of the enterprises by the amount of the tax due and credit that amount to the state as a tax payment. In that sense, socialist countries did not have normal turnover tax administration (nor did they need one), and control was already built into the system of central planning.

The transition to a market economy, and the introduction of comprehensive price liberalization, will sound a deathblow to the present system of turnover taxation. Once the producers and retailers are free to set their prices in accordance with the perceived relation between supply and

---

[4]See International Bureau of Fiscal Documentation (1990).

demand, the authorities will no longer be able to levy a tax "equivalent" to retail-wholesale price differentials, nor will they be able to defend a multi-rate and cascading-type turnover tax. Liberalization of prices will also imply that the tax department will have to actually check monthly declarations of sales by taxpayers and administer the tax properly in order to control evasion. Finally, the authorities will no longer have control of enterprise accounts once the firms are granted autonomy. In other words, the whole socialist system of turnover taxation will have to be replaced.

Payroll Taxes

Next in importance among the revenue sources in socialist countries are social security contributions and payroll taxes, both of which are collected from enterprises.[5] Since incomes of individuals, other than wages in the socialized sector, are small, and since the wage payment to workers was "net" of income tax, the burden of both the social security contributions and income taxes rests with the enterprise and its effect on the economic behavior of individuals and households tends to be minimal.

Theoretically, the workers' share of social security contributions is calculated as a percentage of their net wage and these amounts are then added up to yield gross income. However, gross income is only an accounting entry which serves as the basis for all retirement and benefit calculations. Changes in tax rates do not affect the net wage and social security contributions have little to no effect on the economic behavior of workers. Enterprises paid their share of social security contributions out of a different accounting entry, based on the usual definition of the payroll. Regardless of formal liability, both components of social security contributions represent part of the labor cost of socialized enterprises, over which they have little or no control and which they were unable to shift forward onto consumers or backward onto workers.

Much of the revenue of individual income tax in socialist countries is derived from payroll tax paid by state-owned enterprises on behalf of their workers. As the workers of socialized enterprises are not even aware of the fact that their take-home pay is an after-tax pay, payroll tax, for all practical purposes, has no impact on individual labor supply behavior. Given that the state administers interest rate policy and restricts the ownership of income earning assets, individuals in socialist countries often do

---

[5]Unlike in Western countries, revenues generated by social security contributions are used to finance not only pensions, health care, and unemployment and disability insurance, but also education, culture, science, sports, and similar activities.

not pay tax on interest incomes, dividends, and rental incomes. The personal income tax, thus, applied only to the incomes of performing artists, writers, sportsmen, inventors, and the smallest of retailers and service providers and they alone are required to file tax returns. The scope of personal income tax in socialist countries is, thus, limited. Nevertheless, to the extent any western-style personal income tax existed in socialist economies, it was extremely progressive. Besides, it was so structured as to help discourage private economic activity and to make it difficult for anyone to leave the socialized sector.

These features of personal income taxation clearly are incompatible with the market philosophy, and will, therefore, have to be changed in the course of transition. Most importantly, the reform of personal income taxes will become necessary once wage determination becomes a market-determined process. This will require that various hidden subsidies given to workers (for housing, health care, education, retirement benefits, etc.) be eliminated, and, therefore, that wages be adjusted upward. By failing to establish a clear link between the productivity and benefit levels, the wage policy itself had a built-in egalitarian bias; this role will have to be played by an appropriately structured personal income tax in the future. The entire structure of the tax base and tax rates will have to be redesigned with a view to encouraging instead of discouraging the private sector. Payroll taxes too will have to be restructured to ensure that individuals make appropriate contributions to the social security system.

Foreign Trade Taxes

Unlike advanced market economies, but similar to developing countries, taxes on foreign trade are important in socialist countries. Foreign trade in such countries essentially has the sole purpose of protecting the domestic planning process from outside influences. Consequently, foreign trade tends to be strictly controlled by the planning authorities, which allow only imports of those goods that cannot be supplied in sufficient quantities by domestic producers, and exports of those goods which are in excess supply domestically. Since domestic producers are always guaranteed the predetermined input and output prices in domestic currency, and since the exchange rate is chosen arbitrarily, the foreign trade organization has no objective criteria to guide its decisions. As a consequence, it incurs some losses or realizes some gains in intermediation of imports and exports. It is these gains and/or losses that are recorded in the budget and the use of ad valorem tariffs for fiscal or protective purposes is negligible. To the extent that protection is needed, the preferred device is quantitative restrictions. As a result, nominal tariff rates are relatively low. Moreover, most raw materials and intermediate goods are imported duty free, so the effective rates of protection vary considerably. As far as the fiscal role of tariffs is concerned, customs policy is not considered to be an element of tax policy.

As socialist countries move toward market economies, tariffs will increasingly become an impediment to trade, and trade being an "engine of growth," the role of tariffs will have to be reviewed and reassessed. The fact that tariffs have low collection costs compared with alternative taxes and that ongoing inefficient industries may need some protection in the transition will have to be borne in mind (see Mihaljek (1990b)). But these will have to be weighed alongside the longer-term distortion costs (excess burden) induced by high protective tariffs.

To summarize, the first reason why tax reform is a necessary condition for transition, as well as part of the minimum package of simultaneous reforms, is that the existing tax systems, although rational from the central planning perspective, are incompatible with the functioning of a market economy. In the past, economic agents were not independent decision makers and, therefore, the microeconomic effects of various taxes on economic behavior could be, and were often, ignored. Obviously, the continuation of existing tax systems, with their present features, would be highly inefficient and distortive from the point of view of a market economy.

If macro-fiscal control is to be relied upon during the transition period and beyond, and if firms and households are to be given the right signals, the tax system must become transparent and much more efficient (that is, tax-induced distortions in economic behavior must be minimized), and revenue must be collected at minimum cost. These qualities can be gained only if the existing systems of taxation in socialist countries are thoroughly reformed.

The fact that competitive markets and private enterprises cannot function in an environment characterized by the existing socialist tax system also implies that tax reform cannot be delayed until some later date in the transition process. It must be implemented promptly, because any delay would undermine other economic reforms and, therefore, bring about a stalemate in the transition process.

Simultaneity of Reforms

The second reason for the need of tax reform stems from the interrelated nature of an economic system and the fact that, in order to launch a transition process, a number of reforms must be introduced more or less simultaneously. Over the past year, a consensus has begun to emerge that, once the economy is reasonably stabilized, there are at least ten different types of reform that must be implemented in order to bring about a true change in economic structure. These are: (a) reform of the system of microeconomic management (new incentives, enterprise autonomy, financial discipline); (b) price reform (both the price level and relative commodity prices); (c) creation of competitive markets; (d) tax reform; (e) financial sector reform; (f) external sector reform; (g) reform of the system of macroeconomic management; (h) the establishment of clearly defined property rights over the assets and liabilities of the economy; (i) creation of factor markets (labor, land, and capital markets); and (j) reform of the system of economic information (national accounts statistics and enterprise accounting).

Tax reform, while itself part of this minimum package of simultaneous reforms, must also provide support to other economic reforms. A detailed analysis of the ways in which various measures of tax reform can facilitate the implementation of other reforms on this list, and the feedback of these reforms on tax reform, is beyond the scope of the present paper. In what follows, the nature of this relationship is outlined only with reference to the four most important economic reforms of the transition phase, namely, price reform, financial sector reform, external sector reform, and creation of factor markets.

Price Reform

Besides its immediate impact on the budget, price reform is likely to have a series of fiscal implications at the micro level. On the enterprise side, price reform will mean a new structure of relative prices, which will imply a new pattern of resource allocation, and significant but unavoidable costs of adjusting the existing capacity to new production patterns. On the household side, price reform, combined with the elimination of consumer price subsidies and prospects for unemployment resulting from enterprise restructuring, would significantly erode real incomes.

To help enterprises and households adjust their behavior to a new market environment and, thus, to facilitate price reform, the enterprise profits tax and turnover tax systems of the socialist era will need to be carefully reviewed. To the extent the present enterprise profits tax rates are kept high to finance large budgets and turnover tax rates are kept high to help "clear" the commodity markets, they would become irrelevant and many of the tax rates may have to be reduced. The revenue loss from this reform, if any, should not be a cause for concern as the need for consumer and enterprise subsidies would have been almost completely eliminated by price reform. Some reform of the tax system is, therefore, essential to support price reform; continuation of high tax rates as prices are being liberalized would simply not be economically advisable or politically acceptable.

Financial Reform

The main implication for tax reform of financial sector reform, which consists of the introduction of a two-tier banking system and prudential supervision, creation of money markets, and reforms of the payments system and macro-monetary management, is that the government no longer will have automatic access to central bank credit or money creation for financing of its budget deficits or be responsible for the losses of the banking sector. Instead, the government will increasingly have to rely for this purpose on tax revenues, bond financing, and expenditure control measures.

There is, therefore, a direct link between tax reform and financial sector reforms: the quicker and more successful the tax reform, the easier it will be to achieve the autonomy of commercial and central banks, consolidate their losses, decontrol interest rates, and establish a functioning bond market. The more one hesitates with the reform of major taxes and the institution of the presently nonexisting taxes, the fewer fiscal resources will be at the government's disposal. This will inhibit financial sector reforms because the pressure will be put on banks to perpetuate the old practices of granting "soft" loans to preferred users, with all the negative consequences for financial discipline and market competition.

External Reforms

External sector reforms, which, among other things, will involve the immediate removal of quantitative restrictions and nontariff barriers, such as foreign exchange allocations, will mean opening up the economy and domestic industry to world competition and major price and technology shocks. Should the domestic industry be incapable of facing these shocks in the short run, the levy of tariffs and import surcharges, as transitory measures, may need to be considered to support the process of trade reform. Similarly, designing an appropriate enterprise profits tax to encourage joint ventures and foreign investment can facilitate not only the process of external sector liberalization, but also the restructuring of domestic industry.

Factor Market Reforms

Labor market reform, which involves decontrol of wage and incomes policies, revision of laws which discourage labor retrenchment or protect full employment, and easing of other constraints on labor mobility, can be greatly facilitated if the country's social insurance system, and the accompanying system of payroll taxes, are appropriately reformed. Measures aimed at reform of the social security system should also help mobilize household savings and direct them to the emerging capital market, whereas in the past they were typically invested in unproductive uses, such as hoarding of foreign exchange and black markets.

Capital market reforms, whose main purpose is to ensure a steady flow of investment finance between the deficit and surplus units in the economy, can hardly take place without a thorough revision of personal income taxation. Potential investors in new financial instruments and savers, attracted by the freeing up of interest rates, as well as emerging entrepreneurs, would be strongly discouraged by present highly progressive income tax schedules. Similarly, enterprises would have little incentive to borrow in the capital market if interest payments were not deductible. Tax reform can, therefore, help both on the demand side and on the supply side of capital markets.

Revenues for Macroeconomic Stability

The third reason why tax reform is a necessary condition for transition is that no economy can be transformed in an environment of macroeconomic instability. To achieve stability, fiscal deficits must be under firm control.

Recent trends reveal that most socialist countries are, in reality, experiencing serious budgetary problems, even though they may have, in many cases, nominally balanced budgets. In the past, the adherence to the principle of balanced budget financing was looked upon as an end in itself in socialist economies. Thus, even when recourse was made to deficit financing, this was done as a result of extreme and unavoidable pressures. The insistence on balanced budgets gave rise to two highly destabilizing phenomena: (a) a proliferation of various forms of extrabudgetary financing; and (b) continuous adjustments of tax rates and other fiscal instruments in order to maintain the budget balance at all levels of government. Lack of financial discipline, inflationary pressures, and added uncertainty were the natural outcomes of such policies (see Jurkovic (1989)).

In the near future, other things being equal, budgetary problems may become more serious as market-oriented reforms are initiated. This is because many economic reforms are likely to call for significant additional public outlays in the short run, for example, development of economic infrastructure, consolidation and restructuring of industrial enterprises, financing of bank losses, and institution of transitional welfare programs for the poor and unemployed. While price subsidies, unproductive investment, and spending on the military and internal security, could well decrease or disappear from the budget, these reductions may be slow in occurring. Thus, public expenditure in the transition may not decline as rapidly. On the other hand, the main sources of government revenue (viz., transfers of enterprise profits, payroll taxes, turnover taxes) could decline in the transition as some of the tax rates are lowered, enterprises become nominally independent, and consumer demand falls significantly following price liberalization and contraction of the economy.

Thus, even if a country started from a balanced budget situation, it could well end up in the first few years of transition with a large budget deficit. And, as bond financing, foreign borrowing, and receipts from privatization can, at best, finance only a small part of the deficit in the early years, governments could easily be tempted to create money for financing the budget deficit unless the tax system is reformed.

Reform of the tax system is needed not only to meet the revenue needs of the government budget in the transition period but also to enhance revenue elasticity in order to improve the viability of the budget in the medium term. This is the only way the attractiveness of government bonds can be enhanced and the supply of nonbank financing can be increased for meeting future deficits. However, tax reform will have to be carried out in ways that should not discourage private initiative and enterprise, or hinder the privatization of state enterprises.

Tax reform is, thus, necessary for the transition because it is the only way to ensure that budget deficits can be financed without undermining the overall macroeconomic stability.

Objectives and Constraints of Tax Reform

There is little reason to believe that, for the medium to long run, the desirable properties of the tax system in a reformed socialist economy should be any different from those one would normally prescribe for market economies. However, for pragmatic reasons, tax reform may have to be implemented in two stages, because the constraints of tax reform in the short run (revenue needs of restructuring and limited administrative capacity) make it impossible to immediately introduce the most efficient, equitable, and administratively feasible forms of taxation. Instead, in the transition period, socialist economies may have to concentrate more on rationalization of the existing structure of taxes, making them less distortive while continuing to rely on their revenue yield.

Medium to Long Run

In the medium to long run, the tax system has to aim at the three familiar properties of a good tax system, namely, neutrality (to minimize distortions), equity (to ensure fairness), and simplicity (to ease administration).[6] Achieving an optimum balance among these objectives is just as important for socialist economies in transition as it is for any other country undertaking tax reforms. In fact, since these economies will be installing market-oriented tax systems largely from the ground up, they are in a rare position of being able to design and implement such systems on a truly comprehensive basis, thereby achieving, from the very outset, a much higher degree of integration among different tax elements than would otherwise be possible. This consideration underscores the necessity for policymakers to avoid certain provisions, usually intended as a short-run remedy, which tend to become firmly entrenched in the tax code once introduced and, therefore, the need to fully articulate the nature and characteristics of the desired long-run tax system at the earliest possible stage of tax policy formulation.

Given these objectives, the policymakers will need to address two fundamental aspects of tax design: the trade-off between efficiency and equity (i.e., the extent of the tax system's redistributive role); and the trade-off between economic and administrative efficiency (i.e., the extent to which the tax system can rely on taxes that are inexpensive to collect but which have relatively high distortion costs).

Recent experience with comprehensive tax reforms in market economies has been dominated by two common and simple themes: simplification of existing income tax systems and the expansion of consumption-based taxes, usually by adopting some variants of the value-added tax (VAT). In designing tax systems for the medium to long run, policymakers in socialist countries will, thus, need to overcome certain long-held views concerning the redistributive role of taxation. They will need to recognize that some shift in the relative weights between the conflicting objectives of efficiency and equality of income distribution (in favor of the former)

---

[6]The authors are grateful to Howell Zee for drafting this section.

must be allowed for if market-oriented reforms are going to have their intended effects in stimulating economic growth. This does not mean that the principle of equity must be sacrificed. In fact, horizontal equity is invariably improved when tax simplification involves the elimination of the schedular structure of income taxes. Even vertical equity is often improved when the effect of lowering the statutory marginal income tax rates is more than compensated for by the elimination of various tax deductions and exemptions, mostly benefiting the rich.

The widespread adoption of VAT—the second common theme of recent tax reforms—is due to its well-known property that, in its ideal form, it is the least distortive broad-based consumption tax which, at the same time, has a built-in self-enforcing mechanism. Given its prevalent acceptance around the world, and the increasing interdependence of the global economy, there is little reason for not incorporating this tax as an integral component of tax systems in socialist countries in the long run. This is particularly relevant for the countries of Central and Eastern Europe for whom future membership in the European Community is a real possibility. It must, however, be borne in mind that, if an ideal VAT is not implemented, with all its desirable features (such as the exclusion of purchases of capital and intermediate goods from the tax base, a single-rate structure with few exemptions and a zero rating of exports, and the extension of the tax to the retail stage), its full economic benefit will not be realized. Hence, to the extent possible, deviations from the ideal, in particular the temptation to incorporate multiple rates and exemptions to achieve various political ends, should be avoided. The adoption of a VAT, however, does not preclude the use of excise taxes. Frequently, a judicious application of an excise system in conjunction with a VAT (with minimal deviations) would be able to produce an effective differentiated tax rate structure for final consumer goods which will help meet revenue needs as well as satisfy other social objectives of the authorities.

Finally, policymakers should keep in mind that the performance of any tax system is ultimately limited by the administrative capabilities—legislative, enforcement, collection, manpower training, and record keeping—of the country that adopts it. This points to the importance of ascertaining the administrative needs of the eventual long-run tax systems, and making adequate preparations for them well in advance of their actual implementation. Another crucial aspect of tax administration in the post-reform period will be the division of jurisdictional power over tax and other fiscal matters between the central, regional, and local governments. This issue is, however, dealt with in a separate chapter in this book.

Short Run

Due to the nature of the transition process, and the constraints that tax reform is likely to face in the form of the revenue needs of restructuring and the limited technical capacity of tax administration, the tax reform effort in the short run may have to concentrate on the rationalization of existing revenue sources (enterprise income taxes, turnover taxes, payroll taxes, tariffs). Fiscally and economically more efficient forms of taxation, such as VAT and the comprehensive personal income tax, cannot be introduced rapidly and need not, therefore, be of highest priority. This is, however, not so for explicit and implicit taxes on enterprises. The existing system of profit taxes on enterprises often is among the biggest obstacles for successful reform of microeconomic decision making and must, therefore, be reformed even in the transition.

Three objectives of tax reform that can be identified for the short run are as follows: (a) to meet large revenue needs of macroeconomic stabilization and creation of a social safety net, as some of the existing major sources of revenue (i.e., implicit enterprise profit taxes) evaporate; (b) to start restructuring the existing tax system toward a structure appropriate for the longer run, by making the existing taxes more stable and transparent; and (c) to make the tax system support other market-oriented economic reforms, in ways which must be incentive-enhancing and equity-improving.

Revenue Needs of Restructuring

As a consequence of price reform, the authorities are likely to lose control over output and input pricing and, therefore, over the profit-earning capacity of state-owned enterprises. With privatization, they are likely to lose their receipts in the form of dividends and implicit taxes they used to receive. With the decline in aggregate demand, government revenues from the turnover tax are likely to decline for some time to come. With the possible loss of full employment, the base of payroll taxes is likely to narrow, while at the same time the demands on the social insurance system for payment of unemployment and welfare benefits are likely to increase. Thus, the major revenue sources of socialist economies can be expected to come under stress while other revenue sources, viz., personal income tax, tariffs, etc., will take some time before they can be restructured.

This clearly indicates that the main objective of tax reform in the short run must be to generate sufficient revenue. As noted earlier, if revenue needs of transition are not met, efforts to achieve macroeconomic stability would be seriously affected, and the entire reform effort jeopardized.

Rationalization of Existing Taxes

The first step in the restructuring of socialist tax systems toward a structure appropriate for the longer run is to make the existing taxes more transparent and stable. Domestic and foreign investors need to know what their various tax liabilities would be as and when they undertake specific investments. Similarly, when deciding about their labor supply, individual agents must know what their tax obligations would be if they undertook one economic activity or another.

Not only must the tax system be transparent and free from ad hoc decisions of the type hitherto prevalent in socialist economies, but it must also remain stable for the foreseeable future. This is because many economic decisions are of a longer-term character, so any uncertainty regarding the tax system can be very unsettling for economic agents and, hence, detrimental for resource allocation efficiency and long-term growth.

Support for Other Economic Reforms

As noted earlier, in addition to their positive budgetary effects, the adoption of appropriate measures of taxation can also help support institution of the most important economic reforms. Given that price reforms, financial and external sector liberalization, labor market reforms, etc., can take time, and can have major socioeconomic effects, the potential of interfacing them with tax reform in the transition becomes an important goal in its own right.

In general, as most socialist countries lack tax laws which are detailed enough to allow policymakers to achieve their intentions and, at the same time, safeguard the rights and responsibilities of taxpayers, such tax laws will need to be carefully drafted and processed through Parliament. In the same vein, as most socialist countries lack tax organizations and procedures which are relevant to dealing with taxpayers who are independent of the tax authorities, they too will have to be established and the present tax officials retrained.

Alternatives for Tax Reform

This section begins with a brief discussion of reforms of turnover tax and enterprise profits taxation that have been recently initiated in some countries of Central and Eastern Europe. Next, a few short-run tax reform measures, consistent with the objectives and constraints discussed in the previous section, are outlined. Due to space limitations, the design of longer-run tax reform measures consistent with the general framework for market-oriented economic transformation is not discussed.[7]

Ongoing Tax Reforms

Reform of Turnover Taxation

In many socialist countries of Central and Eastern Europe, tax reform has begun with changes in the system of turnover taxation (see Kopits (1991), and Tanzi (1991)). This is a logical development, because price liberalization normally has priority in the sequence of economic reforms. The main characteristics of turnover tax reforms have been (1) the elimination of price subsidies (i.e., of turnover taxes levied with negative rates); (2) the introduction of ad valorem tax rates; (3) a reduction in the number of tax rates; (4) the introduction of selected excises; and (5) the initiation of work toward the introduction of a VAT.

While all these changes are steps in the right direction, in most cases they have not been accompanied by the necessary widening of the tax base, so the main benefit of the rationalization—higher revenue collected at lower distortion costs—in general has not been realized. In Hungary, for example, a number of basic commodities (especially food products) and most services, accounting roughly for one half of the potential tax base, are effectively exempt from the VAT. This tendency to narrow the scope of tax is due partly to the commitment of the authorities to various social objectives and partly to ignorance about the distortionary effects of partial taxation.

Reform of Enterprise Taxation

Changes in enterprise taxation have constituted the second major area of tax reform in socialist countries. The main features of these changes have been: (1) the elimination of the practice of placing arbitrary claims on enterprise profits; (2) the unification of, and a major reduction in, the rates at which company profits are taxed; and (3) provision of generous tax

---

[7]For recent academic proposals, see Kornai (1990), McKinnon (1989, 1990), and McLure (1990). The main feature of Kornai's proposal is the rejection of the personal income tax; McKinnon would do away with enterprise taxation and rely entirely on VAT; while McLure outlined a proposal for a "simplified alternative tax," which combines an income tax on wage earners and a cash-flow tax on enterprises.

holidays for joint ventures and foreign enterprises in order to attract foreign investment. These changes are generally in line with the long-run strategy of tax reform and the economic transformation. However, there are a few problems in the details of the adopted solutions.

For example, the taxable base still seems to be far from the economic definition of profits, either because many input and output prices still are arbitrarily fixed by the government, or because of the lack of uniform accounting practices, or else because of continuing problems with privatization and assignment of ownership rights. Furthermore, the importance for resource allocation of uniform taxation has not been fully understood, because the new authorities, in the same manner as planners, have singled out a number of sectors (agriculture, food processing, export-related activities) for special tax treatment, thus continuing the old practice of picking the "winners" and the "losers."

Second, the authorities in many countries seem to have misunderstood the importance of tax incentives for attracting foreign investors. One common mistake is to assume that tax holidays for joint ventures or foreign companies, supplemented in some cases with tax-free reinvestments, are sufficient to attract foreign investment, given the presumed comparative advantage in terms of unit labor costs. The fact is, however, that economic, legal, and policy frameworks, that is, the fundamental determinants of economic stability, are far more important for investment decisions than tax incentives are. Yet another mistake is to regard tax preferences for foreign investors as a substitute for inadequate treatment of certain company tax provisions. The tax base in many socialist countries in transition is calculated applying a large number of conservative straight-line depreciation rates with virtually no allowance for loss carryover. Thus, the effective tax rates in many reforming socialist countries remain high relative to rates in comparable market economies, especially on equity-financed investment (see Andersson (1991)).

Finally, the extent of distortions that are introduced through this and similar tax preferences is largely neglected. If domestic residents are treated differently from foreign investors, this could discourage the development of a strong and dynamic entrepreneurial class and could encourage wasteful practices, such as the establishment of fictitious enterprises abroad. Therefore, policymakers in socialist economies in transition need to avoid any deviations from uniformity in the treatment of domestic and foreign companies for tax purposes.

In the way that unified commodity taxation is a logical complement to price liberalization, unified enterprise taxation should be a logical complement to enterprise reform. By extension, the switch to a global progressive income tax can be viewed as an explicit, neutral (across income sources), and potentially fairer revenue-raising instrument to complement wage liberalization (Kopits (1991)). However, only Hungary has reformed its personal income tax so far, while in other countries of Central and Eastern Europe the relevant laws still have not yet been passed.

Short-Run Tax Reform Measures

With price liberalization and liberalization of wage and income policies, implicit taxes on, and subsidies to, enterprises and consumers will be removed. As discussed above, this by itself will require that the governments of socialist countries in transition initiate comprehensive tax reform, and start designing long-term tax systems consistent with the market orientation of the economy. The governments of former socialist countries of Central and Eastern Europe, should also ensure that their longer-term tax systems will be consistent with the tax systems of European Community countries. Socialist countries in transition will also need to start developing their administrative capacity and procedures for implementing the revised tax system.

At the same time, the budgetary needs of the transition will require that tax reform be implemented in the short run as well. Guided by this and other short-run objectives (such as support for market-oriented economic reforms and repealing of those aspects of the existing tax system which are inconsistent with market orientation of the economy), reforms of taxation for the transition period will need to focus on at least the reform of turnover taxes, customs duties, and income taxes. In addition, certain second-best measures may have to be adopted in the interim to support macroeconomic stabilization efforts. Some of the possible short-run tax reform measures are elaborated below. It must be kept in mind, however, that details of tax design and implementation are likely to differ significantly from country to country and that the measures proposed below are by no means universally applicable (they will differ greatly depending on initial conditions).

Turnover Taxes

As indicated above, there should be enormous scope for the improvement of turnover taxation. In the future, as most prices will be market-determined, it will become necessary to introduce explicit ad valorem rates of taxes which apply to market-determined consumer prices. The ongoing reforms in Poland, Hungary, and Romania indicate that reform efforts need to concentrate on at least the following two issues: coverage of the tax base and tax rates.

Concerning the tax base, the reform should seek as broad a coverage of consumption goods as possible, irrespective of whether they are domestically produced or imported, exempting only intermediate products and capital goods as well as exports. This means that food, clothing, and consumer services should not be excluded from the turnover tax net. Such a system would approximate many advantages of the VAT, and it would not be administratively difficult to implement, given the existing institutional infrastructure related to price controls. Should the tax administrative machinery find it difficult to establish and tax the actual retail prices, a fixed markup of, say, 25 or 30 percent, can be applied to the ex-factory price to derive presumptive market prices for tax purposes.

While as a first-best solution, turnover tax should be levied only on consumer goods, in the transition and if the budgetary situation so demands, a small turnover tax of, say, 1 or 2 percent, can be retained even for transactions relating to raw materials, intermediate goods, and capital goods. While this will imply some tax cascading (tax cascading will not be high if the rate of tax is, indeed, low), it may facilitate the administration of a value-added form of consumption tax at an appropriate time.

With regard to tax rates, one of the main tasks of tax reform should be to drastically reduce the number of turnover tax rates. These should, in principle, be uniform, and, if need be, supplemented by additional, and even high, excises on cigarettes, alcohol, gasoline, and selected items of luxury consumption or environmentally damaging goods.

These simple rules should produce a major rationalization of the existing structure of turnover taxes with little to no additional administrative complexities. Since the coverage of the turnover tax would expand, and the tax would be accompanied by a system of excise duties, this rationalization would also help generate additional revenue, depending on the level of the standard turnover tax rate which is adopted. The increase in revenue would also depend on shifts in macroeconomic aggregates, but given that the new prices would be higher, it is not unreasonable to expect some increase in revenue, even though quantities consumed may be lower in the transitional period.

Import Tariffs

Although tariffs are not the first-best form of taxation, from the point of view of open market economies with developed direct tax systems and effective tax administration, they could be used as an important source of revenue in the transition. This is particularly important given that imports are likely to increase as a result of trade liberalization and that trade taxes generally have much lower collection costs than alternative taxes with large revenue potential. Other measures of trade liberalization, viz., exchange rate reform, the elimination of quantitative restrictions, the auctioning-off of quotas, the elimination of foreign exchange restrictions and various import licenses and export subsidies, would be a necessary complement to the program of tariff reform, both from the point of view of the overall objectives of trade liberalization, and because of their positive budgetary effects. The temporary adoption of tariffs could also provide the much needed transient protection to those traded goods industries that have to incur significant adjustment costs in the transition but which are competitive and potentially profitable in the long run.

For a program of tariff reform to be successful, the existing highly differentiated structure of implicit import taxes would have to be replaced by a transparent and much simpler, preferably uniform, set of ad valorem tariffs, applicable to all imports. It is important, however, to strive for as comprehensive a coverage of imports as possible, including any bilateral trade, because exemptions can create significant distortions in the structure of effective protection to domestic industry, and because they generally favor import substituting over export industries. It is also important to have tariffs at reasonably low rates.

In order to avoid the potential problems of longer-term industrial inefficiency, there must be a dated and phased program of tariff reductions. Therefore, concurrently with the initial adjustment in tariffs and the removal of implicit import taxes, the authorities would need to announce a sequence of future tariff reductions, preferably over a short period of three to five years. This would also establish a time frame for their gradual elimination (see Lal (1984)). Once announced, the program would have to be carried out as specified, because any deviations would quickly undermine the credibility of the program.

Income Taxes

The transitional step toward the introduction of a personal income tax can be the introduction of a final withholding tax on wages and salaries of those workers whose incomes have come to be determined by market forces. To begin with, the withholding tax can be a flat tax at a low nominal rate, collected on a pay-as-you-earn (PAYE) basis, without the complexities of family size, number of children, etc. Similar low-rate withholding taxes can also be introduced on other forms of incomes such as interest, pensions, rentals, and the like, without aggregating all incomes earned by an income earner.

In countries in transition with high inflation, enterprise profits taxes can be used as vehicles of bringing into the tax base any profits arising from the inventory holdings by enterprises of finished goods whose prices rise with price liberalization. Consideration could also be given to taxing profits resulting from revaluation of enterprise assets provided the inflation rates remain high. Finally, should enterprises continue to remain state-owned, a charge, in addition to the legislated enterprise profits tax, can be levied to reflect a minimum return on past state equity and toward interest on past loans from the government.

Other Revenue Measures

Socialist countries in transition could also introduce at least a partial property tax while awaiting the adoption of a more comprehensive property tax. This tax could be introduced at the same time as the privatization of land and housing is launched, and it could be based on existing rental values, properly indexed, if no information is available on market-determined rents. This tax would be easy to administer and could be an especially important revenue source for local governments. It would give them at the same time a certain degree of fiscal autonomy.

Finally, there should be some receipts from privatization. Given the uncertainties related to the process of privatization, these receipts could well be relatively small in the short run. Whether small or large, not all of them should be used to finance transitional budgets. A prudent strategy would be to distinguish between a current component of privatization receipts, which are akin to dividend payments to the government and, hence, could be used to finance the restructuring of the economy, and their capital component, which is similar to capital gains and, hence, should be appropriately "sterilized," so as to avoid giving a big boost to aggregate demand. Clearly, there are no set rules for making this distinction and the relevant calculations. To a large extent it will depend on the financing arrangements accompanying the sale of state property. Nevertheless, this distinction is important for the control of inflation and the success of stabilization and, thereby, the program of transition.

References

Alexashenko, Sergei, "Formation of the Tax System in the USSR" (unpublished; Moscow, State Commission on Economic Reform, 1990).

Andersson, Krister, "Taxation and the Cost of Capital in Hungary and Poland: A Comparison with Selected European Countries," *Staff Papers*, International Monetary Fund (Washington), Vol. 38 (June 1991), pp. 327–55.

Davies, R.W., *The Development of the Soviet Budgetary System* (Westport, Connecticut: Greenwood Press, 1979).

Genberg, Hans, "On the Sequencing of Reforms in Eastern Europe," IMF Working Paper 91/13 (Washington: International Monetary Fund, 1991).

Holzman, Franklyn D., *Soviet Taxation* (Cambridge, Massachusetts: Harvard University Press, 1962).

International Bureau of Fiscal Documentation, *Taxation in European Socialist Countries*, Vol. V (Amsterdam: International Bureau of Fiscal Documentation, 1990).

Jurkovic, Pero, *Fiskalna politika u ekonomskoj teoriji i praksi* [Fiscal Policy in Economic Theory and Practice], (Zagreb: Informator, 1989).

Kaser, Michael, *Soviet Economics* (London: Weidenfeld and Nicholson, 1970).

Kopits, George, "Fiscal Reform in European Economies in Transition," IMF Working Paper 91/43 (Washington: International Monetary Fund, 1991).

Kornai, János, *The Road to a Free Economy* (New York: W.W. Norton, 1990).

Lal, Deepak, *The Real Aspects of Stabilization and Structural Adjustment Policies: An Extension of the Australian Adjustment Model*, World Bank Staff Working Paper 636 (March 1984).

Levine, Herbert S., "Soviet Economic Reform: The Transition Stage" (unpublished; Philadelphia, Department of Economics, University of Pennsylvania, November 1989).

McKinnon, Ronald I., "The Order of Liberalization for Opening the Soviet Economy" (unpublished; Stanford, Economics Department, Stanford University, April 1989).

———, "Stabilizing the Ruble: The Problem of Internal Currency Convertibility" (unpublished; Stanford, Economics Department, Stanford University, May 1990).

McLure, Charles E., "A Consumption-Based Direct Tax for Countries in Transition from Socialism" (unpublished; Stanford, Hoover Institution, Stanford University, December 1990).

Mihaljek, Dubravko (1990a), "On the Sequencing of Economic Reforms in Socialist Countries: A Fiscal View," in Essays of the Fiscal Aspects of Economic Reforms in Developing and Socialist Countries (unpublished Ph.D. dissertation, Pittsburgh, Department of Economics, University of Pittsburgh, 1990).

———(1990b), "Optimal Commodity Taxation and Tax Reform in the Presence of Collection Costs: The Fiscal Role of Tariffs," in Essays of the Fiscal Aspects of Economic Reforms in Developing and Socialist Countries (unpublished Ph.D. dissertation; Pittsburgh, Department of Economics, University of Pittsburgh, 1990).

Nuti, Domenico Mario, "Stabilisation and Reform Sequencing in the Soviet Economy," *Recherches Economiques de Louvain*, Vol. 56, No. 2 (1990), pp. 169–80.

Ofer, Gur, "Budget Deficit, Market Disequilibrium and Soviet Economic Reforms," *Soviet Economy*, Vol. 5, No. 2 (1989), pp. 107–61.

Raiklin, Ernest, "On the Nature and Origin of Soviet Turnover Taxes," *International Journal of Social Economics*, Vol. 15, Nos. 5–6 (1988), pp. 3–64.

Svejnar, Jan, "A Framework for the Economic Transformation of Czechoslovakia," *PlanEcon Report*, Vol. V, No. 52 (December 29, 1989), pp. 1–18.

Tanzi, Vito, "Tax Reform and the Move to a Market Economy: Overview of the Issues," in *The Role of Tax Reform in Central and Eastern European Economies* (Paris: OECD, 1991).

CHAPTER 8

Income Tax Reform

Leif Mutén

This paper deals with both individual and corporate income taxation. To begin with, some typical traits of the income tax systems in centrally planned economies are presented.[1] Since many centrally planned economies have already taken the first steps toward reform, the old system will be described in the past tense. Considerable elements of the old system are still in force in several of the countries referred to. The following section describes the necessary modifications to adapt the system to a market economy, and the final section will present the problems of getting from here to there.

Income Tax in Centrally Planned Economies

Individual Income Tax

Typically, in a centrally planned economy, individuals work either for the government, a government-owned enterprise (normally described as nationalized or owned by the people), or for some other collective organization, principally bound by directives issued from the central (party or government) authorities. Since wages and salaries under these circumstances are subject to central decisions, they may be presumed fair and equitable, and accordingly, not in need of any adjustment in the direction

---

[1]Vito Tanzi, in "Tax Reform in Economies in Transition: A Brief Introduction to the Main Issues," IMF working Paper 91/23 (Washington: International Monetary Fund, 1991), offers a general picture of many of the issues dealt with here. Although in parts going into more detail, this chapter will not contain a description of each of the centrally planned economy's tax system studied. All of them show substantial similarities, and the deviations from the common pattern in one country or the other are not of much interest when it comes to analyzing the situation in general. It is only when some particular feature stands out as, in a sense, exceptional, that reference will be made to the country or countries applying it.

of social redistribution or taxation according to ability to pay. This simplifies the system a good deal; instead of individually taxing each wage and salary earner on the basis of his income, one can impose tax, as needed, on the total payroll, and make the employing enterprise or organization pay.

The issue is different when there is an element of private initiative in the formation of income. Circumstances have differed between centrally planned economy countries in this respect. Some did, for instance, accept some activities in the liberal professions; others did not. In a country where, for example, physicians are supposed to work full time for the public health service for a salary, normally no need is seen for an income tax on their earnings as private practitioners. At the same time, private demand quite often brings about a flourishing (black) market for their services, an unused potential source of tax revenue. Other such incomes may be those of authors, composers, and artists. In a strictly planned economy, however, these are funneled through public institutions, and special income tax arrangements may, accordingly, have been found unnecessary.

The crucial point where the market economy and the planned economy differ is that of private enterprise. If the economy is totally collectivized, there is no room for private enterprise at all. What may at all exist, does so illegally, and tax laws are redundant, since the entrepreneurs are liable to confiscation of whatever their earnings from the forbidden activity might have been. Often, however, countries have abstained from nationalization of small enterprises. Tolerated profit-making up to a point implies income formation beyond the direct control of the authorities. Here, therefore, a redistribution motive might come to the fore. Often, of course, this has been coupled with the wish to make life so sour for the entrepreneur that he gives up, opting instead for the nationalization of his business and his own employment in the public sector. An outflow of this attitude has typically been a schedular income tax system, with mildly progressive rates for the cultural workers, and with a stiff progression for the not yet nationalized private enterprises.

With respect to investment income, the picture has been similar. To the extent real property in private hands was still tolerated, a need was perceived for tax on the yield, again, typically, in the form of a schedular tax on rental income.[2] Such a tax may also have included the incomes realized

---

[2]There is a different twist to this story in some of those countries where all private ownership of land has been abolished. If governments have issued "rights of occupancy," sometimes for a very low compensation, to individuals and firms found worthy of the privilege, these occupiers of land have not been subject to

by those who sublet real property. Again, the choice has been one between taxing the activity and treating it as a crime. The schedular taxes were often confiscatory, with high rates on gross rents, and with no, or insufficient, deductions for maintenance, depreciation, and mortgage interest. The property owners had the choice between charging black market rents and using their capital to pay tax.

Interest income was normally not officially tolerated in other forms than interest on government bonds, or on accounts in government banks, or in other centrally steered credit institutions. Just as the incomes from employment in the government sector, the interest payments were centrally fixed, and any further adjustment through an income tax may have seemed redundant. In the same vein, capital gains taxes were virtually unheard of in centrally planned economies, again for the simple reason that such gains were not tolerated in the first place, even though they might well have occurred.

Some centrally planned economies have been confronted with the problem of residents or citizens deriving incomes from abroad. Inasmuch as such incomes were received by residents while staying in the country, they may have been adjusted to the domestic level already by way of converting them at an unfavorable artificial exchange rate. This treatment may, however, have been combined with a schedular tax. Some cases are also known of countries tolerating, or even encouraging their citizens taking employment abroad, but then in a collectively organized form, with the authorities seizing the difference between what the foreign employer pays for the labor and what the workers get to use of their wages and salaries for their own needs. With such arrangements, again, a special income tax may have been seen as superfluous.

Individual income taxation was normally imposed with some personal allowances, in the first place, a basic tax-exempt amount or zero bracket for the taxpayer himself, and more often than not also with some tax relief for dependents. This relief may be granted in the form of a deduction from tax, or possibly, even a refundable tax credit (the more usual form in this case is that of a direct subsidy to children), or in the form of a deduc-

---

taxes intended to hit landowners, since, as a matter of right, they have not been owners. Lacking other taxes, they have been better off with their rights of occupancy than they would have been with full ownership. Obviously, this situation requires either the recognition of the holder of the right of occupancy as a beneficial owner, liable to all the taxes normally levied on landowners, or, alternatively, the introduction of a realistic periodic land rent, to be paid by the occupant to the Government as the beneficial owner, and fixed at a high enough level to equalize the occupant's rights with those of a tenant.

tion from income. If the income tax system is schedular and wage and salary earners are exempt (the tax on wages and salaries being paid in the form of a payroll tax charged to the employers), the need may be perceived for measures of a different kind to take regard to family burdens. Cases are known, in particular, from Romania, of special taxes imposed on childless persons. The logic is that present or past parents will thus get a relative relief. The same relief has been offered to those not yet found old enough to have children. It is only fair to say that such an arrangement, penalizing childlessness, was more to be seen as a measure to promote a higher birth rate than as one to bring about equity between taxpayers with and without children.

Corporate Income Tax

There are several conceptual problems with respect to the corporate tax systems prevailing in centrally planned economies. First of all, payments from government-owned enterprises to government were not necessarily seen as taxes, but rather as simply a matter of cash management, government moving its money from one pocket to the other. Second, much of the taxes paid were turnover taxes, levied on the basis of the established profit margin between inputs at regulated prices, and outputs, again at regulated prices, as well as on planned production and sales volumes. These turnover taxes were normally adapted to a highly discriminatory price policy. If the authorities decided that a certain category of goods should be sold at a relatively high price, and the corresponding margin was paid in as turnover tax to the authorities, this should, in normal terms, be interpreted as a kind of excise taxation. Yet, this arrangement has often run parallel to another one, more akin to the idea of a profits tax, establishing the obligation of enterprises to pay to the Treasury a certain percentage of their gross profits, normally with a ceiling for the gross profit ratio allowed to be retained in the enterprise. This implies, in other words, a 100 percent top marginal profits tax ratio.

The definition of profit for these purposes was not in all respects in accordance with the accounting concepts prevailing in market economies. The definition of costs was usually tainted by the absence of well-defined depreciation rules, or by restrictive rates of depreciation, assuming clearly unrealistic useful lives. Whereas the payments to government may have been defined, at least to some extent, as interest on government capital, there was no entry in the cost accounting for interest on such debt, and as is usual in centrally planned economies accounting, the time value of money was not a working concept. Whereas direct production costs were deductible, there was often insufficient regard taken to overhead costs. The result was that the total payments often exceeded the net profits in the market-economy sense of the word, and that enterprises would have been drained, and actually were so in many cases, if they were not provided with fresh capital from the government.

Another important deviation from the rules prevailing in market economies was the measurement of profitability as the taxable profit in percent of production and distribution expenses rather than of capital invested. Romania, for instance, imposed a 100 percent tax on all profits exceeding 10.5 percent of these expenses. Another peculiarity is the tax on depreciation of assets imposed in the U.S.S.R. and Czechoslovakia.

A system of this kind lends itself poorly to a traditional classification, separating profit distribution from taxes and direct taxes from indirect ones, or, using a more modern distinction, separating taxes on income and property from taxes on goods and services. The proper substitute may well be a combination of measures, including a non-tax element of dividend payments on the equity capital (initially in the hands of the government, but presumably ending up in other hands through privatization measures), an element of corporate income taxation, and an element of taxation on goods and services.

One might have different opinions on what effects the old system has had on the behavior of corporate management. It is, for instance, often pointed out that managers of government-owned enterprises are not threatened by bankruptcy, if they make consistent losses. They are, likewise, not confronted by shareholders craving for dividends, nor do they have to fear takeover bids that may occur in a market economy if confidence in the future performance of corporations slackens and the market rates of their shares fall below the value of their net assets.

Also, in systems of nationalized enterprises, the positive motivation of profit-related bonuses and fringe benefits seems to have been absent. If profits are taxed at 100 percent or more on the margin, even the stimulus involved in being able to undertake desired investments out of increasing profits is taken away. Incentives of a different kind may, however, have been offered: favorable publicity and bonuses granted for exceeding plan objectives, and often not more aboveboard, opportunities to derail production factors into profitable activities in the informal sector, or into fringe benefits such as company housing, stores, etc., available to management. It is likely that incentives of this kind have existed in many or all centrally planned economies. It is less likely that they have always been of a kind stimulating the most efficient economic behavior, measured in terms of market prices.

Income Taxation in a Market Economy
Personal Income Taxation
Income or Expenditure-Based Taxation?

After, or in connection with, the transformation of a centrally planned economy into a market economy, the problem arises, what kind of a tax system to substitute for the old system? Obviously, it is tempting to aim for optimal solutions, particularly in view of the fact that the prevailing system obviously has to be jettisoned, and that fundamental tax reform is clearly seen as needed, the only question being of what kind.

Some might find that the best answer is a system that includes no income tax at all. Those who feel that consumption is a better measure of ability to tax than income, be it objectively, be it for reasons of the disincentive effects on savings accompanying an income tax, will argue in favor of some type of consumption tax. If for reasons of equity or redistribution there is a preference for individualizing the consumption tax and making it progressive, this may be complicated but not impossible. In fact, patterns of progressive expenditure taxes or cash flow taxes have been discussed a long time already, in several countries.

Two practical experiments with a progressive expenditure tax actually undertaken, in India and Sri Lanka, were both given up as failures. Industrial countries seriously considering the same tax, have not come to a positive decision.

It is difficult to generalize about the reasons for this negative attitude. Equity considerations may have been part of them, although there are those who feel that income tax has been oversold as an equity measure. These critics feel that it is more equitable to tax people on how much they take out of the pool of resources (i.e., their consumption), than on what they put in there (measured by their income, if that represents the value of what they produced, or the yield on what they invested). International harmonization has possibly played a more important role as an argument against expenditure taxation. It is hard to see the equity in a system that allows people to make their incomes in a country where expenditure, not income, is taxed, and then spend the money in a country taxing income and not expenditure. The need, if not for harmonization, then at least for approximation of taxes, may be most strongly felt in common market areas, but is certainly a consideration even outside them. Such harmonization or approximation is rendered more difficult if drastic systemic changes are undertaken in some countries and not in others. The international outlook, in a sense, supports conservatism.

In the view of some experts, the very purpose of the expenditure tax, to promote savings, is possibly put in jeopardy in situations where taxpayers expect their consumption standard or the tax rates to be higher in the future. With those assumptions, a progressive expenditure tax should imply an incentive for timing consumption expenditures earlier rather than later. In this discussion, it will simply be assumed that centrally planned economies in transition to a market economy will not go for an experiment in the form of a cash-flow tax or an expenditure tax.

If that is so, then an income tax will be the natural instrument for imposing taxation in accordance with ability to pay. The introduction of the market economy will imply that the government no longer controls the distribution of income, in the sense that it did under central planning, and that therefore, to the extent there is an egalitarian trend in the policy chosen, taxation will be more needed than before as an instrument of redistribution.

Proportional or Progressive Income Tax?

To be sure, redistribution by way of progressive taxation is an objective that is not very fashionable these days. Repercussions on the incentive to work and to take risks, and the negative influence on the compliance with tax laws, are arguments for restraint in this regard. Conceivably, the practical experience of confiscatory taxes on remaining private enterprises and private landlords may be drawn on to convince governments that there are narrow limits to what can be done in a market economy to achieve equal distribution through taxation. Obviously, the message has to be that common happiness will be greater if a larger pie is shared in unequal parts, than if an equally shared pie is kept small as a result of excessive redistributive measures that hamper growth. The problem is to establish some consensus about when redistribution is significantly impeding growth.[3]

If it is intended to use the income tax for redistributive purposes, a global tax on all the taxpayer's income from all sources is clearly the ideal. The same holds, if ambitions just include taxation according to ability to

---

[3] The reason why there are many theories and not just one adhered to by all, is that the tax rate may have both a substitution effect and an income effect, the former, effective on the margin, discouraging the taxpayers' efforts to earn more income, the latter, representing the total income-reducing effect of the tax, normally expected to encourage these efforts. A lump sum tax is optimal in the sense that it has no marginal (i.e., substitution) effect, but just an income effect. The problem is that a lump sum tax is basically unfair if not differentiated according to ability to pay. Yet, any factor used to differentiate the tax will automatically be burdened by the marginal effect that the lump sum tax was conceived to escape.

pay—a principle that in reasonable interpretations will also include a degree of progressivity. A progressive rate for each of a number of schedular taxes would unduly benefit taxpayers with incomes of different kinds at the cost of those whose incomes are derived from one source only. The brackets should be few; for all reasonable purposes, three to five brackets are sufficient.

Worldwide Income Tax or Territoriality?

Similarly, it is desirable, at least in principle, to establish the income tax base for individuals as the worldwide income, so as not to put a premium on investment or other activities abroad, and to establish as fair a measurement as possible of the taxpayer's ability to pay. Moreover, there is a technical argument in favor of worldwide taxation, namely, that a taxpayer who is found to have a standard of living far beyond his declared means should not be offered an opportunity of explaining away this fact by pretending to have had incomes derived from abroad, notably of a kind not easily checked by the tax authority. If, for these reasons, a worldwide income tax seems desirable, there are, on the other hand, administrative difficulties connected with such a tax claim. The ideal may well be a system where, as a general rule, passive income received from foreign sources remains taxable, whereas active income, mainly wages and salaries, but possibly business income derived from permanent establishments abroad, remains exempt from domestic income tax. Also, it is obvious that very little is gained by any effort to extend this claim to tax on foreign-source income to nonresident citizens. With few exceptions (the big one being the United States), countries limit their claim to tax on worldwide income to residents.

Taxation of Income in Kind

Experience tells that if taxation is limited to money income, taxpayers and employers will find ways to escape taxation by giving compensation in kind. The taxation of fringe benefits is a complicated issue. If the tax authority insists on consistent taxation of all benefits in kind, it looks like nit-picking. If it leaves benefits untaxed, taxpayers will use the loophole. Valuation of benefits raises problems, particularly if one tries to tax benefits only at the value they have to the employee. The personal consumption content of housing, company cars, travel for mixed business and recreation purposes, or participation in business entertainment, is often difficult to identify.

Some countries avoid dealing with the taxpayer himself by establishing, instead, either a tax on the value of the fringe benefits charged on the employer, or a separate tax on fringe benefits, likewise paid by the employer. One problem is how to deal with nonprofit employers and with government as an employer.

No solution to the fringe benefit problem is satisfactory. The general trend, however, goes toward more consistent taxation, even at the price of what might look as excessive stinginess on the side of the tax administration. Keeping a strict line here can prevent a development toward a barter economy that in the long run will hurt everybody, taxpayers, employers, and the fiscal authority.

Capital Gains Taxation?

Capital gains are nowadays generally conceived of as being part of income. Are there weighty reasons for giving them preferential treatment? The answer to this will depend on several factors. One has to do with the income tax rate schedule: if the rate is high, the fundamental weakness of a capital gains tax that is limited to realized gains only, the "lock-in" effect, will be more pronounced than if the rate is more modest. No country has successfully applied a tax on unrealized capital gains. Accordingly, if the general rate is not kept reasonably low, a separate capital gains tax rate will be needed, and the Pandora's box of tax shelter operations, turning current income into capital gains, will be opened.

Another issue is that of inflation. The higher the inflation rate, the more unfair will a system of capital gains taxation be, if no adjustment of the base is made for inflation. Again, in the absence of indexation, it is usually found necessary to include some general rule mitigating the tax rate, or reducing the part of the gain liable to tax. In view of the invitation to sheltering current income that this will offer, many countries have seen it as less cumbersome to apply a rule under which the cost base is lifted by a factor based on the movement of the consumer price index, unless inflation is very modest. The justification for indexation of the cost base also applies to the debt side, particularly if a deduction has been offered for nominal debt interest payments.

Indexation of Interest Income?

A similar argument applies to interest income and to the deductibility of interest in general. Without indexation, and with a sizable degree of inflation, the taxation of nominal interest receipts and the deductibility of nominal interest payments may well imply that the real rate of interest received or payable, net of tax, turns lower than zero, even if the nominal rate of interest exceeds the rate of inflation. Again, indexation may be seen as a necessary element in a tax system aimed at functioning well in an inflationary environment.

Individual or Household Income?

The globalization of the income tax would facilitate any measure to take regard to the taxpayer's family situation. A choice would have to be made, to begin with, of which unit to use for taxation: the individual, the married couple, or the whole household? The general tendency, worldwide, is nowadays in favor of separate taxation of husbands and wives. One administrative reason for this is that separate taxation facilitates final withholding taxation of wages and salaries. Two policy problems will also be solved by separate taxation. One is that under a progressive system the joint taxation of married couples discriminates against them in comparison with other forms of cohabitation. The other policy problem, also taken care of through separate taxation, is that with joint taxation, the spouse last deciding to join the labor force will be inhibited from doing so, since she or he will face the marginal rate applicable on top of the other spouse's income. Obviously, the price to be paid for separate taxation is that taxation of different households with the same income might differ depending on whether one or two individuals contribute to the household income. A splitting of the total income into two between the spouses solves the last problem, and may be carried as far as to eliminate discrimination of married couples, but leaves unsolved the third policy issue, the discouragement of entering the labor force.

Family Allowances

With respect to children and other dependents, industrial countries sometimes choose to offer the relief in the form of a subsidy independent of the tax system, offering the same amount per child, regardless of parental income. An intermediate position is that of a refundable tax credit, an arrangement that likewise assures the same amount to each child. If only tax relief is aimed at, it is usually found that a tax credit is more equitable than a deduction from income, although many countries still stick to the deduction from income. Finally, some countries, following an originally French pattern, apply the progressive rate schedule under a family quotient system, splitting the income, for instance, into two for childless couples, into three for couples with two children, and so on. This family quotient system offers substantially more relief for each dependent, the higher the household income. The preferred solution from the technical point of view is to subsidize children outside the tax system and disregard them for purposes of defining the tax burden. If any tax relief is considered, a tax credit should be the preferred method.

Indexation of Rate Schedules and Allowances?

Again, in this context, the inflation problem has to be taken into consideration. For threshold amounts and family allowances, as well as bracket limits in the progressive tax schedule, the erosion of nominal amounts following inflation, if not compensated for by discretionary measures, implies that the effective tax rate goes up with inflation, that a relatively greater number of income earners get caught in the tax net, and that the reliefs for dependents diminish in value.

Many countries have avoided this situation by indexation of the amounts involved. Obviously, strong equity arguments speak in favor of such indexation. It is inconceivable that standards of fairness and equity underlying the original tax system would change with inflation to such a degree as to make a system affected by "bracket creep" and inflationary erosion of exemptions and allowances still remain acceptable under fairness and equity standards prevailing after inflation.

On the other hand, the argument can be made that an inflation adjustment ex post, taking regard of an inflationary movement in the previous year, may have a damaging effect on revenue in the next year, during which there will possibly be much less inflation. Also, a government may well feel that it can make more political hay by allowing inflation to increase taxes without Parliamentary decisions, while at the same time allowing itself to mitigate this invisible inflationary tax increase by way of a highly visible tax reduction decision. And finally, any inflation adjustment on the statute book may be seen as a sign of government tolerating inflation and counting upon it as a normal element.

As a final remark on indexation, it should be emphasized that total indexation of tax systems is usually not practiced in other countries than those with hyperinflation. In other countries, partial indexation may be applied, most often in the field of personal allowances and bracket limits, but also with respect to the capital gains tax base, to depreciation allowances, and to interest payments. Moreover, inflation-hit countries have particular reasons to watch over it that taxes are paid currently, since delays in paying tax implies that the money the tax is paid in is worth less than the money in which the tax base was computed. Measures to compensate for this effect may include strict rules on current payment of tax and high interest rates for late payment.

If countries hesitate with respect to complete or partial indexation, they may go for alternative solutions to the same problem. A case in point is depreciation, where generous depreciation rules and last-in-first-out valuation of inventories are often seen as substitutes for indexation. Also, frequent discretionary changes of allowances and rate bracket limits may be seen as such a substitute, as will the exemption of interest from tax and the nondeductibility of interest paid.

Corporate Income Taxation

Turnover Versus Income Tax

First of all, there must be established a clear distinction between turnover taxes and other taxes on goods and services, on the one hand, and income taxes, on the other. The former will, as mentioned elsewhere in this book, ideally take the form of a value-added tax. Among other reasons, the fact that a VAT in international practice follows the destination principle would make it a mistake to regard the VAT as an alternative to, or part of, the corporate income tax.

Liable Enterprise Forms

Second, there must be a firm basis for deciding what kinds of enterprises are liable to corporate income tax. There is no point in establishing that an individual is liable to personal income tax on his business income as long as he has no more than five employees (a rule sometimes applicable in centrally planned economies), once the market economy principles apply and allow him to hire more labor. On the other hand, there is a tendency among some industrial countries to establish income tax on enterprise units, regardless of legal form, establishing a "tax fence" between the firm as such and its owner. With such a rule, the enterprise income tax can be made uniform between corporations, partnerships, and proprietary firms, and the physical owners, be they shareholders, partners, or proprietaries, will be taxed only on profits they take out of the enterprise in the form of dividend, profit share, or salary.

It is not necessarily the best idea to take this route. The existence of alternative legal forms for businesses gives flexibility, and traditional tax systems have adapted to this by allowing intermediate forms of enterprises to grow. A proprietary owner who wants the corporate form for his business might normally be able to do so by forming what is formally, or at least in reality, a one-man corporation; if the tax law allows him to take out a salary with no, or generous limits, he may be able to achieve the same purpose as the "fence" rule provides for. The use of the partnership form, allowing a separate legal personality for the enterprise while at the same time providing the partners an opportunity of deducting current losses from their current income, may have been abused in many cases for pure tax shelter investments. Yet, there are ways of stopping the abuses while still keeping the advantage of the partnership form for promoting new business ventures, if that is seen as an objective.

The form of a cooperative, either a producer cooperative or a consumer cooperative, is well known, at least as a concept, in many centrally planned economies as well as in many nonsocialist countries. Tax laws around the world contain many provisions giving special relief to cooperatives, either for pure political reasons or for the reason that the cooperative is seen as an extension of the original producers or of consumers, and therefore should not be seen as necessarily subject to the same tax as those doing business for profit.

In reality, the name of cooperatives is very often used as a cover for what is regular profit-making business. There is obviously no point in trying to make a distinction between producing business firms or agricultural enterprises, on the one hand, and producer cooperatives they own, on the other. The issue is somewhat more delicate with respect to consumer cooperatives. The distribution function performed by them might be seen as an extension of the chores otherwise resting on the households. In theory, there is a very fine line between a number of households organizing joint purchases to get lower prices for the higher quantities they buy, and the same households setting up a cooperative retail store to carry on basically the same activity. In all these cases, the guiding principle should, however, be to keep fair competition in the market place. If cooperatives are given special treatment, they may outcompete more efficient, noncooperative enterprises, and they may be abused for purposes of private businesses carried on in the cooperative guise.

For the same reason, it is not recommended to make a difference in the corporate tax rate between different types of corporations. Also, the corporation tax rate should be proportional, not progressive. There is no reason to believe that large investors invest in large companies, small shareholders in small ones, rather the opposite. Technically, the use of progressive rates leads to considerable complication if abuse by splitting up businesses is to be avoided. Usually, the corporate tax rate is chosen at a level not exceeding the top income tax rate (this would induce an escape into partnerships), but not very much below it, either (to prevent abuse of companies to accumulate personal income).

Taxation of Corporations and Shareholders

There is no reason to expect that former centrally planned economies will dispense with the traditional corporate form of business. The problem is how to tax corporations and shareholders. In this regard, the issue facing countries in transition is, to an extent, somewhat easier to deal with, compared with the corresponding problems in countries where privately owned corporations are already in existence and a tax system applied to them has been in force for a long time already. The reason why the situation is simpler in the former centrally planned economies is that whatever new tax system is chosen, there is no windfall gain or loss for shareholders, who have acquired their shares at a rate in which the negative or positive value of the formerly prevailing tax regime has been discounted.

To begin with, a decision should be made about the system to be chosen for the taxation of corporations and shareholders. The "classical" system provides for taxation of corporations on their whole profits, with the income from dividend distributions again being taxed in the hands of the shareholders. This is called economic double taxation of distributed corporate income. The system is often criticized as unjustly discriminating against the corporate form, although those defending the classical system traditionally argue that the use of the corporate form is a privilege that should be paid for. What they have in mind is, in particular, the fact that a shareholder is not personally responsible for a corporation's debt. Critics of the classical system may respond with a reference to economic realities: private owners of closely held corporations very often have to sign personal guarantees for the corporate debt, thus forgoing the privilege assumed to motivate the double taxation.

Even in countries with a classical system, steps may be taken to mitigate the effect of double taxation. As already indicated, there may be a smooth transition from a system of simple taxation to the double one, if closely held corporations are allowed to pay salaries to managing shareholders without limits, or with limits generous enough to make the salary absorb the profit. This implies that double taxation hits only nonbusiness corporations and corporations with shareholders not at the same time working for them. Similarly, countries may redefine what is, for tax purposes, a normal corporation subject to double taxation, by opening the opportunity of partnership treatment (i.e., the taxation of each shareholder on his share of the corporate profit, with no regard to whether it has been distributed or not), for instance to corporations with a limited number of shareholders, all of them taxable individuals. (In the United States, the "subchapter S corporation" is a case in point.)

The same idea can, in principle, be extended to all corporations. It is, however, not realistic to apply the partnership treatment to corporations with a great number of shareholders. The principle of establishing the profit on the basis of the corporate accounts and to tax each shareholder on his share of the profit (or give him a deduction for his share of the loss) is clear enough in theory, but bogs down in a morass of complication, if applied to thousands of shareholders buying and selling their shares throughout the year. Moreover, if the tax authority finds reason to contest the corporation's tax return, the assessments of all these shareholders may have to be kept open, possibly for a long time, until the assessment of the corporation's profits has been settled. One might, however, apply a modified partnership method by combining two rules: one, a rule that gives the corporation a deduction for dividends distributed, and two, a rule that gives corporations and shareholders the right to opt for a dividend to be deemed as distributed, although the corporation has kept the money. Such a rule was recommended by the famous Carter Commission in Canada, but never brought to the statute books.

If the partnership method is generally seen as an impractical way to solve the double taxation problem, two other rules are more close to reality. One is the split rate method, under which distributed profits are taxed at a lower corporate tax rate than profits retained, in the extreme case at a zero rate (i.e., deductible as costs). The other is the imputation method, under which shareholders may take a credit against the income tax on dividends received for all or some of the corporate income tax paid by the corporation with respect to the profit out of which the dividend was paid.

Of these two methods, the split rate method, although seemingly the simpler one, is the one that raises most problems. First of all, it gives relief even where no relief is needed, the recipients of dividends being tax-exempt (charities, pension funds, even foreign shareholders, provided there is not a high enough withholding tax on the dividends). Second, it may be deemed necessary to apply a rather high withholding tax on dividends to prevent distribution and reinvestment from emerging as a better alternative to the retention of profits. Without such a withholding tax, foreign-owned corporations may be in a better position than corporations with domestic shareholders, but the withholding tax may well be seen by the foreign shareholders and their governments as a means of discriminating against them.

The imputation system is more popular and has been adopted by the majority of the EC countries, as well as in a good number of countries outside the Community. It is, however, not without problems. These are of several kinds: incidence, incentive effects, equity, and international discrimination.

The incidence issue refers to the fact that a corporate income tax that is presumed shifted to the purchasers of corporate products or back to the production factors used by corporations cannot at the same time be seen as a prepaid levy on the shareholders' dividend income. Therefore, one has to assume that the corporation tax is basically not shifted, to make it rational to integrate the corporate income tax with the taxation of the shareholders' income. The matter is particularly sensitive in relation to integration schemes that eliminate personal income tax on shareholders with respect to their dividend income. The elimination, through imputation of personal income tax on dividends, may seem to be a misplaced tax subsidy in the eyes of those who feel that corporations shift their taxes onto consumers or production factors. The matter is seen in the same unfavorable light by those who, whatever shifting they assume, feel that corporations should be held separate from their shareholders.

Another issue has to do with the incentive to distribute income rather than to retain it. A theoretical approach is to assume that an imputation system does not stimulate distribution of dividends; the argument is that if the money can grow more quickly by being retained in the corporation than invested by the shareholders, the latter should prefer to let it stay in the corporation. The intuitive approach is more straightforward: if there is a tax relief offered against the double taxation of distributed profits, and no such relief is available for undistributed profits, then those shareholders who want distributions may feel they have an argument against those who want to retain the profits.

If there is economic double taxation of distributed profits, retained profits will be seen as a cheap source of capital, since the economic double taxation reduces the opportunity cost of using such profits to finance new corporate investments. The prevailing theory concerning the cost of capital for corporate investments stresses the need for some degree of neutrality between different sources of financing. In this respect, financing with new equity capital is relatively the most expensive form of financing in a classical system, whereas financing with retained profits is the cheapest form. With an integrated system the relative cost of new equity capital will be lower, and that of retained profits will be higher. With loan interest deductible from taxable profits, borrowed capital will be relatively cheap as a source of financing. It can be argued that complete neutrality presupposes identical treatment of loan capital and equity capital.

The point is often made with respect to countries poor on capital that they should use the classical system as a means of stimulating the retention of capital, in particular if the alternative is distribution to shareholders outside the country, who might not reinvest there. On the other hand, it is generally felt that it would be rational to harmonize the cost of capital for different types of financing, so as to make the cut-off point for new investment basically the same for all investors, regardless of their financing opportunities. It is, of course, doubtful, to say the least, that the ideal of neutrality will ever be even approximately achieved.

The equity aspect leads both ways. The classical system with its economic double taxation can be said to penalize shareholders in corporations distributing all or part of their profits. Imputation implies that all a taxpayer's income, be it earned by himself or by a corporation where he has stock, carries the same tax. The problem is that it does not look like that, since some of the tax is paid in advance by the corporation. Experience has taught that it may be risky for politicians to be shareholders in a full imputation system. Angry voters finding that their shareholding politicians are enjoying "tax-free" dividends while they themselves toil for a wage compensation fully taxed, have on occasion reacted with a backlash.

The international aspect is also complicated. The EC has not been able to harmonize the different approaches to company/stockholder problems. Imputation is more often than not offered to domestic shareholders only, and this, in turn, is often seen as discriminatory against foreign shareholders. Moreover, there is usually a requirement that domestic tax be paid corresponding to the tax credited to the shareholders. If foreign source income is taxed abroad, with a tax credit or exemption applied in the country where the corporation is domiciled, the law in that country may well make it a condition for imputation that a corresponding tax (précompte, A(dvance) C(ompany) T(ax)) be paid before a dividend can be made on which shareholders can collect an imputation credit. This, in turn, may well be a disincentive to foreign activities for companies affected. Accordingly, the imputation system may work in favor not only of domestic shareholders but domestic investment, as well. In some countries, it is felt that this has not been regarded as a disadvantage, rather the opposite.

How Does One Come From Here to There?
Administration Issues

The most important factor in deciding how to reform a tax system is the availability of administrative resources. Laws on the statute book have no beneficial effect, if not implemented. Implementation does not come by itself but must be dealt with by the tax administration. It is dangerous to issue tax laws when compliance cannot be effectively monitored. It is particularly detrimental in countries, such as the former centrally planned economies, where many citizens are used to distrusting the authorities, and where it must be feared that voluntary compliance is rare.

The large part of budgetary revenue emanating from the major government enterprises has traditionally been under the control of the government bank system and of the government audit agencies. Inasmuch as tax authorities have functioned, their tasks have been more limited, dealing primarily with smaller entities, individual income earners, owners of vehicles, etc.

It would be futile to ask this rudimentary tax administration to shoulder the task of introducing and supervising an entirely new system of individual and corporate income taxes, including individual tax returns from all income earners, perhaps over half the population, and information returns in an even higher number. The new system will have to be introduced in a form that safeguards the revenue while at the same time minimizing the administrative burden. Several policy decisions must be based on this basic consideration.

Personal Income Tax

First of all, the number of taxpayer files has to be kept to a minimum. This can be done by applying the tax on wage and salary earners as a final withholding tax, adjusted only in cases of multiple employment. The income tax on these categories would then basically be levied from the employers. Checking the withholding tax payments would be easier, the more standardized the tax rules. If the family situation of an employee could be ignored (separate taxation of husbands and wives, child subsidies rather than dependency allowances), and the tax based on monthly income, the control could be extremely simple.

Other incomes could be dealt with separately. For interest and dividend income, another final withholding tax would be the most practical. For business income, on the other hand, it would seem indispensable to use a system of personal assessment, preferably of the self-assessment kind. An integration with the system of tax on wages and salaries would be required, to prevent a taxpayer from drawing twice on the basic exemption, once from his salary and again from his business income. On the other hand, it would not be in accordance with the principle of extreme simplification to allow wage and salary earners to enjoy a refund of withholding tax on these incomes as a result of declaring a loss from business activities.

With respect to agricultural income, major units should be treated like businesses, whereas small agricultural units should be subject to a simple scheme of presumptive taxation based on area, general quality, and location. In countries with a functioning system of purchasing agencies, it is, in theory, possible to impose a withholding tax on payments to agricultural producers, a tax that could be final for those of them not willing and able to produce proper accounts as a basis for a correct assessment of income. It is likely, however, that in many former centrally planned economies, much of the agricultural income will be realized by direct sales to consumers from producers in local market places. There is no sufficient reason to give these market sales a clear advantage over sales to wholesalers, millers, dairies, and abattoirs. On the other hand, an individual tax on presumed agricultural income, based on precise estimates of each individual crop, or number of animals could easily require as much of an administrative effort as an income tax based on real profits. It is therefore not recommended as a transition measure. The tax in the transition period should be simple.

Capital gains taxation would not be a practical proposal for the transition period. The establishment of a proper acquisition cost for those who receive property in the procedure of restitution of formerly seized property would be utterly complicated. For those who acquire property in the course of privatization, it might be easy enough to establish a basis, where their acquisition is for money. The technique being developed in several former centrally planned economies, however, is based on some voucher system, under which citizens are entitled to a certain amount in vouchers (that may or may not be defined in currency), and will use these to acquire securities. Applying a zero base to these acquisitions would to an extent act counter to the intention behind privatization, whereas little may be known about the actual market value of the vouchers at the time of acquisition.

It would seem easier to establish taxation of private capital gains at a later stage, when market values have been established. One could then use a D-day provision setting the date at which the base value is fixed for the future capital gains tax. In that context, the base value could be applied generally for all investors, regardless of how they acquired their property.

Definitions of capital gains vary between countries. It would seem rational, given the difficulty of introducing a system of private capital gains immediately, to adopt a system under which all business profits are taxed as such, with the capital gains concept restricted to private investments only. For businesses, an opening balance sheet has to be established for business profits tax purposes, as well as for purposes of accounting and control. Under that assumption, all profits referring to business assets could be regarded as business profits, and corresponding losses as business losses. This is the German rule, a country in which private capital gains are taxable as income only if the holding period is very short or the gains occur on the sale of shares representing a major holding. Obviously, the assumption that all gains on business assets constitute current income presupposes consistent treatment as realization for business purposes of all separations of business assets from the business, say, as a dividend in kind or for the private use of the owner of the business.

Corporate Income Tax

The important part in government financing previously taken by turnover tax, profits tax, and profit remittances from government enterprises will, to a large extent, have to be substituted for by a sales tax, preferably a VAT. To some extent, however, it will be indispensable to use corporate profits as a tax base. For this purpose, it will be important to build an organization for the assessment and collection of business taxes, possibly manned by staff earlier engaged in financial control, and rendered redundant in the course of privatization. The effort should be directed toward the more important enterprises first, and imply a financial reconstruction in which realistic opening balance sheets are established, on the basis of which genuine future business results can be computed.

It is important that valuation of assets in these opening balances is made in a business-oriented fashion. In other words, historic prices should not be relevant, and bad debts should be eliminated. The tendency has been for depreciation periods to be too long. This is accentuated even more when regard is taken to technical obsolescence, and disclosed when protected enterprises of a centrally planned economy are exposed to the international market.

It is not possible to generalize about the setting up of new opening balance sheets for government-owned enterprises in centrally planned economies. Arguments can be made for continuity, allowing excessive asset values be depreciated over some time, while at the same time keeping the enterprises responsible for the debt they may have incurred to government banks, and other enterprises. If such a solution is realistic, it mitigates the problems occurring with respect to treasury accounts, as well as those of other creditors. Sometimes, however, the state of affairs in the enterprises is so bad as to necessitate a complete reconstruction, with a drastic write-down of assets, and with elimination of debt that cannot possibly be honored in the future and has to be eliminated for the balance to show a sufficient equity base. This type of reconstruction will obviously have repercussions on creditors, who, in turn, may also need the same treatment. Obviously, the whole problem area is one that includes not only tax legislation, but the commercial code as well.

It is important to go about this procedure speedily, to give the enterprises a realistic financial base and make it possible for them to establish a new accountability to creditors and to the fiscal authority. The procedure is particularly urgent for the major enterprises, and should be pushed forward vigorously, without time consuming perfectionism. For the purpose of assuring that all enterprises have orderly accounts to begin with, opening balances could be established provisionally, with the possibility of revision within a period of six months or possibly a year.

Even if the new balance sheets are produced with the utmost speed, the operation will nevertheless be time-consuming, and there will be need for provisional tax to be levied in the meantime. It is obvious that the usual basis for provisional tax payments (i.e., the latest declared or assessed business profit, usually the one referring to the previous year) will not be available. Given the new principles of taxation, it is also inconceivable to use the traditional base for enterprise taxes or profit sharing. Therefore, as long as there is no opening balance to form the basis for a provisional estimate of expected profit, some other base has to be found for the current year payments of corporation tax. The possible alternatives are two: one, a percentage of gross receipts, and the other a percentage of gross profits. In practical terms, the former is somewhat easier to apply than the latter. The gross profits should, however, normally have a somewhat closer relationship to the net profit than the gross receipts have. For that reason, it is suggested that provisional payments of corporate tax be based on gross profits, obviously at a much lower percentage rate than the final tax on actual profits. As soon as a proper computation of net profits is possible, in other words, as soon as an opening balance has been established, and a net profit can be estimated, it should be permitted to switch over to the estimated net profit as a basis for provisional tax payments. For the final payments of corporate tax, it should be mandatory to use the net profit, but, as indicated above, it would possibly be necessary to keep a certain time period during which adjustments to the established opening balance would be permitted.

Final Comments

In the foregoing, no references have been made to the existence of special rules for foreign investments and joint ventures, these being treated in another chapter. Obviously, all reform measures discussed above have to be considered in the context of concessions already granted. Possibly, if the system is drastically changed, the climate might invite renegotiation, but caution must be exercised to avoid the impression that the country reneges on its legal obligations.

The word perfectionism has been used in the text. It might be worth pointing out that the warning against perfectionism is not a recommendation of laxitude. What is aimed at is realism. Rome was not built in one day, nor is a full-fledged modern tax system to be set up within a year or two. Therefore, it is important to have the proper priorities. These should be, first of all, to take care of the big revenue-raisers first, i.e., the general sales tax (turnover tax or VAT), major excises (tobacco, alcoholic beverages, petroleum products, and automobiles) and the tax on wages and salaries (including social security contributions), as well as taxes on major businesses and corporations. Experience tells that these taxes together represent almost all tax revenue. Other taxes such as estate or inheritance duties, capital gains tax, stamp duties, or license fees, may have significance in other respects but cannot compete as revenue-raisers. Revenue-raising is the number one problem that must be dealt with first.

Likewise, the administrative resources have to be concentrated, at least initially, on the largest taxpayers. In most centrally planned economies, the existing tax administration is oriented toward smaller taxpayers, the larger enterprises being submitted to audit in another context. It is essential to build a new tax administration with its main resources concentrated on the most important taxpayers. Again, priorities have to be set in a realistic fashion.

Once it was thought that the tax instrument would easily lend itself to all kinds of policy measures. Tax incentives were offered to influence individuals and enterprises in the direction of a number of different behavior patterns. In present times, the optimism surrounding this kind of interventionist fiscal policy has faded. There is a widespread understanding that subsidies worth giving in the first place might be better given directly over the budget, rather than in a hidden form as "tax expenditures." There is also a tendency to dismiss fiscal interventionism as over-ambitious, and to revive the old requirement that the tax should be neutral, not influencing the behavior dictated by the market place. While extreme positions of both kinds are counterproductive, it is only realistic to accept that in today's world, fiscal interventionism has few promoters, and that the general tendency is for countries to offer, and investors to demand, broad-based, simple systems with correspondingly low rates.

CHAPTER 9

Introducing Value-Added Taxes
Alan A. Tait

Command economies typically use a simple turnover tax on manufacturers. Such taxes cannot be moved forward or back because the state fixes the prices of outputs and inputs. The sales tax becomes a residual wedge between the retail price and the costs of production. Because the authorities are reluctant to change prices, yet costs of production may have to change (owing, perhaps, to external imported price changes), enterprises often find themselves unable to pay the turnover tax and having to bargain with the tax agencies to postpone their tax payment. The use of turnover taxes to compensate for perceived variations in profitability whether in China (Blejer and Szapary (1989), p. 8), Africa, or Central and Eastern Europe can lead to hundreds, if not thousands (3,000 in Hungary, see Lukács (1991)) of implicit rates. "The tax differed, depending on the codes, sizes, type of packaging, target consumer (children, adults, women, etc.), the nature of the inputs and raw materials used, the machinery and technology employed" (Vucher (1991)). This state of affairs means that the sales tax system of a command economy has no clearly defined, transparent relation to a commonly recognized legal tax base and a commonly applied tax rate structure. To replace such sales taxes by a value-added tax (VAT) must involve substantial changes in the tax coverage and many large changes in relative prices.

Because almost all revenue is derived directly from the (relatively few) state enterprises and cooperatives, officials and tax administrators are not organized to cope with a tax system that involves all enterprises and most income-earning individuals. In centrally planned economies the tax authorities are used to dealing with a few hundred or several thousand large enterprises. The concept of a flourishing, rapidly changing private sector, with many service industries, numerous financial institutions, and a competitive distribution trade, all involving (often small) enterprises that may open and close quite quickly, creating a large turnover in registration, is difficult for them to grasp. The collection, audit, and control mechanisms in no way correspond to a western style administrative system. Therefore, at the same time as profound changes in the political and economic structures are taking place, the whole sales tax administrative structure must be changed.

Further, frequently, centrally planned regimes, as a stabilization instrument, use some form of gross investment tax as a way of taxing capital. Under a typical European Community (EC) style VAT, full credit is given for the tax content of all inputs, including capital goods. To change from taxing capital, often in a highly discretionary way, to not doing so, confronts macroeconomic managers with major problems. The relative prices of capital goods may change too suddenly, and anticipation of such changes may lead to "bunching" of capital goods orders. Also the revenue sacrificed by not taxing capital goods may appear too much to be accommodated at once.

Managed prices also affect external trade. In the command economy the true burden of cascaded, uncertain, and often unknown, domestic sales taxes cannot be identified when goods are exported and therefore cannot be rebated. Nor can complementary taxes be imposed accurately on imports. Such sales taxation probably contributes to a trade deficit that must be compensated through other policy measures, including the exchange rate and this further distorts domestic cost and price structures. The change to a VAT means the sales tax will be fully identified for cross-border trade and will involve a changed attitude to economic and tax management.

This suggests a principal reason why such countries turn to a VAT as their preferred sales tax (and most intend to do so—see Table 1). The existing taxes induce distortions and impose an uneven burden on external trade. The fact that the VAT has been adopted by the EC is perceived, certainly by the economies of Central and Eastern Europe, as a major justification for introducing VAT; it puts them in the mainstream of modern sales-tax reform. Centrally planned economies outside Europe, especially in Asia, also note that the VAT is the premier sales tax recognized by GATT for full rebate on exports. However, the further argument that replacement of direct taxes (unrebated at export) for the VAT (rebated) will help exports is subject to important qualifications (see below).

In addition, some countries in transition simply wish sales taxes to carry a higher share of the revenue burden, and VAT is seen as a proven, reliable, buoyant, revenue source. This implies that the revenue to be replaced need not only be that associated with the old turnover tax. Many countries that introduced a VAT obtained a yield higher than initial estimates (Korea,

Table 1. Countries in Transition Adopting or Planning to Adopt VAT

	Date VAT[1] Introduced or Proposed	VAT Rates[2] Discussed or at Introduction
Bulgaria	Mid-1992	**10**
Czechoslovakia	1992	...
New German Länder	July 1990	7,**14**
Hungary	January 1988	0,15,**25**
Poland	1991/2	5,**18**
Romania	1992/3	**10**
U.S.S.R.	1993/4	...
Yugoslavia	1994	...

Sources: Various country reports.

[1]All dates and percentage rates are provisional and indicative, except for the New German Länder and Hungary.

[2]The zero rate is only mentioned where it covers a significant portion of household consumption, i.e., Hungary, 42 percent. Rates shown in bold are the standard rates applied to most goods and services.

Indonesia, Mexico, New Zealand, Portugal, and Tunisia) and the VAT in economies in transition could replace revenue that could have come from taxes that are more difficult and uncertain to administer (profits and income taxes).

However, the main advantage of a VAT, whether fully articulated or not, for economies in transition, is that the new sales tax structure helps break the vicious circle of the price formation mechanism and ad hoc interventions to correct microeconomic imbalances. It helps the economy move toward a fiscal system characterized with greater certainty for economic agents and more transparency for the authorities. It is worthwhile undertaking only if relative prices are allowed to change. If the governments retain the old habits of intervening through bilateral negotiations between the authorities and enterprises to "arrange" tax liabilities, then the advantages of VAT, allocative fairness and transparency, will be sacrificed. Traders in both public and private sectors liable to VAT must have their tax assessed without favor and must be obliged to pay or be liable to the prescribed penalties. A new attitude in this respect is probably one of the main advantages enforced by the introduction of a VAT.

Institutional Obstacles to Reform

Relative Power of Ministries

It is not often mentioned, but one of the most profound institutional obstacles to reform in centrally planned economies is the fundamental shift in power between ministries (and their ministers). In a command economy the ministry of planning is the most powerful, followed by some of the "heavy" ministries such as agriculture, power, industry, and, of course, defense. At the bottom of the influential heap are the ministry of finance and the central bank. In the command economy, the ministry of finance is simply a collection and accounting agency. The change to a more market-oriented economy involves a fundamental shift of power to the ministry of finance. It should become the most powerful ministry controlling the expenditure of other ministries and administering revenue collection in a dispassionate manner according to a legislated tax code. This means that, in the reform debates, the ministry of finance becomes the major protagonist for the change in taxation but most other ministries and agencies are, at best, lukewarm. The VAT is often one of the earliest tax reforms that the ministry of finance attempts; it also carries crucial implications for prices and administration. As such its introduction can be seen as a major test of the ability of the ministry of finance to establish its authority.

State and Private Sector

The administration of VAT involves substituting a sales tax organization (perhaps linked to a fledgling income tax department) for the traditional command economy organizational distinctions between socialized and nonsocialized sectors. In the usual VAT, the state is only taxable on the sale of goods and services if it competes with similar businesses in the private sector; of course, to all intents in command economies, there has been little or no private sector, so the issue did not arise. However, as the private sector expands the state enterprises cannot be in a tax privileged position. All state enterprises supplying goods and services must be liable to VAT. The rule that it is only when a state enterprise is in competition with the private sector that it is liable to VAT cannot be used in these circumstances. Such competition may not exist yet it must be encouraged. Therefore, all state enterprises must be liable to VAT so that *potential* private sector production is not stifled. This argues for a very broad-based VAT and powerful political voices will be raised against it.

Professions

Another major institutional obstacle is having to rethink and redraft the legal basis for the sales tax. Concepts that are unimportant in socialist economies must be introduced. What constitutes the supply of goods or services? Is the time of delivery, invoicing, availability, or payment of goods to be the definition of the time of supply? What will be the treatment of credit or installment sales? What is a taxable activity? What should be the VAT treatment of groups of companies (especially in a federal structure)? The whole structure of collection, penalties, and appeals for VAT must be rethought and applied to all registered taxpayers including state enterprises.

There are other institutional professional problems in training the VAT administrators, but clearly there may also be a problem to create the accounting profession to audit books of account in the private sector. Financial accounts in centrally planned economies, typically, simply validate the planned real economy. The accountancy profession as known and functioning in market economies does not necessarily exist. For instance, it has been held that in Poland there were only some 1,000 trained accountants, most of whom were contracted to work on the books of state enterprises. But the evaluation of such accounts, by an independent profession, as the "true and fair view of the state of affairs of the company" according to a Companies Act, is a major institutional hurdle.

Communications

Another hurdle is often the state of telecommunications. It simply is not realistic to consider on-line computer systems for VAT if the telephone lines are limited or connections unreliable. Realistic estimations often consider five to ten years to be the minimum time before up-to-date such systems can be set up (International Monetary Fund (1991b), Vol. 3, Chapter V. 4). In the meantime, alternative, more flexible systems must be sought involving stand alone regional computers and courier transfer of information to headquarters.

Such administrative or legal constraints impose their deadening hand on the speed at which the VAT reforms can take place. However, the creation of a timetable for VAT introduction is a crucial way to focus attention on the scale of changes needed and on their sequencing. "The IMF experts were also a great help in working out...a very detailed timetable of the...steps from the decision of principles, through the legislation work, the organization of a new tax administration, recruiting and training personnel, the computerization, to the publicity" (Kupa (1991)).

The Timetable

A detailed, well-articulated, timetable for the introduction of VAT forces those responsible to think carefully about what has to be done, the resources needed, and the sequence of actions. The tax administrations of centrally planned economies may not be used to formulating decision-making in this way, and the timetable formulation, in itself, becomes a teaching mechanism.

Chart 1 shows an abbreviated example of a VAT timetable which can be elaborated with much more detail. Nine broad areas are suggested as a convenient start to concentrate attention on specific tasks.

Some issues that are particularly time-consuming and important in introducing conventional VATs are sometimes thought by the authorities in economies in transition to be less important. For instance, in some countries (e.g., Australia, the United States) a two- or three-year parliamentary cycle is considered almost too short to get the policy and legislative changes (Timetable, Section 1) for VAT agreed to and into the law. In economies in transition, parliaments themselves are changing, there may be a flood of legislation on a broad range of issues, foreign financing may hinge on reforms, and knowledgeable criticism of legislation may be lacking. Such considerations may reduce the time needed to introduce the VAT compared with governments preoccupied with a constitutional timetable that dominates the legislative tactics for major tax reforms. However, the major restructuring of the tax administration and the training in modern tax administration may also lengthen the time needed for the VAT. The timetable shown in Chart 1 suggests 18 months as the lead time needed and this has proven to be a reasonable target, although it is also true that in most cases the initial estimates of the time needed have turned out to be too compressed and have, in nearly all cases, slipped by several months.

The whole problem of information and publicity (Timetable, Section 2) is almost dismissed in many economies in transition. Organizations that have been used to telling a limited number of state enterprises what to do are not tuned to gaining the willing participation of taxpayers in the administration of VAT. Many ex-socialist tax authorities will claim that they can "concertina" the time needed to introduce VAT by chopping out the time needed for taxpayer education. Of course, this is probably not the best way to introduce a new market based sales tax, and yet it can be difficult to shake the authorities' conviction that such taxpayer education is unimportant. The whole idea of writing a *Guide to VAT* for all possible taxpayers, or special pamphlets on specialized interests (farmers, small retailers, secondhand goods merchants, exporters) is often a novelty in these countries, as is the suggestion of advertising around key dates in the VAT timetable (registration, implementation, first returns). Again, seminars to explain the operation of VAT to Chambers of Commerce or professional bodies is treated as a novel idea, as are advisory visits to educate taxpayers

Chart 1. Timetable—VAT Introduction Over Eighteen Months

	Months to Introduction of VAT																		Post VAT		
	1	2	3	4	5	6	7	8	9	10	11	12	13	14	15	16	17	18	19	20	21
1. Policy and legislation																					
Allocate development budget								x													
Establish VAT Development Unit								x													
Appoint staff to Development Unit								x	x												
Resolve outstanding policy issues									x	x	x										
Consult other organizations on law									x	x	x										
Revise current draft of VAT law									x	x	x										
Finalize draft VAT law											x										
Draft law to Council of Ministers											x										
Present law to Parliament											x	x									
Pass law												x	x								
2. Publicity and education																					
General sectoral discussions										x		x	x	x	x	x	x	x	x		
Hold seminars for businesses											x	x	x	x	x	x	x	x	x		
Draft and print VAT Guide													x	x	x	x	x				
Draft and print Registration Guide													x	x	x	x	x	x	x		
Draft and print standard account books																x	x	x	x		
Prepare VAT material for consumers													x	x	x	x	x	x	x		
Prepare trader specific pamphlets													x	x	x	x	x	x			
Advertise registration period																x	x	x	x		
Advertise implementation date																				x	
Advertise first payment date																				x	
3. Organizational																					
Decide organizational structure									x	x	x										
Estimate number of taxpayers									x	x											
Calculate staff needed for VAT									x	x	x	x									
Appoint senior territorial staff													x	x							
Allocate staff to audit positions														x	x	x	x				
Allocate initial processing staff														x	x	x	x				
Allocate remaining staff														x	x	x	x	x			

4. Operational issues
   - Decide broad operational issues
   - Design registration system
   - Design return/payment process system
   - Design audit system

5. Computer development
   - Complete user specifications-registration
   - Develop registration system
   - Test registration system
   - Load registration database
   - Complete user specifications full system
   - Develop full system
   - Test and revise full system

6. Forms
   - Design and print registration form
   - Design and print return form

7. Manuals (Staff instructions)
   - Allocate staff to write manuals
   - Prepare technical manual
   - Processing and procedures manual
   - Advisory activity manual
   - Audit manual

8. Training development and delivery
   - Technical training
   - Return processing training
   - Advisory training
   - Audit training

9. Registration and implementation
   - Issue registration forms
   - Conduct advisory visits
   - Issue first return forms
   - Receive first payments
   - Identify defaulters
   - Pursue defaulters

Task	Schedule marks
4. Operational issues	
Decide broad operational issues	x
Design registration system	x x
Design return/payment process system	x x
Design audit system	x
5. Computer development	
Complete user specifications-registration	x x
Develop registration system	x x
Test registration system	x x
Load registration database	x
Complete user specifications full system	x x x
Develop full system	x x x x
Test and revise full system	x x x xxx
6. Forms	
Design and print registration form	x x x x
Design and print return form	x x x x
7. Manuals (Staff instructions)	
Allocate staff to write manuals	x x
Prepare technical manual	x x
Processing and procedures manual	x x x
Advisory activity manual	x x x
Audit manual	x x
8. Training development and delivery	
Technical training	x x
Return processing training	x x x
Advisory training	x x x x
Audit training	x x
9. Registration and implementation	
Issue registration forms	x x
Conduct advisory visits	x x
Issue first return forms	xx
Receive first payments	xx
Identify defaulters	xx
Pursue defaulters	x

in their obligations, but the authorities are not prepared to allocate much of their efforts and workforce to such suggestions.

The importance of careful design and creation of VAT forms (Timetable, Section 6) can be educational. VAT forms cannot be designed until fundamental decisions are taken about the tax base and rate structure which, in turn, depend on successive legislative actions. In at least one economy in transition the whole question of the design of tax forms was a revelation of modern tax management to the authorities.

Again, the concept of tax manuals (technical, processing, procedures, and advisory—Timetable, Section 7) is often not well understood. The old turnover taxes have been simple to administer and the need for careful management of more complex taxes poses an administrative challenge. Writing such VAT manuals can prove to be much more time consuming than expected.

Training (Timetable, Section 8), in economies where tax reform has been infrequent, is not seen as important, or, at least the time needed to train officials fully to implement the VAT, is easily underestimated. It has already been stated that the VAT is often the start of a major organizational overhaul in tax administration. It is important to concentrate on getting it right for technical training, return processing, and, especially, audit training. The time needed for such training is often not fully appreciated (for a much fuller account of administration and staffing issues for the VAT, see Tait (1991b), Chapter 12).

Some Major Changes
Manufacturers, Wholesalers, and Small Traders

In centrally planned economies the whole concept of a sales tax, including wholesalers and retailers, is alien. Government tax relations have been primarily with state enterprises; monitoring transactions between enterprises has been mainly by checking the physical flow of goods. Although it is possible to introduce a VAT on imports and manufactured goods alone as a way to initiate a VAT (e.g., Indonesia), in the more flexible and market-based economy to which it is assumed the economies in transition are moving, the disadvantages of a VAT concentrated on manufacturing would rapidly become apparent. Vertically integrated firms and firms with implicit agreements with their purchasers would shift profit centers downstream and erode the VAT revenue. Neither "manufacturing" or "wholesale" are clear concepts, and to define them for tax purposes is almost impossible and, in practice, has led to complex formulas, which have left far too much discretion to the tax authorities. From the outset the liability to VAT in economies in transition should be defined for all traders through to the retail stage with an exemption applied only on the basis of turnover.

This means that "small traders" must be defined. It is a characteristic of economies in transition that past economic management has concentrated on production from large scale enterprises. Small entrepreneurs have been discouraged. Therefore, typically at the outset of the transitional stage, small traders will hardly be a problem. One of the first indications of the reform programs working is the emergence of many small trading activities (e.g., Hungary and Poland). The VAT should be designed so that such small trading activities are exempt but, if they are successful and become moderate to medium-size traders, they will be obliged to register for VAT. A characteristic of the authorities when considering the new VAT is often their anxious determination to try and tax all traders and a frequent reluctance to establish an initially generous threshold below which small traders will not be taxed. In a sense, this is a legacy from past administrations where entrepreneurial success and "profits" were frowned upon. Establishing a reasonably high initial threshold for VAT makes administrative sense. "Probably the most crucial function for simplifying the administration of VAT (apart from the number of rates) is the choice of threshold for liability to the tax" (Tait (1991c)). A higher threshold eliminates a mass of small potential taxpayers who often find it difficult to keep the appropriate records, who frequently deal in cash, and who technically find it difficult to cooperate with the tax authorities. A higher threshold allows administrators to concentrate their valuable time on those larger enterprises where more revenue is at risk and where the rewards of better administration will be greater.

A high threshold does give small business a trading advantage. Some firms may be tempted to understate their sales to remain below the threshold or even to divide their businesses to keep each potential registered trader below the threshold. However, it is also found that small traders who are significant suppliers to larger enterprises who are registered for VAT will volunteer to be registered themselves so that their purchasers can claim their credit for the tax content on the small traders sales. This means that small traders should always be given the option to opt into VAT.

In some centrally planned economies there have been extensive schemes levying a presumptive tax on small independent traders (e.g., in Poland). Such presumptive taxes are based on indicators, such as the number of employees, the type of trade conducted, and the location in the country. These lead to a presumed turnover figure and an implicit rate of tax. There may be a temptation, during the transition period, to retain such presumptive schemes on small enterprises as a way of compensating for their exemption from VAT. In most circumstances such schemes, if administered fairly, absorb an unreasonable amount of administrative services which would be much better put to the administration of the full VAT. Given that economies in transition wish to encourage the small trading sector it would seem better to exempt small traders entirely from presumptive taxes.

Agriculture

Of course, in many countries the most common small trader is the farmer. This may not be true in economies in transition. In many of these economies small farms have been amalgamated into large state enterprises or agricultural cooperatives. These agricultural businesses are usually on a large scale and frequently involve extensive manufacturing, such as slaughtering, food processing, plant maintenance, machinery repair and manufacturing, transport, and retailing. In the transitional phase of these economies, which presumably should involve the movement to encourage private farming and farming-related activities, the sensible treatment under VAT would be to treat small farmers under the general rule for small traders. So small farmers would be exempt until their turnover reaches a threshold sufficiently large to require them to register.

Large agribusinesses would have to be completely part of the VAT system and keep their accounts and records in a manner that satisfies the tax authorities. The large agricultural businesses would be able to claim tax credits for their current and capital inputs, but they would be taxed on their value added. Small farmers would not be taxed on their value added, but would have to pay VATs on their inputs; however, as the usual input for a small farmer is restricted to seeds, fertilizers, pesticides, and some simple agricultural machinery, the tax on inputs as a percentage of their sales would not be a major cost. If a small farmer was in a particular form of business where his, for instance, capital costs became a significant proportion of inputs then he would be free to register in the normal manner and claim credit for the VAT on those inputs.

An alternative that has been used, for example, in Hungary, is to apply a zero rate to the major and uniquely agricultural farming inputs, for example, pesticides and fertilizers, but not tools, machinery, or building materials. However, zero rating such inputs invites continuous claims for other inputs to be added to the zero rating formula (Lukács, 1991). Basically, it is better to exempt small farmers and require larger, more capital-intensive farm businesses to register as normal VAT taxpayers.

VAT Base

As in most existing VAT systems, the administrators and politicians in economies in transition would agree that health, education, social, and religious services should not be taxed. Although there are many interesting matters that can be discussed under the tax base, the major changes for these economies probably involve the attitude toward the taxation of food, housing, financial services, and the public provision of goods and services. A brief comment on each is offered.

Food

In most countries the taxation of food is an emotional issue. In the EC food is usually taxable. Indeed, not to tax it can reduce the potential VAT base by up to 25 percent. Given the limited availability of consumer durable goods in many of the economies in transition, the likelihood is that expenditures on food and housing will form a larger proportion of household expenditure than in the countries in the EC. In like manner, this means that to treat these goods under the VAT in a preferential manner will erode the tax base by more than would be the case in other countries. It is therefore a major change for the authorities to face up to the need to tax food under the value-added tax. It is indicative of the political sensitivity of this issue that the 5 percent sales tax introduced early in 1991 in the Russian Republic was already canceled on food before May in the same year (International Monetary Fund (1991b)).

In practice, it is probably unrealistic to seek to include basic foodstuffs under the VAT in economies in transition. The sales of produce directly from the farm with no processing or manufacturing involved (e.g., fruits and vegetables) are difficult to monitor and are probably best exempted. Much the same applies to food sold in its more or less raw or semiprocessed state (e.g., meat and dairy products). Given the large markets in direct sales by smallholders of their own produce in many economies in transition, it is probably impractical to subject such "farm gate" sales to VAT. Rather than using the zero rate or exempting all food sales, exempting basic foodstuffs could be considered.

Not to tax food at all under the value-added tax requires the use of the zero rate (as in the United Kingdom, Ireland, and Hungary). The zero rate for food is an extremely blunt instrument to achieve the desired end, presumably of defending the living standard of the poor. The zero rate favors the rich as well as the poor, and the rich tend to spend absolutely much more on food than the poor. If basic unprocessed foodstuffs are not subject to VAT, the poorer households are protected to a major extent and there will still be a substantial tax base on processed or packaged food. "With hindsight, it would have been more realistic to apply the zero rate to a narrower, more strictly defined group of products, services and introduce a standard rate of about 18–20 percent" (Lukács (1991)).

This processed food can be taxed at the standard rate or at some lower rate. This is the practice in most EC countries where lower rates are applied to food, but the rate is sufficiently high to ensure that VAT is payable and there is no refund. This lower rate applies to all food products including those served in restaurants.

The problem with admitting a lower rate for food is that it creates the potential lobby for other goods and services to be moved to the lower rate. Quite quickly the producers of clothing and electricity would claim that these were necessary goods consumed by low-income families and should be taxed at the lower rate. Thus the value-added tax base can be quickly eroded. Essentially, the lower rate should be used only for food.

Housing

Another major change in attitude is involved with the tax treatment of housing. In many countries in transition housing has been vested in the state. The state has owned the property, and individual property rights have been strictly limited. Where individuals have had the right to own property, they have been able to borrow money at low rates for long-term mortgages, thus creating a quite separate problem for interest rates and bond markets. As far as the VAT is concerned, the idea that it should be applied to all new housing comes as a considerable shock to both the authorities and the public.

Most of these economies in transition are suffering from an acute shortage of new housing. The housing stock is old, or if recently built, is suffering from rapid decay and is in need of substantial repair and maintenance. A VAT that taxes new housing, repair, and maintenance is seen as a politically damaging tax in a country attempting a rapid transition to a free-market economy.

In the conventional VAT all building materials, as well as the value added of builders and repair and maintenance services, are taxed at the standard rate. Attempts to ameliorate this treatment of housing under VAT cause problems. To relieve housing from VAT requires the application of the zero rate (as in the United Kingdom and Hungary). As mentioned previously, this is an extremely crude instrument to achieve a given objective; housing constitutes a major portion of richer household expenditure, and to extend the zero rate to housing gives a large advantage to the better-off households as well as the poor.

Moreover, as repair and maintenance is still taxable under the standard VAT rate, this treatment requires a distinction between "new housing" and repair and maintenance. In practice, this proves extremely difficult. In Hungary, the authorities recognized that in an economy in transition many households would wish to apply their energies to extending or building new houses themselves by their own labor. This was to be encouraged by allowing such households to register for the building they were doing and to claim the full credit for the VAT on the building materials they purchased. This seems a straightforward proposal, but in practice it turned into a major administrative problem for the authorities. Local tax offices were overwhelmed by thousands of individuals presenting hundreds of tax invoices for building materials, which proved extremely difficult to validate as being only for the particular household in question. In fact, such treatment is likely to prove a major loophole in the tax. The long-run solution is to tax new housing under a standard rate VAT, and if the authorities wish to give some encouragement to housing, this is better done through special borrowing facilities, for example, to first-time new housing borrowers.

Financial Services

Another major change in attitude is involved in the treatment of financial services under the VAT. Many of the centrally planned economies have treated market-provided financial services with suspicion and have tended to concentrate the provision of such services in the state. A major part of the transitional movement is the creation and expansion of private-sector financial services.

It is an advantage of the EC form of VAT that financial services are untaxed. That is, the value added they provide is untaxed, but they pay VAT on their inputs and cannot claim it as a credit. This treatment should encourage the expansion of financial services vis-à-vis other goods and services liable to VAT. This may not prove entirely popular with the authorities in economies in transition, but prolonged and thoughtful consideration (for example, in Canada and New Zealand) has convinced these countries that, on the whole, such financial services cannot be taxed under VAT. This should be the preferred treatment in economies in transition and should be welcomed. It would be unwise for those economies to experiment with methods that many sophisticated countries have prudently decided would not pay.

Rate Structure

Many countries that have adopted VAT in recent years (Canada, Japan, Korea, Mexico, and New Zealand) have decided to use a single rate. Even countries that initially used many rates (e.g., France and Italy) have moved toward fewer. Certainly the emphasis is on fewer rates, and recently the EC has recommended that only two rates should be used, a standard rate between 15 and 20 percent, and a lower rate between 4 and 9 percent. Yet, there remain temptations to use multiple rates for VAT and, given the experience of most of the economies in transition that have previously used dozens if not hundreds of sales-tax rates, the temptation to carry these numerous rates into the VAT is strong. Indeed, the change from using many (implicit) rates of sales tax to using only one or two may be a major challenge facing the regimes.

The justifications for using multiple rates of VAT are basically two (for a more extended discussion, see Tait (1991a)). First, in the tax changeover, countries frequently wish to minimize relative price changes. They are tempted to try and match the value-added tax rates broadly to the old tax rates so as to limit the final impact on consumer prices. Second, they fear the effects of using a single rate on a broadly defined VAT base that would penalize lower-income households. Lower rates of VAT could favor goods that are prominent in the budget of low-income households, and higher rates could be levied on goods and services that were an increasing proportion of higher-income household consumption.

Oddly enough, the first justification for using multiple rates, to minimize relative price changes, is one of the least applicable to economies in transition. These economies are faced with massive relative price changes in both goods and factor markets. If the market is to act as an indicator of the relative scarcity of resources, relative prices must be allowed to change. Given that most of these regimes have existed for decades with prices distorted by state intervention, the implied relative price changes to allow the market to operate are enormous. Whether the VAT uses one, two, or three rates becomes a somewhat trivial consideration compared with the massive changes of prices throughout the economy. In these circumstances, the major administrative advantage of having a single rate VAT should dominate the discussion.

The desire to shield lower-income households from the full effect of applying a standard rate VAT across the board is linked to the discussion immediately above. Households will be affected by an enormous range of relative price changes, and the relative net expenditure outcome for each household will vary considerably according to individual household circumstances. Investigations show that VAT is a relatively ineffective instrument to narrow differences in pretax incomes and by extension to eliminate the impact of the tax on the poor. In economies in transition, the introduction of the VAT is likely to be followed closely by the introduction of personal income taxes and the expansion of a security net through enhanced social and welfare transfers. It is generally agreed that help to low-income households can be much more precisely achieved by targeting transfers to low-income households through the income tax and social security systems than by making broad categories of goods and services liable to VAT.

The VAT is not meant to be used for economic and social ends. It is intended primarily as a major buoyant revenue source. Far better to simplify its administration and ensure that it is administered effectively than to erode its efficiency through exemptions and multiple rates. Indeed most economies in transition appear to have accepted these arguments and seem to be moving to accept only two rates (see Table 1).

Effects

Prices

Linked to the discussion in the previous section is the effect of VAT on prices. The authorities in countries in transition have traditionally contained price changes by direct intervention and are uncomfortable with the idea of allowing price changes moving through the entire economy to be reflected in final retail price changes. As already mentioned, a major requirement to be anticipated with the introduction of VAT is a large number of changes in relative prices. Depending on the constituents of the consumer price index, this is likely to produce a major change in the cost of living. The expressed worry is that such a change will be inflationary.

However, why should the introduction of a VAT be inflationary? If the VAT replaces an existing turnover tax to yield an equal revenue, there will be changes in relative prices, but no overall price increase. Indeed, even if the VAT generates a net increase in revenue, a tax increase, other things being equal, should be deflationary rather than inflationary. It is only if other actions are taken through, for instance, indexation and increasing the money supply (indexation has already been mentioned as a possible palliative to price increases in the U.S.S.R.) that a general price increase could occur. In other words, it is not the VAT itself that can be inflationary, but other policies that make it so.

The timing of the introduction of VAT may influence the price effects. If there is great uncertainty about both specific and general price changes, as is likely in economies in transition, then traders (including state enterprises) may use this as an opportunity to widen margins, but again this would only be inflationary if organized labor attempted to recoup the erosion of real incomes by increasing their share to offset the expanded share going to profits.

Experience in other countries that have introduced a value-added tax suggests it is possible to introduce a VAT, and sometimes even to increase the yield of sales taxation, and not to shift, or to increase the rate of change of, the consumer price index. There is no necessary correlation between introducing a VAT and an increase in inflation. Along with all the other price changes associated with market-oriented reform it is difficult to see why the introduction of VAT in an economy in transition should have any effect on inflation. Indeed, all the changes in relative prices associated with an economy in transition are releasing a repressed inflation of the past. This should mostly be a once-and-for-all increase in the price level, provided that monetary and other fiscal policies are supportive (Wolf (1990), p. 5).

Regressivity and Equity

Another major change for the economies in transition is an explicit preoccupation with the effects of taxation on the distribution of income. This may well come to a head with the introduction of the value-added tax and be combined with the first experience of genuinely free parliamentary debate when questions about the distribution of income and wealth can be raised and be subject to a free vote. A straightforward single-rate VAT and few exemptions must mean that the payment by low-income households will be a higher proportion of their incomes (and expenditures) than payments by higher-income households. That is, the VAT will be regressive.

This makes it all the more important that items consumed as household income rises should be liable to the VAT, and this typically means services that have frequently been untaxed in such economies, for example, electricity, telephones, professional services, hotels, and restaurants. The question of whether or not VAT is regressive in these economies is likely to become very political, but it is by no means simple. The question to be asked is whether a VAT is more regressive than the alternative, and further to consider the VAT simply as a unit of the overall tax system and, indeed, as a unit of the overall budgetary system.

VAT is adopted because it is a potentially buoyant revenue source. It is replacing taxes with which the authorities are dissatisfied. If it is replacing taxes that are highly distortionary, using multiple rates, taxing capital and exports, then, the VAT is clearly an improvement.

Also the question must be investigated, since revenue must somehow be provided, about what taxes would be raised if VAT is not introduced. Would excises be increased? Taxes on tobacco, alcohol, and soft drinks are likely to be even more regressive than the VAT. A payroll tax for social security, often levied as a proportional tax, might be even more regressive than the VAT.

Of course, the VAT is only part of the overall tax system. As already mentioned, the VAT is not supposed to be an instrument of income redistribution. Income, property, and wealth taxes are designed to redistribute income and wealth between households and individuals. It is the overall impact of the entire tax system on households that is important and not just the impact of any one element.

Further, even more important than the overall tax system is the overall budget impact. It is widely argued that the government's impact on the relative positions of the poor and the rich is probably even more effectively managed through the way in which the government spends its revenue than the way in which it gets it. Well-designed transfer systems that can accurately target the low-income households at risk are probably more effective than the broad-based and multiple-rate impacts of a sales tax. By focusing attention on the broader issues of the overall budgetary impact of government revenue and expenditure decisions, the VAT introduction may do more to focus debate on the overall impact of government decisions on distribution.

Exports

It is sometimes held that the substitution of a VAT for the hidden turnover taxes will help exports. As the VAT is fully rebated on exports, but the previous sales taxes and direct sales taxes have not been, it is suggested that substituting VAT for these taxes could help the balance of payments and current account.

To evaluate the size of the trade benefit from the changeover to VAT requires assessments on the response of producers to the shift in the ratio of producer prices of exports to producer prices of domestic sales, the response of consumers of exports to price change, and the negative response of domestic consumers to market prices of imports relative to market prices of domestically produced goods. In the circumstances of economies in transition, with the huge relative changes in prices and the uncertainty generated, the impact of VAT on all these various assessments is likely to be relatively small.

The further argument that exports might be encouraged by the substitution of the VAT, rebated on exports, for direct taxes that have not been so rebated, is also subject to great uncertainty. If there is a budget constraint, the government revenue forgone by substituting a VAT (which is rebated) for direct taxes (which were not) must be replaced by raising other domestic taxes. In one way or another, real household income is likely to be reduced, and this is likely to encourage claims for wage increases, which eventually would filter through into manufacturing costs and erode the competitive advantage gained for exports. Any advantage of the VAT substituted for direct taxes would be temporary.

Overall, it is likely that any short-run gain for exports will be brief and that no long-run advantage will be gained from the substitution of VAT for direct domestic taxes (Tait (1991b)).

Federal and State Issues

Another characteristic of economies in transition is that the move to free markets and free elections is frequently accompanied by upsurges in enthusiasm for local minority issues (Czechoslovakia, Ethiopia, Yugoslavia, USSR). This usually raises the issue of local finance and clearly the VAT, as a major revenue source, is eyed as a potential lucrative base for state or republic tax revenue.

As both experience and debate have shown, in a federation VAT is not a good state or local tax. Federal countries that have tried to give varying degrees of freedom to subfederal governments to alter VAT bases and rates (e.g., Argentina, Brazil, Mexico) are not especially happy examples to follow. The lengthy discussions over alternatives for federal/ provincial VATs in Canada showed how unattractive the options were. The protracted debate in the EC, first favoring the country-of-origin principle but now about to be based on the destination principle, exemplifies the practical problems involved. A federal country that has used the VAT satisfactorily (Germany) emphasizes the need for federal legislation to determine the structure, base, and rates of the VAT, and although collection is in the hands of the states (*Länder*), a strong revenue-sharing agreement is needed to ensure equitable distribution between the federal government and the states (and even in Germany any alteration of this revenue-sharing agreement has proved a delicate political matter).

The basic problem is that for VAT revenue to be apportioned within a federation, the VAT content of goods and services crossing (state or provincial) boundaries must be checked and settlements made. The only watertight way to do this is to have customs border controls clearly impractical in a federation. The EC, after protracted debate, has adopted an interim solution from 1993 to 1996 (when perhaps a more permanent "clearing house" system will be developed). After 1993, all controls and payments of VAT at EC borders will be scrapped, as will all customs documents for intra-Community trade (saving some 50 million forms a year, each with 54 questions to be answered). Exporters to other EC members will zero-rate exports. The "time of supply" for VAT payment will no longer be at the frontier, but instead will be at the time the importing firm makes its periodic return. The big problem is that, as goods cross borders tax-free, a potential for fraud on a huge scale arises if the goods can be diverted and sold in a domestic market without a liability to VAT being established. The more states or provinces in a federation, the greater the probability of fraud.

The EC proposes to meet this problem by requiring the largest firms in each country to make quarterly reports of the VAT numbers of their customers in other member countries and the total value of trade with each. In addition, countries can supplement these returns by spotcheck audits. The proposal (by France) to oblige traders to make detailed lists of the value and customers' identity for each transaction to another member country was rejected because it would have placed too large a burden on firms (especially smaller traders—see "World Tax Report" (January 1991), pp. 1–2). Moreover, states or provinces within a federation cannot choose VAT rates that are significantly different. Any country or state maintaining rates strikingly higher than its neighbors would find itself losing trade and would be obliged to bring its rates into line.

All this suggests the unenviable alternatives open to a federation that wants to use VAT for state revenues. While the EC has to adopt such recording obligations on its traders as a move to eventual full integration, it seems bizarre to increase the costs of compliance so massively in a federation simply because of reluctance to agree on a revenue-sharing agreement. It would seem that the sorts of returns needed to establish a statistical validation for a revenue-sharing formula would be more simple to supply and collect than the onerous requirements of the EC. Moreover, if the VAT administration (whether at federal or state level) deals with a unified base and rate structure, the revenue is more secure and fraud less likely.

Basically, VAT is not designed to be a local tax. Let us concentrate on its virtues as a broad-based revenue buoyant tax and not try to tinker with it either for income distribution purposes or to accommodate subnational revenue needs.

References

Blejer, Mario S., and Gyorgy Szapary, "The Evolving Role of Fiscal Policy in Centrally Planned Economies Under Reform: The Case of China," IMF Working Paper 89/26 (Washington: International Monetary Fund, 1989).

International Monetary Fund (1991a), "Soviet cabinet approves crises economy steps," *Morning Press*, May 17, 1991.

——— (1991b), International Bank for Reconstruction and Development, Organization for Economic Cooperation and Development, European Bank for Reconstruction and Development, *A Study of the Soviet Economy*, Vol. 3 (Paris: OECD, 1991).

Kupa, Mihály, "Implementation of Tax Reform in Hungary: Political, Transitional, and Administrative Aspects," *Economies in Transition: The Role of Tax Reform in Central and Eastern European Countries* (Paris: IMF/OECD, 1991).

Lukács, J., "VAT In Hungary," *Economies in Transition: The Role of Tax Reform in Central and Eastern European Countries* (Paris: IMF/OECD, 1991).

Tait, Alan A. (1991a), "Designing a VAT in Eastern Europe: Issues of Base and Rates," *Economies in Transition: The Role of Tax Reform in Central and Eastern Europe* (Paris: IMF/OECD, 1991).

——— (1991b), *Value-Added Tax: International Practice and Problems*, second reprint (Washington: International Monetary Fund, 1991.

——— (1991c), "VAT Policy Issues," *VAT Policy and Administration*, IMF Occasional Paper (Washington: International Monetary Fund, 1991).

Vucher, S., "Problems with regard to the introduction of a value-added tax in Bulgaria," *Economies in Transition: The Role of Tax Reform in Central and Eastern European Countries* (Paris: IMF/OECD, 1991).

Wolf, Thomas A., "Reform, Inflation, and Adjustment in Planned Economies," *Finance and Development*, March 1990.

"World Tax Report," *Financial Times,* January 1991.

PART III

Public Expenditure

CHAPTER 10

Foreign Trade Taxes and Subsidies
Van-Can Thai

Unlike in market-oriented economies, where foreign trade tax and subsidies serve well-known policy objectives (industrial development, trade policy, balance of payments or budgetary revenue), in centrally planned economies they served different objectives. While the price equalization system was aimed in general at insulating domestically controlled prices from variations in international prices and in particular at promoting a planned division of labor and at contributing to specialization among CMEA member countries, it had tax and subsidy consequences. Tariffs were used as an instrument to obtain trade concessions from market-oriented economies rather than to protect domestic industries.

With the demise of central planning and the collapse of the CMEA, a number of former centrally planned economies have already abolished the price equalization system and are in the process of formulating a market-based external tax system. The paper focuses on common institutional features of foreign trade taxation and subsidization shared by selected European and Asian countries in transition; it nevertheless makes reference to individual countries in appropriate cases.[1] It also explores the design of the current foreign trade taxation, taking into account the coordination with other indirect taxes, including the turnover tax or its successor, value-added tax (VAT), the administrative capacity, and various objectives such as stabilization, protection and growth. More broadly, the nature and sequencing of foreign trade tax, tariff and subsidy reform will

Note: The author would like to thank, without implicating, George Kopits who provided guidance and was involved at all stages of this paper; Vito Tanzi for his encouragement and helpful discussions on an earlier draft; and Chris Wu for her able statistical assistance. The views expressed in the paper do not necessarily represent those of the International Monetary Fund.

[1]Specifically Bulgaria, Czechoslovakia, Hungary, Romania, Poland, the U.S.S.R., Yugoslavia, China, and Mongolia.

be discussed in the context of an overhaul of the domestic price system, exchange rate policy, nontariff barriers, and state enterprise sector during the transition period. Within this framework, the paper reviews the foreign trade taxation and subsidization in the past, including the fiscal implications of the price equalization system. It then analyzes the present trends before examining the scope for further reform. Some conclusions are presented in the final section.

System Under Central Planning

The most prominent feature common to the countries under study was that foreign trade taxation assumed a passive role as it was completely subject to central planning. Tariffs practically had no protective role and foreign trade taxes and subsidies have almost exclusively been derived from the operations of the price equalization system which taxed and subsidized both imports and exports.

Besides this common denominator, these countries during 1985–89 also exhibited the following main features. First, almost all foreign trade tax revenue was derived from imports. Second, the structure of foreign trade taxes, although varying from country to country, was more similar to developing countries than to industrial countries. The ratio of import levies to GDP ranging from 1.5 percent in China to 3.8 percent in the U.S.S.R. was closer to the 4.3 percent observed in developing countries[2] than to the less than 1 observed in industrial countries. The two exceptions were Czechoslovakia with less than 1 percent at one end of the spectrum and Mongolia with 17 percent at the other end (Table 1). This ratio despite the falling foreign trade transactions relative to GDP (except Poland) increased in Eastern European countries, reflecting in part the need for more revenue to contain the fiscal deficits. It declined, however, in the other countries owing to a fall in imports relative to GDP, to organizational problems (Mongolia, the U.S.S.R., and Yugoslavia) or to import liberalization (China). Third, export taxes, where they were present (Bulgaria, Poland, Mongolia, and the U.S.S.R.), were levied mainly on "hard" goods. These were goods, such as raw materials or energy products (mainly from the U.S.S.R.), with high demand on world markets and with domestic prices lower than international prices. Export levies varied between 1 percent of GDP in Poland[3] and 3 percent in the U.S.S.R. and tended to decrease over time. Fourth, all countries, except China and Yugoslavia, granted subsidies to exports which accounted for almost all

---

[2]Figures relating to these countries are taken from Tanzi (1991b).
[3]This was about the same percentage as in developing countries.

Table 1. Countries in Transition: Taxes and Subsidies on Foreign Trade, 1985–89
(In percent of GDP[1])

	1985	1986	1987	1988	1989	Average 1985–89
Bulgaria						
Taxes and duties	2.95	3.38	6.24	4.28	3.51	4.07
Imports	1.88	1.86	4.90	2.63	2.33	2.72
Exports	1.06	1.51	1.34	1.65	1.18	1.35
Subsidies	8.02	8.63	9.04	5.30	4.09	7.02
Net Taxes(+)/Net Subsidies(−)	−5.07	−5.26	−2.79	−1.02	−0.58	−2.94
Czechoslovakia						
Taxes and duties[2]	0.53	0.72	1.41	2.15	0.97	1.16
Imports	0.03	0.03	0.03	0.04	0.07	0.04
Exports	—	—	—	—	—	—
Subsidies	1.86	2.53	2.52	2.51	1.83	2.25
Net Taxes(+)/Net Subsidies(−)	−1.33	−1.81	−1.11	−0.36	−0.86	−1.09
Hungary						
Taxes and duties[2]	3.08	3.55	2.83	3.05	4.04	3.31
Imports	2.67	3.00	2.83	2.58	2.87	2.79
Exports	—	—	—	—	—	0.00
Subsidies	4.07	4.08	4.17	4.22	2.62	3.83
Net Taxes(+)/Net Subsidies(−)	−1.00	−0.53	−1.34	−1.17	1.42	−0.52
Poland						
Taxes and duties[2]	3.67	3.58	3.36	4.03	...	3.54
Imports	1.55	1.71	1.92	1.97	...	1.73
Exports	1.19	0.98	0.32	0.20	...	0.83
Subsidies	4.42	3.88	3.21	3.84	...	3.84
Net Taxes(+)/Net Subsidies(−)	−0.76	−0.30	0.15	0.19	...	−0.30
Romania						
Taxes and duties	—	—	—	0.90	0.99	0.38
Imports	—	—	—	...	...	...
Exports	—	—	—	...	...	...
Subsidies	0.76	—	2.11	—	0.30	0.63
Net Taxes(+)/Net Subsidies(−)	−0.76	—	−2.11	0.90	0.69	−0.26
U.S.S.R.						
Taxes and duties	8.37	7.17	7.38	6.16	6.18	7.05
Imports	4.02	3.88	3.82	3.42	3.65	3.76
Exports	4.35	3.29	3.56	2.74	2.53	3.30
Subsidies	...	0.19	0.98	1.11	1.02	0.82
Net Taxes(+)/Net Subsidies(−)	...	6.98	6.40	5.05	5.16	5.90
Yugoslavia						
Taxes and duties	2.64	2.64	2.80	2.97	1.79	2.57
Imports	2.64	2.64	2.80	2.95	1.79	2.56
Exports	—	—	—	—	—	—
Subsidies	—	—	—	—	0.19	0.04
Net Taxes(+)/Net Subsidies(−)	2.64	2.64	2.80	2.97	1.60	2.53
China						
Taxes and duties	2.39	1.56	1.25	1.11	1.15	1.49
Imports	2.39	1.56	1.25	1.11	1.15	1.49
Exports	—	—	—	—	—	—
Subsidies	—	—	—	—	—	—
Net Taxes(+)/Net Subsidies(−)	2.39	1.56	1.25	1.11	1.15	1.49
Mongolian People's Republic						
Taxes and duties	21.90	19.11	18.68	17.70	17.70	19.02
Imports	18.61	16.60	16.17	15.25	16.21	16.57
Exports	3.29	2.51	2.51	2.45	1.49	2.45
Subsidies	6.02	5.19	5.11	3.90	4.03	4.85
Net Taxes(+)/Net Subsidies(−)	15.88	13.92	13.57	13.79	13.67	14.17

Sources: International Monetary Fund (1991); and national data.
[1] Gross social product for Yugoslavia, and GNP for China and Romania.
[2] Including other foreign trade levies.

subsidies to foreign trade. The Eastern European countries needed these subsidies to push the export of their "soft" goods with limited demand on world markets and with domestic prices higher than international prices (e.g., manufactured goods) in order to earn foreign exchange necessary to finance imports. These subsidies were substantial and higher than export tax revenue by two to five times. As a percentage of GDP they tended to decline (except in the U.S.S.R.) principally on account of the policy to reduce subsidies particularly during 1988 and 1989 when economic reforms were pursued more vigorously. Fifth, the combination of taxes and subsidies on foreign trade has in general resulted in net subsidies in Eastern European countries and in net taxes in other countries especially in Mongolia and the U.S.S.R.

Price Equalization System

While the main objective of the price equalization system is to insulate domestically fixed prices from variations in world prices it has fiscal implications. Its mechanism in foreign trade is similar to the domestic turnover taxes. It introduces wedges between controlled domestic prices and import or export prices. These wedges constitute product-specific taxes or subsidies on imports and exports.[4] The price equalization system works as follows. The foreign trade organizations purchase domestic products from production enterprises or wholesale distributors for exports and sell imported products to trading firms at administratively fixed wholesale prices.[5] The difference between these domestic prices and the valuta prices (which are foreign prices converted to domestic currency by using some arbitrary exchange rate[6]) resulted in profits or losses for the foreign trade organizations. Profits are transferred as taxes to the budget and losses are compensated by subsidies from it.[7] In sum, these wedges prevent any pass-through of foreign price changes onto domestically controlled prices.

---

[4]These wedges are called "price differential taxes/subsidies." They also operate as "foreign exchange coefficients" or "DVK" in the U.S.S.R.

[5]The foreign trade organizations, which hold the state monopoly of foreign trade, do not engage in production or distribution.

[6]Usually the official or commercial exchange rates which serve in essence as an accounting device. Sometimes, these exchange rates are multiplied by some coefficients in an attempt to measure the profitability of an industry or a group of products. These are the "foreign trade effectiveness coefficients" or "foreign exchange multipliers" introduced in Hungary in the early 1960s; see Boltho (1971).

[7]Part of profits includes margins for foreign trade organizations. The thrust of reasoning is not changed with all profits considered to reflect in price differential taxes.

The relationship among domestic prices, foreign prices, exchange rates, taxes or subsidies may be expressed as:

$$P_i = P_i^* e\,(1 + t_i) \text{ or } P_i = P_i^* e(1 - s_i), \tag{1}$$

where P_i represents the domestic price of product i, e the exchange rate, P_i^* the price in foreign currency of product i, t_i the ad valorem tax rate on product i, and s_i the ad valorem subsidy rate on product i.

In market-oriented economies, t_i is parametric, P_i and e are determined by market forces, and arbitrage ensures the equality of equation (1). In centrally planned economies, the process is reversed, P_i and e are arbitrarily fixed and t_i is determined by the price equalization system as follows:

$$t_i = \frac{P_i}{P_i^* e} - 1 \text{ or } s_i = 1 - (P_i / P_i^* e). \tag{2}$$

For imports, if the fixed domestic price of an import substitute P_i is higher than $P_i^* e$, t_i is positive, foreign trade organizations realize a profit which is taxed away for the budget. On the contrary, if P_i is lower than $P_i^* e$, t_i is negative and equal to s_i, foreign trade organizations incur a loss which is subsidized by the budget. Equation (2) indicates that the tax rate increases with the increase in domestic controlled price while it decreases with an increase in foreign price or with a devaluation of the exchange rate. For exports this analysis is reversed.

The price equalization system results in a proliferation and variability of tax rates. For each product, there may be one rate; yet the rates may vary from one trading partner to another depending on the terms of agreement set forth in the respective bilateral trade protocols. The rates also change passively with changes in domestic prices, foreign prices, and the exchange rate. In principle, these rate changes should induce a direct reallocation of resources in commodity and factor markets but they do not in centrally planned economies because domestic prices facing firms are unaffected. Instead, these changes influence the allocation of resources indirectly through their effects on the budget and monetary aggregates. It is partly through these channels that domestic prices may not be completely insulated from changes in world prices.[8] Furthermore, the complexity and opacity of these implicit taxes and subsidies combined with the arbitrariness of cost, price, and exchange rate determination distort

---

[8]For more detailed discussion, see Wolf (1980, 1985, 1988).

the pattern of comparative advantages making it very difficult to detect the losers and winners in foreign trade.[9]

Tariffs

In market-oriented economies tariffs aim at well-known objectives. In industrial countries tariffs are used for protection, in developing countries in addition to protecting domestic industries, tariffs also aim at raising revenue for the budget, contributing to reducing balance of payments deficit, or improving income distribution (e.g., higher tariff rate on luxuries). As a cost component, tariffs affect relative prices and influence the choice between domestic and imported goods either for production or consumption. They, thus, indirectly contribute to determining the level and composition of trade. In centrally planned economies tariffs practically did not serve any of these functions. No tariffs existed until 1961, when they were introduced in Czechoslovakia, Hungary, Poland, and the U.S.S.R.[10] as a bargaining tool to obtain trade concessions especially from industrial countries.[11] Tariffs were differentiated between personal and commercial imports.[12] As personal imports were negligible and most commercial imports were conducted by foreign trade organizations in quotas and within bilateral agreement, revenue from tariffs was negligible and, despite their presence, tariffs were redundant in terms of allocative effects.

The redundancy of tariffs in centrally planned economies may be explained by several factors. First, the level and composition of foreign trade were directly determined by the central plan in the form of annual and five-year trade plans. These contained implicit quotas for both imports and exports which reflected tariff-inclusive relative prices of domestic and imported goods. The implicit quotas in these plans were distributed by product and to individual firms with precise import entitlements and export targets. The trade plans were carried out exclusively by foreign trade organizations and mostly within the framework of bilateral trade and payments agreements or protocols which contained detailed

---

[9]Recognizing this difficulty, Hungary started in the 1950s to develop effectiveness indices to simulate the profitability of various exports but as with all indices they had shortcomings. This topic is discussed extensively in Boltho (1971).

[10]China introduced tariffs in the early 1950s.

[11]These countries generally adopted a three-column schedule. The most-favored-nation rates ranged from 0–5 percent for raw materials to 10-50 percent for finished products and the maximum rates were twice the most-favored-nation rates. Imports from the least developed countries were generally exempted; see Familton (1970), pp. 182–83.

[12]Among the CMEA member countries, Hungary did not have this dichotomy in tariffs; see Holzman (1974), pp. 23–25.

specification on quantity, value, and settlement currency (e.g., transferable rubles).

Second, the soft budget constraint (e.g., easy access to budget subsidies and bank credit) has made cost considerations irrelevant to state-owned firms. Although tariffs were a component of production costs, to the extent that enterprises did not need to pass through those onto output prices, tariffs were redundant.

Third, the concern with fulfilling the national plan and the need to ensure price stability and to provide affordable goods for consumers led to domestically controlled prices and to the insulation of these prices from the direct effects of price changes in international markets through the price equalization system.[13] In some cases, changes in world prices were offset with compensatory adjustment in tariffs.

Fourth, the state control over the exchange and payments system in the form of payment restrictions implemented through the foreign exchange plan (the counterpart of trade plan) imposed a binding constraint on imports on the basis of the availability of foreign exchange.

Regarding the administration of foreign trade taxes and subsidies in former centrally planned economies, it was both simple and effective. These advantages were derived from the following main factors. Foreign trade taxation had little role to play. Trade was conducted in implicit quotas under the trade plans and implemented exclusively by foreign trade organizations, and tariffs were redundant. The state was both the taxpayer and the collector. Furthermore, the revenue from the price equalization system could be determined with almost certainty because all the elements in the price equalization system were fixed or planned while the collection of duties and granting of subsidies were effected through bank accounts between a limited number of foreign trade organizations and the budget.

Current Reform Measures

The former centrally planned economies have evolved at different speeds in transforming themselves into market-based economies.[14] Although the pace of restructuring has been accelerated in the last few

---

[13]The insulation of domestic economies from the influence of world markets was also dictated by other considerations including concern for self-sufficiency and national security.

[14]Some countries started earlier (Hungary in 1968), others in the 1970s (China in 1978) and 1980s (Poland in 1981, the U.S.S.R. in 1986), and still others began to embark on this process as recently as 1990 (Bulgaria, Czechoslovakia, Romania, Mongolia).

years, direct control has not completely been abolished and market mechanisms have yet to be fully established, foreign trade taxation/subsidization is in transition between heavy reliance on the price equalization system and market-based instruments of tariffs.[15] It therefore combines: (1) a somewhat modified price equalization system applied essentially to CMEA countries and to bilateral trade agreements that tends to vanish with the acceleration of the reforms in 1991; (2) tariffs applied to other countries and transactions; and (3) nontariff barriers in the form of licensing, explicit quotas, and export earning retention schemes. Further, these elements may be accompanied by exchange rates ranging anywhere between multiple practices, a fixed nominal rate, or a nearly fixed real rate.

Modified Price Equalization System

With the demise of central planning and the attempt of the government to replace direct control by indirect instruments to regulate the economy—often by mimicking the market mechanisms—the elements that enter in the calculation of price equalization system taxes and subsidies, namely the quantities of exports and imports, the domestic and foreign prices and the exchange rates have lost their former degree of certainty. Domestic prices are no longer fixed as they were liberalized.[16] Foreign prices have become less certain as trade conducted under bilateral protocols has contracted and unconstrained trade in convertible currencies has expanded. Export and import volumes have become more uncertain as planning was abolished, foreign trade organizations' monopoly was phased out or eliminated, and the right to trade has been extended to other enterprises. Furthermore, enterprise reforms have made both prices and quantities more variable as enterprises have been authorized to have more autonomy in investment, production, pricing and marketing, to compete more among themselves, and to trade directly with foreign markets while they have been more subject to hard budget constraint and more exposed to international competition. Exchange rates have become more flexible to reflect more closely changes in economic conditions and current account convertibility was achieved in Poland in 1990 or has been

---

[15]Selected trade and economic reforms are summarized in the Appendix Table.

[16]Prices were liberalized in a big bang as in Poland in 1989 or more often have been decontrolled, although at variable intensity, in a gradual manner as in China and Hungary, or in steps as in Bulgaria and Czechoslovakia.

underway in other countries.[17] With these systemic changes, the automatic price equalization system lost its rationale and has to be abandoned completely or modified as done in a number of countries in transition.

The main modification of the price equalization system has been the discontinuation of the automatic full transfer of profits and subsidization of losses and the provision of more incentives and financial discipline to enterprises. However, this modification has been accompanied, in some countries, by negotiations between the government and enterprises.[18] As the transformation to the market system has been accelerated in 1991, the price equalization system, whether modified or not, has practically been abolished.[19]

Tariffs

The reforms in economies in transition have led to a more important role for tariffs. These have now been more actively used in countries which had them prior to the reforms (Czechoslovakia, China, Hungary) or have recently been introduced in countries where they had not existed (Mongolia in 1990). They are applied almost exclusively to trade with convertible areas.[20] There is a separate tariff schedule for individuals, but

---

[17]For example, in early 1991 Hungary has adopted a four-year economic program. Among the objectives are the authorization for Hungarians to hold foreign currencies without restrictions by 1993 and full convertibility of the forint by 1994.

[18]In Hungary, since early 1990, enterprises have retained profits and practically borne all costs. However, the amounts of retained profits and subsidized losses may still be subject to negotiations with the government; see Abel, Hillman, and Tarr (1991). In Romania, while the price equalization system on imports remains unmodified, enterprises are encouraged to export especially to the convertible currency area to earn export subsidies. They negotiate with the government on target prices for their exports which constitute the criteria to pay taxes or to receive subsidies on foreign trade. In Poland, the price equalization sytem was abolished in early 1990 for the convertible area while it has remained applicable to the ruble area, administratively fixed price products, and some contract (free) price products.

[19]In the U.S.S.R., the price equalization system abolition was announced for January 1991 together with the decision of the CMEA to conduct trade among its former members at world prices and in convertible currencies in the context of overall price and trade liberalization. However, it is still unclear how the price equalization system abolition has been implemented in the U.S.S.R. as prices have not been substantially liberalized and the trade arrangement between the U.S.S.R. and the former members of CMEA has remained practically unchanged mainly because of the shortage of hard currencies.

[20]In China, tariffs apply to all countries and are a component of the foreign prices in the calculation of price equalization taxes.

practically all tariff revenue is generated by commercial imports.[21] Imports from developing and from CMEA countries are generally exempt from customs duties. Imports from other countries benefit from preferential rates if they have concluded the most-favored-nation clause; for the rest, the rates are much higher and in general double the most-favored-nation rates. The rates tend to increase with the degree of processing and vary across countries. Exemptions are usually granted to import of raw materials, equipment, and capital goods. The most-favored-nation rates are in general less than 90 percent and the average rates are relatively low. Some countries impose surcharges mainly on consumer goods.[22]

In general, there are no export taxes.[23] In a few countries where they are present, they are levied mainly on raw materials and energy products to ensure adequate supply for domestic use (Bulgaria, China, Mongolia, and the U.S.S.R.) or to raise revenue (mainly the U.S.S.R.). Except in Mongolia and the U.S.S.R., revenue from this source is relatively minor. Direct subsidies on imports are minimal while those on exports are levied in some countries but these tend to be limited and are gradually abolished.[24]

Implicit Taxation

Since tariffs cannot provide the same degree of certainty in the determination of the level and composition of foreign trade as could the former foreign trade and foreign exchange plans, licensing, quotas, and other exchange restrictions, which, in many respects, are equivalent to implicit taxation, have been used to keep some control over trade.

Licensing is generally required for imports as well as exports. Import licensing is aimed at protecting domestic industries, responding to balance of payments difficulties (Bulgaria, China), or ensuring the use of foreign exchange for priority activities (China). Its coverage may be extensive (45

---

[21]Poland unified the individual and commercial tariffs in 1990.

[22]For the U.S.S.R., the surcharges apply to both imports and exports and to all countries including the CMEA countries, and are in fact the ad valorem rates implicit in the now defunct price equalization system. As they capture the large difference between the world market price equivalent in rubles and the substantially distorted domestic prices, they may reach as high as 500 percent.

[23]To the extent that the price equalization system still applies although modified, there are implicit taxes.

[24]Hungary subsidizes exports of agricultural products and processed food to the convertible area.

percent of imports in China), limited (6 percent in the U.S.S.R.),[25] or restricted to a small number of strategic or sensitive commodities such as crude oil, natural gas, ammunition, and narcotics (Czechoslovakia). Its coverage is nevertheless being rapidly reduced in countries engaged in trade liberalization.[26]

Export licensing is dictated by concern to ensure supply and avoid shortage in domestic market (Bulgaria, China, the U.S.S.R.), to restrict exports to certain CMEA trade partners with which trade surplus has emerged (Bulgaria),[27] or to observe export quotas in bilateral trade agreements or voluntary export restrictions with industrial countries (China, Bulgaria, Czechoslovakia).[28]

Quotas are relatively limited and imposed both on imports and exports.[29] Their main purpose is added insurance to provide an adequate supply of specific commodities in domestic market, to observe bilateral agreements and voluntary export restrictions, or to limit the use of hard currencies for consumption.[30]

All export earnings, before reform, were required to be surrendered to the central bank at the official exchange rate. As an incentive, part of export earnings is now allowed to be retained by enterprises to be used for their imports or to be sold at the market-determined exchange rate. Poland abolished this scheme in 1990 as its exchange rate has become market determined and its currency convertible. Implicit subsidies were also provided to stimulate exports in the form of preferential interest rates or income tax rebates as in China and Hungary. These export incentives were abolished in Poland in 1990 or are to be abolished in Czechoslovakia and Romania in 1991 due in part to their costs and relative ineffectiveness.

---

[25]The low level of import licensing may be explained by concern to increase the supply of commodities in shortage in domestic market.

[26]Hungary has been engaged in a three-year liberalization program starting from January 1989. By the end of 1991, 90 percent of trade in convertible currencies will be liberalized and by 1992 complete import liberalization will be achieved.

[27]This is explained by the inability of a surplus country to use its credit balance in transferable rubles in a third country.

[28]Bulgaria has five voluntary export restrictions for textiles and Czechoslovakia has seven voluntary export restrictions for metallurgical products, textiles, and mutton with industrial countries.

[29]There are no import quotas in Czechoslovakia. Quotas in Poland are specified in value and quantity in licenses.

[30]Hungary imposes a total quota on the value of consumer goods imports settled in convertible currencies.

Agenda for Future Reform

As trade liberalization is a key component of the reform in economies in transition, foreign trade taxation has a determinant role to play. The objective, pace, and sequencing of foreign trade taxation reform in the period ahead are dictated by those of trade, exchange, and payments reforms, which have to be undertaken in coordination and ideally in conjunction with other domestic reforms, notably, price liberalization, enterprise restructuring, bankruptcy laws, and overall fiscal reform.[31] In the immediate future, two measures that cover both imports and exports need to be taken. First, the undesirable effects of the overvalued exchange rate in terms of implicit subsidization of imports and taxation of exports that distort the allocation of resources and carry an anti-export bias should be eliminated by establishing a realistic and unified exchange rate that reflects market forces; concomitantly any remaining price equalization system practices and other multiple currency practices have to be abolished immediately. Second, with increasing price liberalization and opening up of the economies to foreign trade, nontariff barriers (licensing, quotas) have to be replaced by explicit ad valorem tariffs; experience in Mongolia shows that this can be implemented very quickly. Against the background of these two measures, the following sections will discuss possible reforms for taxes and duties on imports and exports. As the former centrally planned economies have recently embarked on these reforms, the experience of similar reforms in market-oriented economies may provide some useful directions.

Import Taxes and Duties

While tariffs have no role in the long term as trade is liberalized they may have an important revenue role in the short term. First, import tariffs can provide additional revenue to reduce fiscal deficit for stabilization without which other structural reforms may be jeopardized. Second, given the difficulties to increase revenue from other taxes because of social and political implications, tariffs would be a viable alternative; they could also provide the necessary time for overall fiscal reform to be implemented. Third, as illustrated by developing countries with inadequate administrative capacity, the relative ease to raise revenue from tariffs implies low cost for their administration. This is an important consideration for efficiency as it can be shown that tariffs are the first best to raise

---

[31]For an overview of the fiscal reform, see Kopits (1991).

revenue when collection costs are taken into account.[32] Fourth, as the changes from inward- to outward-looking policy would take some time to be carried out, in exceptional circumstances tariffs—subject to preannounced sunset provisions—can provide some temporary protection for those industries which cannot compete with foreign producers in the short term but which may prove viable in the medium term after the necessary restructuring has taken place.

Base

To raise revenue for the budget and at the same time to minimize distortions in the domestic allocation of resources, tariffs should be imposed on an ad valorem basis and on as broad a base as possible. This means that there should preferably be no exemptions, as experience with Hungarian tax reforms shows that attempts to fine tune taxes with various exemptions to promote equity have resulted in unnecessary administrative burden and distortive incentives.[33] Therefore, tariff exemptions and preferential tariff rates should be abolished as rapidly as possible and no new ones should be granted, except those governed by international conventions (e.g., diplomatic exemptions). The exemptions under contractual obligation should continue to be observed but should not be renewed at expiration. Tariff exemptions often granted to capital, equipment, and intermediate goods imported by foreign investment enterprises should also be eliminated. This preference distorts the structure of protection and has little impact on foreign investment as this is likely to be determined more by other factors, such as macroeconomic stability, access to foreign exchange for profit repatriation, availability of imported inputs and services, a disciplined and skilled labor force, adequate infrastructure and telecommunications, a transparent legal and regulatory framework, or protection of property rights, than by tax concessions. However, as discussed below, tariff exemptions should be allowed on imports used in the production of exports, which should be free of all indirect taxes.

The dismantlement of nontariff barriers could also increase budgetary revenue for the short term. Quotas should be replaced with equivalent tariffs. If licenses could not immediately be abolished they should be auctioned to siphon off the monopolistic revenue from the license holders to benefit the budget. This approach would preclude the discretionary allocation of quotas and licenses, thereby eliminating the sources of possible administrative complication, corruption, and rent-seeking activities.

---

[32]See Mihaljek (1990).
[33]See Gray (1990).

Furthermore, a more flexible exchange rate policy would often entail a depreciation to a more realistic level, leading to a larger tax base and higher tariff revenue.

Structure and Rates

The structure of import tariffs applied to this comprehensive base should meet a number of criteria. Tariffs should not be too high to encourage smuggling or too differentiated to create distortions in protection across industries. After all, differentiated rates cannot be justified because at present it is difficult to pick out the winning or losing products or industries given the little knowledge (except they are very large) about distortions between costs and domestic prices and between these and world prices. Furthermore, even if the pattern of protection is known, a protection policy based on current comparative advantages would miss out on dynamic gains resulting from the growth of economy and the eventual emergence of new winners. Yet in the mean time, existing import protection has an established and vocal constituency to retain the rents from such activity. For these reasons, tariffs should be neutral among different products and should preferably be uniform. Although uniformity is not optimal under conventional efficiency criteria, because of imperfect competition, economies of scales, or smuggling, it may be justified when consideration is given to transparency, administrative simplicity, and lack of incentive for rent-seeking activities.[34] As a point of departure, the uniform rate should at least be revenue neutral such that it could raise at least the same revenue as the foreign trade taxation it replaces given the priority for stabilization.[35]

The determination of this uniform rate should be undertaken within the broader framework of the revenue potential of the entire tax system that is needed to reduce the fiscal deficit for the stabilization of the economy. As revenue from tax on income and profits and tax on turnover or its successor value-added tax (already implemented in Hungary in 1988 and planned to be introduced soon in Czechoslovakia, Bulgaria, Poland) has shown to decline on account of the temporary shrinking of the tax bases

---

[34]See Mihaljek (1990) and Panagariya (1990). It is worth noting, for example, that Chile has a uniform rate of 15 percent and Bolivia aims at unifying its two rates, 10 percent and 17 percent, in 1991.

[35]The amounts of revenue generated by a uniform tariff and by the former system may be equal but are not strictly comparable because of the difficulty to account for all qualitative, administrative, and structural differences between the two systems.

during the initial phase of economic reform,[36] tariffs should provide an increasing part of the needed revenue. Therefore, the uniform rate might need to be higher than the revenue-neutral rate but preferably should not exceed about 20 percent.[37]

How should tariffs be restructured? The first action is to unify the personal and commercial schedules as was effected in Poland in 1990 to reflect the goal of neutrality of tariffs among different economic agents. While it is preferable to create a system with a unique schedule with a uniform rate to raise the required revenue, the existing setting in the majority of economies in transition might lean toward a two-schedule system consisting of a general schedule and a reduced-rate schedule. The former would apply to imports from all countries, the latter to countries with a most-favored-nation clause, while developing countries would benefit from the general system of preference.

Should there be a lower tariff rate on imports of necessities and a higher rate on luxury imports? Experience, especially in developing countries, shows that it is more effective to provide targeted subsidies to low-income groups[38] and to levy excises on luxury products—to avoid unintended protection for domestic producers of luxuries—for equity reasons.

The tariff level should also be coordinated with other taxes to determine the potential revenue contribution of each tax to the overall revenue need of the budget. In the short term, as discussed earlier, tariffs could play an important role in face of declining revenue from other taxes. But in the medium and long term there should be a gradual shift to domestic taxes, especially to consumption tax in the form of value-added tax and possibly personal income taxation as tariffs would be reduced to a minor role with trade liberalization in general or with accession to customs union or free trade zone (e.g., EC or EFTA) for European countries in transition in particular. The coordination between foreign trade taxes and domestic taxes, which could be implemented quickly, should also aim at

---

[36]Most significantly, the restructuring of enterprises is likely to negatively affect income, output, and employment. The hardening of the budget constraint and the greater financial autonomy would lead to a more accurate determination of (lower) profits. The closing down of unsalvable enterprises and the streamlining of the rest would result in a reduction of costly production and bloated labor. Production would also suffer from lack of work discipline.

[37]For the period 1985–89 the average actual tax rate on imports was about 51 percent in the U.S.S.R. and Mongolia and 1–12 percent in the other countries. The average for developing countries is estimated at 20 percent; see also Mihaljek (1991), Chapter IV.

[38]Former centrally planned economies have had a long experience in handling the subsidization of targeted groups.

reducing the number of rates. There should be a uniform rate on foreign trade and another one on turnover or consumption taxes applied equally to imported goods and domestically produced import substitutes. With this arrangement, the distortive effect of a differential consumption tax between imported and domestic products is avoided and the uniform tariff rate represents clearly the extent of protection to be reflected in the cost differential between foreign and domestic goods. This arrangement would also minimize distortions and provide transparency and simplicity for administration. For countries such as Bulgaria, Czechoslovakia, Romania, Poland, and possibly the U.S.S.R., which are reforming the turnover tax and planning to introduce a value-added tax, they should take this opportunity to adopt this approach. For countries such as Hungary, which have multiple rates in their VAT and tariffs, a steady reduction in the number of rates may be pursued simultaneously with the harmonization of the tax rates on consumption of imports and domestically produced goods. This would definitely improve the allocative efficiency and effectiveness of taxation. Finally, beyond the short-term revenue requirement for controlling the fiscal deficit and for easing the reliance on other forms of taxation (especially on capital and payroll) there should be a gradual reduction of tariffs in the medium to long term. If a country has a dual schedule system, this overall rate reduction could be implemented by reducing the higher rate schedule before reducing the lower rate schedule—an approach, for example, apparently begun in 1990 in the U.S.S.R. This reduction would be best achieved by collapsing the highest rates and radially reducing all other rates.[39] The gradual reduction should be dated and phased over a period of, say, two to five years.[40] The timetable should be announced and should be strictly observed. This would provide clear signals to all economic agents to adjust in response to changes in relative prices resulting from tariff reductions. Any deviation or reversal would destroy the credibility of the liberalization and would raise

---

[39]This is a combination of the "concertina" method and the "radial" method for tariffs reduction. The first method at each stage of reduction reduces all the highest rates to the level immediately below while leaving the other lower rates unchanged; see Bertrand and Vanek (1971). The second method at each stage reduces all rates by the same percentage applied to the rates existing prior to the current stage of reduction. See Thomas, Matin, and Nash (1990), p. 13.

[40]These were the time periods for Mexico and Chile in the 1980s to reduce their tariffs to a relatively uniform rate structure of about 15 percent in addition to eliminating most of the quantitative restrictions; see Thomas, Matin, and Nash (1990). This approach was first applied in the trade liberalization program in the Southern Cone (Argentina, Chile, Uruguay) in the 1970s.

doubt about its sustainability. The latter can be ensured with an adequate macroeconomic policy stance.

For economies in transition the issue of whether to reduce tariffs and remove other trade barriers unilaterally or to delay it to obtain concessions in multilateral negotiations under GATT is broadly relevant. Undoubtedly, unilateral trade liberalization, especially as regards the removal of trade barriers, is the best strategy because of the internal benefits it confers in terms of internal allocative efficiency and competitiveness. Nevertheless, having reached a moderate level of ad valorem duty rates (as in Czechoslovakia), further rate reductions (to most-favored-nation or zero rates) should be conditioned on reciprocal concessions by trading partners.

Export Taxes and Subsidies

A major objective of trade and industrial policy in economies in transition is to promote exports which have proved successful in many countries, especially in South East Asia. Essential ingredients of an export-oriented strategy include the maintenance of a realistic exchange rate, import liberalization (to eliminate anti-export bias), and—with some exceptions[41]—the removal of export taxes.

The elimination of export taxes should not pose major revenue problems for the budget. First, export taxes may be replaced by other levies. In China and the U.S.S.R., for example, export taxes are levied almost solely on raw materials, minerals, or energy products to ensure adequate supply for domestic industries that may be replaced by royalties, rental payments, or taxes on sales designed to manage natural resources and to protect the environment in a more rational way. Second, the loss in export tax revenue may largely be offset by the reduction of export subsidies. Although export subsidies might be successful in some instances—if subject to a finite time limit, in the case of genuine infant industries—they should ultimately be eliminated because they are rarely cost-efficient (in comparison to a realistic exchange rate policy) and are more likely to be countervailed by other countries.

To promote exports, the elimination of tariffs has to be accompanied by other policies. Above all, exports from primary sectors have been proved

---

[41]For a given country, exports may be taxed to take advantage of some monopoly power of its exported products on world markets or to substitute for other forms of taxation such as taxation of agriculture income. But these export taxes may be applied only temporarily as they become rapidly ineffective with adjustments in world demand and supply in the former case or can be replaced with more efficient forms of taxation in the latter.

favorably influenced by realistic prices and exchange rates, low protection of industries, and lack of restrictions on foreign investment. Exports of manufactured products depend to a large extent on foreign investment and this is likely, as mentioned earlier, to be influenced far less by subsidies and tax preferences than by other sound economic policies and institutional factors.[42]

Import tariffs have an anti-export bias. To promote exports this bias has to be eliminated by freeing inputs used in the production of exports from import tariffs and other indirect taxes. This is the policy pursued by all economies in this study. Its actual implementation has mostly taken the form of outright duty exemption or, temporary admission. Other forms of duty-free schemes such as drawbacks of indirect taxes and duties, in-bond manufacturing plants (Hungary, Poland), and export-processing zones (China) have been used by economies which have had longer experience with tariffs and more elaborated customs administration. The choice of a particular scheme should be based on a careful consideration of its costs and benefits and on the administrative capacity and technical expertise of each country.

Administration

As the effectiveness of the trade tax reform depends on the ability of administration to implement it, the administration of foreign trade taxation would need to be improved substantially and quickly. This complex and urgent task has to start immediately, especially in countries where customs administration is still rudimentary, because it involves multiple decisions on organizational structure, recruitment and training of personnel, changes in nomenclature (e.g., Bulgaria, Romania, the U.S.S.R.), valuation practices (Mongolia, Bulgaria), or tariff position.

The reform may take a few years to reach a fairly adequate operational capability. This time length depends on the initial customs administration conditions, the pace of the reform, and other factors in individual countries. Some countries such as Romania have to create its customs administration literally anew and others such as Hungary, Poland, and Yugoslavia can build it up from their existing arrangements. Mongolia started its customs administration reform in October 1990 and less than a year later has a fairly well functioning system. However, there have been problems associated with control and valuation of imports. The U.S.S.R. customs administration was created five years ago and as of June 1991 is still being

---

[42]The experiences of different countries are documented in Thomas, Matin, and Nash (1990).

organized. The slow pace of reform in this country as in Yugoslavia is further complicated by the resolution of the issue on the responsibilities of the central government and other levels of government in the collection and sharing of budgetary revenue and by interrepublic relations. A solution should be found before a customs reform can effectively be implemented.

Conclusions

The examination of foreign trade taxation under central planning, in the current reforms, and of the agenda of policy actions in the period ahead suggests a number of observations.

First, the reform in foreign trade taxation as in other domestic taxes is a difficult and complex task. It has to be undertaken at the same time and in coordination with other reforms, not only in areas of taxation but also in the overall context of fiscal policy. It also has to depend on other broader systemic reforms, in particular on trade liberalization, the pace and sequencing of which have to be coordinated with the liberalization of commodity markets, financial sector, capital control, and the reforms of exchange rate and enterprises. This encompassing approach is much more demanding than the more partial approach in market-oriented economies where the reform of trade taxation can be undertaken relatively independently as other features of a market-based economy are already in place.

Second, a change in attitude must take place to give the foreign trade tax reform the maximum chance of success; this requires the elimination of the planning instinct believing that policymakers can consistently make better decisions than the market.[43] This attitude change implies that tariff rate differentials, special incentives in the form of exemptions, subsidies, licensing, quotas, and other nontariff barriers have to be replaced by a system of ad valorem tariffs. The rates should be fairly uniform to provide transparency, simplicity, effective administration, and efficiency in resource allocation. Admittedly, as these countries gain access to free trade areas or sign reciprocal trade concessions, there is scope for preferential rates or exceptions.

Third, tariffs can contribute significantly to the revenue needed for economic stabilization in the initial phase of the transition. In the medium term, tariffs have to be gradually reduced. The reduction should be dated, phased, and announced at the very outset of the program; any deviation from this program should be avoided so as not to jeopardize its credibility.

---

[43]The change in attitude has been discussed in Tanzi (1991a) and Kopits (1991).

Fourth, foreign trade subsidies should be abolished—with very few, if any, exceptions—concomitantly with the adoption of a realistic exchange rate policy.

Fifth, the success of foreign trade tax reform depends on the ability of the administration to implement it. Given the currently inadequate customs administration—a legacy of former central planning and price controls—the task of improving it in the short term is both complex and urgent. Nevertheless, the modernization of customs administration, including the introduction of internationally accepted standards on nomenclature and valuation, needs to start immediately as it will take time to build up the capability to implement tariff reform and other related activities to ensure compliance with new foreign trade laws and regulations.

References

Abel, I., Arye L. Hillman, and David Tarr, "The Government Budget Consequences of Reform of CMEA System of International Trade: The Case of Hungary," in *Socialist Economies in Transition*, ed. by A. Hillman and B. Milanovic (forthcoming, 1991).

Bertrand, T., and J. Vanek, "The Theory of Tariffs, Taxes, and Subsidies: Some Aspects of the Second Best," *American Economic Review*, Vol. 61 (December 1971), pp. 925–31.

Boltho, A., *Foreign Trade Criteria in Socialist Economies* (Cambridge: Cambridge University Press, 1971).

Familton, R.J., "East-West Trade and Payments Relations," *Staff Papers*, International Monetary Fund (March 1970), pp.170–213.

Gray, Cheryl W., "Tax Systems in the Reforming Economies of Europe," World Bank Working Papers, WPS 501 (September 1990).

Havrylyshyn, O., D. Tarr, "The Role of Trade Liberalization in Transition to a Market Economy," in *Proceedings of OECD Conference on Transition to a Market Economy* (Paris: OECD, forthcoming, 1991).

Holzman, F.D., *Foreign Trade Under Central Planning* (Cambridge, Massachusetts: Harvard University Press, 1974).

International Monetary Fund, and others, *A Study of the Soviet Economy* (Paris: Organization for Economic Cooperation and Development, 1991).

Kenen, Peter, "Traditional Arrangements for Trade and Payments Among the CMEA Countries," IMF Working Paper 90/79 (Washington: International Monetary Fund, 1990).

Kopits, George, "Fiscal Reform in European Economies in Transition," in *The Transformation of Central and Eastern Europe to a Market Economy*, ed. by P. Marerand S. Zechini (Paris: OECD, 1991).

Marrese, M., and J. Vanous, *Subsidization of Trade With Eastern Europe* (Berkeley: University of California Press, 1983).

Mihaljek, Dubravko, *Essays on the Fiscal Aspects of Economic Reforms in Developing and Socialist Countries*, unpublished Ph.D dissertation, University of Pittsburgh, 1990.

——, "Tax Reform in Socialist Economies in Transition," unpublished, Fiscal Affairs Department (Washington: International Monetary Fund, 1991).

Oblath, Gabor, and D. Tarr, "The Soviet Subsidization and Eastern Europe: The Case of Hungary," (Washington: EMTTE, 1991).

Panagariya, Arvind, "How Should Tariffs be Structured?" World Bank Working Papers, WPS 353 (February 1990).

Schrenk, Martin, "The CMEA System of Trade and Payments: the Legacy and the Aftermath of Its Termination" (unpublished, Washington: the World Bank, 1991).

Tanzi, Vito, "Quantitative Characteristics of the Tax Systems of Developing Countries," in *The Theory of Taxation for Developing Countries*, ed. by David Newberry and Nicholas Stern,(New York: Oxford University Press, 1987).

—— (1991a), "Tax Reform and the Move to a Market Economy: Overview of the Issues," in *The Role of Tax Reform in Central and Eastern European Economies* (Paris: OECD, 1991).

—— (1991b), *Public Finance in Developing Countries* (Brookfield, Vermont: 1991).

Thomas, Vinod, Kazi Matin, and John Nash, *Lessons in Trade Policy Reform* (Washington: The World Bank, 1990).

Wolf, T.A., "On the Adjustment of Centrally Planned Economies to External Economic Disturbances," in *East European Integration and East West Trade*, ed. by P. Marter and J. M. Montias, (Bloomington, Indiana: Indiana University Press, 1980), pp. 86–111.

——, "Economic Stabilization in Planned Economies: Toward an Analytical Framework," *Staff Papers*, International Monetary Fund (March 1985), pp. 78–131.

——, *Foreign Trade in the Centrally Planned Economy* (New York: Harwood Academic Publishers, 1988).

CHAPTER 11

Taxation of Foreign Direct Investment

Erik C.F. Offerdal

For many countries in transition to market economies, attracting foreign direct investment has become a cornerstone of the reform programs. It is not difficult to understand why. Investment with direct foreign participation may provide the kind of technology transfer that these countries are eagerly searching for—knowledge about foreign markets, management and marketing techniques, access to financing and financial management, modern production technology, computer systems, and telecommunications equipment. In addition, it is probably anticipated that such investment will create employment opportunities that will compensate for the dismantling of inefficient state enterprises, and also turn out to be an important source for government tax revenue.

This paper will use the countries in Eastern Europe as an illustrative example of economies in transition; however, the issues concerning foreign investment certainly extend beyond this region. To limit the scope, the paper will focus on direct investment, defined as equity investment with the intention of exercising substantial or complete control over operations, as opposed to portfolio investment, which can be in either debt or equity form, and has no control over operations. It is interesting to note that direct investment in Eastern Europe so far has been primarily in the form of joint ventures, rather than subsidiaries of multinational enterprises. This is largely a result of laws that make joint ventures the only viable alternative in the early stages of reform.

A general policy question is raised in this chapter. How should Eastern European countries design their tax policy to encourage foreign direct investment? It will be argued that emphasis should be placed on two elements: *simplicity* in the tax code, with a minimum of tax incentives

Note: Comments by Leif Mutén and Krister Andersson are greatly appreciated.

toward foreign investors, and on *coordination* of tax policy, both with other capital-importing countries in Eastern Europe and with capital-exporting countries. There are three reasons for this emphasis. First, it is quite likely that a foreign investor may be more attracted by such features as a stable macroeconomic environment, a transparent regulatory framework, and absence of restrictions on repatriating profits, rather than specific tax incentives. Second, the issues involved in taxing border-crossing income flows are quite complex, and the tax administrations in all Eastern European countries are already overburdened with the rapid pace of change in the taxation of domestic entities. Third, the total tax burden of an enterprise investing in Eastern Europe depends not only on the tax code of the host country of the joint venture, but also of the home country where the enterprise is headquartered. Without a proper coordination of tax policies there is a clear possibility that either the effects of tax incentives will be eliminated, or the revenue base for the capital-importing country will be eroded, or both.

Prior to the watershed events in 1989 most countries in Eastern Europe had very little foreign investment, and a tax system geared toward central planning. Since attracting foreign investment has now become an important policy priority, these countries will have to establish a two-stage work program. The first stage is to identify the determinants behind such investment, and review the main issues in designing tax policy towards wholly or partly foreign-owned entities in their countries. The second stage will be to compare this review with the tax reforms, and other changes in the regulatory environment that have been put in place over the last year, and thus to formulate a strategy for further reform. This paper attempts to give a preview of this work program.

Important Determinants of Foreign Direct Investment

Before embarking on a discussion of tax policy toward foreign direct investment, it is useful to identify determinants influencing such investment flows. Most research on foreign direct investment has focused either on flows of capital between industrial countries themselves, or on capital export from industrial countries to developing countries. However, Eastern European countries do not fit neatly into either one of these categories of industrial or developing countries, and it is not clear how the special circumstances of these countries will influence foreign investors.

As a group, the countries in Eastern Europe have an extensive and diverse industrial base, albeit one with a largely obsolete capital stock.

They have a well-trained and well-educated workforce, they represent a vast new market, and some of the countries have a reasonably well developed physical infrastructure.[1] Finally, they represent a distinct geographical region, with immediate geographical proximity to the EC, which may become an important source of capital exports to the region. All these indications suggests that the area should be unusually attractive for foreign investors.

Oddly enough, the economic transformation to becoming market economies taking place in these countries may, in the short run, represent the most formidable obstacle to foreign investors. All these countries have an institutional infrastructure (legal systems, regulatory and government agencies, financial institutions) largely incompatible with a market economy that will take some years to change. The transition is, by its very nature, an exercise in trial-and-error reforms, and although the endpoint of this process is relatively well defined, there is no clear-cut path from "here" to "there." If the current gyrations in the macroeconomic environment are added into this, it becomes evident that investment in this region is fraught with unusual short-term uncertainty.[2]

In assessing what factors may affect foreign direct investment to the region, it is useful to turn to the large body of research on determinants behind international capital flows. A survey by Lizondo (1990) divides theories explaining international capital flows into three groups: one assumes perfect markets, a second takes its point of departure in various market imperfections, and a third encompasses more miscellaneous theories. Most hypotheses appear to have some empirical support, but none is robust enough to reject the others.

The focus of the theories assuming perfect markets has concentrated on three variables explaining foreign investment. The first of these variables is the differential between rates of return in the investor country and in the host country, in the assumption that capital is perfectly mobile and will tend to flow toward high-return countries. The second variable is the risk involved in investing in various countries and explains foreign investment as a portfolio diversification at the corporate level since investors will try to minimize their exposure to risk by channeling capital to countries with different and uncorrelated risk profiles. The third variable is the size of the

---

[1] In some areas, however, notably telecommunications, the infrastructure is less developed.

[2] The riots in Romania in late September 1991 against the government's reform program being a case in point.

market in the host country, on the assumption that producing locally for a large market will be less costly than producing for exports in the home country. Of these three variables, market size has the fewest theoretical underpinnings, but yet, according to Agarwal (1980), has been empirically most successful. The reason why the two former variables have not met with empirical success may lie in the serious problems related to measuring actual and expected profits, both of which may differ from reported profits. This difference between reported and actual profits arises because of transfer pricing practices of transactions between a subsidiary and the parent firm, and among subsidiaries.

The second group of theories focuses on market imperfections, which have given rise to an industrial-organization explanation of foreign direct investment. If a firm engages in foreign investment, despite the inherent disadvantages of language barriers, different legal systems, and the like, it must have offsetting advantages, such as brand name, protected technology, or preferential access to financing or to markets.

Of more direct interest to this study, however, is the third group of theories, dealing with how such factors as the macroeconomic environment, political stability, tax incentives, and government regulations encourage or discourage foreign direct investment. It is fairly intuitive that economic and political instability (which often go together) may contribute to an unfavorable investment climate. The potential for large and unexpected changes in the legal or fiscal framework (e.g., expropriations, a change in the tax structure), or abrupt changes in the macroeconomic environment (e.g., spiralling inflation and exchange rate volatility) may all reduce the expected yield from an investment abroad. That empirical analysis of these factors (see Lizondo (1990) for references) has met with mixed results may again be suggestive of the difficulties in measuring these variables. As regards tax policy and tax variables, the majority of empirical research has focused on foreign investment in the United States and on United States' investments abroad, and the empirical results have been somewhat inconclusive. Government regulations that may have a disincentive effect have been studied in Agarwal (1980) and OECD (1989). These regulations usually take the form of authorization procedures, requirements of employment levels and technology transfer, limits on foreign ownership, and limits on repatriation of profits. Empirically, such regulations appear to have had a definite impact on foreign investment, both by introducing additional costs that reduce the profitability of a specific project, and by creating an environment that may be interpreted as hostile toward foreign investment.

Issues in Taxation of Foreign Direct Investment

When the countries in Eastern Europe are designing their policy toward taxation of foreign investment, four issues will have to be addressed: the jurisdictional basis of taxation, which (if any) tax incentives they wish to implement, the definition of minimum presence, and attribution rules for income of enterprises operating in several countries. These issues have been elaborated, although in different contexts, by Conrad (1989), Musgrave (1986), Mutén (1983), and Sinn (1987), and are summarized below.

Jurisdictional Basis

When a corporation invests abroad through establishing or expanding a foreign subsidiary, overlapping jurisdiction of taxation may arise. This can be illustrated by a simple, two-country example, where the following notation is introduced for one country:

t_{RD}—the effective tax rate on *Residents' Domestic* source income,
t_{ND}—the effective tax rate on *Nonresidents' Domestic* source income,
t_{RF}—the effective tax rate on *Residents' Foreign* source income,

and t^*_{RD}, t^*_{ND}, and t^*_{RF} are the corresponding effective tax rates for the other country. The equilibrium condition for an investor—the condition that would leave him indifferent between investing at home and abroad—is that the after-tax return is equal at home and abroad, i.e.:

$$r(1-t_{RD}) = r^*(1-t^*_{ND}-t_{RF}), \text{ and} \tag{1}$$
$$r^*(1-t^*_{RD}) = r(1-t_{ND}-t^*_{RF}). \tag{2}$$

Both investors will have to answer to two tax authorities; in the home country of the investor, and in the host country of the investment. The possibility of multiple taxation of foreign investment, and therefore of heavier taxation, depends as much on the provisions of the home country of the corporation as the host country of the subsidiary. Two opposite jurisdictional principles can be applied to avoid this overlap, known as the residence or source principles. The residence principle implies that all residents of a country are taxed on their worldwide income, regardless of its source. In terms of the example above, this implies that:

$$t_{RD} = t^*_{ND} + t_{RF}, \text{ and } t^*_{RD} = t_{ND} + t^*_{RF}, \tag{3}$$

and all income accruing to a resident is taxed equally, irrespective of its source. The source principle, on the other hand, implies that all income earned within the boundaries of the source country is taxed there, no matter where the ultimate recipient of the income resides. In this case, the example above would yield:

$$t_{RF} = t^*_{RF} = 0, \ t_{RD} = t_{ND}, \ \text{and} \ t^*_{RD} = t^*_{ND}, \tag{4}$$

and all income from the same source is taxed equally, irrespective of the residence of the owner.

If all countries applied only one or the other of these principles, the jurisdictional issues would be quite straightforward, since all capital income would be taxed only once. However, most countries apply different combinations of the two, giving rise to the possibility of double or even triple taxation of border-crossing income flows.[3] Specifically, capital-exporting countries that apply global income taxes (e.g., the United States) tend to use a semblance of a residence principle, taxing the worldwide income of all its residents, with some credit for taxes already paid on foreign source income, and applying the source principle to nonresidents. Other capital-exporting countries, particularly those applying more schedular tax systems (e.g., France) tend to use a source-based principle, largely exempting the foreign source income of its residents.

In practice, a major source of multiple taxation is the coordination of the personal and corporate tax code—both in the host and home country. This can be illustrated by the case of a corporation with a subsidiary in an Eastern European country.

If profits generated in the subsidiary are retained and the home country defers any tax liability on the parent company and its shareholders arising from undistributed income (including capital gains), there is no double taxation. The subsidiary is a separate legal entity in the host country and it is taxed once. However, if the profits are repatriated to the home country, the distribution can take two alternative channels: either through distributions to individual shareholders, or through distributions to the parent company. In either case, the integration of the personal and corporate tax codes becomes crucial.

If the recipient is an individual shareholder, the distribution will be taxed at three levels: through the regular corporate tax in the host country, through a withholding tax at the personal level in the host country,[4] and finally through the personal income tax in the home country of the shareholder. Whether these three levels also imply multiple taxation of income depends on three factors. First, whether the host country applies

---

[3]Or, hypothetically, to no taxation—if a resident of a country applying the source principle invested in a country that applied the residence principle.

[4]As can be seen from Table 1, most Eastern European countries impose such a withholding tax.

the so-called classical system of corporate taxation, in which both retentions and distributions are subject to the full corporate tax, or whether there is some relief for dividends, and if so, whether this is extended to foreign shareholders. Second, whether the home country tax credit for host-country withholding taxes is sufficient. Third, whether and to what extent the home country will impose regular income taxes on dividends received.

Profit repatriation directly to individual shareholders is, however, empirically insignificant, the major portion of distributions being channeled through parent companies. In that case, dividends received by the parent company will become part of taxable income in the home country, that is, an additional layer of corporate taxation, before the income reaches the shareholder, unless the home country grants a tax credit for taxes paid in the host country. In some integrated systems, this tax may take the form of a special levy, imposed as a counterpart to the tax credits enjoyed by shareholders, in case dividends are paid out of tax-exempt foreign-source income.

While no country applies the pure residence or source principles, the pure forms of these two principles have interesting implications for the efficiency of the world allocation of investment and saving. With the residence principle it follows from condition (3) that the tax factor for domestic and foreign investment is equal and therefore that the domestic and foreign before-tax rates of return are equal, that is, $r = r^*$. That the before-tax rate of return will also equal the marginal productivity of capital implies that under this principle the world allocation of capital is efficient. With the source principle, on the other hand, it follows from the arbitrage equilibria (1) and (2) and condition (4), that the after-tax rate of return will be equal domestically and abroad. Since the after-tax rate of return will equal the saver's intertemporal substitution of consumption, it follows that under this principle, the world allocation of savings will be efficient.

Tax Incentives

The types of tax incentives a capital-importing country may introduce can be distinguished along two different lines. First, whether the incentives take the form of lower tax rates, or the form of exemptions or deductions from the tax base. Second, investment incentives in the tax code may be general, applying to both domestic and foreign investors, or they may be geared toward foreign investors only.

Examples of tax-rate incentives primarily take the form of tax holiday provisions, in which an investment is exempt from taxes for an initial period. The definition of the tax base will be the result of provisions on depreciation schedules, carryover provisions for losses, treatment of capital gains, tax credits, inventory valuation, and foreign exchange gains and losses. Measures, such as accelerated depreciation schedules, full or partial exemption of capital gains, and investment tax credits, have been used by most industrial countries and many developing countries over the last couple of decades and raise important issues about the neutrality of the tax system. While some of these incentives have had the intended effect in increasing the volume of investment, more often than not this investment has failed to translate into improved economic growth performance. The reason is fairly straightforward and has been the subject of extensive research over the last few years: these incentives create differences in taxation that result in an inefficient allocation of capital among industries, assets, forms of financing, and forms of ownership. Tax reform in western industrial countries now emphasizes reducing these distortive effects by introducing lower and more uniform tax rates on a broader tax base.

In addition to the issue of neutrality, the combination of various incentives raises important questions about tax design. As pointed out by Mintz (1990), a tax holiday combined with accelerated depreciation allowances may actually penalize an investor in a long-lived asset by preventing depreciation deductions during periods of peak profitability.

Incentives that apply only to foreign investors raise two issues. One issue is that they create an additional incentive for domestic corporations (i.e., corporations domiciled in the capital-importing country) to establish domestic subsidiaries with fictitious foreign ownership to allow them to take advantage of such incentives. The difficulties in uncovering such schemes, and therefore of containing abuse, should not be underestimated. Second, and perhaps more important, the effectiveness of such incentives is ultimately out of the host country's control and depends entirely on how the home country establishes the foreign tax credit given to the parent corporation. This issue usually falls under the label of "tax sparing," referring to whether the home country "spares" the parent company from including the value of the incentives in calculating the tax credit, that is, that this credit is calculated as if full tax had been paid, not reduced by these incentives.

Minimum Connection

A country that is host to direct investment from abroad will, as with other types of taxes, have to define what constitutes a taxable activity, that is, when a certain economic activity is sufficient to become liable for filing returns and subject to taxation. The usual concept in this regard is the "permanent establishment" criterion, but the definition of this varies. From a revenue point of view, there is a clear incentive for capital-importing countries to expand the tax net for foreign investors as much as possible. This, however, neglects the cost of assessing and collecting taxes from "smaller" activities, which may be quite formidable.

Attribution Rules

When a corporation operates in several countries that apply combined residence/source principles of taxation, the problem will arise of how to define net taxable income in each of the countries it operates. This is discussed in some detail in Conrad (1989), Musgrave (1986), and Mutén (1988). Two methods are possible.

The first method is to assess all subsidiaries on the basis of separate accounting, assuming that they maintain an arms-length principle in transactions between themselves and the parent company. However, for many interenterprise transactions markets will not exist which define arms-length prices, especially in transactions that may be at the root of establishing the subsidiary, for example, shared technology, research and development, and management techniques. The resulting interenterprise transfer prices may therefore be somewhat arbitrary and will, in all likelihood, be designed by the enterprise to minimize its total tax liability by shifting profits to low-tax countries.[5]

The second method is to use an allocation formula of consolidated worldwide income of the multinational company, where each country in which the multinational operates is allocated a share of taxable profits based on the share of total value of assets, total payroll, total sales, or some other measure in that country. Mutén (1988) discusses two problems with this method, its international equity implications and the underlying unitary basis. First, this method will tend to be systematically biased in favor of capital-exporting countries, in that both the major part of the assets, the payroll, and sales may be in the corporate headquarters in the home country. An unfairly high share of the total taxable income, and therefore the tax revenue, would therefore be allocated to the home country. Second, the unitary principle underlying the consolidation of worldwide profits implies the use of a single currency. If large exchange rate changes have occurred during the period, the question of which currency to use

---

[5]As Conrad (1989) has pointed out, this arises because differences in tax systems create incentives to shift profits, and not because of inherent problems in separate accounting.

becomes far from trivial, since the calculation of worldwide profits in a devalued currency may show a profit, while recalculation in an appreciated currency may show a loss. It goes without saying that in a period in which Eastern European countries are moving toward currency convertibility, the resulting exchange rate fluctuations could have quite dramatic tax consequences if this method is applied.

Current Taxation of Foreign Direct Investment in Eastern Europe

Table 1 gives an overview of the current tax treatment of foreign direct investment in six Eastern European countries (Bulgaria, Czechoslovakia, Hungary, Poland, the Soviet Union, and Romania[6]). This selection of countries is based principally on the availability of information. One of the most interesting conclusions that can be derived from Table 1 is that tax incentives clearly emphasize tax rates rather than the tax base.

All countries have provisions for tax holidays, ranging from 2 to 5 years, but with somewhat different definitions of the starting point; foundation of the company (Czechoslovakia), start of operation (Poland), and first profitable year (the Soviet Union and Romania). Four countries (Bulgaria, Czechoslovakia, Hungary, and the Soviet Union) combine this with a reduced regular tax rate compared to what applies to domestic firms, usually a reduction of 15–20 percentage points.

None of the countries has a standard accelerated depreciation schedule, or any other compensation for implicit increases in the tax base owing to inflation, but two countries (Czechoslovakia and the Soviet Union) allow accelerated depreciation for foreign companies. This depreciation allowance is particularly generous in the case of the Soviet Union. Some countries (Bulgaria, Hungary, and the Soviet Union) allow loss carryforward provisions, although in the case of Bulgaria this provision is limited to foreign investors only.

The Soviet Union is a special case among these countries in that it allows an appropriation to a reserve fund equal to 25 percent of the equity capital in the firm as a deduction from taxable income and, in addition, allows a full tax credit for the same appropriations, plus for interest expenses and R&D expenses. It would appear that this, combined with the generous depreciation allowances, will enable most foreign investors to reduce their tax liability to negligible levels. One might wonder whether

---

[6]Yugoslavia has been omitted from this comparison because of the paucity of information on foreign direct investment.

Table 1. Taxation of Foreign Direct Investment in Eastern Europe

	Bulgaria[1]	Czechoslovakia[2]	Hungary	Poland	Soviet Union	Romania
Tax rates						
Standard CIT, domestic enterprises	62 percent	55 percent	35 percent for first FT 3 mill., and 40 percent thereafter.	40 percent	45 percent	Progressive schedule of 67 brackets, 5 percent to 77 percent tax rates.
Excess profits tax	No	No	No	No	Yes, 80–90 percent rates.	No
JVs	42 percent	40 percent	28/32 percent[3] (see also tax holidays).	40 percent	30 percent	As for domestic firms.
Deductions						
Accelerated depreciation	No	Yes, for JVs only	No, straight-line with very detailed schedule.	?	Yes, JVs can choose their own schedule.	No
Appropriation to reserve fund	No	No	No	?	Yes, up to 25 percent of equity capital.	
Interest	No	Yes	Yes	?	Yes	Yes
Loss carry-forward	Yes, may be carried forward up to 5 years (JVs only).	No	Yes, may be carried forward up to 2 years.	?	Yes, if reserve fund is not sufficient, losses may be carried forward up to 5 years.	No
Exemptions						
Tax holidays	5 years for certain high-tech industries.	2 years from foundation of JV.	5 years with 14/16 percent tax rate and 21/24 percent tax thereafter if company is in manufacturing or a hotel.[4] 5-year full tax holi-	3 years from start of operation.	2 years (3 in Far East) from first profitable year.	5 years in manuf., agricult., and construction, 3 years in expl. of natural resources, 2 years in trade and services. All from first profitable year.

Other	day, and 14/16 percent tax thereafter if company is in priority sector.[5]	5-year tax holid., 20 percent tax rate, and full exemption from customs duties in free-trade zones. Dividends and other profits distributions are not treated as taxable income. Companies may declare themselves as free-trade zones, exempt from customs.	Dividends and other profits distributions are not treated as taxable income.	Companies may declare themselves as free-trade zones, exempt from customs.
Credits				
Reinvested profits	Full credit			50 percent credit for reinv. profits, or 25 percent credit if certain conditions on imports of raw materials, job creation, and domestic purchases are met.
Other	Ex-post reduction in tax liability available on application for JVs in "public interest" industries.			All appropriations to reserve fund, interest expenses, and R&D expenses.

Table 1 (concluded). Taxation of Foreign Direct Investment in Eastern Europe

	Bulgaria[1]	Czechoslovakia[2]	Hungary	Poland	Soviet Union	Romania
Withholding	10 or 15 percent for dividends, 15 percent for interest and royalties.	?	20 percent for dividends and interest unless reduced by tax treaty.	15 percent for dividends, 10 percent for interest	30 percent statutory rate, effectively reduced to 5–15 percent by tax treaties.	15 percent statutory rate, but tax treaties may exempt partially or totally.

[1] Tax incentives are available only to enterprises with at least 50 percent foreign ownership.
[2] Tax incentives are available only to enterprises with at least 30 percent foreign ownership.
[3] If foreign shareholding is at least 20 percent or Ft 5 million.
[4] If more than 50 percent of turnover is from manufacturing or hotel business, total share capital exceeds Ft 25 million, and foreign ownership share exceeds 30 percent.
[5] There are also regional incentives available, both reduced tax rates for 5 years and deductions for 30 percent of capital investments. Tax incentives in Hungary are cumulative, so a company may obtain both a "preferred industry" and a regional tax rate reduction.

the tax holiday provision, starting at the first profitable year, is redundant in this case.

There are also some interesting differences with regard to the incentive to financing investment. Bulgaria has a very strong incentive against debt financing, giving full tax credit for retained earnings and no tax deduction for interest expenses. Hungary has an opposite incentive, allowing full exemption of dividends and other distributed earnings, and full deductibility of interest.

None of the countries has any explicit provisions for foreign exchange gains or losses. These may be particularly important items for investors in the region.

Table 2 gives an overview of some important government regulations for the same six countries. All countries actually accept up to 100 percent foreign ownership of an enterprise, although several (Hungary, Poland, Bulgaria) require prior government approval for a foreign majority stake. Some countries have requirements on domestic management (Bulgaria). Only Hungary and Bulgaria allow unrestricted repatriation of profits in hard currency and guarantee compensation at market value in the case of expropriation.

Recommendations for Further Tax Reform

Although the fiscal reforms introduced in Eastern European countries over the last two years (somewhat longer in the case of Hungary) have been an impressive achievement, there is clearly room for further improvement in the treatment of foreign direct investment. Future reform should focus on: international coordination, elimination of most incentives, and improving tax administration.

It follows from the discussion in the previous sections that the issues involved in taxing border-crossing income flows are quite complex. The total tax burden of an enterprise investing in Eastern Europe depends not only on the tax code of the host country of the joint venture, but also on the tax code of the country where the parent company is domiciled. Coordination of tax policies should therefore be pursued vigorously, both toward capital-exporting countries and toward other capital-importing countries in Eastern Europe. This coordination should be organized through bilateral tax treaties, based on the OECD or UN model treaties. These model treaties will clarify many of the issues discussed above: jurisdictional basis, minimum presence, and attribution rules, and will also define host-country withholding taxes, home-country tax credits, and clarify the basis for tax sparing. Establishing such bilateral tax treaties will

Table 2. Joint Venture Regulations

	Bulgaria	Czechoslovakia	Hungary	Poland	Soviet Union	Romania
Maximum foreign ownership percentage	Ownership may exceed 49 percent up to 100 percent but approval of the competent state authority is required.	Since 1989, 100 percent foreign ownership is permitted.	Ownership may exceed 49 percent up to 100 percent, but approval of the competent state authority is required.	Ownership may exceed 49 percent up to 100 percent, but approval of the competent state authority is required.	Since 1989, 100 percent foreign ownership is permitted.	Since January 1990, 100 percent foreign ownership is permitted.
Management requirement (foreign vs. national)	Joint management by Bulgarian and foreign partner required.	Legal and actual relationship between Czechoslovak and foreign partner determined under mutual agreement.	Management can be foreign. No obligation to have a Hungarian board member.	General manager can be Polish.	Legal and actual relationship between Soviet and foreign partner determined under mutual agreement.	Management can be foreign.
Profit repatriation	Profit transfer in hard currency is guaranteed.	Profit share of foreign partner can be transferred abroad, but must be financed from joint venture's own foreign currency receipts.	Profit transfer is allowed (and conversion of profits into hard currency is guaranteed by the government).	Must sell 15 percent of annual hard currency profits to a Polish foreign trade bank. Balance of hard currency profit is remittable.		Repatriation of profits up to 8–15 percent of contribution to registered capital (depending on industry) is allowed.

	Bulgaria	Czechoslovakia	Hungary	Poland	Soviet Union	Romania
Foreign currency accounts/credits (joint ventures)	Accounts can be in leva and in foreign currency. Credits can be obtained from both Bulgarian and foreign banks.	Accounts and credits at either Czechoslovak or foreign banks, or from either Czechoslovak or foreign banks.	Joint ventures are subject to same law as Hungarian companies.	Account at Polish foreign trade bank obliged. Account at foreign bank allowed. Credits can be obtained from both Polish or foreign banks.	Accounts and credits at or from either Soviet or foreign banks.	Account at Romanian bank obliged. Account at foreign bank allowed. Credits may be obtained from both Romanian or foreign banks.
Retention rights	Same as Bulgarian firms: average of 50 percent of hard currency earnings can be retained.	70 percent of hard currency earnings can be retained.		85 percent of hard currency earnings can be retained (compared to Polish firms 0 percent).	100 percent of hard currency earnings can be retained.	Same as Romanian small private firms: 50 percent of hard currency earnings can be retained.
Expropriation of capital	Government guarantees compensation at market value in the currency of investment.	No specific provision as yet, but these are in preparation (e.g., intergovernmental agreement).	Expropriation or nationalization not precluded, but government guarantees compensation at market value in currency of investment.	No specific provisions or guarantees in this respect.	International agreements protect foreign investments.	Expropriation or nationalization not precluded, but government guarantees compensation at market value.

send a signal to potential investors about the intentions and the direction of tax policy in Eastern Europe and thus contribute to reducing the uncertainties of investing there. Also, the model treaties may aim at establishing capital export neutrality, that is, that foreign and domestic investments are taxed similarly.[7] Given the complexities of tax legislation in the various industrial countries, with different jurisdictional bases, for example, it would be an almost hopeless task for Eastern European countries to achieve the same neutrality without tax treaties.

The countries in Eastern Europe comprise a close geographical region. They are all undergoing the same reform process, and all are very actively trying to solicit foreign direct investment. An open competition between them, using tax incentives as instruments to attract foreign investors, could lead to a situation observed elsewhere (in Africa, for instance) of a destructive erosion of the revenue base, without necessarily achieving much in terms of investment.

The possible trade-offs between generous tax incentives for foreign investment and possible tax revenue is well known, and analyzed in some detail by Musgrave (1986). If such incentives are effective in attracting foreign investment that carries with it a positive welfare effect for the economy, their use may indeed be warranted. However, as discussed above, there is little empirical evidence on the elasticity of foreign investment to these incentives, and it is thus an open question whether the loss of revenue is for naught. Indeed, this may be considered as an analogue to a discriminating monopolist: if a single producer knows the demand elasticity of each of his customers, and if there is no opportunity for trade between customers, he can charge a different price to each customer and capture the consumer surplus. Similarly, if an Eastern European country knows the elasticity of each potential foreign investor with respect to tax incentives, it might be possible to develop individual incentive "packages" that could attract foreign investment with minimal revenue loss. However, as long as this information is not known,[8] blanket incentive schemes will necessarily imply an income transfer from the country's Treasury to inframarginal investors, who would have made their investment irrespective of tax incentives.

---

[7]In a recent paper, Razin and Sadka (1991) show that the residence principle, which achieves capital export neutrality directly, is indeed the outcome of an optimal tax exercise for a small, open economy, fully integrated in world capital markets.

[8]Even if this information *is* known, it is an open question whether the benefits of the investment would justify the nightmarish tax enforcement problems that would ensue from such individual tax incentives.

A more effective approach to establishing a climate that is attractive to foreign investors is having a tax code that is transparent and predictable, with low and uniform tax rates applied to a broadly defined concept of income, and with necessary provisions built in to account for purely inflationary gains or losses. Eastern Europe should follow this route. First, in addition to creating an attractive investment climate, this approach also has the advantage of establishing a relatively neutral tax system, with minimal distortive effects on capital allocation and potential economic growth within the country. Second, all countries in Eastern Europe have started developing ambitions about applying for membership in the EC as soon as the initial stages of the transition to market economies are complete. Such membership will necessarily imply a harmonization of capital taxation toward the EC standard, which is precisely one of low tax rates applied to a broad tax base. Rather than postponing such harmonization until possible membership is imminent, there is a good case for moving in this direction now, when the tax systems in all Eastern European countries are being developed. Third, and related to this, foreign investors will be concerned about inconsistencies or abrupt changes in tax policy over time, that is, investing when taxes are relatively low, and then facing higher taxes when operations have started.[9] The discussion by Hewitt (1990) is particularly instructive in this regard.

An additional tool to improve communications with potential foreign investors would be to set up a one-stop-shop foreign investment agency as a single interface between foreign investors and host country governments with both authority and expertise to handle all inquiries, authorizations, and approvals.

The tax reform process in the Eastern European countries so far has put an enormous strain on a tax administration entirely unfamiliar with the institutional arrangements of a market economy. The reform process has focused primarily on establishing a legislative framework for income and VAT/turnover taxation, and only now is attention being turned toward building the administrative apparatus necessary to monitor and enforce this legislation. The discussion in previous sections has pointed to several areas where foreign investment will further complicate tax administration. Most prominent among these are enforcing appropriate transfer-pricing practices and legal ownership arrangements within the tax treaties.

---

[9]An interesting case in point is Romania, which avoided this time inconsistency when reforming its profits tax by keeping all joint ventures with foreign participation established prior to the new tax code under the old tax code.

References

Agarwal, J.P., "Determinants of Foreign Direct Investment: A Survey," *Weltwirtschaftliches Archiv*, Vol. 116 (1980), pp. 739–73.

Boskin, M. J., and W. G. Gale, "New Results on the Effects of Tax Policy on the International Location of Investment," in *The Effects of Taxation on Capital Accumulation*, ed. by M. Feldstein (Chicago, University of Chicago Press, 1987).

Conrad, Robert F., "Considerations for the Development of Tax Policy When Capital is Internationally Mobile," World Bank Working Paper 47 (Washington: World Bank, 1989).

Fuente A., and E. Gardner, "Corporate Income Tax Harmonization and Capital Allocation in the European Community," IMF Working Paper 90/103 (Washington: International Monetary Fund, 1990).

Greene, Joshua, and Delano Villanueva, "Private Investment in Developing Countries," *IMF Staff Papers* (Vol. 38), March 1991.

Hewitt, Daniel P., "Optimal Tax/Expenditure Competition Strategy in the Presence of Time Inconsistency: The Case for Investment Tax Abatements," IMF Working Paper 90/59 (Washington: International Monetary Fund, 1990).

IMF Tax Policy Division, "Tax Policy and Reform for Foreign Direct Investment in Developing Countries," IMF Working Paper 90/70 (Washington, International Monetary Fund, 1990).

Jun, Joosung, "Tax Policy and International Direct Investment," NBER Working Paper No. 3048 (Cambridge, Massachusetts: National Bureau of Economic Research, 1989).

———, "U.S. Tax Policy and Direct Investment Abroad," NBER Working Paper No. 3049 (Cambridge, Massachusetts: National Bureau of Economic Research, 1989).

Kopits, George, "Effects of Tax Changes on Direct Investment Abroad," in *United States Taxation and Developing Countries,* ed. by R. Hellawell (New York: Columbia University Press, 1980).

Lizondo, J. Saul, "Foreign Direct Investment," IMF Working Paper 90/63 (Washington: International Monetary Fund, 1990).

Mintz, Jack, "Corporate Tax Holidays and Investment," *The World Bank Economic Review,* Vol. 4, No. 1 (1990).

Musgrave, Peggy, "Coordination of Taxes on Capital Income in Developing Countries," World Bank Discussion Paper DRD286 (Washington: World Bank, 1986).

Mutén, Leif, "Some Topical Issues Concerning International Double Taxation," in *Comparative Tax Studies*, ed. by S. Cnossen (Amsterdam: North-Holland, 1983).

———, *Transfer Pricing Rules or Unitary Method—Where Are We Heading?* (Uppsala: Iustus Publishing, 1988).

OECD, "Investment Incentives and Disincentives: Effects on International Direct Investment" (Paris: Organization for Economic Cooperation and Development, 1989).

Razin, Assaf, and E. Sadka, "Vanishing Tax on Capital Income in the Open Economy" (Unpublished, 1991).

Sanchez-Ungarte, Fernando, "Rationality of Income Tax Incentives in Developing Countries," in *Supply-side Tax Policy,* ed. by V. Ghandi (Washington, International Monetary Fund, 1987).

Sinn, Hans-Werner, *Capital Income Taxation and Resource Allocation*, Vol. 35 in *Studies in Mathematical and Managerial Economics* (Amsterdam: North-Holland, 1987).

Appendix

Selected Economies in Transition: Selected Trade and Economic Reforms, June 1991[1]

	Bulgaria	Czechoslovakia	Hungary	Romania	Poland	U.S.S.R.	China	Yugoslavia	Mongolia
Abolition of central planning	yes	yes	yes	yes	yes	yes	partial	yes	yes
Abolition of trade plan	yes	yes	yes	yes	yes	yes	partial	yes	partial
Abolition of foreign exchange plan	yes	yes	yes	yes	yes	yes	partial	yes	partial
Abolition of foreign trade organizations' monopoly	yes	yes	yes	yes[2]	yes[2]	yes	partial	yes	yes
Foreign trade organizations as agents in foreign trade	yes	yes	yes	yes	yes	yes	yes	yes	yes
Firms may trade directly	yes	yes	yes	yes	yes	yes	some	yes	yes
Abolition of Price Equalization	announced	yes	modified	modified	yes	yes	partial	...	announced
Import tariffs	yes	yes	yes[3]	yes[4]	yes	yes[4,5]	yes	yes	1991[6]
Surcharge[7]	yes	yes	...	no	...	yes	yes	yes	no
Exemption									
Developing countries	yes	yes	yes	yes	yes	yes	yes	yes	no
CMEA	no	yes	yes	yes	yes	yes	yes	yes	partial
Foreign investment firms' capital and equipment	no	yes	yes	yes	yes	...	yes	yes	partial
Raw materials, equipment	no	yes	yes	yes	yes	yes	yes	yes	yes
Export tariffs	yes[8]	no[9]	no	no	no	some[10]	some[11]	no	no[12]
Indirect tax rebates on exports	...	...	...	...	yes	yes	yes	yes	no
Import subsidies (direct)	...	no[13]	...	no	...	yes	limited	no	yes
Export subsidies (direct)	...	no[13]	yes[14]	no	no[15]	yes	no	limited	yes
Import restrictions									
Quotas	no[16]	yes[17]	limited[18]	no	some[19]	yes	no	limited	yes
Licensing (percent of total)	no[20]	limited[21]	yes	yes[22]	yes[19,23]	6[23]	45	no[24]	yes
Export restrictions									
Quotas	some[25]	some[26]	...	yes	some[25,26]	yes	yes	no	yes
Licensing (percent of total)	some[25]	some[27]	yes	some[28]	yes	70	55	...	yes

Appendix
Selected Economies in Transition: Selected Trade and Economic Reforms, June 1991[1] (concluded)

	Bulgaria	Czechoslovakia	Hungary	Romania	Poland	U.S.S.R.	China	Yugoslavia	Mongolia
Bilateral trade agreement	some	some	some	some	some	some	some	some	some
Export earnings retention (percent)	10–50	no	...	0–50	abol-ished	variable	80–90	...	variable
Unified exchange rate	yes	yes	yes	no	yes	no	no	no	no
Convertibility	limited	limited	1994	no	yes	no	no	no	no
Price liberalization (percent of sales)	90[29]	90[30]	90[31]	yes[32]	90[31]	no	45	extensive	60[33]
Enterprises									
Increasing autonomy	yes	yes	yes	yes	yes	some	some	yes	yes
Increasing financial discipline	yes	yes	yes	some	yes	no	limited	no	some
Privatizing public enterprises	discussed	1991	1989	1991	1990	housing	no	discussed	discussed[34]
Allowing private business activity	yes	yes	yes	yes	yes	limited	limited	yes	yes
Liquidation and bankrupcy law	discussed	discussed[35]	yes	discussed	yes	yes	limited	yes	yes[34]

Sources: International Monetary Fund and the World Bank.
[1] Unless otherwise indicated.
[2] Monopoly remains for oil and oil products in Romania and for coal, copper, and sulphur in Poland.
[3] Tariffs applied to convertible area.
[4] Reform in progress
[5] Tariffs were 0–70 percent on 300 items before reform. The U.S.S.R. envisaged adopting the Harmonized System from January 1991 with rates 0–100 percent and averaging 10 percent.
[6] Rate range is 0–100 percent and applied to all countries.
[7] Surcharge rates are 15 percent in Czechoslovakia, 100–300 percent in Romania, 20–80 percent in China, 10 percent of equalizing burden tax and 10 percent surcharge in Yugoslavia, and 100–300 percent in the U.S.S.R. In the latter country the rates are lower for the CMEA than for other countries.
[8] Introduced in 1990.
[9] Limited to some noncommercial exports (e.g., by tourists).
[10] Rates are 5–50 percent on raw materials and energy products.
[11] From 10–100 percent on raw materials, foodstuffs and minerals.
[12] Established in March 1991 and abolished in June 1991.
[13] Abolished in 1991.

14 For exports of processed food, agricultural products to convertible area. But no subsidies were granted for exports outside of export quotas to CMEA countries.

15 10–30 percent but abolished with other export incentives in 1990.

16 Prohibition of imports of 26 products for protection purposes.

17 Introduced in 1991 on cattle, beef, and butter.

18 Competition among firms to fill quotas.

19 Licenses specify quotas and values.

20 Abolished in 1990.

21 Applies only to oil, gas, narcotics, arms and ammunition.

22 For statistical purposes.

23 Licensing includes general and one-time licenses.

24 Except a few products under international agreements and controlled for noneconomic reasons.

25 For centrally balanced items including raw materials, food, and other products to prevent domestic shortage.

26 Including voluntary export restrictions to industrial countries.

27 Includes raw materials, agricultural products to prevent domestic shortage, and items under voluntary export restriction.

28 On products subject to price control and on those imported at subsidized exchange rate.

29 Percentage of turnover liberalized in February 1991.

30 As of end June 1991, another 4 percent is scheduled for end 1991.

31 Three-year liberalization program beginning in 1989 with cumulative liberalization of about 90 percent at end 1991.

32 Virtually complete as of August 1991.

33 60 percent of GDP.

34 June 1991.

35 To be adopted soon.

CHAPTER 12

Public Expenditure: Policy Aspects
Ke-Young Chu and Robert Holzmann

This paper discusses public expenditure policy issues in economies in transition, focusing on those in Europe but also discussing those in Africa and Asia. The next two sections discuss the present economic environment in economies in transition, the role of public expenditure policy, and how economic reform interacts with public expenditure policies, based on recent experiences in several economies in transition. The last section presents some conclusions.

What Have They Inherited?

The present economic environment in economies in transition inevitably affects their public expenditure policies. Most European economies in transition may be classified as middle-income countries, while most African and Asian economies in transition are low-income countries.[1] Traditionally, European economies in transition have not officially recognized the existence of the poor. However, poverty is becoming an important policy issue, although, in absolute terms, European poverty issues are not the same as those of poorer African and Asian economies in transition.[2]

Prior to the reform, economic growth in most economies in transition had been stagnant; conditions have worsened in many of them in recent years. Many have large domestic and external imbalances. The industrial structure in many European economies in transition, which have rela-

---

[1] The discussion is based on statistical data as of the late 1980s, before many of the economies in transition started their reform processes. The basic economic and social indicators discussed in this section have not since changed significantly.

[2] As of 1989, per capita GDPs for six Eastern European former centrally planned economies have been estimated at about US$2,500 on average and for the U.S.S.R. at about US$1,800 (International Monetary Fund (1990)). Income estimates for economies in transition are particularly difficult. Widely divergent estimates can be obtained, depending on what domestic prices and exchange rates are used.

tively large primary and secondary sectors, does not necessarily reflect their comparative advantage. The capital stock is inefficient and unproductive, reflecting the past state-dictated investments. In some European economies in transition, transforming a large inefficient military industry to an efficient nonmilitary one is a major challenge. For many, the break-up of CMEA trade, the increase in oil prices, and the slow world economic growth have resulted in large external imbalances and made foreign private and public creditors extremely cautious about investment in economies in transition—necessitating a further reduction in their domestic absorption.

The social indicators in economies in transition are diverse (Table 1). Mortality rates for children under five years of age range between 15 and 30 per thousand in European economies in transition, between 33 and 80 in Asian economies in transition, and 83 and 214 in African economies in transition. Czechoslovakia has the lowest under-five mortality rate (15), and Angola the highest (214). School enrollment rates are also diverse. Ethiopia has the lowest primary school enrollment rate of 35 percent and an even lower secondary school enrollment rate of 15 percent. The sec-

Table 1. Economies in Transition: Social Indicators
(As of the mid- or late 1980s)

	Mortality Age under five years (Number of deaths per 1,000 live births)	Life Expectancy at Birth (Years)	School Enrollment Ratio[1] Primary	Secondary (Percent)
Europe				
Bulgaria	16	72	104	75
Czechoslovakia	15	71	96	38
Hungary	18	70	97	70
Poland	19	72	101	80
Romania	24	70	97	79
U.S.S.R.	30	71	...	...
Yugoslavia	27	72	95	80
Africa				
Algeria	83	64	96	54
Angola	214	45	93	13
Ethiopia	189	47	35	15
Mozambique	197	48	68	5
Asia				
China	33	70	132	43
Mongolia	80	62	102	92
Viet Nam	51	66	102	42

Sources: The World Bank, *Social Indicators of Development, 1990*; The World Bank, *World Development Report*, 1990; and IMF (1990).
[1]School enrollment ratios exceed 100 percent in some cases because the children who are older than statutory school ages remain enrolled.

ondary school enrollment rate of 5 percent in Mozambique is dismal, but in some other countries, such as Angola, China, Czechoslovakia, and Viet Nam, the rate is also very low.

Public Expenditure

Analysis of public expenditure in economies in transition is severely hampered by distorted product and factor prices, including controlled product prices, nontransparent public-sector compensation systems, unrealistic interest rates, and a multitude of exchange rates, some highly overvalued. The quality of data is problematic in many economies in transition, as a result of both distorted prices and misclassification, and the share of public expenditure in GDP and the composition of public expenditure may not provide a realistic picture of its economic or functional mix.

A unique characteristic of economies in transition, of course, is the domination of their public sector in both the production and use of their domestic output. In most European economies in transition, on the production side of GDP, the domination is almost complete: state-controlled production accounts for some 90–95 percent of GDP. The domination of the state sector explains its pervasive role in investment.

Official statistics suggest that, based on national account data, the share of government consumption in GDP in European economies in transition ranges between 4 percent and 10 percent (although one of the countries shows 20 percent). These extremely low shares (compared with the share of about 20 in other countries) suggest severe statistical problems, as well as represent distorted prices, rather than reflect a limited share of government consumption.[3] The share of private consumption varies, with about 50–60 percent in European economies in transition and 50–70 percent in some African economies in transition. The shares for European economies in transition are somewhat below those for many industrial countries (60–70 percent).

Based on budgetary data, the resources commanded by the general government (including central and local governments) are larger in economies in transition than in more market-oriented economies. For exam-

---

[3]The May 1991 issue of the IMF's *International Financial Statistics* indicates that as of the late 1980s, the share was 4 percent and 6 percent, respectively, for Romania and Poland, and 9 percent and 11 percent, respectively, for Yugoslavia and Hungary; Czechoslovakia was an exception, showing 20 percent. The ratio was 19 percent for Algeria and 24 percent for Ethiopia. In the case of industrial countries, the ratio ranged between 17 percent and 20 percent, except for Sweden and Finland, which showed above 25 percent.

ple, in the late 1980s the ratios of general government expenditure to GDP in the European economies in transition averaged about 55 percent. The ratio for Poland was about 50 percent; the ratios for Yugoslavia and Romania were between 40 percent and 45 percent. These levels are substantially higher than in market-oriented developing countries, whose ratios tend to average some 30 percent, or even industrial countries, whose ratios tend to average some 40 percent.[4] These ratios, however, are not extraordinarily high compared with those of some industrial economies with extensive welfare systems. For example, in 1988, the ratios of general government expenditure to GDP in the Netherlands, Norway, and Sweden were close to 60 percent, and those in Austria, Belgium, Ireland, and Luxembourg exceeded 50 percent.

The economic mix of general government expenditure indicates grossly distorted prices. In the late 1980s, transfers to households and enterprises in European economies in transition ranged between 10 percent to 30 percent of GDP (Table 2). Compared with market-oriented industrial economies, the high share was largely due to the relatively high share of transfers to enterprises in European economies in transition. The wage bill, as it appears in the budget, is relatively small. For example, in 1989, the public sector wage bill for Bulgaria, Czechoslovakia, Hungary, Poland, and Romania accounted for only 5–8 percent of GDP, but this low share reflected low monetary wages, complemented by transfers and other indirect payments.[5] Low-interest payments in European economies in transition in general are due to artificially low interest rates.

The functional mix of general government expenditure indicates the importance that some of the European economies in transition attach to social security and housing, the latter expenditure being a component of the compensation package. Thus, in 1988, expenditure on these programs in Hungary, Romania, and Yugoslavia accounted for 10–20 percent of their general government budget. These shares were substantially higher than in market-oriented countries and than their own shares of expenditure on health or education. Some economies in transition have had a heavy burden of military expenditure. One of the most comprehensive sources of international data on military expenditure (SIPRI data) indicates that in 1972–88, in European economies in transition, military expendi-

---

[4] International Monetary Fund (1990), pp. 112–13. The ratio of 30 percent of general government expenditure to GDP in developing countries compares with about 25 percent for the central government. It is likely that the ratios for some economies in transition are higher if all the extrabudgetary entities are included.

[5] The labor share of GDP is also lower in economies in transition than in market-oriented industrial economies (see the next section).

Table 2. European Economies in Transition: Composition of General Government Expenditure
(In percent of GDP)

	Bulgaria	Czechoslovakia	Hungary	Poland	Romania	U.S.S.R.	Yugoslavia
General government expenditure, 1989							
Total expenditure	60	69	64	48	45	56	41
Major components							
Goods and services	24	24	22	13	15	21	9
Of which: wages and salaries	5	7	8	8	5	...	...
Interest payments	3	—	3	—	—	1	—
Transfers to households	10	13	16	10	11	8	19
Of which: social security	10	12	14	9	8	8	...
Subsidies and current transfers to enterprises	15	19	16	17	1	18	13
Capital expenditure	5	6	7	7	18	8	—
Central government expenditure, 1988	...	...	58	39	37	...	7

Sources: International Monetary Fund, *Government Finance Statistics Yearbook* (1990); Kopits (1991); and World Bank, *World Development Report* (1990).

ture on average accounted for roughly 10 percent of GDP—12 percent for the U.S.S.R. and from 1.4 to 4.6 percent for other European economies in transition. Angola's military expenditure accounted for nearly 20 percent of GDP (Hewitt (1991)).

Policy Issues

Market-oriented reform in centrally planned economies has important implications for public expenditure policy, since it requires, inter alia, a redefining of the eventual role of the public sector vis-à-vis the private sector. Economies in transition must also define the role the public sector should play during reform.

The large role of the public sector was inevitable in a command economy, where the government intervened heavily in production, allocation, and distribution through the operations of general budget (budgets of state, local authorities, and the numerous extrabudgetary funds), socialized enterprises, and fiscal functions of monetary authorities and financial intermediaries. Despite their large role, public sector financial operations were subservient to the quantity-based plan and were only a residual of the planning process for assuring, together with credit and cash plans, the consistency of financial balances at administratively determined prices.

The market-oriented reform compels economies in transition to reduce, or even eliminate, many government activities and to shift these functions—partly or fully—to the emerging private sector. Reform should be aimed at reducing public ownership, cutting the scope of the budgetary resource intermediation, and virtually eliminating traditional subsidies to households and enterprises.

However, even in a market-oriented economy, the public sector has an essential role to play. The general budget becomes a major instrument of macroeconomic policy. The government has to provide public goods and services that the private sector either does not provide or provides less-than-socially-optimal quantities. In addition, the government redistributes income between individuals, groups, and generations.

For most economies in transition, it is still unclear whether they will choose a market system like that in the United States or like that in Scandinavia. However, it is clear that the economic and political dynamics will conflict. For example, the limited private sector in economies in transition is likely to compel them to provide transitory budgetary support of private initiatives; however, public intervention should be designed to avoid conflict with the growth of private activities. The intervention and its resource implications will also conflict with the demand for lower taxes;

this demand will grow as economies in transition adopt a tax system based more on personal income and consumption.

Economic Reform and Public Expenditure Policy

Public Expenditure Policy During Transition

During reform, the public sector should reduce macroeconomic imbalance, increase the efficiency of resource use, promote sustained economic growth, and foster social objectives.

Economic and political considerations as well as the starting position of economies in transition dictate that public expenditure policy should play a major role in stabilization. Thus far, all European economies in transition have rejected monetary reform as a way to deal with the inherited monetary overhang. In many of these countries, the absence of domestic financial markets precludes the possibility of nonmonetary financing of even a small deficit; in addition, a weak external payments position does not allow them to borrow from abroad. Moreover, the revenue position of the budget during reform is likely to weaken (Tanzi (1991a)). All of these factors indicate that a substantial cut in budgetary outlays is a central element in securing stable prices during transition.

On purely economic grounds, budgetary restraint should be easy because many expenditure programs are inefficient and unnecessary. Economies in transition can reform or eliminate many public programs and improve allocative efficiency. Prime candidates in this respect are the large budgetary subsidies to consumers and enterprises that range between 10 percent to 30 percent of GDP, or up to 50 percent of total budgetary outlays in some years (see Holzmann (1991a), Ahmad in this volume). A drastic cut and the eventual elimination of these traditional subsidies will not only improve the budgetary position, but will also be indispensable for enhancing allocative efficiency. In many economies in transition, including those in Europe, military expenditure consumes a much higher share of resources than in market-oriented economies, and a substantial reduction of their military expenditure should be possible.

The role of the public sector as a guarantor of employment has been a major source of inefficiency. While the nontransparency of the compensation system involving entitlements in various forms has made it difficult to estimate the wage bill at shadow prices, the public sector wage bill, as it appears in the budget, has been mostly moderate. As the reform proceeds, however, public sector wages and salaries should become more competitive vis-à-vis the private sector. The public sector will have to abandon its objective of employment guarantee. At the same time, the wage structure will have to change, with more pronounced wage differential for more efficient provision of public services.

As the reform proceeds, the investment expenditures of socialized enterprises will rely more on their own retained earnings and even on financial markets. The privatization of these enterprises should reduce even further their dependence on the state budget. However, economies in transition face a difficult task of having either to provide budgetary support to restructure state enterprises prior to privatization or to hand them over to domestic and foreign investors at scrap value. Rising unemployment will increase the pressure for the government to attempt restructuring with a continued emphasis on providing employment opportunities.

At the same time, many economies in transition will have to redefine the role of the central or federal government vis-à-vis that of republics or local governments. In the past, the central budgetary authorities determined expenditure priorities for the local authorities. Such an approach is not only likely to be inconsistent with ongoing political reform, but is also inefficient (see Hewitt and Mihaljek in this volume).

The growth orientation of public expenditure should involve at least the following. First, public investment programs for physical infrastructure and human capital should be strengthened and be made to maximize their complementarity with private investment, while taking into account the possibility that private sector responses may not be fast enough. Second, the poor prospects for the foreign as well as domestic private financing of large investment requirements point to the importance of potential public sector contributions to the national savings (Tanzi (1991b)). Third, public outlays (or tax expenditure) should support private initiatives to compensate for market imperfections (such as the lack of a broad-based commercial banking system) and the uncertain business climate. Fourth, budgetary outlays should also be required to clean the balance sheet of socialized banks and enterprises from past commitments, as a necessary step for avoiding "bad equilibria" reflecting the absence of capital markets (Calvo and Frenkel (1991)).

The public sector should also be instrumental in protecting the poor and the environment. The traditional social programs (particularly pension, sickness, and family benefits) should be made more efficient and targeted to the poorest and most vulnerable. In addition, economies in transition in general need social safety net programs to protect the poor during the transition. European economies in transition should introduce or strengthen programs for unemployment insurance and social assistance for protecting the most vulnerable during reform (see Holzmann (1991a and 1991c), Kopits (1991), and Ahmad in this volume). The environmental problem (largely owing to distorted energy prices, the bias toward heavy industry, and ineffective regulations) will be partly contained as more appropriate prices of energy products emerge; however, many European economies in transition may not be able to improve the quality of the environment without some budgetary expenditure.

Implications of Economic Reform for Budgetary Expenditure

These needs for budgetary outlays during the reform point to the need for a speedy reform of traditional expenditure programs. The reform process itself, however, will affect the level and composition of public expenditure.

The reform will change the way GDP is produced, used, and distributed. The corresponding changes in macroeconomic aggregates will influence public expenditure as well as revenue. As economies in transition grow, their primary and secondary sectors will contract, forcing them to adopt burdensome unemployment and early retirement provisions (as experienced by many Western industrial countries in the 1970s and 1980s). At the same time, as the reform proceeds successfully, the improvement of the efficiency of resource use will enable economies in transition to reduce their relatively high fixed investment and stock-building without reducing growth—although during transition, they will have to increase public investment substantially. Finally, the wage component of GDP is relatively low in economies in transition (approximately 35 percent), compared with market-oriented economies (55 percent), reflecting the importance of in-kind entitlements (e.g., housing, health, and education) in the compensation package, in which monetary wages tend to become a residual. This compensation system allows for relatively high earnings of socialized enterprises, but requires high revenue from earnings and turnover taxes. While the reform will reduce the revenue base by increasing the wage share, it will also reduce the need for many expenditure programs.

At least temporarily, however, the budget is likely to be burdened by former implicit subsidies that are likely to become explicit as the reform proceeds. A successful reform program requires an adjustment in relative prices through domestic price liberalization, the move toward positive real interest rates, and an appropriate exchange rate policy. The mostly upward adjustment of real interest rates and exchange rates, however, has potential wealth and distributional effects, requiring additional budgetary subsidies for some of those with net financial liabilities. This budgetization of implicit subsidies will also result from housing credits and foreign debt.

In centrally planned economies, interest rates did not play an allocative role. Households' choice of instruments for financial savings was limited essentially to deposits in specialized state banks, which paid very low deposit rates, and this allowed the banks to grant housing credits at low interest costs. As tight monetary policy and competition among financial institutions drove real interest rates toward positive levels, this cross-subsidization became unsustainable. For social and political reasons, many of these countries avoided a full pass-through of higher deposit rates, which would have resulted in a substantial burden for households facing large outstanding debts and compressing real wages, thus creating political pressure for new subsidies.

Former centrally planned economies also extensively used exchange rates as planning instruments. In addition, the socialized enterprises had to obtain foreign loans in convertible currency indirectly through a state-owned bank that extended credit in domestic currency—often at low interest rates; the exchange rate risk was therefore taken over by the financial intermediary, resulting in major hidden subsidies to socialized-sector enterprises. Devaluation implies large valuation losses of financial institutions; for economic and legal reasons, however, they cannot pass the losses on to the enterprises. These losses require either direct budgetary transfers or lower nontax revenues from the financial institutions.

Since virtually all foreign debt was contracted and extended on similar terms, with the domestic counterpart having been eroded in most countries by high inflation, both the principal and interest of the whole foreign debt becomes a liability of the budget. Consequently, the large foreign debt problem in most of these countries has become not only a balance of payments problem, but also a budgetary problem; any debt reduction will ease both balance of payments and budgetary difficulties for years to come.

Recent Experience in Reform Countries

The relationships between economic reform and public expenditure in European economies in transition (Bulgaria, Czechoslovakia, Hungary, Poland, and Romania) are similar in many respects, but also different owing to their varying starting positions as regards macroeconomic imbalances, prior reform attempts, and expenditure priorities.

In all European economies in transition, expenditure restraint has been a major instrument for stabilization. Some countries have attempted to reduce the share of general budgetary outlays drastically as a percent of

GDP by cutting traditional subsidies (particularly for foodstuffs) substantially. The cut was partly offset by the need to create new subsidies and transfers (such as for housing and foreign debt). Moreover, they have not been able significantly to reduce transfers to enterprises. Many of them have also reduced capital expenditure, wages, and defense outlays, although some increased (in real terms or as a percentage of GDP) social security outlays. This latter increase, however, is not due to increased income support for the most vulnerable but is a result of the slow reform of traditional social programs which exert additional expenditure pressure in a more market-oriented environment.

Since all European economies in transition are still attempting to stabilize their economies, their public expenditure composition does not yet reflect market orientation; nor does it have a growth-oriented posture. On the contrary, the composition of expenditure still tends to reflect their former command systems, while the revenue side increasingly reflects their market-based environment. Such a situation aggravates macroeconomic instability, makes structural change even more difficult, and requires a speedy and drastic reform of major expenditure programs, particularly the further reduction in traditional subsidies, military outlays, transfers to socialized enterprises, and a major reform of social security programs. With the tax system reform and the corresponding revenue position improvement, these measures should allow for introducing badly needed growth-oriented expenditure.

Among African and Asian countries, China has more reform experience than any other country, beginning a wide range of reforms in 1978. Some countries, such as Angola and Mongolia, are just beginning reform processes. While all these countries have started or are starting their reform processes with large macroeconomic imbalances, most African and Asian economies in transition have lower living standards and less trained manpower than their European counterparts. Although reducing macroeconomic imbalances is as urgent as in European economies in transition, in African and Asian economies in transition, the state has a larger role in strengthening the nutrition, health, and education of the poor.

China's approach to reform has been aimed at enhancing the role of individual state enterprises and increasing the flexibility of its system to replicate the functioning of the market-oriented system, while keeping the widespread state ownership (Blejer and others (1991)). Decentralization has enabled state enterprises to retain a larger fraction of their earnings and to finance their investment directly from their own earnings. As a consequence, the ratio of state expenditure to GDP declined from 34 percent in 1978 to 23 percent in 1988, largely reflecting a similar decline in state capital outlays. The decline in expenditure has been limited by the continuous subsidization of state enterprises and consumers. The state enterprises have continued to need subsidies because price reform has been incomplete; urban consumers have needed subsidies because of food price increases.

Mongolia began a major reform effort in 1990 by eliminating the State Planning Committee (Milne and others (1991)). The medium-term reform plan calls for a reduction in expenditure from 65 percent of GDP in 1988–90 to 50 percent of GDP in 1991–95. The reform has helped eliminate many subsidies. Increases in domestic prices have enabled the Government to eliminate most subsidies to the agricultural sector, loss-making state enterprises, and importers. Enterprises are expected to finance an increasing proportion of their investments either from their own resources or by borrowing.

Concluding Remarks

Economies in transition share common policy issues. Redefining the role of the state is the most obvious. All economies in transition have to determine how fast they want to establish private property rights, create competitive product and factor markets, eliminate distortions in prices, and transfer the state's activities relating to the production of private or semi-private goods to the private sector. In spite of these common issues, there is great diversity among economies in transition. Their living standards, macroeconomic problems, and social conditions differ substantially. The speeds of their reforms have also differed. Some are attempting not only to establish private ownership, but also to privatize state-owned land and state enterprises. Others are moving slowly, retaining state ownership but enhancing the autonomy of state enterprises.

The role of public expenditure policy in economies in transition depends on, inter alia, their initial economic conditions and their intentions regarding the speed of the reform. Most economies in transition have to reduce public expenditure to improve their fiscal balance. Many have to reform their inefficient consumer and enterprise subsidies and reduce defense outlays; at the same time, they have to allocate the limited public financial resources to the most pressing needs, which differ among economies in transition. European economies in transition must improve their infrastructures to pave the way for efficient private investment. They also must reform their social security systems and improve the quality of the environment. Many African and Asian economies in transition have to enhance their human capital as a basis for sustained growth.

The reform process results in changes in the level and composition of public expenditure, but these changes should not be assessed in isolation. As some prices are liberalized, subsidies that were implicit will become explicit, and the level of measured public expenditure will tend to increase. Coping with the impact of a less-distorted price structure is less obvious, but very important. An increase in official prices and changes in relative prices will change the composition of public expenditure. For example, an increase in consumer prices, while reducing subsidies, will necessitate an increase in both public sector wages and social safety net programs.

Successful public expenditure reform is a critical condition for economic reform. Public expenditure reform, however, depends on reforms in taxation, pricing, public enterprises, and fiscal devolution. Successful public expenditure reform also depends on the country's commitment to reducing the state's direct role in production, allocation, and distribution, containing the level of public expenditure within a sustainable macroeconomic framework, improving the efficiency of public programs, and enhancing its indirect role in inducing efficient private economic activities and productive investment.

References

Blejer, M.I., D. Burton, S. Dunaway, and G. Szapary, *China: Economic Reform and Macroeconomic Management*, IMF Occasional Paper 76 (Washington: International Monetary Fund, January 1991).

Borensztein, E., and P.J. Montiel, "Savings, Investment, and Growth in Eastern Europe," IMF Working Paper 9/61 (Washington: International Monetary Fund, 1991).

Calvo, G.A., and J.A. Frenkel, "Transformation of Centrally Planned Economies, Credit Markets, and Sustainable Growth," paper presented at the joint Austrian National Bank-International Monetary Fund Seminar on Central and Eastern Europe: Roads to Growth (Austria), April 1991.

Hewitt, Daniel P., "Military Expenditure: International Comparison of Trends," IMF Working Paper 91/54 (Washington: International Monetary Fund, 1991).

Holzmann, R. (1991a), "The Social Safety Net," in *The Transition to a Market Economy in Central and Eastern Europe*, ed. by P. Mahrer (Paris: Organization for Economic Cooperation and Development, 1991).

——— (1991b), "Budgetary Subsidies in Centrally Planned Economies in Transition," IMF Working Paper 91/11 (Washington: International Monetary Fund, 1991).

——— (1991c), "Adapting to Economic Change: Reconciling Social Protection with Market Economies," paper presented at the ILO Tripartite Symposium on the Future of Social Security in Industrialized Countries (Geneva), October 1991.

International Monetary Fund, *Government Finance Statistics Yearbook* (Washington, 1990).

———, and others, "Summary and Recommendations," *The Economy of the USSR* (Washington, 1990).

Kopits, G., "Fiscal Reform in European Economies in Transition," IMF Working Paper 91/43 (Washington: International Monetary Fund, 1991).

Milne, E., J. Leimone, F. Rozwadowski, and P. Sukachevin, *The Mongolian People's Republic: Toward a Market Economy*, IMF Occasional Paper 79 (Washington: International Monetary Fund, April 1991).

Tanzi, V. (1991a), "Mobilization of Savings in Eastern European Countries: The Role of the State," in *Economics for the New Europe*, ed. by Anthony B. Atkinson and Renato Brunetta (London: Macmillan, 1991).

—— (1991b), "Tax Reform and the Move to a Market Economy: Overview of the Issues," in *The Role of Tax Reform in Central and Eastern European Economies* (Paris: OECD, 1991).

CHAPTER 13

Government Budget and Accounting Systems

A. Premchand and L. Garamfalvi

The success of the formulation and implementation of appropriate fiscal policies is dependent, to a very substantial extent, on the strength of the fiscal institutions in general, and budget and accounting systems in particular. These systems in the centrally planned economies had extensive influence on a number of countries that adopted central planning at a later stage and on countries that had a mixed-economy orientation. These systems had also some impact on the literature on planning and budgeting. Despite this extensive influence, however, the literature available on the subject is relatively small. The need for heightened awareness of the various aspects of these systems, both in theory and practice, arises from two interrelated considerations. The first is the extent to which the systems had contributed to fiscal distress and to the consequent general disillusionment with the economic system. The second is the type and extent of improvement needed in the systems to be adapted to meet what are perceived to be the general needs of a democracy and a market economy. This paper therefore is devoted to a description of the budget and accounting systems in centrally planned economies—their features, themes, and limitations—and a discussion of the issues and vulnerable areas, as well as the ways in which the transition may be made to market orientation.

Some caveats relating to the description of the systems and discussion of issues should, however, be noted at the very outset. The features described have developed over a period of time. While historical antecedents are briefly alluded to wherever appropriate, the description refers to the features found in the late 1980s.[1] The picture is drawn from a variety

---

[1]Readers interested in an extensive discussion of the development of the sys-

of countries and should therefore be viewed as a composite rather than as an individual country description.[2] The systems had widespread application of varying intensity. In addition to the U.S.S.R. and Eastern European countries, the systems in Algeria, Angola, Benin, China, Congo, Cuba, Ethiopia, Guinea, Lao People's Democratic Republic, Mongolia, Mozambique, Myanmar, Somalia, Tanzania, and Viet Nam represent variations on a theme and have a common framework. In some cases, the framework as applied in some of these countries was, for all intents and purposes, the same as was in practice in the U.S.S.R. In some countries, some features of the Soviet system were adapted to the local conditions, while in others they became additional features to the traditional machinery. The discussion of the features primarily relates to those that are common to these economies and follows more the orientation of an economist than that of either an accountant or a student of public administration. Moreover, the evaluation of the system is not in comparison with any ideal system, but primarily in terms of the strengths and weaknesses relative to the expected goals and tasks.

Structural Aspects of the Systems

The approaches to decision making and the values that underlie the decisions basically reflect the institutions, structures, systems, and techniques used by governments. In this regard, centrally planned economies offer some uniform features. Essentially, the budget and accounting systems in government reflect a value chain in which the role of each one and the complementarity among the components in the decision-making pyramid are carefully designed. As Pryor (1968) noted some time ago, the institutions responsible for public expenditure management are more hierarchically organized in the centrally planned economies than in the market economies.

Important among the major instruments used by the government is the budget itself. Supplementing the fiscal policy articulated through the budget is the credit policy, which seeks to provide necessary monetary resources for the production system. In many cases, credit is used as an extension of fiscal policy and the banking institutions provide funds, often

---

tems since the early days of the Russian revolution may see Davies (1958) and Campbell (1963). The official Soviet Government publication, *Soviet Financial System* (1966), is also, not withstanding some turgid prose, a essential reading.

[2]Two case studies, of China and Poland, respectively, are provided in Premchand (1990).

supplied from the budget and from their own resources as well, for the purposes specified by the government. These development financial institutions, although called "commercial," do not receive or accept funds from the public, but are used as conduits to pass on funds to selected projects and programs specified by the government. Thus, an understanding of the working of the fiscal policy would require an analysis of the budget as well as the operations of the development financial institutions. (In the overall paradigm of central planning, though the budget is given some primacy, redistribution of national income also takes place through the credit system, and through the mechanism of price planning.)

The national budget in centrally planned economies, following a principle of "democratic centralism," includes the budgets of the central government, regional levels of government (republics, provinces, and so forth), and local levels of government (communes, municipalities, and prefectures).[3] The arrangement is an extension of one of the basic themes of centrally planned economies, namely, "unified leadership and decentralized management," although the origins of inclusion of provincial and local governments in the central budget would appear to be more rooted in expediency than in any ideal.[4] The provincial and local budgets are, however, prepared in conformity with the guidelines provided by the central ministry of finance, and the budgets so prepared are reviewed and consolidated by the central governments. Both types of budgets—central and local (including provincial)—are expected to be in balance with no deficits. During more recent years, however, this came to be applied with some relaxation in that central governments were permitted to have deficits while local budgets were to be balanced. The experience in this regard differs among countries. For example, in China, provincial governments are expected to be in balance but during recent years have tended to accumulate payment arrears which, in a way, means that budgetary deficits have occurred.

The budgets also reflect the extensive linkages between government and public enterprises. In centrally planned economies, the state intervenes in all types of economic activities and practically all economic activ-

---

[3] There are variations on this theme. An important exception to this is Yugoslavia where each republic has its own budget. The federal budget is responsible for one third of the total public sector finances.

[4] During the initial years after the revolution in the U.S.S.R., the republics were permitted to draw up their own budgets, but as their response for the mobilization of financial resources needed for "socialist reconstruction of the economy" was less than expected, their budgets were integrated with the central budget and "national budgets" came to be prepared. See Soviet Financial System, p. 84.

ities are under state ownership. Traditionally, the state provides from its budget all the capital needed for the establishment of its enterprises, provides the needed inputs, and buys the outputs. The capital, until recently, was provided in the form of a grant, although as an integral part of recent reforms aimed at instilling an awareness of the costs of capital, some capital is provided in the form of a loan. It is, for this reason, that discussions of the capital structure of an enterprise, the relative roles of equity and debt, and the computation of the rate of return, tend to be somewhat alien in nature in centrally planned economies. In return for the capital provided, the state demands and receives in turn, in addition to turnover taxes, a share of the profits as well as a share of depreciation reserves.

The umbilical linkages between the government budget and enterprise budgets have, in most cases, two types of impact. First, is the growth of extrabudgetary funds. These are different from enterprise budgets which anyway are not included in the national budget. These funds were usually set up to provide a measure of managerial autonomy to budget units with own revenues to ensure a more efficient use of resources. The common characteristic feature of their financial relationship with the state budget is that if own revenues are not sufficient for carrying out tasks entrusted to a fund, they are entitled to receive subsidies from the state budget. Although the reasons for setting up extrabudgetary funds might have differed among countries, there appear to be four categories of funds.

(1) *Separate state funds*—financed from earmarked fiscal revenues not transiting through the state budget and from subsidies from the state budget. These funds are entrusted with major tasks such as environmental protection, water supply development, road network development, and are supervised by agencies at the ministerial level.

(2) *Budgetary establishments*—authorized to engage in profit-making activities in addition to their budgetary tasks. This category includes research institutes attached to universities or to university hospitals.

(3) *Special support funds*—engaged in the provision of goods and services on a small scale, such as providing recreational facilities to employees of a ministry or day care for the children of employees, or other nonpecuniary benefit.

(4) *Auxiliary funds*—set up as management units in support of activities, such as maintenance and repair of administrative buildings.

Extrabudgetary funds, which have grown in number, spawn a variety of activities, are frequently equivalent in size to the state budget,[5] and have

---

[5]This is the case, for example, in China. See the country study in Premchand (1990).

tended to blur the distinction between what is basically a budgetary task of the government and the task of an enterprise. More significantly, the unitary nature of the budget, while insisted upon in theory, remains obscure in practice.

The second impact is on the cash nature of the budget. The budget system in centrally planned economies is, in principle, cash oriented, in the sense that transactions are recorded when money is received or paid rather than at the point when liability has arisen. In practice, however, given the close links between the government budget and the enterprises, transactions may take place without any movement in cash. Thus, taxes due are routinely adjusted against subsidies to be paid or capital to be transferred.[6] In addition, the budget itself shows total revenues net of subsidies paid to enterprises.

The systems in centrally planned economies also reveal a greater role for the central bank. All receipts and outlays of the state are received and paid out by the central bank and its offices. The central bank, in addition to meeting the day-to-day needs of the state, furnishes the initial accounts to the government which then prepares, on that basis, an annual financial report. The bank has thus a major role in the process of control over budgetary compliance.[7]

The budget system in centrally planned economies has another notable feature that merits recognition. This relates to its classification of the budget transactions. On the revenue side, the approach of the classification is to make a distinction between taxes, profit remittances (included as a part of receipts from state-owned enterprises and institutional units), and other revenues. On the expenditure side, however, a distinction is made between productive and unproductive expenditure. (Lenin considered that the practices of bourgeois economists in regard to classification bordered on "official financial trickery."[8]) This distinction, which in a manner may be considered as an extended application of the one made by Adam Smith between productive and unproductive labor, separates the outlays on industry, agriculture, transport and communications, and related efforts as expenditure in the productive sphere, and outlays on social

---

[6]This type of adjustment which started in the U.S.S.R. several decades ago was refined and formalized in the organization of the Social Accounting Service in Yugoslavia. This agency, set up in 1959, is the only financial recording agency for all the entities of the public sector. Thus, there are no delays in the payment of corporate taxes to the government or subsidy payments to the enterprises, for these are all carried through cashless book adjustments.

[7]For an illustration, see the country study on Poland in Premchand (1990).

[8]See *Soviet Financial System*, p. 225.

services, defense, and administrative services, as unproductive.[9] The systems do not, however, make any distinctions between current and capital outlays.

The government accounting system follows a two-pronged approach in that double-entry bookkeeping is utilized for production and enterprise type of activities, while a single-entry system is used for normal service-type activities of the government.[10] As Campbell noted, these systems are "virtually identical with traditional capitalist accounting."[11] During the budget implementation stage, spending ministries are free to authorize the budget allocations after the approval of the budget. In most cases, the productive agencies are each assigned a government-owned development bank, which acts as a payment agency. In some cases, the bank is also responsible for compiling the accounts of the agency for which it is acting as a banker. In most countries, following the Soviet practice, taxes are paid every ten days and accounting reports covering both receipts and expenditure are compiled for each segment of ten days and for the month.[12]

Financial Planning and Budgeting

One of the enduring contributions of central planning systems both to practices and to the literature on budgeting is financial planning.[13] Financial planning aims at building a proper bridge between production plans and their financial implications. Planning in centrally planned economies is essentially done in terms of five-year and annual plans that in turn are based on the material balances approach under which the linkages among

---

[9]From the national accounts standpoint, the system in CPEs makes a distinction between that part of the national income which is allocated to the accumulation fund (material production) and the part allocated to the consumption fund (nonproductive).

[10]See Campbell (1963), and the country study on China in Premchand (1990). The major differences are in regard to the treatment of profits (which are distributed to various funds) and valuation of assets, which is invariably done in terms of historical cost.

[11]See Campbell (1963), p. 11.

[12]Pryor (1968) makes a reference to other features of CPEs such as that budgets are usually explained rather than debated. This aspect has, however, undergone some changes during recent years in several countries. For example, in China, the budget for 1991 was returned to the government for additional work before final approval.

[13]Financial planning was ushered in as an integral part of the New Economic Policy announced by Lenin. Since then, both terms—New Economic Policy and Financial Planning—have become part of policymakers' jargon. During the last two decades, financial planning came to be practiced by industrial and developing countries, with varying degrees of success. For a detailed account of these practices, see Premchand (1983).

various sectors are analyzed in terms of physical inputs and outputs. The tasks of the state sector are conceived, in this process, primarily in material terms, which are then converted into financial terms.[14] But not all activities of the state are converted into cash, for, as already noted, several transactions may not involve any cash disbursements as appropriate adjustments are made in the accounts. Thus, separate cash plans are prepared. But these cash plans form only one of the many components of the system as a whole (others include the financial plans of enterprises, collective farm sectors, capital investment plans, and so forth). The financial plans normally cover a period of one year and thus are coterminous with the budget rather than with the medium-term financial plans.

The basis of financial estimates is derived from the physical goals specified in the plan. Each sector of expenditure is given guidance on the level of standards (or norms) in physical terms. These are then converted into "standards in financial terms," which, simply stated, are a translation of the physical standards into monetary terms, calculated at prices specified by the government. Such standards are indicated for the whole economy, while "budgetary standards" are applicable to the outlays financed from the budget. Costs derived from these standards are labeled as standard costs, although they refer primarily to the cash flows rather than accrued costs. These costs are applicable for ongoing activities as well as projects under construction and the maintenance aspects of completed projects and are computed, approved, and enforced by the central agencies such as the state planning commission and the ministries of finance.

On the basis of the above-mentioned standards and related assumptions about the broad needs of the country, initial plans are prepared with reference to which guidance is provided to the departments and the budgetary process is initiated.

Budgetary Process

The budgetary process, as usual, involves a number of organizational steps that are common with other mixed and market-oriented economies. The various phases involved in budget preparation are illustrated in Table 1. It should, however, be added that the timetable shown therein is

---

[14]Here again, it would appear that the emphasis on material or physical aspects was a natural alternative in the U.S.S.R. during the early years after the revolution. During this period, high inflation was rampant and the value of money was being eroded progressively. Planners preferred the emphasis on physical aspects, which were then converted, for purposes of budget, into financial terms. Since then, material balances have become a firm fixture in the landscape of planning (see Davies (1958)).

illustrative only and the actual practices vary among countries. Similarly, the nature and the number of participating institutions may also vary among countries. Some aspects of the process illustrated in Table 1 deserve elaboration. The first relates to the process of review of investment plans and outlays proposed for construction, which also tend to dominate the budget. General guidance is provided as to the areas where investment is needed and the kind of production targets that are expected to be fulfilled. On this basis, the concerned agencies prepare a number of project proposals for review by the planning agency. Their scrutiny, which has varying levels of screening and which now is a common feature of investment planning in general, has come to be replicated in mixed economies. The major difference between the centrally planned economies and mixed economies is primarily the prices assumed for the purpose. In the former, prices reflect the valuation of the concerned official. In the latter, it is a linear extension of the market forces.

The second relates to the impression about the financial structure in centrally planned economies and the notion that all directives flow from the top down. This is true, but only partially, in the sense that all budgetary programs are reviewed, approved, and monitored by a central body which is usually the planning organization. But before final decisions are made, there is a substantial input from all concerned into what is included in the plan and the budget. During this phase, there is room for bargaining at every level. In some cases, this bargaining could even lead to a budget that is different from the financial equivalent of the plan prepared by the planning organization. Depending on the "systems politics" or the relative power of the planning and finance organizations, the plan may set the framework for budgets, or negotiated budgets may set the basis for plans. In addition, once the plans and the budgets are approved, operational flexibility is given to the agencies, subject, of course, to the compliance of various process controls (discussed further on). This operational freedom provides a relief from the high degree of centralization that may be implicit in the process.

The third aspect concerns the role of the legislature, and the role of the budgeteer in the process. Every financial system usually has an institution that is considered to be dominant by virtue of the responsibilities vested in it. Power comes from that dominant position. There is one seat of power in centrally planned economies which, for all external appearances, resides outside the government. This is the party congress. Its influence is not measurable, but practically nothing moves without its knowledge, involvement, and active assistance. Broadly, it is comparable to a legislature, but the way in which financial business of the government

Table 1. The Budget Preparation Process

Principal Activities	Participating Institutions	Timetable
1. Preparation of an annual draft plan based on the medium-term plan. The annual draft plan includes preliminary targets and limits for output and labor productivity. The draft plan is communicated to the ministry of finance, branch ministries, functional ministries, and to the national bank for information.	Central planning authority	February–March
2. Preparation of instructions, forms, and schedules for forthcoming budget year. Preparation of a preliminary balance of revenues and expenditures corresponding to annual draft plan. The preliminary balance accompanied by comments, explanation, and instructions is sent to branch ministries, functional ministries, and to the national bank for information.	Ministry of finance Branch ministries Functional ministries National bank	March–April
3. Branch ministries prepare budget instructions for enterprises, based on the preliminary balance.	Branch ministries Enterprises	April
4. Preparation of budget estimates for the forthcoming year in enterprises, branch ministries, and functional ministries.	Branch ministries Functional ministries	May
5. Discussions of budget estimates, negotiations, and bargaining in view of "readjusting" targets and limits for outputs and inputs.	Central planning ministry Ministry of finance Branch ministries Functional ministries National bank	May–June
6. Preparation of a revised annual draft plan.	Central planning authority	June
7. Preparation of a revised balance of revenues and expenditures corresponding to the "revised" annual plan.	Ministry of finance	July–August
8. Budget negotiations between the ministry of finance, branch ministries, and functional ministries.	Ministry of finance Branch ministries Functional ministries	September
9. Preparation of the draft budget and submission to the council of ministers.	Ministry of finance	September
10. Discussion of the draft budget by the council of ministers. If approved, submission to the national assembly.	Council of ministers	October–December
11. Approval by the national assembly.	National assembly	November–December

is carried out by this body is different from any legislature. It has no taxing powers; it has no specified role for the introduction and processing of money bills. But none of them can take shape without the approval of the party.[15] The life of a budgeteer in centrally planned economies is relatively smooth. The plan specifies the allocations and the basis for them, as well as the expected outcome. The plan is the basis on which spending agencies prepare their proposals. The plan also provides the basis for the budgeteer's existence in central and spending agencies. Inasmuch as everything is specified, his role is confined to fine-tuning the phasing of outlays submitted to him.

Also, insofar as a plan always concentrates on the incremental spending, the issue for the budgeteer is to deal with the increment, ignoring the ratcheted level of previous year's spending. Thus, each year's level becomes a part that is consigned to history and efforts are devoted to the slicing of the increment to the extent that such slicing is not fully indicated in the plan. Here again, the approach is one of fine-tuning rather than one that seeks a structural involvement. This atmosphere guarantees a minimum, and provides a certainty to the budgeteer that his counterparts in other systems would envy.

The certainty comes from a picture that is totally artificial. Macroeconomic stability is assumed. Prices are fixed by the government and do not reflect the market scarcities. It is this aspect which undergoes a total transformation as economies are opened and as prices, for the most part, are fixed by the market. The macroeconomic picture can no longer enjoy the stability (which, anyway, as noted above, is a doctored one) and will reflect the basic strengths and weaknesses of the economy. In the new environment, the primary task of the budgeteer is to come out of his long isolation and to recognize the impact of the macroeconomic aspects on the budget and the impact of the budget on the economy. This requires him to forecast, to carry his colleagues in the spending agencies with his forecast, to formulate his budget on the basis of that forecast, and to provide himself with contingency mechanisms to cope with the changes in the economy.

The control framework in centrally planned economies has been analyzed traditionally in terms of (a) preliminary financial control, (b) current financial control, and (c) post factum control.[16] The first type of

---

[15]It is not uncommon that the party adds its own proposals to the budget. In China, these are popularly known as "comrade-so-and-so" projects. This phenomenon is comparable to the pork-barrel approaches in Western democracies.

[16]See *Soviet Financial System*, p. 347. Davies (1958), however, sought to

control is carried out during the review of budget estimates process to verify the accuracy of conversion of material values into financial terms. The second type of control is essentially a process or compliance control exercised within an agency at the time of incurring expenditure, and the last type of control is exercised after the transactions are completed and is a type of audit control. This brief description, however, does not do justice to the overall framework of controls that exists in centrally planned economies.

The control framework, reflecting the value chain system associated with centrally planned economies, has evolved over the years and covers budget transactions, extrabudgetary funds, outlays under the credit plan, and the outlays of the state enterprises for capital construction. The framework is also unique in that it reflects the unitary structure of the government. It is a vast one and includes policy controls, regulatory controls and process, and ad hoc controls. In addition, there are controls that relate to quantitative restrictions on the supplies of material inputs and of vital elements such as electricity (these are illustrated in Table 2).

In theory, it would appear that this ambitious framework offers a series of specified opportunities for interaction with agencies to coordinate their fiscal activities and to ensure, by and large, that the tasks undertaken are in accordance with agreed plans. Of specific importance is the fact that these controls are also applicable to the transactions of the provincial or decentralized levels of government. Policy guidance from the central government is both a part and an extension of the national plan. The two main components of this are the indicative guidance of the level of expenditures for each province for the next year and, more specifically, the level of investment to be undertaken regardless of the sources of financing. This guidance in turn reflects two concerns—the level of investment in the economy and the need to maintain a balanced budget in the provinces. By its very nature, it thus tends to be broad and the main responsibility for ensuring that the resources are effectively used to meet the local needs rests with provincial governments. As an integral part of this effort, the central government also takes into account the level of administered

---

analyze them in terms of "technical," "economic," and "efficiency" controls—technical control seeks to ensure that funds are spent for the purposes intended, while efficiency control refers to the use of resources. Economic controls are those that seek to ensure allocative efficiency (p. 203). The last one refers to the controls exercised at the budget formulation stage, while technical controls are the same as process or compliance controls. Davies concluded that, in practice, there were no efficiency controls except in terms of the logic of the norms or standards for each type of service.

Table 2. Framework of Controls

Policy Controls	Regulatory Powers	Process Controls	Ad Hoc Controls	Physical Controls
Direction of macroeconomic management	Determination of budgets for earmarked purposes	Review and consolidation of agency budgets	Determination of supplemental budget allocations to agencies; Determination of provincial transfers to the center	Specification of physical aspects of projects
Determination of investment		Approval of investment budgets; Review of payments	Determination of central transfers to provinces	
Determination of price subsidy policies	Determination of extra-budgetary funds and their activities	Quarterly monitoring of central and provincial budgets and reporting to the cabinet	Determination of change in the annual budget in light of changing economic events	
Determination of domestic and foreign borrowing	Determination of loan component of national key projects	Submission of annual accounts	Determination of transfers from enterprises	
	Yardsticks for personnel and wages	Determination of domestic bond issues		
	Specification of budget and accounting rules	Determination of foreign loans		
	Specifications on the use of circulation funds utilized by enterprises	Monitoring of credit plan implementation		

prices, as well as the level of subsidies (both on specified commodities and those reflecting the operational losses of enterprises) and the levels of domestic and external borrowing. Thus, responsibilities for policies concerning the essential components of macroeconomic management are vested with the center. The impressive range of controls should not, however, be mistaken for effective controls.

Strengths and Weaknesses

The preceding brief discussion may give the impression that in all unimportant matters the systems in market economies and centrally planned economies are generally identical; the important differences are the extent of state ownership and its involvement in the economy, and as a corollary the emphasis on central planning. These systems have, however, revealed strengths and weaknesses over the years. Essentially, the weaknesses arise largely from the practices in each and every area of budgeting and expenditure controls, and the strengths are in the area of accounting and payment processes. Since the strengths are fewer than the weaknesses, it is appropriate that they are considered first.

The accounting system, which is primarily intended to insure against dishonesty and to provide documentation on the transactions of the government, is designed on the model of a commercial system and has been largely successful in providing timely data. That said, it should be noted that the central planners have tended to rely more on the extensive statistical system than on the accounting data generated for their policymaking and monitoring. Another area of strength is the relative abridgement of the payment process. The assignment of a bank to each spending agency has reduced the red tape and the numerous steps of verification associated with a number of other systems. That this aspect may have been given less importance may have been entirely due to the fact that in the dirigisme of planning, the focus is all on the upstream activities, that is, policymaking.

The weak areas are, however, too many. Basically, the systems have undergone little change over the years. That very feature would appear to have undermined its strengths. Further, some seeds of problems would appear to be inherent in the system. On the structural front, the establishment of numerous extrabudgetary funds has tended to overshadow the importance of the budget. In such a context, the real content of fiscal policy has been less clear. It could be argued that fiscal policy's lower profile was inherent in central planning and, therefore, the creation and functioning of extrabudgetary funds may not have been as problematic as it might appear. This has to be tempered, however, by a recognition of the contradictions in the approaches of the budget, on the one hand, and extrabudgetary funds, on the other, and the frequent incidence of fiscal perversity in the activities of the extrabudgetary funds.

Another weak area has been the role of bargaining in the budgetary process. Although the extensive enumeration of plans and their components should, in theory, minimize the importance of bargaining, in practice it would appear that this has been quite prevalent. The organizational rationality has been such that each agency has endeavored to obtain enlarged budgetary allocations. Where this was not possible, resort was made to extrabudgetary transactions. Apart from this circumvention, as Davies noted, "the actual operation of a direct planning system . . . inevitably involves the emergence of illegal or semi-legal operations,"[17] by which the units or agencies have made efforts to adjust to realities and somehow or other scramble for materials and other inputs to carry out the specified projects. This contributed to the pursuit of a track parallel to the budget. Furthermore, insofar as legal channels are concerned, agencies have tended to manipulate data and selectively use "outside" support to obtain protection or a dilution in the directives of the central agency. The result has been that budgetary outcomes have often been different from estimates. To some extent, the role of bargaining could have been minimized through the formulation of a budget law. While centrally planned economies have had a number of decrees and associated regulations, they did not have a budget law as in other systems, to guide and discipline the budgetary process. The absence of such a law has tended to encourage bargaining.

The framework of control, while giving the impression of a neat and precise division of labor, has been and is a fragmented one, with too many institutions participating—often with overlapping spheres of control. By including all conceivable activities, the framework has lacked priorities and selectivity. More significantly, given the dependence on the transformation of material balances into financial terms, the budget and related planning did not provide for any margins of slippage or contingencies. The budgeteer, in that context, has looked to bargaining as an administrative safety net.

The major vulnerable area, however, concerns the way in which the resource constraint is internalized in the various stages of the budgetary process. In centrally planned economies, little allowance has been provided for the macroeconomic dynamics of resource shortage. As a Soviet official publication stated, "Socialist finance is always very stable. Financial

---

[17]See Davis (1958), p. 181.

282 • FISCAL POLICIES IN ECONOMIES IN TRANSITION

resources are growing continuously. There are no budget deficits and there is always a surplus of revenue over expenditure."[18] It added that "the issue of currency is not used as a source of revenue." This approach has had a twofold effect. First, since the calculations of requirements have been made in terms of materials, or what has come to be known as volume terms, the agencies have had no need to think of financial implications. They were to be financed regardless of cost.[19] Second, the focus of the agencies' efforts has been on the increment in the aggregate. There has been, therefore, an innate compulsion to demonstrate a need for more resources, rather than to manage effectively the already available resources. Thus, each year's expenditure levels have become the base for ratcheting upwards and they have tended to become progressively so as financial benevolence on the one hand, and defense needs on the other, have become, in most cases, inexorable. The absence of knowledge of resource availability may have become a powerful incentive and those responsible for budgets in the agencies would appear to have been less than aware of the claims of the additions on the resources. In that context, budgets that were not to have incurred deficits began to experience them and bank financing has become an automatic exercise. Normally, the emergence of the deficits would have contributed to the formulation of policies aimed at avoiding deficits. In the event, a weak budgetary machinery became, it would appear in retrospect, an unwitting ally to a policy failure. This combination may have contributed to the collapse of the system sooner than later. While it is always possible to argue that policy failure alone may have contributed substantially to this, the contribution of the budget machinery in building up a ratcheting expenditure process cannot, by any means, be minimized.

Toward a Market Economy

The issues referred to above need to be addressed, even if there were no efforts made to move toward a market economy. They acquire, however, greater urgency in the context of movement away from central planning. The systems need to be strengthened to meet the growing demands, and to reorient the systems so that they can be made more responsive.

---

[18]*Soviet Financial System* (1966), p. 61.

[19]During the 1970s, expenditure planning in the United Kingdom was done in volume terms. This very soon contributed to a crisis and by 1981 forced the authorities to switch to a cash basis. For a more detailed account of this experience, see Premchand (1983), Chapter VI.

A movement to a market economy implicitly assumes a corresponding movement toward political freedom and the establishment of democratic forms of government. While there are variations on the theme or the content of a budget in a democracy, its two essential features are transparency and accountability for results. The former ensures that funds are applied for the process approved by the legislature. The budget itself should be transparent so that the full purpose of the outlays and the results likely to accrue are made clear. While it is recognized that some of the controls described earlier do ensure that funds are applied for the approved purposes, the exercise of the controls in the new setup will be more transparent so that, where necessary, the legislature itself could also oversee the day-to-day activities of the government. Transparency does not mean an open invitation to the legislature to micromanage. Rather, the intent is to provide a window of opportunity to monitor the performance of the executive part of government.[20]

Accountability imposes additional tasks on the executive in that it has to ensure delivery of goods and services in an economic, efficient, and effective manner. As already noted, there is little incentive for government departments in centrally planned economies to economize; history also shows that there has been little concern for the delivery of services. These tasks impose, therefore, numerous additional responsibilities on the budget system.

The first imperative is to formulate the budget in the context of a macroeconomic framework with an explicit recognition and assessment of the linkages between the budget and the economy, and a reasonable assessment of prospective income and what can be achieved at what cost. Recent experience makes it abundantly clear that resources are—contrary to the previously cited assertion about socialist finance—limited, and that bank financing is finite. In this changed context, the capacity of the budget system needs to be strengthened so that resource realities are recognized at every stage. This would involve planning of a different type. It requires forecasting, on a rolling basis, the implications of each program and source of revenue so that there could be an explicit recognition of the parameters and determinants of each program and of the influence of policy decisions and other nonpolicy changes on programs. Spending agencies need to be informed of the ceilings on resources. These approaches, together with contingency plans or articulation of fall-back positions in the event of changes of assumptions or actual developments,

---

[20]Poland has already enacted legislation specifying the role of the legislature in regard to budget matters. Hungary has formulated draft legislation in this regard.

would show all concerned the impact of current policies and the margins available for expansion or the effort needed for scaling down some operations. In turn, these efforts result in the education of the public about the prospective benefits and impending burdens. Working within a macroeconomic framework would imply that resource allocation would no longer be a matter of ensuring increments, but downward adjustments too. The budgetary process needs to adapt itself to that significant change. The type and extent of change involved, for example, in the preparation of budget estimates, is illustrated in Table 3.

The budgetary machinery also needs to be changed in two other associated aspects. As indicated before, the national budgets in centrally planned economies also include the budgets of the local levels of government. This, however, has contributed to a good deal of overlap and frequent duplication in the efforts of central and local governments. There is now a need to clearly define the respective roles, responsibilities, and jurisdictions of the various levels of government in regard to revenues and expenditures. Further, as central banks attain a measure of autonomy, the relationship between them and the government, particularly in regard to the function of central banks as payment agent and as providers of short-term finances, would need to be specified.

The budget itself would need a good measure of consolidation in these economies. Apart from shedding the functions that have become redundant in the context of privatization, the opportunity has to be taken to draw the contours of coverage of the budget.[21] As an integral part of this effort, the extrabudgetary accounts would have to be rationalized.

Introduction of the above-mentioned changes would also require supplementary organizational modifications in the ministries of finance. Apart from undertaking the type of rolling financial planning, the ministries may have to assume some of the functions that would cease to be performed by the central banks.[22] Moreover, the ministries would have the obligation to monitor the implementation of the budget so as to ensure that the

---

[21]Viet Nam has delinked state-owned enterprises from its budget in 1989. The system of taxation has moved from a sharing of profits to the taxation of profits. Financing of subsidies and capital expenditures (including circulation funds) from the budget has been stopped.

[22]Viet Nam is one of those few who have shifted these functions from the Central Bank (State Bank of Viet Nam) to the Ministry of Finance. A national Treasury has been established to be responsible for collection and payment of government monies, for the compilation of government accounts, and for the coordination of domestic and foreign borrowing. A similar effort initiated in Yugoslavia in 1990 did not make much progress, however, in view of the subsequent major political developments in the country.

Table 3. Impact of Market Orientation on the Government Budget: An Illustration

Budget Items	Centrally Planned Economic System	Market-Oriented Economy
Revenues:		
Taxes on nonagricultural cooperatives and private sector	Private sector's role not significant in the economy. Revenues are negligible.	The importance of private sector activities will dominate economic activity. Income taxes will gradually increase in importance and become a major revenue source.
Turnover tax	Value of turnover constrained by price controls; revenues stagnant.	Free market pricing will ensure buoyancy of turnover taxes if rates are ad valorem.
Profit tax	Profits are regulated; revenues are stagnant.	Profits determined by market demand conditions and corporate profit taxes will increase in importance as market expands. Tax administration should be developed to avoid lags in payment and evasion.
Commodity taxes	Sales taxes on goods and services constrained by price controls	Sales taxes are collected on a monthly basis. Highly elastic with price developments and could be a reliable source of revenue.
Agricultural tax	Insignificant, and cumbersome as it was in part paid in commodities. Difficult to value.	Income taxes on agriculture are difficult to assess, but indirect levies such as land taxes or sales taxes are easier to collect in cash rather than in commodities.
Trade taxes	Revenues constrained by artificial transfer prices from COMECON, and distorted exchange rates did not reflect scarcity value of traded goods.	Market-related exchange rates help dampen excess demand, and taxes on international trade are very important sources of revenues. Difficult to evade and easy to collect, and elastic if rates are ad valorem.
Taxes and transfers from SOEs (state-owned enterprises)	Lags in price adjustment reduce profits, the most important source of taxes—based on turnover. Taxes collected reflected extent of subsidized inputs.	Nonprofitable SOEs will be subject to restructuring. Profits will be affected by autonomy of enterprises on decisions of production, pricing, and investment. Switch to corporate profit taxes may imply a decline in relative contribution of SOE during transition, as surpluses of SOEs will no longer reflect input subsidies which were eliminated.
Crude oil exports	Local value depends on exchange rate paid by special trading agreements.	Free market price and appropriate exchange rate will provide full value for the exports.

Table 3 (continued). Impact of Market Orientation on the Government Budget: An Illustration

Budget Items	Centrally Planned Economic System	Market-Oriented Economy
Nontax revenues	Fees set at artificially low levels.	Inflation adjustment of fees and cost recovery measures will improve receipts.
Expenditures:		
Wages and salaries Basic wages	Fixed wages are supplemented by commodity rations.	Automatic adjustments indexed. If wage adjustments are not fully indexed with inflation, the wage bill can be controlled in real terms.
Transfers Social Security Fund	None, because prices are subsidized.	Social security funds will cost government in the short run but the cost will be much less than provision of subsidies under centrally planned economies.
Transfers for working capital of SOEs.	SOE losses and working capital requirements automatically covered irrespective of efficiency considerations. Open-ended subsidies of SOE operations.	Very limited. Reliance on banking system finance encourages financial discipline and more efficient utilization of resources; lower outlays.
Subsidies Food procurement Production Exports	Major expenditure items. Production subsidies to cover SOE losses and consumption subsidies result from prices set at below cost. If costs cannot be reduced, the subsidies are open ended and inefficiencies increase government expenditures and contribute to inflation and cost hikes in a vicious cycle.	Subsidies for production by SOEs eliminated. Open-ended subsidies for consumption goods abolished. Prices will improve resource allocation and solve problem of excess demand. Limited subsidies to essential inputs can be phased out as markets develop.
Interest	Depend on size of debt (domestic, foreign); interest rates and exchange rates which were held down artificially reduced outlays but had serious distortive effects on the economy.	Depends on size of debt; interest rate reform and free exchange rates will increase outlays, but should encourage more responsible borrowing for clearly more productive uses.
Goods and services Administrative expenditures Operating and maintenance Services (education and health)	All purchases determined according to plans and reflect dominant role of public sector. Costs do not reflect market value and thus do not encourage efficient utilization of goods and services.	Volume of purchases will decline in real terms as more activities are taken over by private sector. However, costs will reflect market prices which will require higher unit cost. Value for money considerations should be encouraged to improve efficient use of outlays.

Other (including security and military)	Depends on size of operations; lack of correct valuation of resources may encourage excessive outlays.	Depends on size of operations; private contracting for supplies will eventually reduce outlays; exchange rate changes will increase outlays for import content.
Capital expenditures	Large outlays; determined according to material balances in plan. Evaluations distorted by using artificial prices, interest rates, exchange rates which may result in wrong priorities for investment. Excessive emphasis on heavy industry, self-sufficiency, and protection.	Much smaller outlays limited primarily on infrastructure, as private sector takes responsibility for investment in the economy guided by markets. Appropriate prices and interest costs will guide investments to most competitive and efficient sectors.
Fiscal deficit (excluding grants and government financing requirements)	The deficit is determined according to plan. Excessive fiscal deficits should be avoided but if they occur are not considered economically significant since price changes are controlled; thus, excess liquidity (monetary balances) generated from government dissavings will have to be offset by "forced" household savings. This is manifested in shortages of supplies relative to demand at the official prices.	The fiscal deficit is of critical importance to economic management throughout the year. The size and financing of the deficit affect economic activity and money supply. Deficit financing is the most important cause of inflation as prices are free to move and excess liquidity chasing a limited supply of goods represents excess demand. To curtail excess demand deficit financing (particularly printing of money) will have to be reduced by control of the deficit. The choice of fiscal deficit financing requires delicate coordination with monetary policy instruments (domestic debt management) and external sector policies (external debt management).
Foreign borrowing (net) Former trade blocks within centrally planned economies	Barter trade transactions are the means of payment. The relative competitiveness of different countries is not measurable; loans have a large implicit grant element determined by noneconomic factors such as solidarity considerations.	Trade and loans among all countries are denominated in convertible currencies. Since repayment will be in hard currency, true international competitiveness of utilization of borrowed funds will determine the purchasing power of the domestic currency.
Convertible currencies	Budgetary impact is dependent on the amount of debt contracted.	All debt is contracted and repaid in convertible currencies. Flexible exchange rates imply constant revision of debt revalued in local currency cover which has to be mobilized even when there are external payment arrears.

Table 3 (concluded). Impact of Market Orientation on the Government Budget: An Illustration

Budget Items	Centrally Planned Economic System	Market-Oriented Economy
Domestic borrowing Banking system	A balancing item by default in the financial plan; affecting the monetary balances held by the public with no outlet but savings at the banking system. Fully accommodating monetary policy ensures inflationary financing of the deficit; but inflation is not immediately recognized in the state-owned sectors.	Of critical importance to the level of credit in the economy. Liquidity in the economy increases by a multiplier effect at commercial banks and directly results in inflationary pressures (as more money chases a limited supply of goods). This excess demand also spills over to the external sector as excess demand for imports which causes a deterioration in the balance of trade. With flexible exchange rates the price of foreign currency (the exchange rate) will also devalue. Short-term monitoring of bank borrowing by government is a critical condition for financial management and stabilization program.
Nonbank borrowing	Not practiced.	An important stabilization policy instrument for *short-term* financial management. Interest rates will have to be remunerative. The instrument draws down liquidity from the economy for a short period to allow the fiscal measures to take hold (they usually do so with a lag). Without correcting the fundamental fiscal problem, interest payments by government add to the deficit and liquidity soon after.
Arrears	Regarded as an accounting problem.	Regarded as a form of credit with exactly the same monetary implications. Nonpayment to government of liabilities by taxpayers or borrowers has the same effect of government lending to them in terms of liquidity in the economy and inflation. Arrears are an inflationary instrument of financing. External arrears are inflationary unless their value is sterilized in blocked accounts, and are frequently contributing to erosion of the real value of the currency.
Below-the-line accounts and contingent liabilities	Not significant; as the whole economy is largely public sector.	Domestic banks lending to SOEs, or foreign banks lending for projects, will seek to reduce their exposure to the swings affecting market conditions through acquiring a lower risk of sovereign debt. Unless the uses of loans were efficient, the contingent liability will turn to a real expenditure by government in due course. Control of government guarantees is a financial management practice.

macroeconomic policies are on track. These aspects imply that finance ministries should have the capacity both to induce and deter certain actions.

Further, with a view to minimizing the role of "bargaining," in the process, a kind of budget law needs to be formulated. Such a law should not be a mere codification of the existing practices; rather, it should be the framework that embodies the above-mentioned changes and specifies the role of the legislature, ministries of finance, central banks, central and local government nexus, the role of spending agencies, and associated aspects.

Along with the above, accounting systems need to be strengthened so as to ensure the preparation of comprehensive accounts and provision of adequate cost information on various services. More important, it would have to serve the purposes of departmental management rather than being oriented exclusively, as has been the case, to the statistical demands of the central planner. This user orientation will, however, be successful only when the user himself is more aware of his own needs as a manager. This transformation is not merely inevitable, but a priority at this stage.

Management of Change

The changes indicated may, in theory, be introduced either in one sweeping action or more gradually. It has to be recognized, however, that the systems now existing in centrally planned economies have been developed over a period of years and, inevitably, change will also be gradual. Moreover, the recent experience with institutional development suggests that it is a medium-term task, more suited to long-distance runners than to sprinters. Also, it should be noted that the dismantling of central planning has not so far contributed to any major change in the way in which government budgets are formulated and implemented in these countries. While there have been expressions of intent to change the systems, change itself has been negligible.

But any effort at reform requires that more attention be paid to the management of change so that problems that may arise can be anticipated and addressed. This requires a strategy for the implementation of changes. Such a strategy has to be evolved, taking into account the financial and human resource shortages, differentiation in content to meet the heterogeneous requirements of the users, phasing of implementation, and more important, the availability of contingency mechanisms in the event of emergence of a new set of problems. Furthermore, due attention needs to be paid to the cost of proposed changes and their technological underpinnings. Plans of action need to be tested to ensure that there is a feedback mechanism to address the problems. Also needed is a comprehensive understanding of the causation between action and result. Some changes may have instant results, while some will have long lags. The organizational bottlenecks such as inertia, legal obstacles, efforts at self-preservation, protection of territorial turf, comfort of the status quo, and ambivalence about the future also need to be taken into account. Values that have been acquired over four decades and that have become ingrained into thinking would take some time to replace. Meanwhile, the price that the community pays for this inertia is that its fiscal policy becomes a captive to the archaic systems. A beginning in this long journey is overdue.

References

Campbell, R.W., *Accounting in Soviet Planning and Management* (Cambridge, Massachusetts: Harvard University Press, 1963).

Davies, R.W., *The Development of the Soviet Budgetary System* (Cambridge, England: Cambridge University Press, 1958).

Premchand, A., *Government Budgeting and Expenditure Controls* (Washington: International Monetary Fund, 1983).

———, ed., *Government Financial Management: Issues and Country Studies* (Washington: International Monetary Fund, 1990).

Pryor, F.L., *Public Expenditures in Communist and Capitalist Nations* (London: George Allen and Unwin, 1968).

U.S.S.R., *Soviet Financial System* (Moscow: Progress Publishers, 1966).

Other sources consulted in the preparation of the paper include the following:

Abalkin, L.I., *Economic Reforms in the European Centrally Planned Economies*, Economic Commission for Europe (New York: United Nations, 1990).

Berend, T.I., *The Hungarian Reforms, 1953–1988* (Cambridge, England: Cambridge University Press, 1990).

Gallik, D., C. Jesina, and S. Rapaway, *The Soviet Financial System* (Washington: U.S. Department of Commerce, 1968).

Knight, P., *Economic Decision-Making Structures and Processes in Hungary: The Dilemmas of Decentralization* (Washington: World Bank, 1984).

CHAPTER 14

Social Security

George Kopits

Perhaps ironically, countries that have lived for decades under *socialism* are experiencing a *social security crisis* of major proportions. Existing social security schemes impose a heavy fiscal burden on these countries' productive structure, provide insufficient protection for the elderly and the indigent, induce waste and misallocation of resources, inhibit incentives to work and to save, and are vulnerable to considerable abuse. Social security reform ranks among the most complex yet urgent tasks in the transition to a market-oriented economy. The challenge ahead is not only of a technical but also of a political and social nature. Accordingly, the reform is expected to take into consideration the inertia of certain contractual obligations (e.g., age requirement for old-age pension) and constitutional rights (e.g., to free health care). In broader terms, despite the abolition of socialist central planning and official recognition of unemployment and poverty, governments of transition economies have been reluctant to undertake wide-ranging social security reform.[1] Sweeping reform is viewed with fear by large segments of the population that risk losing entitlements to which they have become accustomed over generations.

This paper highlights the salient features of social security institutions and practices in economies in transition, identifies major problems, and examines options for reform. The discussion focuses on programs that provide insurance for contingencies, such as old age, disability, sickness, maternity, and unemployment. Social assistance programs, including family allowances and various targeted transfers to low-income households,

---

Note: The author is indebted to Michael Bell, Gérard Bélanger, János Kornai, George Mackenzie, Gyula Pulay, and Milan Vodopivec for useful comments.

[1]Unlike China and some regions of the U.S.S.R., most Central and Eastern European countries had fairly developed Western-type social security systems prior to the postwar imposition of socialist central planning.

are mentioned peripherally. Employer-provided benefits fall outside the scope of this study.

Legacy of Socialist Planning

Broadly speaking, under socialist central planning, income equality and welfare were to be ensured by price controls on goods and services intended to satisfy merit wants—as defined by the planners—by a compressed wage structure, and by constitutionally guaranteed employment, free health care, and education. Moreover, through the workplace, employees had access to old-age, disability, and survivors' pensions, and sick pay, maternity benefits, and family allowances. State-owned enterprises provided free vacations at designated resorts, housing, access to consumer goods (often at a discount), and other benefits in kind. Although initially the coverage of social security schemes was limited largely to the industrial sector, eventually it was expanded, at least in principle, to the entire labor force, including agriculture and services. Social security benefits were largely financed from payroll tax contributions by employers, and if necessary, supplemented with general revenue. Enterprise-specific benefits in kind have been treated as a cost to the enterprise or as a charge to the enterprise's social fund.

Overall, it was thought that high growth at capacity along with price stability, given adherence to the plan, would obviate joblessness and poverty. In this ideologically grounded scenario, there was no need for institutional arrangements to provide unemployment relief and social assistance. However, the scenario failed to materialize; over time, in practically all socialist economies, growth rates decelerated, productivity fell, and widespread commodity shortages emerged, deviating from the above conceptual framework. Governments were compelled to adjust relative prices in line with cost developments, and to allow some wage differentials and a second economy for supply-side reasons. At the same time, mounting redundancies were hidden in the state enterprises' work force and treated dysfunctionally through the existing social security schemes. In particular, eligibility for old-age and disability pensions and for sick pay was liberalized to help absorb redundant labor. But many households, facing shortages and price increases, remained disenfranchised as their income level sank below the poverty line; poverty was either neglected or alleviated on an ad hoc basis by local jurisdictions. In some countries, the claims on social security benefits increased owing to worsening demographic trends, as reflected in a relatively high old-age dependency ratio (Table 1). The rise in social security benefits besides large consumer subsidies

Table 1. Countries in Transition: Dependency Ratios, 1980–2020[1]

	1980	Estimate 1990	Projection 2000	2010	2020
Bulgaria					
Old-age dependency	18.0	20.6	27.0	29.2	33.6
Youth dependency	33.5	29.8	27.5	28.9	29.5
China					
Old-age dependency	7.9	8.7	10.7	11.9	16.8
Youth dependency	59.3	39.0	39.5	33.2	30.7
Czechoslovakia					
Old-age dependency	19.7	18.3	19.0	20.0	26.2
Youth dependency	38.3	35.7	30.7	31.5	30.8
Hungary					
Old-age dependency	20.8	20.3	22.6	24.8	31.6
Youth dependency	33.9	28.9	26.2	27.6	27.9
Poland					
Old-age dependency	15.4	15.4	18.0	18.7	25.7
Youth dependency	37.0	38.7	32.3	31.3	32.2
Romania					
Old-age dependency	16.3	15.7	19.3	20.9	23.7
Youth dependency	42.3	35.1	33.8	33.1	31.3
Yugoslavia					
Old-age dependency	14.2	13.4	19.2	24.0	27.4
Youth dependency	36.8	34.1	31.1	30.6	29.9
U.S.S.R.					
Old-age dependency	15.8	14.4	18.6	20.5	23.3
Youth dependency	38.1	39.2	35.0	31.7	32.0

Source: World Bank.

[1]Old-age and youth dependency ratios are defined as the population of over 64 years and below 15 years of age, respectively, as a percentage of active population aged 15–64 years.

imposed a heavy financial burden requiring even more frequent hikes in payroll tax rates, with adverse implications for equity, allocative efficiency, and external competitiveness. By the end of the 1980s, in most European economies in transition, the cost of social security benefits plus various consumer subsidies totaled at least one fifth of GDP.

Old-Age Pensions

Old-age pensions in former socialist countries suffer a number of fundamental shortcomings: they provide disincentives to work and to save, are costly, offer inadequate protection in an inflationary environment, and may be riddled with inequities. These deficiencies stem mainly from the length of qualifying service periods, retirement age, benefit accrual formula, calculation of pension base, statutory replacement rates, and treatment of inflation (Table 2), as compared with relevant provisions in OECD member countries.[2]

In a number of transition economies, the service period necessary for eligibility is rather short, especially given the generous inclusion of non-working periods (maternity, studies, military service) as qualifying service years. Except for Poland, the retirement age, set at 60 for men and 55 for women, is both rigid and low by international standards and discriminates by sex. Under certain circumstances, a further cut in the retirement age in the event of redundancies is provided by statute in some countries (Bulgaria, Hungary, Yugoslavia) and on a case-by-case basis elsewhere. In a few countries (Bulgaria, Czechoslovakia, U.S.S.R.) a social minimum pension is available for the elderly who have never held a job or are not eligible otherwise.

The benefit accrual rate per year worked declines over the service period in some countries. After rising sharply at the minimum period, the yearly increment may fall until it reaches zero upon reaching the maximum years of service. The statutory replacement rate (i.e., the ratio of benefits to the pension base) ranging from about 50 percent to 80 percent or more, is high compared with most OECD member countries. However, the rate is applied to a pension base calculated on relatively low undifferentiated wages. Departing from the definition of the base on the full amount of earnings, some countries (Czechoslovakia, Hungary, U.S.S.R.) have introduced a regressive formula whereby the base may fall to zero (equivalent to a ceiling) at higher marginal earning levels.

The pension base contains an upward bias insofar as it is calculated in reference to earnings in the best years (at the extreme, one year in China) from a recent period. It has been found that employers and employees often collude in raising salaries to artificially high levels in the years prior to retirement. The combination of this pre-retirement practice and the legal replacement rate leads to generally high effective replacement rates at the time of retirement, relative to lifetime income. With high inflation, however, the retirement benefit tends to collapse rapidly to the minimum pension level because ad hoc adjustments for price increases are typically provided for minimum pensions only.

The relatively low fixed retirement age and short service period mask unemployment relief. Meanwhile, these eligibility provisions, coupled with flat or nearly flat benefit accrual formula (i.e., zero or near-zero marginal replacement rates) at retirement, weaken the work effort. Further, the prospect of alternative work anticipated upon early (including disabil-

---

[2]See OECD (1988b).

Table 2. Countries in Transition: Old-Age Benefits and Eligibility Requirements, 1991

| | Statutory Replacement Rate (In percent of pension base) | | Benefit Accrual Rate, Yearly | Pension Base/Earnings | | Minimum Pension (In percent of minimum wage) | Automatic Indexation | Standard Retirement Age (Age) | | Early Retirement (In years)[3] | Prior Service Period (In years) | | Social Pension[2] (Age) |
	Minimum	Maximum		Marginal Ratio (In percent of earnings)	Period (In years)			Men	Women		Minimum	Maximum	
Bulgaria	30–55[4]	67–92[4]	2	100[5]	3 (5)	75	—	60	55	3	12½/10[6]	31	70
China	60	80	...	100[7]	1	—[8]	—	60	50–55	—	10	...	—
Czechoslovakia	50	60	1	100 to 0[9]	5 (10)	72	—	60	53–57[10]	...	25	35	65
Hungary	53	75	2 to 0.5	100 to 0[9]	3 (5)	93	from age 70	60	55	3	20	42	—
Poland	55	80[11]	1	100	3 (12)	35[12]	from age 80	65	60[13]	—	25/20[6]	...	—
Romania	...	61–92[4]	1 to 0.5	100	5 (10)	33	—	60	55	—[14]	...	...	—
U.S.S.R.[15]	55	75	1	100 to 0[9]	5 (15)	100	full	60	55	—	25/20[6]	...	65/60[6]
Yugoslavia[15]	35/40[6]	85	2/3[6]	100	10[16]	—	full[17]	60	55	5	20/15[6]	40/35[6]	—

[1]Number of best years out of total years (shown in parentheses) prior to retirement.

[2]If ineligible for any other pension; means test may apply in some countries.

[3]In years prior to standard retirement age, for other than occupation-specific reason (e.g., hazardous working conditions) or disability. Subject to certain eligibility requirements, including fulfillment of minimum service period.

[4]Varies inversely with level of pension base. For Bulgaria, minimum and maximum rates are based on assumption of 2 percent annual accrual in reference to full pension rates of 55–80 percent at 25 years of service for men and 20 years for women. For Romania, minimum and maximum rates are based on assumption of 10 additional years beyond full pension period (30 for men, 20 for women) at 1 percent annual accrual for first 5 years and 0.5 percent thereafter, in addition to full pension rate of 54–85 percent.

[5]Rate is 30 percent or 40 percent on bonus payments, depending on occupation.

[6]For men and women, respectively.

[7]Standard wage (i.e., without bonus and allowances).

[8]Flat amount of 30 yuan, cannot be related to a minimum wage.

[9]Marginal ratio declines regressively with the level of earnings (i.e., zero implies a ceiling on the pension base).

[10]Varies according to number of children raised.

[11]Assuming 45 years of service.

[12]Percent of average monthly wage in the state enterprise sector.

[13]Retirement age is 55 for women with 30 years of service.

[14]For 1990 only, five years before standard retirement.

[15]Since the second half of 1991, complete administrative and financial separation of social security operations among most republics.

[16]Best years over entire service period, fully indexed.

[17]Adjustment to last year's inflation rate.

ity) retirement and a relatively high average effective replacement rate at retirement may actually reduce the propensity to save.[3] In sum, eligibility requirements for old-age benefits are on the whole biased in favor of low-wage female employees with a short service period and against high-wage male employees with a long service period and few nonworking years.

Health-Related Schemes

Over time, eligibility for partial disability pensions has been eased considerably in most former European socialist countries. Also, sick pay is provided rather liberally to employees of state-owned enterprises (for periods of one year or more in Czechoslovakia, Hungary, and Yugoslavia) without an initial waiting period (Table 3). Neither the employer, nor the employee, nor the certifying physician is at risk. On the contrary, each benefits from the decision to place the employee on partial disability pension or sick leave: the employee benefits in the form of paid leisure or alternative work opportunity, the employer benefits from not having to bear the burden of a redundant worker,[4] and the physician from a gratuity payment by the employee. In contrast, the duration of maternity allowances varies widely between an anti-family stance (one to two months in China)[5] and a pro-family attitude (two years or more in Bulgaria and Hungary),[6] depending on national demographic trends. Replacement rates (up to or near 100 percent in most countries) are rather attractive for all health-related cash benefits.

Thus, while a portion of these benefits serve a genuine need—especially in the case of full and permanent disability—in view of the rather poor health of the population in this region, considerable scope exists for abus-

---

[3]Under market-like conditions, the negative wealth effect of a high replacement rate is likely to more than offset a weak positive effect of a low retirement age, in the context of the extended life-cycle saving hypothesis. However, in an inflationary environment, absent indexation of pensions, the expected erosion of the initially high replacement rate may strengthen the incentive to save for the post-retirement period. The net effect of social security on voluntary saving has not been investigated in socialist or post-socialist economies, where household saving consists mostly of forced saving. For evidence regarding market-oriented developing and industrial countries, see, for example, Kopits and Gotur (1980); for more recent analysis on major industrial countries, see Hutchison (1991).

[4]In this respect, China and Yugoslavia constitute exceptions by requiring employers to bear the cost of at least the initial 30 days of sick leave.

[5]The Chinese authorities have pursued aggressively policies to contain population growth not only through short maternity leave, but also through such practices as the loss of jobs, by either one or both parents on the birth of their second child.

[6]Andorka (1991) found evidence that the generosity of family allowances had an influence—albeit perhaps temporary—in boosting birth rates in Hungary.

Table 3. Countries in Transition: Health-Related Cash Benefits and Eligibility Requirements, 1991

| | Statutory Replacement Rate (In percent of earnings) | | | Sick Pay Duration/Obligation (In days)[4] | | | Maternity Benefit Duration[2] (In months) | Prior Service Period | | |
	Disability Pension[1]	Sick Pay	Maternity Benefit	Employee	Employer	Government (In months)		Disability[3] (In years)	Sickness (In months)	Maternity (In months)
Bulgaria	40–100	70–90[5]	100[6,7]	—	—	8	24	0–5	3	—
China	80–90[8]	40–100[9]	100	—	unlimited[10]		1–2	—	—	—
Czechoslovakia	25–60	70–90	90	—	—	12	6	0–5	—	9
Hungary	51–100	75–85	65–100[2,7]	—	3	12	25	0–10	—	6–9
Poland	50–80	75–100	100[7]	3[12]	—	9	6	1–10	1–6	—
Romania	60–100	50–85[11]	50–94	—	—	6[12]	4	1–22	—	—
U.S.S.R.[13]	55–75	50–100	100[7]	—	—	4[14]	4	1–15	—	2
Yugoslavia[13]	45–85	60–100	100[7]	—	30	unlimited[10]	3–9[15]	1	18[16]	12[16]

[1] Rate generally varies according to degree of disability, with top rate provided for total disability.
[2] Including period before confinement in Bulgaria, Czechoslovakia, Hungary, Romania, and U.S.S.R.
[3] Required period increases with age of beneficiary. In most countries, there is no prior employment requirement for employees under 20 years of age.
[4] Initial days of sickness.
[5] For workers, 120 percent of basic wage (excluding bonus and allowances).
[6] Rate is 100 percent from 45 days prior to birth until up to 180 days after childbirth. Afterward, benefit is equivalent to minimum wage until the end of second year of leave.
[7] Plus lump-sum grant.
[8] Additional lump-sum benefit provided if disability is related to work.
[9] Rate declines over time and depends on occupation.
[10] Until recovery or determination of permanent disability.
[11] Rate increases with years of service in brackets between less than two years to over eight years of service.
[12] For first three days only one half of normal benefit is provided by government, assuming that the beneficiary must absorb the other half reduction in benefit.
[13] Since the second half of 1991, complete administrative and financial separation of social security operations among most republics.
[14] Disability pension thereafter.
[15] Duration varies across republics.
[16] One half of period if continuously insured.

ing partial disability pensions and sick pay, which amount to a form of hidden unemployment compensation—even following the recent establishment of formal unemployment compensation schemes (Table 4). Information on the actual recourse to these schemes is uneven, but it appears that in some countries the number of individuals on disability pension and the average length of sick pay surpass substantially comparable OECD averages.[7]

For the most part, the health-care system is characterized by gross waste and misallocation of resources owing largely to the absence of incentives and information necessary for cost-efficient use. Much like in the state enterprise sector, health-care delivery and financing suffer from the lack of cost accounting. Neither health-care providers (administrators, physicians, technicians, nurses) nor consumers have knowledge or consciousness of the cost of medical services, and there are hardly any risks or rewards associated with the degree of efficiency in health-care use. Waste is also prevalent in the consumption of pharmaceuticals—to the extent they are available—dispensed freely or at highly subsidized prices.

Notwithstanding the principle of free universal access, in practice quality health care can be obtained primarily through an elaborate system of informal gratuity payments. Gratuities are provided mainly to physicians (rather than health-care technicians or supporting services), as determined by market forces and habit.[8] A proportion of health-care services is tied up in justifying sick pay and disability benefits, in exchange for gratuity payments. Also, institutional health care is often provided in lieu of social assistance (especially for the aged), which has not yet been developed in most of these countries; in some instances, this arrangement has been facilitated by a large excess capacity in hospital beds.

Financing

In socialist centrally planned economies, payroll-based social security contributions have been an important source of financing benefits; in fact,

---

[7]For example, in Hungary, the average length of sick days is almost one month a year. For a comparative analysis of health-care delivery and financing in OECD member countries, see OECD (1987); for a summary update, see Schieber, Poullier, and Greenwald (1991).

[8]By now, in most present or former socialist economies, informal gratuities (in the form of payments in cash or in kind) are an accepted, and often expected, supplement to relatively low fixed medical salaries. For an analysis of medical gratuities in Hungary, see Galasi and Kertesi (1991); inequities in the provision of health-care services are discussed in Orosz (1990).

Table 4. Countries in Transition: Unemployment Compensation and Eligibility Requirements, 1991

	Year of Establishment	Statutory Replacement Rate *(Percent of previous wage)*		Compensation Limits *(Percent of minimum wage)*		Compensation of New Entrants	Maximum Duration of Compensation *(In months)*		Subject to Personal Income Tax	Required Prior Employment[1] *(In months)*
		First Year	Subsequent Period	Minimum	Maximum		General	New Entrants		
Bulgaria	1990	100–50[2]	—	100	—	100	9	9	—	—
China[3]	1986	50–75	50–75[4]	...	...	—	24[4]	—	—	...
Czechoslovakia	1991[5]	60–50[6]	50	100	—	40	12	12	—	12 (36)
Hungary	1989[7]	70	40	95	300	100	24	6	yes	12 (48)[8]
Poland	1990	70–40[9]	—	44	73	110–125	unlimited	6	—	6 (12)[8]
Romania	1990	35–60[11]	—	100	—[10]	44	6	6	—	—
U.S.S.R.[12]	1991	45–75[13]	—[14]	100[15]	—	—	6	—	no	...[16]
Yugoslavia[12]	1972	50–100[17]	50–100[17]	80[18]	400[18]	—	18–36[19]	—	yes	12 (18)

[1] Previous employment requirement out of a given total period shown in parentheses. For example, in Yugoslavia, beneficiary is required to have been employed 12 months during the past 18 months.

[2] First month (paid by the employer) at 100 percent, declining 10 percentage points each month until reaching 50 percent by the sixth month; for additional three months, benefit is equivalent to minimum wage.

[3] Coverage limited to contract workers and to employees in enterprises closed down under the bankruptcy law.

[4] Benefit provided in the second year only if coverage of five years or more.

[5] In 1990, a combination of a severance payment paid by the enterprise and unemployment compensation of up to one year paid by the government, was available.

[6] Rate declines from 60 percent in the first half, 50 percent in the second half of the year. For structurally unemployed workers and those on vocational training, the rate in the first half is 65 percent and 70 percent, respectively.

[7] In 1986–88, job search subsidy paid by enterprise dismissing the employee and by the government.

[8] Alternatively, new entrants in labor force who have just completed studies are also eligible.

[9] Rate declines from 70 percent to 60 percent after first three months, and further to 40 percent after nine months.

[10] Maximum is the average wage level.

[11] Replacement rate increases with service years, with maximum rate reached with over 15 years.

[12] Since the second half of 1991, complete legal, administrative, and financial separation of social security operations among most republics.

[13] In most republics, 75 percent rate applied during the first three months of unemployment, 60 percent in the following four months, and 45 percent in the remaining months.

[14] Some republics may provide an additional 45 percent replacement for an additional year.

[15] 550 percent in the Ukraine.

[16] Four months in Russia.

[17] Statutory replacement rate varies across republics. Benefit increases with the growth of net earnings in the republic.

[18] Compensation limits vary across republics.

[19] Maximum duration (varying across republics) for men and women with 30 and 25 years employment record, respectively. With longer employment record, duration is unlimited. With employment record of less than 30 years for men and 25 years for women, duration of payments is usually reduced according to a declining scale.

these contributions, as well as other payroll taxes, constituted the only major form of parametric taxation. With few exceptions (notably, Yugoslavia), contributions were lumped with the rest of general revenue in the state budget and, along with other revenue, were used to pay for benefits.

The share of social security benefit payments in general government expenditure has risen steadily as a result of expansion in coverage, liberalization of eligibility requirements, increased inefficiency, and in some cases, demographic pressures. Sagging labor productivity over the last decade or so contributed indirectly to liberalized eligibility for covert unemployment compensation and to the stagnation of the contribution base. These factors led to a rising deficit in social security operations, which, in turn, prompted increases in contribution rates. In some countries, the financing of certain assistance-type benefits (especially family allowances and health-care services to noncontributing households) with payroll tax contributions has also contributed to the increase in rates.

The collection of social security contributions has been left in the hands of state-owned enterprises which in the past were willing and able to discharge their obligations under a soft budget constraint. However, as the constraint tightened—under some budgetary and credit discipline—these enterprises have been facing payments difficulties, reflected in contribution collection lags. Meanwhile, the emergence of a second economy—legally or de facto exempt from payroll taxation—and a weak administrative capacity for identifying employees on whose behalf contributions are to be made, has resulted in an increasing erosion of revenue from social security contributions.

By international standards, social security contribution rates in economies in transition are high and rising. In three countries (Bulgaria, Czechoslovakia, Hungary), statutory social security contribution rates stand above 50 percent, and only in one country (China) is the rate below 20 percent (Table 5). Except for a couple of countries, the entire contribution is legally borne by the employer. Absent integrated labor markets and given price and wage controls, it is difficult to determine the incidence of payroll taxation in socialist economies. As these economies open up and are liberalized, however, its incidence will resemble increasingly that in market-oriented economies, for which economy-wide simulations suggest that at least to some extent payroll taxes are reflected in labor costs.[9] Consequently, with the privatization of industry, high social security contribution rates are likely to depress employment and—insofar as the rates

---

[9]See OECD (1986).

Table 5. Countries in Transition: Social Security Financing and Contribution Rates, 1991[1]
(In percent of wages)

Country/Coverage	Statutory Contribution Rates			Financing from Budget
	Employee	Employer	Total	
Bulgaria				
ODS/Z/W/F	—	50.00[2]	50.00	Balance
H	—	—	—	All
U	—	3.75	3.75	Balance
Total	—	53.75	53.75	
China				
ODS	—[3]	18.00[3]	18.00[3]	Balance
Z/W/H	—	—	—	All
U	—	—[4]	—	Balance
Total	—	18.00	18.00	
Czechoslovakia				
ODS/Z/W/U	—	50.00	50.00	Balance
H	—	—	—	All
Total	—	50.00	50.00	
Hungary				
ODS/Z/W/H	10.00	43.00	53.00	None
U	0.50	1.50	2.00	Balance
Total	10.50	44.50	55.00	
Poland				
ODS/Z/W/F	—	43.00	43.00	Balance
H/U	—	—	—	All
Total	—	43.00	43.00	
Romania				
ODS/Z/W	3.00	22.00	25.00	Balance
U	1.00	4.00	5.00	Balance
H	—	—	—	All
Total	4.00	26.00	30.00	
U.S.S.R.				
ODS/Z/W	1.00	26.00[5]	27.00	None
U	—	1.00[6]	1.00	Balance
H	—	—	—	All
Total	1.00	27.00[5]	28.00	
Yugoslavia[7]				
ODS	...	...	16.00–19.00	Balance
U	...	...	0–0.80	Balance
Z/W/H	...	...	8.70–10.00	Balance
Total	...	...	...[8]	

[1]Only employees' (as distinct from self-employed) programs are shown. The contribution base is not subject to a ceiling in these countries.

[2]Highest statutory rate. Lower rates (35 percent and 45 percent) are applied according to a scale inversely proportional to the retirement age.

[3]Typical rates; rates for contract workers are split into 3 percent from the insured and 15 percent from the employer. Actual rates vary considerably across enterprises and jurisdictions.

[4]Rate for contract workers is 1 percent.

[5]Originally, the employer's contribution rate was scheduled to rise to 37 percent and total rate to 38 percent in 1995. In some republics, actual rates are subject to change by 1992.

[6]Typical rate; actual rate and base vary among republics. May be supplemented with voluntary contributions.

[7]Typical rates; actual rates vary across republics.

[8]A variety of additional contributions are required for child care, education, culture, and other uses. All contributions amount to more than 45 percent of wages.

Notes: ODS = old-age, disability, survivors' insurance; Z = sickness and maternity; W = work injury; U = unemployment compensation; H = health care; and F = family allowances (if financed from contributions).

are differentiated by industry or sector—to distort the allocation of resources across economic activities. Furthermore, without border tax adjustment,[10] high payroll taxation is likely to inhibit external competitiveness, placing an added burden of adjustment on the exchange rate.

Initial Reform Measures

Since embarking on a comprehensive market-oriented transformation, in 1989–90 a number of former socialist economies have introduced certain amendments in the social security system.[11] These steps involved separation of social insurance operations from the state budget and the creation of an unemployment compensation scheme, along with active market labor programs. In addition, efforts are under way to develop a social safety net, thus substituting targeted subsidies for consumer price subsidies.

In most socialist economies, until the late 1980s, social security operations were consolidated with the rest of the state budget. Since then, virtually all governments—with the notable exception of Czechoslovakia—have sought to redefine the status of social security schemes. The separation of social security programs from the budget was prompted in part by an attempt to link payroll-based contributions and benefits.

Although in Poland a separate Pension Fund had already existed as an extrabudgetary fund, as of 1987 the Social Insurance Fund took over the responsibilities of the former Pension Fund as well as the expenditures on sick leave, family allowances, and maternity benefits, to be financed fully with social security contributions. In 1989, Hungary shifted social security operations from the state budget to the Social Insurance Fund, under the authority of the National Social Insurance Directorate. At the outset, the Fund covered old-age, disability and survivors' pensions, sick pay, family allowances, and pharmaceutical benefits. The following year, the remaining health-care benefits were exchanged for family allowances between the Fund and the budget. For 1991, the budget of the Social Insurance Fund was subject to legislative debate and approval, separately from that of the state budget. A similar step was taken in the U.S.S.R., whereby, effective January 1991, social security operations were moved off budget,

---

[10]Payroll taxes are treated as income taxes which tend to be absorbed by the taxpayer. By contrast, adjustment is provided on imports (through taxation) and exports (through refund or exemption) for taxes on sales or value added and other internal levies, on the basis of the destination principle, assuming full forward shifting.

[11]For an overview in the context of fiscal reform in European transition economies, see Kopits (1991).

placing pensions, maternity, and child-rearing benefits under the Pension Fund, and sick pay, child-bearing, and death benefits under the Social Security Fund. At the same time, Romania introduced two separate Social Security Funds: one to provide retirement benefits and another for all other benefits, except health-care expenditures, which remain under the state budget.

The separate status of social security funds was to be underscored by administrative and financial autonomy. This often required a further hike in social security contribution rates to close the emerging deficit on social security operations that had been covered heretofore with general revenue. In some countries (Hungary, Romania, U.S.S.R.), the authorities aimed at generating a surplus with a view to substituting a funded system for the PAYG (pay-as-you-go) approach.

Concerned about the social implications of industrial restructuring and given the limited scope for coping with them through existing social security programs, the authorities introduced formal unemployment compensation and active job creation programs. Apart from unemployment compensation provided openly in Yugoslavia since the early 1970s, such schemes were unknown in socialist planned economies until the recent official acknowledgement of unemployment. In 1986, limited unemployment compensation was provided in China (for contract workers in state enterprises and workers dismissed owing to bankruptcy)[12] and in Hungary (euphemistically called job search benefits, paid through enterprises by the government to laid-off workers). A broadly applicable formal unemployment compensation scheme was adopted by Hungary in 1989. Since then, all neighboring countries have enacted similar schemes (Table 4).

In general, the unemployment compensation schemes introduced in Central and Eastern European countries are comparable to those found in most OECD member countries. However, the benefits provided by the former tend to be more generous as regards either the replacement rate (Bulgaria), or the duration of the benefit (Hungary and Poland), or both (Yugoslavia). Also, in some cases, the requirement of prior employment is fairly liberal or nonexistent (Bulgaria and Poland). In their present form, unemployment compensation seems to be viewed in some countries as social assistance to jobless households rather than as temporary income support for short-term unemployment to those who already have joined the labor force. Hence, there is a real risk in some countries that unem-

---

[12]As the bankruptcy law has been applied rarely so far. China's unemployment compensation scheme can be regarded as experimental.

ployment benefits may induce labor force participation and continued reliance on such benefits, imposing a considerable fiscal burden.

Given that an important component of unemployment during transition is by definition structural and to alleviate undue recourse to cash benefits, some countries (Bulgaria and Hungary) introduced active labor market programs: manpower training, as well as wage subsidies to enterprises to hire the unemployed. This approach has been made imperative by industrial restructuring, particularly in the wake of trade liberalization, which has rendered obsolete the skills of a significant portion of the labor force formerly engaged directly or indirectly in the production of nontradables or of exports to the CMEA market prior to its collapse.

Future Options for Reform

Apart from the economic distortions and inadequate protection under existing social security institutions, the level and coverage of benefits are financially unsustainable over the foreseeable future in several transition economies.[13] Through the medium run, an economy-wide revival in economic growth and labor productivity is not likely to materialize, resulting in increased claims on unemployment benefits and in a shrinking revenue base. A cutback in subsidies and bank credit will impair the ability of state-owned enterprises to meet their payroll tax liability, as already evidenced by the buildup in contribution arrears in some countries. Meanwhile, newly established private enterprises will be able to evade—more successfully than their Western European counterparts—the contribution obligation, given a weak tax administration. Finally, a rapidly aging population in some countries (especially Bulgaria and Hungary) will impose an added demand on retirement and health-care benefits in the long run, to be financed by a shrinking work force (Table 1).

In view of these prospects, stop-gap adjustments in some benefits or increases in payroll tax rates, as practiced in the past, no longer represent a viable solution. Instead, fundamental reform of social security has become an urgent task for ensuring the medium- to long-term sustainability of the system, and more immediately, adequate protection during enterprise restructuring and price liberalization; overall, the reform should contrib-

---

[13]Ideally, this view would need to be corroborated with a fully-specified macro model such as the one developed for example in Aaron, Bosworth, and Burtless (1989) for the United States. However, Central and Eastern European economies undergoing radical structural transformation lend themselves only for simple long-term policy scenario calculations. See such scenarios for Hungary in Kopits, Holzmann, Schieber, and Sidgwick (1990) and for the U.S.S.R. in International Monetary Fund and others (1991).

ute significantly to economic growth. The reform effort needs to encompass both the benefit and the financing sides: rationalization of eligibility for old-age and health-related benefits, adjustment of the level and coverage of cash benefits, overhaul of health-care delivery and financing, clearer institutional distinction between financing insurance- and assistance-type schemes, encouragement of private pensions and insurance, and a significant reduction in payroll tax rates.

An additional issue that merits attention involves the degree of decentralization of social security programs across jurisdictions (republics, provinces). China and Yugoslavia imposed differential contribution rates and benefit payments throughout their territories. Recently, in both the U.S.S.R. and Yugoslavia, social security operations have disintegrated among republics; most republics acquired independent control over budgetary and extra-budgetary schemes. Other countries are facing the dilemma of separating pensions, health care, and unemployment compensation along republic lines. The large size of certain countries or political, economic, and demographic differences within them argue for separate schemes. However, some of these differences could provide a rationale for unifying the programs throughout each country on grounds of pooling insurance risks.

Restructuring Benefits

Arguably, a precondition for rationalizing eligibility for traditional benefits is the creation of appropriate programs for unemployment relief and social assistance, so that a given program no longer has to be used inter alia to fulfill these functions, but can be devoted solely to provide insurance for a well-defined contingency (old-age, disability). Practically all economies in transition have introduced unemployment compensation schemes and are strengthening assistance to low-income households. However, the existing *unemployment compensation* tends to be both insufficiently applied but too generous where provided. On the one hand, with the possible exception of the former German Democratic Republic, Poland, and parts of Yugoslavia,[14] the authorities have been reluctant to allow for open unemployment; unemployment rates in transition economies are for the most part still considerably below those in, say, France, Italy, or Spain, despite a much higher efficiency and effective capacity

---

[14]However, Vodopivec (1990) shows that in Yugoslavia, job security and overemployment prevail through a complicated system of (often implicit) levies and subsidies that results in massive inter-enterprise income redistribution and inefficiency.

utilization in the latter. On the other hand, the prior employment requirement for unemployment compensation needs to be tightened in some countries (Bulgaria, Poland, Romania, U.S.S.R.) and the compensation period could be reduced in others (China, Hungary, Poland). The first measure is necessary to prevent leakages to those who enter the labor force just to claim benefits; the second is predicated on the understanding that there are more effective means for alleviating the large-scale structural unemployment anticipated in transition economies, namely, manpower training, possibly in combination with wage subsidies for private enterprises to hire the unemployed—subject to appropriate safeguards.[15]

With a view to enhancing cost effectiveness, eligibility for *old-age benefits* must be streamlined in several important respects. First, through the phase-in, over ten years or so, of a flexible retirement age with a range (perhaps of up to three years) around a standard retirement age of 65 years (for both men and women), replacing the present low fixed retirement age differentiated by sex. Second, introduction of a constant annual accrual factor in the statutory replacement rate during the service period, in combination with a sharper increment (decrement) for retirement after (before) the standard retirement age, replacing an often variable or zero accrual rate. Third, phase-in of determination of the pension base on the basis of lifetime income and reduction in noncontributory period (retaining at most maternity and military service). Fourth, phase-in of a regressive calculation of the pension base in relation to the level of earnings, until reaching a ceiling—as done in Czechoslovakia and the U.S.S.R. and nearly so in Hungary. And fifth, repeal of early retirement provisions[16] which lose their rationale with the adoption of an actuarially adjusted replacement rate under the proposed flexible retirement age and with the introduction of unemployment compensation and training programs. These measures need to be buttressed with administrative innovations: assignment of a unique identification number to each insured employee or self-employed (preferably identical to the taxpayer identification number) and to each employer; maintenance of a record of lifetime contributions by, and on behalf of, each insured employee or self-employed; and joint administration of income taxes and social security contributions by a single tax authority.

---

[15]For some potentially useful lessons from wage subsidies implemented in major industrial countries, see the analysis in Kopits (1978), and a recent survey in OECD (1988a).

[16]Early retirement provisions have been abandoned or significantly curtailed in Western Europe; see Holtzmann (1988).

As a departure from past practice, instead of ad hoc adjustments of the minimum pension for inflation (and indexation of pensions above an advanced age, as in Hungary and Poland), the authorities should endeavor to establish an automatic indexation mechanism (for current rather than lagged inflation, as in Yugoslavia) at all pension levels, so as to maintain the relative distribution of benefits and replacement rates (following the example of the U.S.S.R.). However, at the initial stage of the transition, a case can be made for granting one-time adjustments for changes in key commodity prices as weighted by the consumption basket of beneficiaries, in compensation for the effect of removing consumer price and rental subsidies.[17] By the same token, elderly individuals who for some reason are disenfranchised from receiving a minimum pension should qualify for a social pension upon reaching a certain age (as in Bulgaria, Czechoslovakia, U.S.S.R.) and meeting a means test. Hence, the social pension may be administered as part of the social assistance program, rather than under the old-age insurance program.

The introduction of unemployment compensation argues for the drastic cutback or, preferably, abolition of *sick pay* as a social security benefit. Specifically, the employer should be made financially responsible for the employee's sick leave for at least the first four or six weeks (or for the sick leave accumulated by the employee) of sickness; the social security system could thus be responsible beyond that period. Such an approach would reduce the present propensity to abuse. Similarly, eligibility for *disability pensions*, especially on the basis of partial disability, should be subject to much stricter screening by the social security administration. But for those who are genuinely disabled, it is essential to develop rehabilitation services—with a view to possibly reintegrating the disabled into the work force—which are notoriously deficient or absent in former socialist countries.

There is a basic need in the *health-care area* for mounting a comprehensive and consistent information system at the macroeconomic and microeconomic levels. In particular, a minimum flow of data on operating and fixed costs of health-care services provided through various channels is indispensable for cost containment, performance evaluation, reimbursement, and budgeting purposes. Consideration should be given to the adaptation of scoring physician services or of productivity-based norms for hospital services, developed in Germany and the United States. Such

---

[17]At this stage, retirees may not be fully compensated for price inflation insofar as they are expected to share in at least part of a downward adjustment in real wages.

methods could be useful for monitoring health-care expenditures and perhaps for remunerating health-care services. Partly on the basis of improved information, informal gratuities should be fully incorporated in physicians' salaries and fees, and remuneration of other health-care providers should be adjusted to reflect openly productivity and market conditions. A logical companion to these measures would consist of reliance on partial financing through co-payments by health-care users, ranging from relatively moderate shares (say, 20–30 percent of approved market price) in the case of basic procedures (done at lower rates for pharmaceuticals and certain procedures in Hungary and Yugoslavia) to larger shares or full payment for nonessential services (including some types of plastic surgery). Consistent with the principle of universal access, co-payments could be waived for low-income households that meet a means test.

The availability of social insurance for old-age, disability, survivorship, and health care does not preclude private insurance for such contingencies. Indeed, if properly regulated, private pensions, private life and health insurance, and private health-care services would provide a welcome complement to social insurance schemes. Moreover, private pension and insurance funds could make a useful contribution to the development of financial markets in transition economies.

Pay-As-You-Go or Funding?

Much like in market-oriented industrial countries,[18] several former socialist countries are actively debating whether to finance social security through a funded system or a PAYG (albeit separate from the budget) system. Among those who favor funding, some argue for an initial endowment to the social security fund from the transfer of ownership of former state-owned enterprises or from the proceeds of privatizing such enterprises. According to a more radical option—along the lines of the Chilean model—the old-age component of current social security contributions would be earmarked as premiums into newly established private pension funds.[19]

There is little room to quarrel about the superiority of the funding principle for purposes of intertemporal stabilization. Initially intended for implementation in many market-oriented economies, the funding principle was abandoned as it became politically convenient to finance budget

---

[18]For a recent summary of the various arguments, for example, largely from a British perspective, see Barr (1987), chapter 9.

[19]See the reform proposals in Hanke (1990) and Deutsch (1991). For a discussion of the Chilean and other Latin American cases, see Mackenzie (1991).

deficits with accumulated social security surpluses. It is, therefore, highly doubtful that economies in transition will be in a position to exercise sufficient restraint in preserving the integrity of a fully funded social security system, which may be required to finance, at a significantly negative real interest rate, budget imbalances that—especially in the absence of financial markets—cannot be readily financed by the nonbank public.[20] Furthermore, the increase in the contribution rate that may be required to build up an actuarial reserve (or even a liquidity reserve) in the fund would add to an excessively high payroll tax—a nonviable option, as noted earlier. The alternative of assigning the ownership of state-owned enterprises or transferring privatization proceeds, despite its sound logic in a partial context, is open to question on two counts. For one thing, it is uncertain whether such proceeds would be sufficient to generate the necessary resource flow. For another, a solid case can be made for utilizing revenue from privatization to redeem large government debt held by commercial banks or other financial institutions—either accumulated from past budget deficits or from the assumption of nonperforming liabilities of state-owned enterprises—rather than for transferring them to the social security fund.

On theoretical grounds, privatization of the old-age pension program merits consideration. Indeed, there are major efficiency gains to be derived from the operation of private pension funds freely competing for voluntary contributions. Protection of beneficiaries could be assured through prudential regulations and a minimum pension guaranteed by the government. Furthermore, such funds could make an important contribution to the privatization of state-owned enterprises and to the development of financial markets and institutions. Transplanting, however, the Chilean experience—notwithstanding its apparent success to date—to former socialist economies may prove difficult in the absence of financial markets. The transition from a PAYG social security system to fully funded private pensions is in practice precluded by the difficulty of meeting the

---

[20]So far, none of the countries intent on establishing a funded system have really succeeded in this endeavor. In Hungary, for example, the small surplus accumulated at the end of 1989 was used to purchase Housing Fund bonds largely to finance an interest subsidy on outstanding mortgages—tantamount to backdoor financing of the state budget deficit. Indeed, it can be argued that this captive source of financing made possible a delay in phasing out the interest subsidy. In the U.S.S.R., upon implementation of the 1990 social security reform legislation, a surplus equivalent to 11 percentage points of the new contribution rate was earmarked for subsidizing enterprise restructuring, which should be viewed as a budget expenditure.

claims of the existing stock of beneficiaries.[21] Therefore, a more realistic option would be to encourage the establishment of private pension funds as a *complement* to the PAYG social security system. To this end, the payroll tax for social security should be trimmed and the tax base should be subject to a ceiling—consistent with a similar approach on the benefit side.[22] It is worth emphasizing the importance of appropriate regulation of the management and portfolio composition of such funds, particularly in view of the risky investment climate prevailing in these economies; this need, however, should not be construed as a convenient constraint on the funds for investment solely or primarily in government paper.

In any event, as observed already, social security contributions are excessive in most former socialist countries, with potentially substantial adverse effects on economic performance. Hence, from the outset, the authorities should endeavor to reduce significantly or at least contain further increments in contribution rates (especially the employer's share), as permitted by net budgetary savings from restructuring old-age and health-related benefits, along the lines suggested above, broadening the contribution base, to include all earnings from primary, full-time, secondary or part-time employment, and the limitation of payroll tax contributions to finance only insurance-type benefits, while shifting all assistance-type benefits to the state budget. Earmarking earnings-based contributions to an extrabudgetary account to pay for insurance-type benefits would enhance the rationale of the contributions on the basis of the benefit principle of taxation. At the same time, social assistance, including family allowances, a minimum social pension, health-care services to noncontributing low-income households (along with exemption from co-payments) should be financed with revenue from more sector-, factor-, and trade-neutral taxes such as the value-added tax, envisaged for introduction in most transition economies.

References

Aaron, H.J., B.P. Bosworth, and G. Burtless, *Can America Afford to Grow Old?* (Washington: Brookings Institution, 1989).

Andorka, R., "Politiques démographiques natalistes et leur impact en Hongrie," *Politiques de Population: Etudes et Documents*, Vol. 4 (April 1991), pp. 87–125.

---

[21]For an analysis of the effects of the Chilean transition on capital accumulation and intergenerational distribution, see Arrau (1991).

[22]As an added incentive, contributions to private pension funds should be deductible from (and benefits from such funds should be included in) the personal income tax base. The same income tax treatment should, of course, apply to social security contributions and benefits.

Arrau, P., "La reforma previsional chilena y su financiamiento durante la transición," *Colección Estudios CIEPLAN*, Vol. 32 (June 1991), pp. 5–44.

Barr, N.A., *The Economics of the Welfare State* (Stanford: Stanford University Press, 1987).

Deutsch, A., "One Pension System in Transition: The Case of Hungary," paper prepared for the International Studies Association (Vancouver, March 21, 1991).

Galasi, P., and G. Kertesi, "A hálapénz ökonomiája," ["The Economics of Gratuities"], *Közgazdasági Szemle*, Vol. 38 (March 1991), pp. 260–88.

Hanke, S.H., "Reflections on Yugoslavia's Transition to a Market Economy," paper presented at the Cámara de Comercio e Industria (Madrid, November 13, 1990).

Holtzmann, R., "On the Relationship Between Retirement and Labor Market Policy," in *Structural Problems of Social Security Today and Tomorrow* (Leuven: ACCO, 1988).

Hutchison, M., "Private Saving, Public Saving, and the Structure of Government Expenditure: International Evidence," paper presented at Western Economic Association meetings (Seattle, June 29–July 3, 1991).

International Monetary Fund, World Bank, Organization for Economic Cooperation and Development, and European Bank for Reconstruction and Development, *A Study of the Soviet Economy*, Vol. 1 (Paris: OECD, February 1991).

Kopits, G., "Fiscal Reform in European Economies in Transition," in *The Transformation of Central and Eastern Europe to a Market Economy,* (Paris: OECD, 1991).

——, "Wage Subsidies and Employment: An Analysis of the French Experience," *IMF Staff Papers*, Vol. 25 (September 1978), pp. 494–527.

Kopits, G., and P. Gotur, "The Influence of Social Security on Household Savings: A Cross-Country Investigation," *IMF Staff Papers*, Vol. 27 (March 1980), pp. 160–90.

Kopits, G., R. Holzmann, G. Schieber, and E. Sidgwick, "Social Security Reform in Hungary," Fiscal Affairs Department, International Monetary Fund (Washington, October 12, 1990).

Mackenzie, G.A., "Selected Issues in Social Security in Latin America," paper presented for the Iberoamerican Conference of the Association of Pension Fund Administrators (Santiago, April 17–19, 1991).

Organization for Economic Cooperation and Development (OECD), *OECD Employment Outlook* (Paris: OECD, 1986).

——, *Financing and Delivering Health Care* (Paris: OECD, 1987).

—— (1988a), *Measures to Assist the Unemployed* (Paris: OECD, 1988).

—— (1988b), *Reforming Public Pensions* (Paris: OECD, 1988).

Orosz, E., "Inequalities in Health and Health Care in Hungary," *Social Science and Medicine*, Vol. 31 (August 1990), pp. 847–57.

Schieber, G., J. P. Poullier, and L. M. Greenwald, "Health Care Systems in Twenty-Four Countries," *Health Affairs,* Vol. 10 (Fall 1991), pp. 22–38.

Vodopivec, M., "The Persistence of Job Security in Reforming Socialist Economies," World Bank PRE Working Paper WPS 560 (December 1990).

CHAPTER 15

Social Safety Nets

Ehtisham Ahmad

Social protection policies or safety nets are needed in the transition from administered or planned economies to more market-oriented systems so as not to impose unacceptable cuts in living standards of vulnerable groups. Some of these safety nets would be operational only during the transition period, while others are expected to remain as an integral part of a market-based economy. Temporary social safety nets include variants of limited subsidy measures as well as targeted employment programs. These may be classified as protective or compensatory measures during the transition period and may be distinguished from the institutional arrangements subsumed under "formal social security" measures that operate to cover normal life-cycle contingencies.

Temporary social safety nets are relevant in a variety of cases. These would be expected to assist the rapid systemic changes being undertaken, as in Eastern European countries, and the more measured adjustments toward a market mechanism in China and other Asian countries. Similar issues arise in many developing countries that have operated systems of administered prices, often involving overvalued exchange rates. Thus transition issues also involve the establishment of prices reflecting opportunity costs and the forces of demand and supply as well as appropriate exchange rates. Major relative price changes may be involved, particularly for items of basic consumption. These adjustments form the foundation for long-term sustainable growth and an eventual improvement in overall living standards. However, in the short term they may hurt the poor (particularly those outside the labor market including small children and the aged), as well as workers receiving administrative wages or subsisting in the informal sector.

Many centrally planned economies in Eastern Europe have had highly developed formal social security arrangements for retirement and long-term risks (see the paper by Kopits in this volume), as well as allowances for the special needs of large families, maternity, and so on. In principle the expectation was that these formal arrangements, together with a full employment guarantee, would have provided an all-encompassing safety net in the centrally planned economies. Consequently, neither involuntary unemployment nor poverty was officially recognized. The evidence suggests, however, that prior to the transition the social security system was inadequate in preventing poverty and need. In addition, the system of wage and employment guarantees served to stifle incentives and the operation of the labor market.

Transfers associated with a widespread coverage of the formal social security system, together with the operation of a wage-based employment system, can form the basis of compensation arrangements for major price changes at the beginning of the reform process. Full wage or transfer indexation or adjustment, however, may not be sustainable from a macroeconomic or budgetary standpoint. The extent of a justifiable compensation is subject to considerable uncertainty. For instance, it may not be appropriate to devise compensation mechanisms for the "gainers" during the process of adjustment. Further, in economies where reforms have been under way for some years and in the "developing" centrally planned economies (Algeria or China), substantial groups are generally not covered by the formal social security instruments. Those in a growing informal sector, including many among the most vulnerable of the population, cannot be easily reached through the traditional instruments of wage adjustments and formal transfers based on social security. Thus, changing employment patterns and growing, often long-term unemployment also point to the need to establish formal as well as more targeted cover for these individuals.

The revenue base in transition economies in Eastern Europe restricts the scope for social safety nets. A shift often takes place from administered prices, 100 percent profits taxation, and turnover taxes to tax systems more common in market-based economies (Tanzi (1991)). This usually entails a loss of revenues in the short term.[1] In addition, extensive enterprise restructuring, accompanied by the emergence of nascent private activities, restrict the potential revenue base in the short term. This crisis on the revenue side constrain freedom of maneuver with respect to additional expenditures for formal components of the social safety net.

---

[1]In China, the government revenue to national income ratio fell from 41.4 percent in 1978 to 23.2 percent in 1989, although this decline was partially compensated by a decline in government expenditures (Hussain and Stern (1991)).

Many countries may be considered in transition from systems of administered prices to the market mechanism. The former communist regimes in Eastern Europe as well as formerly socialist Algeria and Mozambique are undergoing rapid transition. In China the transition has been more prolonged. Non-socialist states including Jordan, the Islamic Republic of Iran, India, and Pakistan, have had central planning and price control for a considerable time. We shall focus on the U.S.S.R., China, the Islamic Republic of Iran, and Algeria. Institutional details are of particular importance, as it is essential to relate policy advice to the ability of regimes in transition to administer suggested options.

Living Standards and Policy Constraints

The structure of wages, given guaranteed employment, has been a key element of social protection policy in the centrally planned economies, together with formal social security transfers for the aged and those unable to participate in the labor force. Since wages were administratively determined, real living standards depended on the supporting system of administered prices and on substantial in-kind transfers. In principle this system should have precluded poverty. In practice it did not, because of incomplete coverage of the wage-benefit system, and the inadequacy of the transfers involved. Despite growing evidence, the existence of poverty was not officially admitted in the Soviet Union and China until the mid-1980s.[2] Typically, pensioners, families with young children, and workers in the unorganized or informal sectors faced a high risk of poverty. In most countries, guaranteeing full employment to the entire population was simply not feasible. Until 1983, in China guaranteed employment had been possible only in the urban, formal sector,[3] and this was sustained largely through strict controls on rural-urban migration (Ahmad and Hussain (1991)). In other developing centrally planned economies, such as Algeria, rapid population growth made guaranteeing employment in the formal sector impossible to achieve.[4] In general, those who do not

[2]See International Monetary Fund (1991) for a discussion for the U.S.S.R., and Ahmad and Wang (1991) for a review of the Chinese experience.

[3]The employment guarantee in China has in principle been abandoned, with the introduction of the contract responsibility system for new entrants to the formal sector work force since 1983. However, the continuation of the employment guarantee for the majority of existing formal-sector workers has ensured that industrial transformation would be a slow process.

[4]Open unemployment in Algeria at the beginning of the 1990s was 25 percent of the labor force.

have regular employment in the organized sector tend to be excluded from the formal system of transfers and associated in-kind benefits.[5]

As a direct consequence of the system of administered wage determination, standards of living of large groups might be described as "marginally adequate" in relation to the subsidized price system. Thus, immediately preceding a price reform, one normally expects to find a bunching of households within a narrow range at relatively low levels of per capita expenditure.[6] In the U.S.S.R., for instance, minimum pensions were set at 70 rubles a month in 1981, and this level was maintained until 1990.[7] At this level less than 15 percent of the population would have been classified as poor in 1988/9, although Goskomtrud estimated a poverty line for 1988 at 100 rubles.[8] However, over 45 percent of the population was concentrated between 75 rubles and 150 rubles per capita per month at the time, and it is evident that small changes in a poverty line would make large differences to the numbers classified as poor. It is in practice, in most countries, difficult to identify the poor clearly in terms of administratively simple groups or categories, and the identification is more difficult in a country where there are extended family networks, and housing is shared by several generations of relatives. Individual incomes are difficult to identify at the best of times and are, in any case, not a helpful indicator in an extended family environment. To document household incomes, including intra- and inter-household transfers, as well as the income imputed for self-owned housing and the direct or indirect subsidy for housing services by the state, is daunting. Difficult as it is to establish a proper benchmark in the pre-reform period, the issue is even more complicated during a period of rapid relative price change.

Using an income-cutoff point to determine who should be compensated for relative price adjustments may be misleading, because of the difficulty in establishing an initial benchmark and assessing real changes in living standards. Furthermore, in some countries, many who would have fallen below the cutoff point prior to the reform would benefit as a result of the reform. This is particularly so in China, where rural households gained substantially as a result of the readjustments in relative prices. A

---

[5]In China, informal-sector workers in cities were reported to be around 50 million in 1989, as opposed to roughly 135 million workers in the large-scale formal sector. Roughly 90 million workers (or 17 percent of the work force) in rural, township, and village enterprises did not benefit from the formal social insurance mechanisms.

[6]Ahmad (1991b).

[7]The minimum pension level was raised to 130 rubles in 1991.

[8]This would have led to 25 percent of the population being classified as poor.

fairly equal distribution of poverty was replaced by rapidly increasing real incomes, particularly in rural areas, albeit at the expense of increased variance of income levels. Thus, in China, the social safety net has essentially been reduced by policy makers to protecting the urban mass, very poor rural regions (through grain transfers), and extending social security cover as widely as possible.[9] In the U.S.S.R., there is a regional discussion that complicates the design of compensatory mechanisms. Most of the poor are in the Central Asian republics, although the impact of the adjustment is likely to be more severe in the European republics. In sum, the additional social safety nets needed during the transition may have to be placed under the losers rather than only those below an arbitrary income level.

Reforming Subsidies

Administered pricing systems, common to most centrally planned economies, are an opaque web of implicit taxes and subsidies. This web has affected almost all sectors of activity, although to illustrate the effects on living standards we shall concentrate primarily on basic consumer items.[10] A principal objective was to keep prices low so as to support the real incomes of net consumers. This pattern was sustained without substantial explicit budgetary outlays through a combination of low procurement prices and overvalued exchange rates. In order to provide appropriate production incentives, adjustments in procurement prices and exchange rates have made the complex system of subsidization more transparent.

Effects of General Subsidies

The system of administered prices involves a fixed price at which individuals are free to purchase unlimited quantities of a given good, and when the price is set below cost, there is a general subsidy involved. The amount of the subsidized good consumed determines the amount of subsidy that each individual receives. Because of consumption patterns, the rich receive a substantially higher transfer in absolute terms than the poor, even for items commonly thought of as "poor man's food," such as bread. In Algeria in 1989, for instance, the richest decile received four times the absolute transfer accruing to the poorest decile on account of the general

---

[9]See, for instance, Ahmad and Wang (1991).

[10]For a discussion of interest rate and industrial subsidies, see the paper by Chu and Holzman in this volume.

subsidy on bread, five times the transfer on account of the subsidy on flour and rice, and six times the transfer arising from the subsidy on packaged milk. None of the subsidized items involved a lower transfer to the richer income groups relative to the poorer.

General subsidies often result in an inequitable regional redistribution. In China, prior to the reforms of 1979, low agricultural procurement prices[11] taxed relatively poor farmers for the benefit of somewhat better-off formal sector workers. In the U.S.S.R., subsidized meat and dairy products are more important in the budgets of households living in the higher-income European republics, but are less important for households in the poorer Central Asian republics. The per capita consumption of meat and meat products, milk, and eggs in Uzbekistan is roughly half that in the Russian republic, and the consumption of potatoes a third. The subsidies thus benefit the rich more than the poor.

The maintenance of general subsidies on particular goods, when there has been a partial deregulation, generates price distortions leading to waste and misallocation of resources. In Algeria, the Islamic Republic of Iran, and China, for example, the low price of bread has led to wasteful consumption. Because animal feed is relatively expensive, and since prices of livestock products and meat are determined by the market, it has been profitable to feed the subsidized bread to animals. A subsidy designed for consumers is diverted to profits for middlemen.

Excess demand for some products with administered prices has led to shortages and queues and the development of parallel markets. In the U.S.S.R., this has disrupted normal channels of supply, as producers refuse to provide goods at the administered prices. Thus, the objective of maintaining administered prices to protect consumers is vitiated. Producer price adjustments together with artificially low consumer prices can be maintained only through large budgetary subsidies, but these are not sustainable in the face of declining revenues. In the U.S.S.R., a 60 percent adjustment in procurement prices in 1990[12] led to an estimated increase in budgetary subsidies on foodstuffs from 10 percent of GDP to around 18 percent, exacerbating budgetary pressures.[13] In Jordan and Algeria, there

---

[11]These were only partially compensated by subsidized prices for agricultural inputs.

[12]This adjustment brought procurement prices close to international prices at the official exchange rate. Of course, to the extent that the official exchange rate was overvalued, a further adjustment in procurement prices would have been needed to avoid implicit taxation of farmers, albeit at the expense of higher budgetary subsidies if fixed consumer prices were to be maintained.

[13]See International Monetary Fund (1991).

has been a phenomenal rise in budgetary subsidies resulting from price adjustment of imported foodstuffs associated with an adjustment in an overvalued exchange rate. The basic problem has therefore been to restrict or reduce explicit budgetary expenditures so as to impose the least burden on a mass of the population heretofore relying on the combination of administered prices and wages.

Policy Alternatives for the Transition

The patterns of the overall distribution of expenditures and of employment in particular countries have immediate consequences for public policy and the formulation of reforms during the transition. Fine targeting mechanisms to provide support on the basis of current income levels will be inadequate, since the price changes will be large. Further, the operations of formal social security instruments, particularly for the unemployed and the informal sector, constrain the extent to which these should be used to provide support during a transition. These formal instruments could face insolvency or administrative collapse during a transition. Nevertheless, there is a need to utilize these effectively as part of a permanent social safety net once the effects of the price shocks have been absorbed.

Cash Compensation and Means Testing

A commonly proposed reform option is to abolish the current system of subsidies altogether and to substitute direct cash compensation to individuals. These may provide lump-sum or one-off compensation to all, or on a means-tested basis. Alternatively, compensation may be provided through adjustments in wages, pensions, and other transfers, particularly in the early stages of reform, if wage and transfer adjustments are capable of providing for all vulnerable groups. Cash compensation may be easy to deliver (but only on a universal or categorical basis),[14] and the objective for the post-reform period should be to provide for life-cycle contingencies through social security cash transfers. For the transition period such compensation may not be entirely practicable.

Sharp price adjustments envisaged involve a high degree of uncertainty. If market forces are allowed to operate, how much compensation is needed will not be known in advance. Thus, inadequate compensation could cause great difficulty, especially given the concentration of families

---

[14]Categorical transfers would be targeted on certain categories of individuals, such as the aged, children, or the unemployed, without attempts to target any further, such as on an income or means-tested basis.

at low income levels, as in Algeria or the U.S.S.R. Overcompensation could exacerbate inflation.

If the compensation is paid through adjustments in wages and social security transfers, the reduction in subsidies would be offset by increased budgetary expenditures on public sector wages. The overall effect on the budget, or the viability of the social security system, would depend on the specific proposals. The ability of the state to adjust wages during the transition, or to provide additional subsidies to the social security system is likely to be constrained given budgetary limitations, particularly where the coverage is less than universal and the most vulnerable are outside formal cover. Increases in payroll contribution rates may not be possible since they are often high already (50 percent in Hungary). In the U.S.S.R., social security reform proposals in 1990 were designed to eliminate a substantial budgetary subsidy, but the contribution rates were to be quickly increased from around 12 percent of the wage bill to 37 percent.[15] High payroll contributions for social security benefits may constrain the development of a nascent private sector and may be unenforceable. Further reduction in the base may however necessitate increased contribution rates.

For the income- or means-tested versions, it may be impossible to determine who should be compensated, since individual incomes are known imperfectly. The basis of individual income is inadequate in the extended family context. Then there are the grey areas of the informal sector and the unemployed. If an income test is to be applied, the standard threshold has to be determined, posing difficulties with 100 percent marginal tax rates at the point of withdrawal. If the cutoff point lets in 70 percent of the population, as it well might, given the overall distribution of income in countries such as Algeria, the administrative bother and cost hardly seems worth the effort. In the context of rapidly changing prices, means testing is virtually impossible.

Categorical Transfers and Allowances

Categorical classifications, for households with children, for example, also pose difficulties in providing a basis for compensation for relative price changes. Many planned economies with systems of child allowances, often with varying benefits for larger families, have been motivated by a pronatalist approach to population size. These measures are probably not appropriate for countries such as China and Algeria where

---

[15]Additional payroll contributions would be needed to finance the unemployment insurance scheme.

the growth of the population poses a serious problem for the provision of social services.

In the U.S.S.R., outlays for family allowances have been more limited than expenditures on pensions, largely on account of the low level of benefits conferred.[16] However, new benefits, or adjustments necessary to improve the living standards of particular groups, would have major budgetary consequences. In Poland and Hungary, family allowances have been fairly generous and have formed a substantial element in the real wage packet of workers.[17]

To limit the budgetary consequences of changes in family allowances, means testing is often recommended. This testing suffers from the administrative difficulties mentioned above, as corroborated by evidence relating to means-tested family allowances in the U.S.S.R. In the Soviet republic of Uzbekistan, 43 percent of households qualified for assistance for family allowances on the basis of formal sector wages during 1989–90, but it was not possible to assess incomes from private activities, such as sale of produce from garden plots and home-grown consumption.[18] Enforced means testing would complicate the administrative ease with which the family allowance might be implemented.

The absence of an income cutoff should not be taken as evidence of poor targeting per se. For instance, in the U.S.S.R., wages until 1990 had been set so that a family with children would need two earners to cover basic needs. With the appearance of one child, 30 percent of households would fall below the official poverty line (with unchanged prices). With more than one child 50 percent of single earner families would be so classified. This is a typical case as younger couples with low incomes tend to have small children, and the arrival of a child restricts the options for earning a second income. Thus, the family benefit, if universal, may well

---

[16]In 1983, family allowances formed only 2 percent of benefit expenditures on formal social security in the U.S.S.R., or around 0.28 percent of GDP (ILO (1988), p. 101). However, in Hungary, family allowances were 14 percent of total benefit expenditures or around 2.6 percent of GDP in 1983, and had increased to 3 percent of GDP in 1989.

[17]In Hungary in 1985, family allowances for two children were of the order of 17 percent of the average wage in manufacturing, and given the increasing level of benefits, four children's allowances were 40 percent of the average wage. See Kopits and others (1990). In Poland, the benefit per child is 8 percent of the average wage, or roughly equivalent to the Hungarian level, whereas in the United Kingdom the figure is around 2.5 percent.

[18]See International Monetary Fund (1991), Chapter IV, No. 6.

be appropriately targeted, since young children are a vulnerable group.[19] However, if the family allowance is payable only to workers in the formal or public sectors, it might benefit the relatively well-to-do, and under such circumstances replacing family allowances by wage adjustments may be a simpler administrative option.

If a universal system of family allowances exists, limiting the duration of benefit may be more cost effective than imposing an incomes test. In order to discourage pronatalist incentives, benefits should not be increased for additional children. Such benefits should, however, be included as part of taxable income for the personal income tax, to claw-back benefits to the rich.

Limited Rationing

A major objective of reform in the centrally planned economies is to permit the operation of a free market mechanism, so that both producers and consumers can respond to appropriate incentives, but this usually requires fairly large price adjustments.[20] It may be possible to institute market clearing prices and reduce subsidy outlays, and still protect the vulnerable through a system of rationing of a limited number of items essential for the poor. The case for rationing is strongest where there is a wide difference between the consumption patterns of different groups and the government lacks the means fully to control incomes and transfers (Weitzman (1977)). During rapid price change and uncertainty concerning outcomes, such rationing can provide a degree of assurance to the most vulnerable households. Rationing can be of many types, reflecting differing administrative, retailing, and supply possibilities.

In principle, rationing designed for transition periods should be set at relatively low levels, but enough, for example, to cover the current quantities consumed by the poorest one or two deciles. Above ration purchases should be at open market prices. The poor would then be largely protected from the effects of the price changes, although higher income groups would be affected to the extent of their consumption beyond the ration. This system has built-in targeting mechanisms: the quantities involved are limited so that the benefits would be rather less for the rich

---

[19]Targeting attention to children may be a desirable objective regardless of income levels.

[20]In Algeria, even with an overvalued exchange rate (DA 16.2 to the U.S. dollar) in early 1991, the price increases required to eliminate explicit subsidies on key consumer goods ranged from 157 percent for wheat to 376 percent for sugar.

than with the general subsidy.[21] In addition, the process of registration and collection of ration coupons would tend to exclude the rich. A ration, which is in principle universal, would also permit the government to hold the line on minimum pensions (as well as minimum wages) during the transition period. It would thus protect social security funds from sharp adjustments and potential disequilibria, as well as the budget from the effects of major changes in public-sector wages.

The choice of commodity to ration, as well as the appropriate administrative details, would depend very much on national or regional characteristics. In Eastern Europe and the western republics of the U.S.S.R., meat and dairy products are consumed by poorer groups, but in developing administered economies, such as Algeria, Iran, and Jordan, as well as in the Central Asian Soviet republics, meat and dairy products are consumed mainly by the well-to-do, and subsidized bread, sugar, and edible oils are more important for the poor. In the U.S.S.R. in 1989, the quantities of meat, meat products, and eggs, consumed by the poorest 15 percent of households or those below the poverty line were roughly 40 percent of average consumption of these items. For milk and dairy products, the ratio was around 55 percent.[22] In Jordan and Algeria, consumption by the poorest one or two deciles of items such as sugar, milk, and rice is similarly around half the average consumption of such commodities. This indicates the possibility of significant reductions in subsidy outlays relative to existing generalized subsidies.

Ration systems can operate through private or government retail outlets. With private retail outlets, there can be either market-based sources of supply or simultaneous supply of both market-based and subsidized goods. When private retailers supply both subsidized and free market varieties of the same product, arbitrage is possible. Preventing arbitrage can drain administrative resources. However, experience suggests that it is possible to minimize administrative outlays, and rationing can be based on a single-market based price system at the retail level.

A form of rationing, which permits a single price at the retail level, would eliminate arbitrage possibilities. Given a ration entitlement based on the per capita expenditures of the poorest groups, individuals could purchase coupons or stamps at the local outlet. Coupons could be resold, if desired, and this would improve welfare. Forbidding resale is generally

---

[21]With a general subsidy, the transfer to an individual is a function of his level of consumption, and richer persons receive a greater subsidy because they consume more than the poor. A ration should limit the subsidy to quantities consumed by the poor, thus reducing the subsidy to the rich.

[22]See International Monetary Fund (1991), Vol. 2, pp. 204–5.

not implementable and would require a large policing effort, which would reduce the acceptability of the system. Coupons would be presented to the retailer, who would provide the stipulated quantity without charge, and any excess purchased above this would be charged at the prevailing market price. Thus, only one price would be relevant to the retailer: the market price. The retailer may be reimbursed in kind, along with a small handling charge, when a certain number of coupons are redeemed. An alternative is to reimburse in cash, depending on administrative feasibility. This fairly simple system would need no verification or monitoring of the retail transactions.

An alternative is to provide the consumer with coupons, on application, free of charge, but to allow the retailer to charge the subsidized price for the quantity stipulated. The state would then agree to underwrite the quantities sold (against the submission of coupons) at the subsidized price plus a handling margin. Yet another possibility is to separate channels of supply, with state outlets providing the rationed goods, and private retailers allowed to charge market clearing prices. Much depends on the private retailing infrastructure, and the options would need to be assessed in relation to private and public administrative capabilities.

Once market prices have been established, and there has been an impact on demand and supply patterns, the authorities should gradually close the gap between the ration and market prices. This should be linked to adjustments in the minimum wage or pension, but not to automatic indexation of all pensions or wages.[23] As the gap between the subsidized and market prices narrows, the rich will have less incentive to use the system, leading to greater self-targeting.

Other Targeting Mechanisms

It should be possible to institute fairly quickly mechanisms to deliver subsidized milk to clinics for infants and lactating mothers, if continued targeting of nutritional supplements to vulnerable groups is desirable, during and after the transition period. Feeding at school is another possibility. This provision for all infants, lactating mothers, and so on, is on a "categorical basis," or without additional targeting of income or assets. "Categorical" targeting mechanisms could provide support for some of the poor and vulnerable in conjunction with an improved set of formal social security arrangements, if the need arises.

---

[23]Wages should be determined by collective bargaining, subject to the minimum wage and aggregate cash limits.

Formal Social Security Arrangements

Given the problems associated with the establishment of a nascent private sector in centrally planned economies, together with the introduction of efficient tax mechanisms, such as the VAT and income taxes, it may be advisable not to begin with high payroll taxes or personal contribution rates (which may be administratively unfeasible or unimplementable) and not to impose substantial financing requirements on the budget during the transition. Thus, significant expansion in the type and level of benefits associated with the existing social security system should not be attempted without regard to the contribution base and financing options. High payroll taxes are likely to lead to a contraction of the contribution base. To some extent the rationing discussed above limits expenditures in the short term, although demographic forces and employment patterns may require structural change in the system (see the article by Kopits, this volume). A social safety net that would permit the rapid restructuring of public sector enterprises is needed and this process involves the introduction of combinations of unemployment insurance, retraining facilities, and public works programs. Finally, in many countries there is a residual category of need for individuals not covered by formal social security programs or other safety nets, such as public works, and these persons would qualify for social assistance in some advanced countries. In-kind and cash transfers for such persons would need to be instituted in a cost-effective fashion.

Unemployment Insurance

While there has been substantial turnover in employment through voluntary "quits," in the U.S.S.R.,[24] involuntary unemployment had not been formally recognized as a possible contingency until recently. This has changed drastically in the last five or six years. China introduced an unemployment insurance program in 1986, and most Eastern European countries now have some form of cover. Unemployment insurance has recently (June 1991) been enacted and implemented in the Russian Republic.

Many unemployment insurance programs included lax eligibility criteria, substantial severance pay, high replacement levels,[25] and fairly long duration of benefits. The initial replacement rate in Bulgaria was 100 per-

---

[24]Oxenstierna (1990).

[25]The replacement level is defined as the unemployment benefit expressed as a proportion of the pre-termination wage.

cent, declining to 50 percent by the sixth month, and 70 percent in Hungary and Poland, but declining over time.[26] Reforms in Hungary provide for an earnings-related benefit in the first phase of unemployment, to be followed by a flat-rate benefit at the minimum wage, with provisions for early retirement for workers who have few employment prospects but who would qualify for retirement on the basis of contributions. In Poland, the replacement rate declines to 40 percent after the ninth month, subject to the minimum benefit, but benefits are provided for an indefinite period. In China, unemployment benefits have been available to contract workers and employees of bankrupt enterprises, with a replacement rate of between 60–75 percent of the worker's standard wage[27] for the duration of the first year and 50 percent for the second year. The true replacement rate in terms of the workers' gross emoluments, including benefits in kind and bonuses, is somewhat lower, at around 28–42 percent of previous earnings.[28] In the U.S.S.R., the 1990 unemployment insurance legislation is among the most tightly defined in the centrally planned economies. It stipulated three month's severance pay along with benefits at 50 percent of tariff wages[29] for six months. As in China, the true replacement rate in the U.S.S.R. would be well below 50 percent because of the loss of bonuses and in-kind benefits. During the succeeding six months, support is to be conditional on participation in training programs or public works, and thereafter eligibility for unemployment insurance is re-established for an additional period of six months.[30]

The benefit formulae described above, particularly for China and the U.S.S.R., are not generous in comparison with international practice. In Germany, the benefit formula stipulates a payment of 63 percent of previous after-tax returns for 52 months, to be followed by unemployment assistance at a rate of 56 percent. France provides benefits for 14 months at between 57 and 75 percent of previous earnings. The period for which unemployment insurance is to be paid, indefinite in Poland and two years in China, is somewhat longer than in the developed countries.

Eligibility criteria for unemployment benefits also vary in the centrally planned economies. Poland is the most generous and provides for dis-

---

[26]Holzmann (1990).

[27]The base for determining the standard wage was to be taken as the average of the standard pay during the last two years of work in an enterprise.

[28]World Bank (1990).

[29]Tariff wages are the basic cash wage, determined according to type of employment, skill, and seniority. They do not include bonuses or in-kind payments, which may form a substantial element of the gross earnings.

[30]For details, see International Monetary Fund (1991), Vol. 2, pp. 160–66.

missed workers, voluntary quits as well as fresh entrants to the work force. Such provisions for unemployment benefits tend to encourage the entry of particular groups, such as housewives and students, into the formal labor force.[31] U.S.S.R. legislation sets down strict eligibility criteria for the earnings-related insurance, but there is a flat rate provision at 75 percent of the minimum wage for first time job seekers and those with no work history—although training assistance is based on the minimum wage for these persons. This is to minimize the disincentive effects of the cover provided.

Financing estimates for unemployment insurance costs have been based on conservative estimates of the extent of unemployment likely to be generated by restructuring state-owned activities. Poland had anticipated that around 200,000 persons would be unemployed in 1990 (1 percent of the work force), in setting a contribution rate of 2 percent on employers.[32] By March 1991, unemployment had reached 1.3 millions (7 percent of the work force) and a Government committee estimated that almost 2 million would be unemployed by the end of 1991. The contribution rates are inadequate to meet anticipated costs, and there are proposals to tighten eligibility criteria for benefits and to limit payments to 12 months. These proposals would be in conjunction with public works programs and retraining, as well as with encouraging foreign investment and other employment-generation programs. The Hungarian unemployment insurance program was, until 1990, financed directly from general revenues, largely because of the already steep contribution rate imposed on account of the retirement program.

The U.S.S.R. had proposed a 1 percent contribution rate from the wage fund of enterprises to finance the unemployment insurance system. However, this would be adequate only for an unemployment rate of 2 percent of the labor force.[33] It is likely that unemployment will be higher than the

---

[31]Almost two thirds of the recipients of the Polish unemployment benefits in 1990 were from such categories, with laid-off workers constituting but one third of the registered unemployed. See Holzmann (1990).

[32]During 1990 the budget estimate was revised to allow for 400,000 unemployed (2 percent of the work force). It was expected that contributions would account for 61 percent of the revenues of the labor fund in 1990 (Holzmann (1990)).

[33]The U.S.S.R. faces serious inter-republican problems in the implementation of an unemployment insurance system. The major claimants at present would be the Central Asian republics, which would run deficits needing to be financed through transfers from the more industrialized European republics. Much of the restructuring would take place in the latter, thus making the likelihood of inter-republican transfers somewhat bleak. (International Monetary Fund (1990), Vol. 2).

estimated 2 percent in the U.S.S.R. As seen in the extreme case, east Germany, unemployment was at 850,000 workers in mid-1991 (9.5 percent of the work force), despite 1.91 million workers engaged on short-run employment schemes. An additional 500,000–700,000 workers are expected to be added to the unemployed mass by the end of 1991. Thus the provision for the unemployed, whose numbers and duration of unemployment are increasing, places stress on the financing ability of the state. It also highlights the need to examine more targeted methods of provision in order to restrain costs.

Public Works

Public works provide a method of targeting assistance for the unemployed without relying on means testing. Providing low wages (at or around subsistence level, sometimes with an element of direct provision of food) and requiring a work test together form a self-targeting mechanism that reduces the work disincentives involved in unlimited assistance payments. Experience from adjustment in countries such as Chile, during the 1970s and 1980s suggests that these schemes are unlikely to be too expensive, even with unemployment levels that exceeded those in east Germany.[34]

The U.S.S.R. program for the provision for the unemployed includes short-term activities in agricultural production, infrastructure and environmental renewal, social services, and child care, among others. Seasonal activities would also be included. The law envisages two-months contracts with the possibility of extension for another two months. These would be organized and financed by local authorities, with co-financing by the Employment Fund. Longer contracts (for one or two years) are envisaged for activities expected to continue over the medium term and eventually to be financed entirely by local authorities.

A second strand of policy in the U.S.S.R. is to encourage self-employment on a large scale. This is achieved by providing credit and assistance with project design and administration, supplies of inputs, and training. However, as in the case of the *Fonds d'emploi de jeunes* in Algeria, the per capita costs of such programs can be fairly high relative to the basic safety net of public works at or around the minimum wage. These activities would thus have to be monitored carefully and encouraged to operate on market principles in order to avoid merely replacing subsidized large-scale enterprises with subsidized small-scale activities.

---

[34]Ahmad (1991a).

Social Assistance

A final element in the series of social safety nets involves social assistance for individuals with no other source of sustenance. This element should be designed to provide permanently for the poorest and the indigent, rather than being limited to protecting the vulnerable during the transition. In the developed countries, social assistance is generally provided locally on a means-tested basis. Because of the stigma attached to the means test and of administrative difficulties, take-up rates are low and many of the truly poor who should have qualified do not apply. These difficulties also obtain in the centrally planned economies. In Hungary, local councils provided financial support to persons over 70 who do not qualify for retirement pensions. While there were 200,000 such persons in 1988, only 25 percent of them received assistance, which was well below the minimum pension.[35]

In China, there is a community-based provision termed the "five guarantees" (*wu bao*), which provides assistance to persons on a categorical basis—the elderly, orphans, widows, the disabled—with the stipulation that they should have no able-bodied relatives. Unfortunately, severe stigma is associated with the lack of support from kin and the extended family in China, so that take-up rates have been somewhat restricted.[36] The state still has a role to play, however, since very poor communities have limited resources to devote to transfers for the five guarantees.

A more effective provision by nongovernmental foundations operates on similar categorical principles in Iran. Again it employs local knowledge to establish the lack of family support and gives priority to the elderly, orphans, widows, and the disabled. The stigma is less than in China; there are virtually no errors of exclusion, and very few errors of inclusion. Benefits are provided in cash as well as kind. Food, health care, and education are priorities. Occupational training is stressed, for instance in traditional Iranian handicrafts, such as weaving and carpet making, as well as other productive activities. The Foundations are nationwide organizations, benefiting from charitable contributions and support from the State budget. Thus, the problem of co-variate risk—poor communities being unable to cater for the indigent in times of stress—is mitigated through the pooling mechanism of a national organization.

---

[35]According to the World Bank, the average payment was Ft 2,300 in 1988, as against the minimum pension of Ft 3,600.

[36]Ahmad and Hussain (1991).

It is thus possible to provide basic assistance to the most indigent in an effective manner, although formal means testing remains administratively cumbersome and socially divisive.

Concluding Remarks

To speed the efficient transition to market-based economies, temporary social safety nets are needed to protect large groups. Measures should be designed to minimize budgetary outlays and provide minimum guarantees. While these should be provided without arbitrary cutoff points (for administrative convenience), for efficiency and in order to mobilize political support, they should not be seen as permanent entitlements. Such temporary safety nets should be withdrawn gradually as the market mechanisms begin to operate, entailing intervention in commodity pricing and in the labor market. The transition should aim for a system of sustainable growth, and the protection of the vulnerable with the eventual establishment of effective permanent social security and assistance mechanisms.

References

Ahmad, E. (1991a), "Social Security and the Poor: Choices for Developing Countries," *The World Bank Research Observer*, January 6, 1991.

———(1991b), "Poverty, Inequality and Public Policy in Transition Economies," processed, to be presented at the IIPF Conference in Leningrad.

———, and S.A. Hussain, "Social Security in China in a Historical Context," in Ahmad et al, 1991.

———, J. Dreze, J. Hills, and A.K. Senn eds., *Social Security in Developing Countries* (Oxford: Clarendon Press, 1991).

———, and Yan Wang, 1991, "Inequality and Poverty in China: Institutional Change and Public Policy, 1978 to 1988," *The World Bank Economic Review*, 3, May.

Holzmann, R., "Unemployment Benefits During Economic Transition: Background, Concept and Implementation," *Forschungsberichte*, Ludwig Boltzmann Institut, Vienna, Austria, forthcoming in *The Transition to a Market Economy in Central and Eastern Europe*, ed. by P. Mahrer and S. Zecchini (Paris: Organization for Economic Cooperation and Development, 1990).

Hussain, S.A., and N.H. Stern, "Effective Demand, Enterprise Reforms and Public Finance in China," *Economic Policy*, Vol. 12 (1991).

ILO, *The Cost of Social Security* (Geneva: International Labor Office, 1988).

International Monetary Fund, the World Bank, Organization for Economic Cooperation and Development, and the European Bank for Recovery and Development, *A Study of the Soviet Economy* (Paris: OECD, 1991).

Kopits, G., R. Holzmann, G Schieber, and E. Sidgwick, *Social Security Reform in Hungary*, (Washington: International Monetary Fund, 1990).

Oxenstierna, S., *From Labor Shortage to Unemployment? The Soviet Labor Market in the 1980s* (Stockholm: Swedish Institute for Social Research, 1990).

Tanzi, V., "Tax Reform and the Move to a Market Economy: Overview of the Issues," in *The Role of Tax Reform in Central and Eastern European Economies* (Paris: OECD, 1991).

Weitzman, M.L., "Is the Price System or Rationing More Effective in Getting a Commodity to Those Who Need it Most," *Bell Journal of Economics*, Vol. 8 (1977).

World Bank, *The Reform of Social Security in China* (Washington: World Bank, 1990).

CHAPTER 16

Fiscal Federalism
Daniel Hewitt and Dubravko Mihaljek

Reform of the systems of intergovernmental fiscal relations in Central and Eastern Europe is both complementary to and a necessary part of the economic and political reforms underway. As these countries transform themselves from planned economies to market economies and from communist regimes to democracies, the previous assignments of fiscal functions and power sharing arrangements between different levels of government are no longer viable nor desirable. Each country must institute a system of intergovernmental fiscal relations compatible with the emerging order.

The initial conditions and the reforms currently under consideration indicate major differences among these countries. The federal states of Czechoslovakia, the Soviet Union, and Yugoslavia have three distinct levels of government: the federation, republics, and communes. The primary intergovernmental fiscal issue is the delineation of powers between the federal government and the republics. In contrast, the unitary states of Bulgaria, Hungary, Poland, and Romania have essentially two levels of government: central and regional-local governments. The primary intergovernmental fiscal issue is to what extent decentralizing expenditure functions and tax collection to subnational governments is politically and economically desirable.

This paper examines federalism issues and issues of decentralization within unitary states separately by (i) identifying possible problems that might arise if currently discussed reform proposals are adopted; (ii) discussing the tradeoffs that policymakers face in designing their intergovernmental fiscal systems; and (iii) analyzing alternate systems in developed market economies, with a view to deriving relevant lessons from these varied experiences.

Prior to 1990, Central and Eastern European countries had rigid unitary intergovernmental fiscal systems (with the exception of Yugoslavia). An economic plan guided both enterprises and government agencies. The

Ministry of Finance, acting under auspices of the planning agency, managed budgetary procedures. The center determined all aspects of tax policy: the tax base, tax rate, exemptions and deductions, method of collection. Taxes were collected primarily through state banks via automatic transfers from public enterprises (Tanzi (1991)). Republic and local government autonomy in fiscal matters was confined to appointing local budget officials (who were then responsible to the center) and filing expenditure requests to higher-level authorities. Since the plan generally provided for uniform levels of services, it precluded independent local decisions on the level or composition of expenditures.

Enormous redistribution was carried out within the system, giving rise to extensive bargaining, similar to that in western democracies, and tended to soften the rigid edifice of the command economy. At the same time, bargaining made the system of intergovernmental finance less transparent and caused frequent deviations from proclaimed policy.

The excessively centralized systems described above are no longer compatible with the emerging market-orientation and incipient democracy. Once Soviet control began to loosen in 1989, and the political and economic reforms began to take shape, similarities in intergovernmental fiscal arrangements in these countries rapidly disappeared. Three trends have emerged. Czechoslovakia, the Soviet Union, and Yugoslavia have federal constitutions that confer special status on the republics, insuring that the republics are much more than just an intermediary level of government between the federal and local governments.[1] Intergovernmental fiscal relations are increasingly becoming a more charged economic and political issue in these countries. The republics now appear to be gaining power at the expense of the federal governments and even preempting the emergence of increased local autonomy. In Yugoslavia, and more recently in the Soviet Union, the federal government depends on annual contributions from the republics for a portion of its funding. This represents a sharp divergence from existing federal systems in the West, in which the center tends to be a major tax collector and the flow of intergovernmental transfers is predominately from the top down. The primary reform issues

---

[1] Economists apply the term fiscal federalism to both unitary states and federations. However, a polity is a federation only when the assignment of powers is secured by extraordinary legal protection, such as a constitution that cannot be amended by a simple majority (Benson (1961)). A confederation is an intermediate case between a federation and independent countries and is usually defined as an alliance of sovereign states united for joint action—such as free trade or defense (in German *der Staatenbund* or alliance of states, as opposed to *der Bundesstaat* or the federal state).

in the three federations are therefore the balance of fiscal power and the assignment of tax and expenditure functions that the republics should cede to the federal government.

The four unitary states have central governments which have undisputed jurisdiction and cede powers to local governments in order to enhance national well being. The primary reform issue in these countries is the extent to which decentralization is desirable and compatible with political and economic changes. Hungary and Poland are developing decentralized systems in which local governments are likely to have a great deal of autonomy in expenditure and tax matters, while the regional governments are likely to remain insignificant and under the control of the central government. In Romania and Bulgaria, the system continues to be predominantly centralized, leaving lower levels of government with relatively little autonomy. In the federal states, the devolution of governmental functions from the republics to local governments is a parallel issue likely to gain more political exposure once the primary federal institutions are more clearly defined.

Federal States and Minimum Central Government

Although the federal constitutions of Czechoslovakia, the Soviet Union, and Yugoslavia designate their republics as sovereign nation-states, these constitutional arrangements were not in force previously. Instead, it has been argued that a "Bolshevik federation" existed, in which democratic centralism, the organizing principle of the Communist Party, had ascendancy over federalism as the principle of state order.[2] With the demise of communist party rule, the absence of a sound foundation for federalism became apparent, and the political vacuum has been increasingly filled by nationalist political groups.

Provided these countries remain united, a federal government with minimum powers is the most likely outcome. This section constructs an approximate description of the minimum functions of a central government within a federation by relying on economic theory, actual practice in these countries, and the accumulated experiences of contemporary Western federations. In examining the general characteristics of contemporary federations, special consideration is given to the institutional arrange-

---

[2]A Bolshevik federation is characterized by dualism of the state and the Communist Party (Kristan (1990)). Democratic centralism is a Leninist doctrine in which Party decisions are in theory democratically adopted after free discussions "from the bottom up" and then implemented without question through directives "from the top down."

ments in Yugoslavia and Switzerland, since these countries have perhaps dealt with the issue of a minimum central government most intensely in recent years.[3] Using this information, a list of high priority federal functions and a list of low priority federal functions is formulated. A hypothesis is that setting up a federation in which the central government has insufficient powers is likely to have excessively high economic costs.

Specific Fiscal Federal Arrangements

Yugoslavia

The unique fiscal system in Yugoslavia has evolved in the direction of a federation with minimal federal powers.[4] Rather than being a simple federal system—with central, republic, and local governments—until recently a parallel system of Self-Governing Interest Communities existed with responsibility for about two thirds of total public services. Different Self-Governing Interest Communities operated at the republic and local levels overseeing health care, education, social security (retirement, disability, and unemployment), and most public infrastructure. Each had its own source of revenue consisting of either an enterprise income or a payroll tax.[5]

Using 1986 as a base year, total public expenditures in Yugoslavia amounted to approximately 33 percent of GDP, of which the federal government, the republics, and the local governments accounted for 7 percent, 5 percent, and 3 percent, respectively, and the Self-Governing Interest Communities accounted for about 18 percent. Federal revenue collection was restricted to customs duties (24 percent of total revenues) and the federal sales tax (36 percent). Contributions of republics to the federal government (39 percent) were the other primary source. Republics collected income and payroll taxes from the enterprises (26 percent of 1986 total revenues), republic sales taxes (19 percent), the share of federal sales taxes (45 percent), and the qualifying republics received development grants and loans (5 percent). The communes collected local sales

---

[3]See Alexashenko (1991), and International Monetary Fund (1991) for more information on fiscal federalism in the Soviet Union. See Kocarnik and Bakes (1991), and Prust (1990) for more information on Czechoslovakia. Owing to the continuing fluidity of the situation in these federations and space limitations, a description of their current fiscal arrangements is not provided.

[4]See Jurkovic (1989), Mates (1991), and Mihaljek (1990) and the chapter on Yugoslavia in the companion volume for more details.

[5]This system was reminiscent of a Lindahl solution (Mihaljek (1986)). Beginning in 1991, it was largely abandoned in favor of more standard budgetary accounting.

taxes (49 percent of local revenue), income taxes (34 percent), and property taxes (3 percent) and received intergovernmental grants (8 percent).

Federal government expenditures consisted of defense (70 percent), veterans' social insurance (16 percent), federal administration (6 percent), and grants to republics (4 percent). Expenditures of the republics consisted of contributions to the federal government (48 percent), economic services (16 percent), and social services (8 percent). Local expenditures consisted of public services (75 percent), social services (3 percent), and economic services (4 percent).

The federal development fund was designed to finance investment in the less developed republics and the province of Kosovo. The fund, which was financed by taxes on enterprises, comprised about 1.5 percent of GDP. A large portion of the loans went directly to enterprises in qualifying republics. The system did not work well; the developed republics complained that overall transfers were excessive, misused, and did not contribute to economic development; the recipient republics complained of the insensitivity of donor republics to their economic problems.

Intergovernmental Finance in Developed Market Economies

The systems of intergovernmental finance in Western federations have evolved gradually, much like their market and political institutions; the present systems result from historical circumstances and political events and reflect cultural traits. In contrast, the socialist countries are starting with relatively open-ended situations, in which the past offers few institutional guidelines owing to the enormous transformations taking place. Thus, the challenge in reforming their systems of fiscal federalism is to create government institutions compatible with what will exist in the future. For these reasons, examination of the existing fiscal systems in Western federations is appropriate. Though no single model of an efficient federal system exists, these federations exemplify the range of possible solutions.

Among the six major Western federations (Australia, Austria, Canada, Germany, Switzerland, the United States), the share of local expenditures in total government expenditures varies from 7 percent in Australia, to 26 percent in Switzerland; the states' or provinces' share of total expenditures varies from 16 percent in Austria, to 48 percent in Canada.[6] The share of local receipts of transfers from higher-level governments varies

---

[6]Figures in this section come from International Monetary Fund, *Government Finance Statistics Yearbook*, unless otherwise stated.

from 16 percent of total local revenue in Switzerland to 48 percent in Canada; the share of intergovernmental grants in total receipts of states or provinces varies from 16 percent in Germany to 50 percent in Australia. Each country has unique features. In Australia local government is of modest importance and the state governments depend heavily on federal transfers; Switzerland is characterized by strong local governments with relatively little dependence on transfers; the United States has a pass-through transfer system from the federal government to state government to local government; Germany and Austria have a high degree of horizontal fiscal equalization; and in Canada provincial revenue collection is relatively high (Bird (1986)).

Unworkable intergovernmental arrangements have often been observed (e.g., in the United States during the Confederate period). But a wide variety of systems do work. The determining factors in such cases often have to do less with the particular pattern of tax and expenditure assignments than with administrative and common-sense aspects of the system. As a result, even in countries that are more satisfied with their systems (Austria, Switzerland, and Germany, as opposed to Canada, the United States, and Australia) policymakers are constantly considering alternative reforms. The most common reform is aimed at simplifying the system of intergovernmental grants; recently some have sought to increase regional equalization and harmonize the taxes levied by different levels of government.

Switzerland

Switzerland, perhaps the most decentralized Western federation, is widely regarded as having something close to the minimum central government functions. In its long history, Switzerland has passed through several cycles of federalism and confederatism.[7] Since the mid-nineteenth century, the powers of the central government have been steadily increasing, primarily because the cantons have recognized the desirability and feasibility of increased benefits of coordination. Throughout, a system which combines representative democracy with approval by referendum and requires an extraordinary majority to enact most federal-level changes has been in force.

Overall government expenditures stood at 27 percent of GDP in 1989, split almost evenly between the three levels of government. Federal gov-

---

[7]Although Switzerland is formally a confederation, many Swiss fiscal federalism experts use the term federation, see Bieri (1979) and Frey (1977); Switzerland figures come from Dafflon (1991).

ernment expenditures comprise social security (21 percent), defense (19 percent), transportation and roads (14 percent), and education (9 percent). Canton expenditures consist of education (28 percent), health (17 percent), other social services (12 percent), and transportation and roads (11 percent). Local expenditures are allocated to education (22 percent), health (15 percent), other social services (11 percent), and environment (10 percent).

Central government revenues come from direct federal turnover and excise taxes (52 percent), personal and corporate income taxes (41 percent), and nontax revenues (7 percent). The cantons depend upon personal income taxes (32 percent), intergovernmental grants and federal revenue sharing (27 percent), nontax revenue (19 percent), and other direct taxes on businesses and wealth (18 percent). Localities' revenue sources consist of direct taxes (50 percent), nontax revenues (32 percent), and intergovernmental grants and revenue sharing (18 percent).

Significant intergovernmental grants and revenue sharing in the budgets of the cantons and localities indicate the importance of equalization in the Swiss fiscal federal system. The distribution of these funds is based on various formulas dependent upon tax effort and tax capacity, among others. The objective of intergovernmental transfers is to enable the cantons to provide similar levels of services without imposing excessively heavy tax burdens relative to other cantons. Dafflon (1991) estimates that 27 percent of the transfers from the center to the cantons are exclusively for income equalization.

Overall, the Swiss system appears quite successful. The gap between cantons with high and low per capita incomes has diminished since the 1950s. Moreover, "the resistance of the rich cantons is amazingly weak, probably in large part because a considerable portion of the financial help . . . to the poorer cantons flows back to them" (Frey (1977), p. 101). However, because of the restrictions placed on the fiscal powers of the central government, activist macroeconomic management of the economy is essentially forfeited (Bieri (1979)).

Minimum Powers of a Central Government Within a Federation

No scientific method exists for determining the minimum powers of a central government within a federation.[8] The minimum powers are linked to the advantages of maintaining a federation, as opposed to separating

---

[8]See Kolm (1985) for discussions of the concept of the minimum functions of a government and a methodology to identify them.

into fully independent countries or forming a confederation. Certain central government activities have the potential to significantly increase collective welfare within each republic; alternatively, decentralization of certain activities to the individual republics would result in significant welfare losses. These activities can be classified as *minimum functions* of a central government. Another class of activities exists whose potential gain from central coordination are of a lower order of magnitude; centralization in these cases is a matter of country preference rather than economic efficiency.

High Priority Federal Functions

The most compelling economic functions of a central government within a federation are promoting internal free trade, facilitating international trade, maintaining macroeconomic stability, and providing public goods that benefit the entire country.

The benefits of *free trade*, long established in economic theory, are now widely accepted by politicians and the public, and supported by evidence that the potential economic gains from free trade are high. The maintenance of a free trade zone implies substantial regulatory powers for the federal government, but only modest expenditure. The appropriate federal regulatory powers to promote internal trade include:
   a. regulation of movement of goods and factors between republics;
   b. enforcement of inter-republic private contracts;
   c. settlement of federal level disputes between republics;
   d. prohibition of discrimination based upon republic origin of: (i) products, (ii) workers, (iii) capital; prohibition of discriminatory commodity taxation;
   e. promotion of market competition;
   f. coordination of business and labor regulations in order to simplify the economic environment in which these factors function; and
   g. supply and control of a common currency.

The second major function of the center is the formulation of *foreign trade* and foreign relations policy, a nearly automatic consequence of having a free trade zone. This function implies federal control over customs policy, collection of tariffs, exchange rate policy, and certain diplomatic functions.

Substantial gains to centralization also exist in *macroeconomic stabilization* policy. Maintaining macroeconomic stability in a country is by its very nature a collective activity and follows immediately from free-trade functions (Pisany-Ferry (1991)). Given a common currency, one centralized agency must control money creation. If monetary policy is decentralized, there would be an incentive for each republic to create excessive amounts of money to realize short-run gains. The resulting cost, an inflation tax, would be borne by the entire federation. In this manner, each republic would compete for seigniorage, and the result would be excessive inflation. Centralized inflation policy implies federal regulation of banks as well.[9]

Other macroeconomic stabilization powers of the federal government are presently somewhat more controversial. To ensure macroeconomic stability, the federal government must be able to contain its budgetary deficits through *recourse to its own revenue sources*.[10] Recent and past experience as well as theory indicate that contributions from member republics are not a reliable means for financing federal operations. The system in operation in Yugoslavia, and more recently in the Soviet Union, has resulted in disgruntled republics withholding contributions.[11] From economic theory, such behavior is predictable as a consequence of problems arising from maintaining a cartel arrangement, or, equivalently, the free-rider problem. Provided the other republics or members of a union make their contributions, a republic can maximize its own welfare by evading payment. Owing to the non-excludibility of national (country wide) public goods, the resulting loss in federal services would be small in relationship to the savings realized by withholding its contributions. Furthermore, withholding contributions or the threat to withhold payment could enable a republic to increase its influence over federation policies.[12]

For these reasons, the federal government must be able to collect funds directly from economic agents within republics, without depending upon

---

[9]Some authors advocate privately issued money, for overviews see King (1983) and *Cato Journal* (1989). Regardless, a common country-wide monetary regime is required, and therefore the regulation of the monetary system is still in effect a federal function.

[10]This does not preclude the federal government from contracting out revenue collection to republics or private banks. The crucial element is the power to collect indirect or direct taxes from federal residents.

[11]Financing federal government operations through contributions from member states has not been widely used in the past; other instances include the U.S., Germany, and Switzerland in their formative stages. A parallel example is the contribution system of the United Nations Organizations where both the United States and the Soviet Union have withheld payments at different times to register displeasure with certain collective decisions.

[12]The free-rider problem does not arise with intergovernmental transfers from the center to lower levels of government. Experience indicates that governments suffering financial crises tend to eliminate upward transfers first, but do not tend to rely inordinately on cuts of downward transfers to other levels of government or individuals.

explicit compliance by the republic governments. Customs duties and the value-added tax are logical federal taxes; with both, uniform tax rates throughout the federation are advisable, in one case to prevent distortions and, in the other, to avoid excessively complicated accounting procedures. If these taxes are not sufficient or their rates are limited by constitutional controls, other own sources of revenue must be ceded to the center, such as federal excise duties.

Another macroeconomic tool that could be crucial to sound management of a federation is a *limitation on republic and local government budgetary deficits*. In the extreme, large budgetary deficits can cause macroeconomic instability. If moral suasion is insufficient to control large deficits during a crisis, the federal government may need to resort to some form of regulatory control.

The final compelling candidate for minimum functions is *national (country-wide) public goods*. The two primary examples are defense and interregional economic infrastructure, both of which offer advantages of economies of scale. Interregional economic infrastructure, such as transnational transportation systems, can promote economic development and therefore make centralization more attractive. However, regional and local economic infrastructure can be effectively provided by republic and local governments.

Lower Priority Central Government Operations

Certain activities of central governments in Western federations reflect national preference, and no compelling economic efficiency arguments seem to guide their assignment. Negotiation between the republics could lead to a consensus for the inclusion of such activities in the domain of the federal government. However, a federation can endure decentralization of all these activities without suffering significant welfare losses, and given the high value that some republics attach to sovereignty, there is no reason to insist on automatic centralization of low priority activities.

Regional Equalization

A country's system of intergovernmental finance reflects that country's concepts of justice and normative views of the role of the state. Therefore, the extent of federal equalization of state and regional income varies widely among the Western federations. For instance, the Australian and German systems enact extensive regional redistribution; Canada provides more provincial-based redistribution; and the United States tends to let regions fend for themselves.

Presently, no consensus for centralized regional redistribution exists in the three federal states under consideration; the republics are unwilling to sacrifice autonomy in order to enhance regional and local equality. Instead, most development aid is likely to be determined on a bilateral republic basis, while only a reserve fund for disaster relief could be envisioned at the federal level in the near future.

Social Insurance, Health, and Education

Expenditures on social insurance, health, education, and other social programs account for the largest share of central government expenditure in all the Western federations. Government supply of social insurance can be justified because the presence of risk may lead to incomplete private markets. The economic justification for public support of health and education is to enhance economic development through investment in human capital, and to promote equality.

The reasons for assigning these functions to the *federal* government is to ensure equal access to all citizens, and to enhance regional economic equality. Given this equalization-based argument, social insurance, health, and education cannot be designated as minimum functions of a central government within a federation. Furthermore, some would argue that regional uniformity is not desirable in some circumstances. An advantage to decentralization is that it allows regional governments to adjust the mix of social expenditures in accordance with the preferences and needs of its citizens (see below). Thus, correction of market failures can take place at republic and local levels. Interrepublic negotiation, possibly assisted by the federal government, can correct interrepublic market failure or benefit spillovers.

Economic Infrastructure and Environmental Protection

Most public infrastructure is either regionally based (e.g., local transportation, support of industry and agriculture), or need not be supplied by government at all (e.g., energy). Where economic infrastructure has interregional elements (e.g., flood control, transnational transportation), there are potential gains to centralization. However, even for these functions, cooperation between two or more republics to internalize the externalities often can solve the allocation problems (following the Swiss example). The same applies to environmental protection.

Consequences of Insufficient Federal Powers

To sum up, the (high priority) minimum federal powers that emerge from this analysis are: (a) regulation of interregional trade; (b) control over the exchange rate and regulation of foreign trade; (c) control over the money supply, own revenue sources, and some limitations on sub-central government deficits; and (d) supply of national (country-wide) public goods where significant economies of scale exist.

Ceding insufficient powers to the center to carry out its assigned tasks can involve substantial welfare losses. In all cases, decentralization of the (high priority) minimum functions would hinder the smooth functioning of the economy, and, in certain circumstances, destroy economic initiatives, thus leading to diminished economic activity. Republic level limitations on free trade and factor mobility would lower collective welfare and the GDP. Decentralized control of foreign trade could lead to trade restriction and a consequent hinderance of domestic economic activity and economic development. Decentralized macroeconomic stabilization policy could lead to inflation, unemployment, and disruption of financial markets. Decentralized supply of national public goods would normally lead to suboptimal levels of public expenditure and, in the case of interregional economic facilities, a decrease in economic activity.

How strong are these minimum powers compared with the current proposals for reform of the federal systems in Czechoslovakia, the Soviet Union, and Yugoslavia? In some respects they are stronger: joint foreign economic policy, own revenue sources for the federal government. In some respects they are weaker: limited federal involvement in social security, transportation, energy, and economic infrastructure.

Fiscal Decentralization Within Unitary States and Republics

The previous section examines assignment of powers between the central government and republics within a federal system. This section analyzes assignment of powers between local governments and the central government within a unitary state and the parallel issue of delineation of authority between local governments and republics within a federation. The appropriate power-sharing arrangement in a given country depends upon collective goals and priorities, both social and economic. Nevertheless, certain general guidelines exist that can be applied to all countries.

Fiscal Decentralization in Central and Eastern Europe

Up till now the Central and Eastern European countries have had excessively centralized systems of government and will undoubtedly move in the direction of greater decentralization (except possibly Yugoslavia). The current trend toward devolution of power to local governments varies considerably. Hungary and Poland have initiated reforms that portend of a fundamental shift towards decentralization; a brief review of their systems follows.

Poland

In 1988, central government expenditures in Poland accounted for nearly 40 percent of GDP, of which one tenth were intergovernmental transfers. Revenues were derived from enterprise taxes (30 percent), social security and payroll taxes (24 percent), and the turnover tax (27 percent). Local government expenditures were 14 percent of GDP; grant receipts were 27 percent of revenues, enterprise taxes were 25 percent, and turnover tax revenues were 12 percent. In 1989, partial indicators show that over 40 percent of voivodship (or provincial) expenditures were for health, 10 percent for education, and 9 percent for economic services. The localities used 42.5 percent of their resources for education, 15 percent for economic services, and 9 percent for health.[13]

The recently enacted reforms set up a unitary system with the voivodships remaining part of the central government and the localities or communes becoming independent entities. The localities have been given responsibility for municipal services including primary education, water and sanitation, roads, housing, fire prevention, sports, and culture. Their most notable source of power is ownership of local housing within their jurisdiction and commune-subordinated public enterprises. The most notable absence from local responsibility is health. Revenue assignments are as yet unspecified, except that the turnover tax is being replaced by a value-added tax with revenues reverting to the center (Prud'homme (1990)).

Hungary

In 1989, central government expenditures in Hungary were 56 percent of GDP, of which one eighth were intergovernmental transfers. Central

---

[13]Figures in this section are derived from International Monetary Fund, *Government Finance Statistics Yearbook*, and government publications. A full functional breakdown of expenditures in Poland is not available.

government revenues came from turnover taxes (32 percent), social security taxes (29 percent), enterprise profit taxes (15 percent), and nontax revenues (15 percent). Expenditures consisted of social security (29 percent), economic services (25 percent), and other social services—education, health, housing, recreation (8 percent). Local government expenditures were 15 percent of GDP, of which education was 31 percent, health was 19 percent, housing and recreation were 12 percent, transportation was 11 percent, and other economic services were 11 percent.

Fundamental changes in the structure of intergovernmental relations were introduced in 1990.[14] Localities are responsible for municipal services, education, health, and social care. Counties have been given responsibility for transportation. Revenue collection is to be highly centralized, less than one fifth of local revenue is to come from own revenue sources. General purpose grants and special purpose grants, with equalization features, are expected to provide half of local revenues; social security system funding of local health expenditures and the local share of personal income tax collections will provide 30 percent. Although the local revenue sources are still unspecified, they will probably consist of fees, land taxation, and asset-based revenue from land, housing, and possibly public enterprises.

Expenditure Assignment

The activities that are appropriate for a central government within a unitary state are not necessarily limited to the minimum functions of a central government within a federation. Lower priority activities are also candidates for centralization within a unitary state and at the republic level within a federation. From an expenditure standpoint, the most important of these functions are regional equalization, social insurance, health, and education. Since all of these activities have significant redistributional consequences, the essential issue is the amount of redistribution that is to be enacted and the extent to which redistribution activities of the government should be centralized.

Redistribution

While the appropriate level of government-sponsored redistribution is unquestionably a country-specific normative choice, the central government has significant efficiency advantages over local governments in

---

[14]The reforms established 3200 decentralized entities consisting of 3000 villages, 140 towns, 21 town-counties, 22 districts of the capital, and 19 counties (Banda (1991), Hungarian Ministry of Finance (1991)).

enacting family-level income redistribution. The primary reason is that the ability of localities to provide support for low income groups is severely limited by interjurisdictional mobility of the poor, the rich, and businesses. Local redistribution induces relocation by providing an incentive for families that benefit from the policies to move in, and an incentive for those that the locality asks to pay for the programs to move out. The greater the extent of mobility, the more difficult and costly it is to redistribute income. In contrast, centralized redistribution of income between regions within a country or a republic tends to provide a disincentive for interregional mobility and is administratively compatible with family-level income redistribution. Additionally, the tendency of central governments to provide uniform services to all regions, and to impose equal tax rates in all regions, promotes regional and family-level equality. Many consider regional uniformity of education, health, and other human services to be socially desirable. Centralized redistribution policy implies substantial expenditure activities—or at least financing responsibility—for the central government in a unitary state, or for republic governments in a federation.

Local Public Goods

In countries with a relatively strong taste for equalization, the rubric of income redistribution can be legitimately used to justify extensive centralization in the supply of government services. However, from an allocative efficiency standpoint, there is wide scope for decentralization. Virtually every type of municipal service is amenable to local control, as are most other traditional government activities (other than the aforementioned national public goods).

The ancient organizational principle of subsidiarity holds that decisions should be made by the smallest group that is directly affected. In delineating how much government decentralization is desirable, a similar concept emerges by analogy from the theory of decentralized markets. Since competitive (decentralized) markets are more efficient, centralized controls by government should be limited to cases where a clearly identified market failure exists. The same rule is appropriate for intergovernmental relations: unless there is a compelling reason to centralize, decentralization is always preferred. An extensive body of economic literature supports decentralization of local public goods, that is, programs that provide benefits within a limited geographic area.

Perhaps the most important advantage to decentralization is the natural motivation for local governments to act efficiently. Competition of local governments with other localities for residents and businesses creates strong incentives for local governments to find the policies that satisfy the desires of current or potential residents and businesses. The possibility of mobility of economic agents between adjacent localities ensures that both land values and the economic vitality of a community are linked to the quality of local government policies—residents and businesses communicate their desires to local governments by "voting with their feet."[15] Although there are problems with this model—income distribution and benefit spillovers—if the realm of local powers is confined to basically nonredistributive functions, and assignment of tasks takes account of benefit regions, decentralization can work to improve the efficiency of government.

Additional advantages accrue to having smaller units of governance. First, since there is a reverse correlation between group size and the cost of reaching decisions, localities can use more simplified decision making processes, such as New England town meetings. Second, citizens can more easily monitor public policies because of their proximity and the relative simplicity of smaller units. Third, smaller bureaucracies are more efficient because they avoid the pyramid effect. Finally, decentralization permits variety. There is a greater possibility to adapt the mix of local public services to regional needs and individual preferences. This non-uniformity of services among localities can facilitate a segmentation of individuals based upon preference groups and thereby enhance global welfare. However, if segmentation is based on income levels rather than preferences, regional diversity merely functions to prevent income equalization rather than serve citizen preferences.

The Trade-Off

In practice, a centralized system (a) provides service standards to each locality, (b) applies equal taxes, and (c) facilitates regional and personal redistribution. At the opposite extreme, decentralized systems (a) allow autonomy to localities, (b) enhance responsiveness of local governments, and (c) provide for relatively modest redistribution. In theory, a strict autonomy-equity trade-off is not necessary; both goals can be accomplished via a decentralized system embellished with complicated inter-governmental grants. In practice, however, an extensive system of grants

---

[15]Tiebout (1956) proposed this idea, which has been subsequently extensively analyzed (e.g., Gordon (1983)). Until recently, only modest effort has been devoted to its analogous effect on businesses. Research indicates that localities that seek to attract businesses to their region will also select optimal policies (Gerber and Hewitt (1987), Oates and Schwab (1988)). In fact, the result is more robust, because distributional considerations do not unduly complicate the analysis.

causes nontransparency and effectively limits local autonomy. Therefore, attempts to institute regional equalization diminish the advantages of decentralization. Such countries as Canada and Australia are continually reforming their systems in an attempt to obtain simultaneously local autonomy and regional equalization. In practice, Canada has achieved a large measure of local autonomy with fairly limited equalization, while Australia has a great deal of income equalization with limited autonomy. Neither has managed to do both with unmitigated success and each suffers from excessive complexity.

On the other hand, using the fiscal federal system as a means of redistribution is not ideal and may be inappropriate in Central and Eastern Europe. There are many ways to carry out redistribution of income; economic theory suggests that asset-based schemes are the most efficient. Since these countries are undergoing massive transformations in all areas, there is little reason to burden the fiscal federal system with responsibility for redistribution when better methods exist. Overall, this analysis favors extensive decentralization of expenditure responsibilities in both the unitary states and within the republics.

Tax Assignment

In considering tax assignments, property taxation is the only inherently local tax, while customs duties are the only inherently central tax. However, centralized tax collection often has administrative advantages. For example, if labor and capital are highly mobile, highly redistributive taxes should be centralized to avoid locational distortions. But this does not provide an a priori justification to exclude localities from using any given tax. Widely different patterns of tax assignments exist in the industrialized nations, and no one system has compelling efficiency advantages over another. Furthermore, no economic justification exists for prohibiting overlapping tax assignments, and in many countries different levels of government indeed use the same taxes without negative consequences.

Thus, like with expenditure assignments, we cannot offer convincing generalizations regarding the optimal tax assignments. These should be viewed as matters of collective preference, common sense, and influenced by existing administrative arrangements.

The pattern of tax assignments observed among the Western unitary states, however, does not show the same degree of diversity as in the federal states. The localities tend to rely on property taxes and intergovernmental grants as the main sources of revenue and tend to supply municipal services and education. The central governments in Spain, Italy,

Greece, France, and the United Kingdom all split their revenue sources fairly evenly between social security taxes, indirect taxes (excises and value-added taxation), and individual income taxes. The main expenditure functions of the central governments in these countries comprise social security, health, and defense, with significant expenditures on education and economic services. Current reforms are moving the intergovernmental systems in many unitary states toward greater decentralization (Denmark, Greece, France, and Italy).

Practical Guidelines

Although there is a great deal of latitude in designing well-run fiscal federal systems, a certain number of practical guidelines can be gleaned. First, a *transparent* system of intergovernmental relations is desirable, in which the level of government responsible for each service and the associated funding are clearly identifiable. The advantages of decentralization rely on direct citizen involvement in local government decisions. Experience indicates that the public will not bother to be informed about the intricacies of excessively complex systems. Even experts can disagree on the facts in countries with complicated fiscal systems and this can lead to distorted policies based upon public misunderstandings. Second, the arrangement should be *simple* in order to minimize administrative, compliance, and legal costs. Third, the financial setup should ensure *marginal cost taxation*. On the margin, the level of government that makes a particular expenditure decision should be responsible for raising the associated revenues. This provides an important automatic expenditure control mechanism and is a necessary condition for constructive local competition between governments.

Finally, within a decentralized system certain types of uniformity are beneficial. *Tax base harmonization* can enhance administrative simplicity and decrease compliance costs, as can coordination of certain business regulations. Coordination of policies should be instituted at an early stage; experience indicates that it becomes excessively costly and administratively difficult to coordinate policies once they are already in place.

Conclusions

Two general conclusions emerge from the analysis of the intergovernmental fiscal systems in Central and Eastern Europe. In federal states, the federal government can perform certain high priority functions to the benefit of all. Republics should guard against excessive decentralization that strips the federal government of minimal powers necessary to perform these functions efficiently. From an economic standpoint, dissolution of a federation is preferable to the problems that might arise from a federal government that is too weak. In contrast, within the republics and in unitary states, extensive decentralization of governmental powers to communes or localities is compatible with economic efficiency.

The analysis has, by necessity, glossed over some very crucial issues. One such issue is the widespread institutional arrangement of public enterprises supplying municipal and social services (particularly in remote regions). Privatization of these enterprises could lead to pressure for local governments to underwrite the financing of their public services. This raises some difficult legal and economic issues. How will the localities fund these services, and are these services appropriate for public supply in their present form? To what extent might these services themselves be privatized or funded through user fees?

The paper did not cover the specific intergovernmental institutions in Bulgaria, Czechoslovakia, Romania, and the Soviet Union. In the two federal states, the fiscal arrangements are very much in flux and appear to be headed in the direction of looser federations. These countries will undoubtedly struggle with some of the fiscal issues that Yugoslavia has experimented with over the past two decades. The two unitary states are still in the early stages of defining the nature of their political and economic reforms and the issue of decentralization of government activities remains uncertain.

References

Alexashenko, Sergei, "Reform of the Fiscal System in the Soviet Union: Main Complexities and Possible Solutions," paper prepared for the Senior Policy Seminar on Intergovernmental Fiscal Relations and Macroeconomic Management organized by the World Bank, New Delhi, India, February 1991.

Banda, Jenö, "Who's in Charge Here, Anyway?" *The Hungarian Observer* (Budapest), Vol. 4 (1991), pp. 10–11.

Benson, G.C., "Values of Decentralized Government," in *Essays in Federalism*, ed. by G.C. Benson, and others (Claremont, California: Institute for Studies in Federalism, 1961).

Bieri, S., *Fiscal Federalism in Switzerland*, Research monograph No. 26, Centre for Research on Federal Fiscal Relations (Canberra: Australian National University, 1979).

Bird, Richard, *Federal Finance in Comparative Perspective* (Toronto: Canadian Tax Foundation, 1986).

Cato Journal, Special Issue on Alternatives to Government Fiat Money, Vol. 9 (Fall 1989).

————, *Federal Finance in Theory and Practice With Special Reference to Switzerland*, (Bern: Verlag Paul Haupt,).

Dafflon, Bernard, "Revenue Sharing in Switzerland," paper prepared for the OECD Conference *Fiscal Federalism in Economies in Transition*, Paris, April 1991.

Frey, René L., "The Interregional Income Gap as a Problem of Swiss Federalism," in *The Political Economy of Fiscal Federalism*, ed. by Wallace E. Oates (Lexington: Lexington Books, 1977), pp. 93–104.

Gerber, Robert, and Daniel Hewitt, "Decentralized Tax Competition for Business Capital and National Economic Efficiency," *Journal of Regional Sciences*, Vol. 27, (3/1987), pp. 451–60.

Gordon, Roger, "An Optimal Taxation Approach to Fiscal Federation," *Quarterly Journal of Economics* (1983), pp. 567–86.

Hungarian Ministry of Finance, "The Finances of Local Self-Government Bodies," in *Public Finance in Hungary* (Budapest, 1991).

International Monetary Fund, *Government Finance Statistics Yearbook* (Washington: International Monetary Fund, 1990).

———, The World Bank, Organization for Economic Co-Operation and Development, European Bank for Reconstruction and Development, *A Study of the Soviet Economy*, Vol. 1 (Paris: OECD, February 1991).

Jurkovic, Pero, *Fiskalna politika u ekonomskoj teoriji i praksi [Fiscal Policy in Economic Theory and Practice]* (Zagreb: Informator, 1989).

King, Robert J., "On the Economics of Private Money," *Journal of Monetary Economics*, Vol. 12 (July 1983), pp. 127–58.

Kolm, Serge-Chrisophe, *Le Contrat Social Liberal* (Paris: Presses Universitaires de France, 1985).

Kocarnik, Ivan, and Milan Bakes, "Fiscal Federalism: Experience of the Czech and Slovak Federal Republic," Paper prepared for the OECD Conference *Fiscal Federalism in Economies in Transition*, Paris, April 1991.

Kristan, Ivan, "Federalism and Democratic Centralism: Yugoslav Practice and the Constitutional Reform," *Review of International Affairs*, Vol. 41, (July 5–20, 1990), pp. 4–8.

Mates, Neven, "Fiscal Reform Issues in Yugoslavia" (Unpublished paper, Fiscal Affairs Department, International Monetary Fund, May 1991).

Mihaljek, Dubravko, "Economic Reforms in Yugoslavia in the Post-War Period: Lessons for Socialist Economies in Transition" (Unpublished paper, Fiscal Affairs Department, International Monetary Fund, May 1990).

———, "Financing of Public Services in Yugoslavia: A Lindahl Equilibrium Model for the Labor-Managed Economy," *Economic Analysis*, Vol. 20 (2/1986), pp. 135–68.

Oates, Wallace E., and Robert M. Schwab, "Economic Competition Among Jurisdictions: Efficiency Enhancing or Distortion Inducing? *"Journal of Public Economics*, Vol. 35 (1988), pp. 333–54.

Pisany-Ferry, J., "Maintaining a Coherent Macro-Economic Policy in a Highly Decentralized Federal State: The Experience of the EEC," paper prepared for the OECD Conference *Fiscal Federalism in Economies in Transition*, Paris, April 1991.

Prud'homme, Rémy, "The Rise of Local Governments in Poland" (Unpublished paper, Créteil, Laboratoire d'Observation de l'Economie et des Institutions Locales, Université de Paris XII-Val de Marne, July 1990).

Prust, Jim, and others, *The Czech and Slovak Federal Republic*, IMF Occasional Paper 72 (Washington: International Monetary Fund, 1990).

Tanzi, Vito, "Tax Reform and the Move to a Market Economy: Overview of the Issues," in *The Role of Tax Reform in Central and Eastern European Economies* (Paris: OECD, 1991).

Tiebout, Charles, "A Pure Theory of Local Government Expenditure," *Journal of Political Economy*, Vol. 64 (1956), pp. 416–24.

Index